Teaching and Learning at a Distance

Foundations of Distance Education

SEVENTH EDITION

Michael Simonson
Nova Southeastern University

Susan Zvacek
SMZTeaching.com

Sharon Smaldino
Northern Illinois University

Information Age Publishing, Inc.
Charlotte, North Carolina • www.infoagepub.com

Library of Congress Cataloging-in-Publication Data

CIP data for this book can be found on the Library of Congress website
http://www.loc.gov/index.html

Paperback: 978-1-64113-626-6
Hardcover: 978-1-64113-627-3
E-Book: 978-1-64113-628-0

Printed in the United States of America.

ABOUT THE AUTHORS

Michael Simonson is a program professor at Nova Southeastern University in the Instructional Technology and Distance Education program. He earned his PhD from the University of Iowa in Instructional Systems. He works with schools, organizations, and corporations to assist them to integrate instructional technology and distance education into teaching and training, and on the development of virtual schools. He was named Professor of the Year for the Fischler School of Education at Nova Southeastern University for 2012–13. Simonson has authored four major textbooks dealing with distance education, instructional technology, instructional computing, and instructional media. His two most recent books received first place book awards from the Association for Educational Communications and Technology. Mike has more than 150 scholarly publications, and in excess of 200 professional presentations dealing with distance education and instructional technology. He is editor of the *Quarterly Review of Distance Education, Distance Learning Journal,* and *Proceedings of Selected Research and Development Papers* presented at the annual conventions of the Association for Educational Communications and Technology. He was an external evaluator South Dakota's Connecting the Schools and Digital Dakota Network projects, and is a consultant for the U.S. Army Research Institute. He also works with various health care professional systems such as the University of Miami's School of Nursing, and Nova Southeastern University's Health Professions Division. Simonson was honorably discharged as a captain from the United States Marine Corps (Ret.).

Susan M. Zvacek has been involved with higher education for more than 20 years and has worked in community college, corporate, and university environments. Currently, she is associate provost of teaching and learning at the University of Denver. Her scholarly work has been primarily in the field of educational technology, with publications and presentations at national and international conferences on topics such as higher order thinking skills, distance education, and the assessment of learning using online tools. She is one of the founding directors of the Exemplary Course Program for Blackboard, the longest running project of its kind, reviewing and recognizing outstanding course design for online and blended teaching environments. Consulting, workshops, and keynote presentations have taken her to the Czech Republic, Cyprus, Slovakia, Austria, Germany, Portugal, Estonia, and the United Kingdom, as well as across the United States. Dr. Zvacek holds a BA in speech from Iowa State University, a master's in education from the University of Utah, and a PhD in curriculum and instructional technology, also from Iowa State University.

Sharon E. Smaldino is a professor emeritus and former L. D. and Ruth G. Morgridge Endowed Chair in Teacher Education at Northern Illinois University. She also served as the director of partnerships. Sharon received an MA in elementary education from the University of Connecticut and her PhD from Southern Illinois University, Carbondale. She focused on working with faculty and P–12 teachers to integrate technology into the learning process. Having presented at state, national, and international conferences, Sharon has been an important voice on applications of technology in the classroom and in distance education. In addition to her teaching and consulting, Dr. Smaldino has served as president of AECT, has served on the board of directors of International Visual Literacy Association, and president of the AECT Foundation Board of Directors. She has written articles for state and national journals on her primary research interests—effective technology integration and distance education for learning. She has worked on several grants that identified technology as an important aspect of ensuring quality learning environments.

BRIEF CONTENTS

CONTENTS

Preface

Teaching and Learning at a Distance is written for introductory distance education courses for preservice or in-service teachers, and for training programs that discuss teaching distant learners or managing distance education systems. This text provides readers with the basic information needed to be knowledgeable distance educators and leaders of distance education programs.

The teacher or trainer who uses this book will be able to distinguish between appropriate uses of distance education. In this text we take the following themes:

The first theme is the definition of distance education. Before we started writing the first edition of *Teaching and Learning at a Distance* we carefully reviewed the literature to determine the definition that would be at the foundation of our writing. This definition is based on the work of Desmond Keegan, but is unique to this book. This definition of distance education has been adopted by the Association for Educational Communications and Technology and by the *Encyclopedia Britannica.*

The second theme of the book is the importance of research to the development of the contents of the book. The best practices presented in *Teaching and Learning at a Distance* are validated by scientific evidence. Certainly there are "rules of thumb," but we have always attempted to only include recommendations that can be supported by research.

The third theme of *Teaching and Learning at a Distance* is derived from Richard Clark's famous quote published in the *Review of Educational Research* that states that media are mere vehicles that do not directly influence achievement. Clark's controversial work is discussed in the book, but is also fundamental to the book's advocacy for distance education—in other words, we authors do not make the claim that education delivered at a distance is inherently better than other ways people learn. Distance delivered instruction is not a "magical" approach that makes learners achieve more.

The fourth theme of the book is equivalency theory. Here we present the concept that instruction should be provided to learners that is equivalent rather than identical to what might be delivered in a traditional environment. Equivalency theory helps the instructional designer approach the development of instruction for each learner without attempting to duplicate what happens in a face-to-face classroom.

The final theme for *Teaching and Learning at a Distance* is the idea that the book should be comprehensive—that it should cover as much of the various ways instruction is made available to distant learners as is possible. It should be a single source of information about the field.

ORGANIZATION OF THE TEXT

Teaching and Learning at a Distance has three types of chapters—foundation chapters, teaching and learning chapters, and managing and evaluating chapters. Chapters 1 through 4 provide a conceptual, theoretical, and research-based foundation for the rest of the text. Chapters 5 through 9 provide educators with the practical skills and information they need to function in a distance learning environment. Chapters 10 through 12 discuss managerial and administrative concerns in distance education environments.

Chapter 1 discusses the status of distance education and also explains what distance education is and its impact on education. This chapter concludes with a vision for schools and learning that is possible because of distance education.

Chapter 2 reviews definitions of distance education that have been and still are used. Since distance education is a field with a long history, that background is discussed. This chapter covers the field, beginning with correspondence study and up through today. Finally, theories related to the practice of distance education are presented, including a proposed American theory of distance education called equivalency theory.

Chapter 3 reviews the extensive research on distance education, including specific areas of practice as well as more general and comprehensive summaries of what the research says. *Teaching and Learning at a Distance* is a research-based textbook based on a thorough study of the empirical information about distance education. This research-based approach is found in all chapters, but is emphasized in Chapter 3.

Chapter 4 presents comprehensive information about the technologies used in distance education systems. Technology generally, and instructional or communications technology specifically, are broadly defined, and this chapter includes discussions, explanations, and many visuals to provide the reader with practical knowledge about how information is communicated and how synchronous and asynchronous distance education systems operate. The use of the Internet and the World Wide Web for distance education is discussed extensively, also.

Chapter 5, the first of the teaching and learning chapters, presents instructional design, which is the systematic process of using technology followed by educators. This chapter presents the procedures to be followed when courses, or components of courses, are designed for distance delivery. In this edition the Unit-Module-Topic approach for organizing instruction is emphasized.

Chapters 6 and 7 explain the unique responsibilities of the instructor and learner involved in distance education. It is clear from the research and from practical experience that learning and teaching at a distance are not significantly different from traditional education. However, there are some special responsibilities and expectations for students and instructors involved in distance education.

Chapter 8 is one of the most important chapters of the book. Handouts, study guides, and visuals are important tools and techniques of the effective educator, generally, and the distance educator, specifically. The interactive study guide with its word pictures, visual analogies, and visualization is a significant tool used in distance education systems.

Chapter 9 presents thoroughly revised techniques for assessing learning, assigning grades, and determining academic progress of students in a distance learning environment. Many educators question the fidelity of assessment at a distance. This chapter provides research-based approaches for valid assessment of learning.

Chapter 10 deals with the rules, regulations, and procedures related to intellectual property that the distance educator needs to understand. This edition reflects major updates in the interpretation of intellectual property, ownership, and copyright case law, providing a more comprehensive and applied perspective. Distance educators transmit information, much of which may be copyrighted.

Chapter 11 illustrates how distance education has become an enterprise, even a business, and discusses the techniques for managing and leading an organization dedicated to the delivery of distance instruction. Of special emphasis is the idea of the distance learning leader.

Chapter 12 discusses the evaluation of distance teaching and distance education systems, and gives specific examples of procedures to follow. New examples and approaches are included in this chapter. Assessment and evaluation are closely related, but evaluation is special to the distance educator.

FEATURES OF THIS EDITION

- Chapter **goals and objectives** provide an organizational plan for the student and structure the information.
- **A Look at Best Practice Issues**, a new feature found throughout the text, presents critical issues in the field of distance education. This feature is designed to be the starting point for discussions about how distance education is changing teaching and learning.
- Dozens of new **visuals** have been added to clarify ideas and explain procedures, and references and resources have been updated in each section and every chapter to make this book as current and relevant as possible.
- Chapter **scenarios** and /or **discussion questions** are provided to review key ideas.
- Stronger emphasis is placed on **how to design, deliver, and evaluate** online instruction as distance education has matured and the importance of online, World Wide Web–based instruction has grown.
- Increased coverage of course management systems is provided.
- Finally, each chapter has a comprehensive list of references and suggested readings.
- In some instances, nonprint resources, especially web locations, are provided.

ADDITIONAL RESOURCES

Support Materials for *Teaching and Learning at a Distance: Foundations of Distance Education*

The materials listed next were created by the authors of this book and are available for use by students and instructors using *Teaching and Learning at a Distance: Foundations of Distance Education* or by those interested in distance education.

Many additional materials, including PowerPoint slides, documents, links to references, and podcasts can be found at:

http://www.nova.edu/~simsmich/distance_ed_res.htm

Links to podcasts and videos listed below can also be accessed at:

http://www.tresystems.com/publications/

Chapter 1: Foundations of Distance Education

- Simonson on the five themes at the foundation of *Teaching and Learning at a Distance: Foundations of Distance Education* https://vimeo.com/76984144
- Simonson Discusses Richard Clark's "Mere Vehicles" Statement

  https://vimeo.com/77513306

- Distance Education in South Dakota – The Capital City Conclave on Distance Education

  Part 1: https://vimeo.com/49383526

  Part 2: https://vimeo.com/49384048

- Star Schools: Three Statewide Approaches to Distance Education

  Part 1: https://vimeo.com/49381680

  Part 2: https://vimeo.com/49382319

  Part 3: https://vimeo.com/49383086

- Army and Navy Staff Officer Training and Distance Education

  http://www.youtube.com/watch?v=m3B5jfm_vww&list=PLLfZk-j6DDwUq2lfiE-dgbt4YRxSyeJ1_&index=8

- Distance Education in Turks Caicos

  http://www.youtube.com/watch?v=dJKr-baGi_s&list=PLLfZk-j6DDwUq2lfiE-dgbt4YRxSyeJ1_&index=9

- Wired for Success: Alabama's ACCESS to Distance Learning

  http://www.youtube.com/watch?v=s73YkD0GY

- Global Collaboration for Healthcare

  http://www.youtube.com/watch?v=2CLIO0SEbww&list=PLLfZk-j6DDwVk59HaCj45PIcjjkXZNT6J&index=11

- Distance Education in Portugal – Interview with Dr. Pedro Reis https://vimeo.com/8100057

Chapter 2: Definitions, History, and Theories of Distance Education

- Virtual Schools – A series

  https://vimeo.com/album/5215261

- Simonson on Equivalency Theory

  https://vimeo.com/77512842

- Transactional Distance Theory

  http://www.youtube.com/watch?v=Qph1gbQhK_8&list=PLLfZk-j6DDwUq2lfiE-dgbt4YRxSyeJ1_&index=3

- Definition and Background of Distance Education—a classic video from the Iowa Star Schools project

  https://vimeo.com/77514955

- Research and Theory

  http://www.youtube.com/watch?v=WqbBBFnNUiA

Chapter 3: Research and Distance Education

▪ Simonson on Trends in Instructional Technology and Distance Education

   https://vimeo.com/35260851

Chapter 4: Technologies, the Internet, and Distance Education

Chapter 5: Instructional Design for Distance Education

▪ Simonson on Organizing Online Courses

   http://www.youtube.com/watch?v=qzwRIMzZZdA&list=
   PLLfZk-j6DDwUq2lfiE-dgbt4YRxSyeJ1_&index=6

▪ The Curriculum—this classic video was produced as part of the Iowa Star Schools project

   https://vimeo.com/77516590

Chapter 6: Teaching and Distance Education

▪ The Shadow technique for involving online students in their distance delivered courses

   https://vimeo.com/76985274

▪ Simonson on Grading Threaded Discussions

   http://www.youtube.com/watch?v=8VT_35m15Lc&list=
   PLLfZk-6DDwUq2lfiE-dgbt4YRxSyeJ1_&index=7

▪ Retention of Students in Online Courses—A Presentation to Faculty

   https://vimeo.com/76984837

▪ The Teacher—This video is part of the classic series produced as part of the Iowa Star Schools project

   https://vimeo.com/77515914

Chapter 7: The Student and Distance Education

▪ Top Ten Tips for Student Success in Online Courses

   https://vimeo.com/50630107

Chapter 8: Support Materials and Visualization for Distance Education

▪ Mini-Flipping a Classroom—A Five Part Series

   https://vimeo.com/album/4542884

- Digital Media Single Concept Videos for Distance Education—a series of video definitions of terms used by distance educators in the creation of teaching and learning materials.

  - Narrowcasting

    http://www.youtube.com/watch?v=NM2R_BYs-Rg&list=PLLfZk-j6DDwVk59HaCj45PIcjjkXZNT6J&index=1

  - Storyboards

    http://www.youtube.com/watch?v=NwjXTcfe1ck&list=PLLfZk-j6DDwVk59HaCj45PIcjjkXZNT6J&index=2

    http://www.youtube.com/watch?v=AmrTD9StoDM&list=PLLfZk-j6DDwVk59HaCj45PIcjjkXZNT6J&index=8

    http://www.youtube.com/watch?v=mwoWqGd_KIE&list=PLLfZk-j6DDwVk59HaCj45PIcjjkXZNT6J&index=27

    http://www.youtube.com/watch?v=v0aFjLE6Rpo&list=PLLfZk-j6DDwVk59HaCj45PIcjjkXZNT6J&index=28

    http://www.youtube.com/watch?v=cbr3LsLLR7w&list=PLLfZk-j6DDwVk59HaCj45PIcjjkXZNT6J&index=29

- Mash-up

  http://www.youtube.com/watch?v=tm4biZ69OR0&list=PLLfZk-j6DDwVk59HaCj45PIcjjkXZNT6J&index=3

  http://www.youtube.com/watch?v=spOWx2ARm_I&list=PLLfZk-j6DDwVk59HaCj45PIcjjkXZNT6J&index=20

- Podcasts

  http://www.youtube.com/watch?v=UZcu5m8zH64&list=PLLfZk-j6DDwVk59HaCj45PIcjjkXZNT6J&index=4

- Aggregators

  http://www.youtube.com/watch?v=jughwdnbaKA&list=LLfZk-j6DDwVk59HaCj45PIcjjkXZNT6J&index=5

- VoIP

  http://www.youtube.com/watch?v=vCnVLRpv3-w&list=PLLfZk-j6DDwVk59HaCj45PIcjjkXZNT6J&index=6

  http://www.youtube.com/watch?v=zeiSiUJlwNw&list=PLLfZk-j6DDwVk59HaCj45PIcjjkXZNT6J&index=18

- Twitter

  http://www.youtube.com/watch?v=wTDRTGVkGyY&list=PLLfZk-j6DDwVk59HaCj45PIcjjkXZNT6J&index=7

- HD Technologies

  http://www.youtube.com/watch?v=VtqMRQMXaRc&list=
  PLLfZk-j6DDwVk59HaCj45PIcjjkXZNT6J&index=9

- CODEC

  http://www.youtube.com/watch?v=xiix10GIQjg&list=
  PLLfZk-j6DDwVk59HaCj45PIcjjkXZNT6J&index=10

- iTunes U

  http://www.youtube.com/watch?v=0zBe6RcrXRo&list=
  PLLfZk-j6DDwVk59HaCj45PIcjjkXZNT6J&index=12

- MPEG

  http://www.youtube.com/watch?v=eLyLBkn5-xk&list=
  PLLfZk-j6DDwVk59HaCj45PIcjjkXZNT6J&index=13

- PDA

  http://www.youtube.com/watch?v=bdqeXFu3QDM&list=
  PLLfZk-j6DDwVk59HaCj45PIcjjkXZNT6J&index=14

- QR Code

  http://www.youtube.com/watch?v=S2t_wz-Rru4&list=
  PLLfZk-j6DDwVk59HaCj45PIcjjkXZNT6J&index=15

- SCORM

  http://www.youtube.com/watch?v=Gwo0QmfvTtQ&list=
  PLLfZk-j6DDwVk59HaCj45PIcjjkXZNT6J&index=16

- Smartphones

  http://www.youtube.com/watch?v=IAJOrI7HzG4&list=
  PLLfZk-j6DDwVk59HaCj45PIcjjkXZNT6J&index=17

  http://www.youtube.com/watch?v=_Z6S3vZzPI4&list=
  PLLfZk-j6DDwVk59HaCj45PIcjjkXZNT6J&index=30

- .GIF

  http://www.youtube.com/watch?v=UYjpcOVuI6A&list=
  PLLfZk-j6DDwVk59HaCj45PIcjjkXZNT6J&index=19

- .mov

  http://www.youtube.com/watch?v=XlPP5Cn4PPU&list=
  PLLfZk-j6DDwVk59HaCj45PIcjjkXZNT6J&index=21

- Episodes

  http://www.youtube.com/watch?v=onzy2dqUHog&list=
  PLLfZk-j6DDwVk59HaCj45PIcjjkXZNT6J&index=22

- Screencast

  http://www.youtube.com/watch?v=aAymX6ej43Q&list=
  PLLfZk-j6DDwVk59HaCj45PIcjjkXZNT6J&index=23

- White Balance

  http://www.youtube.com/watch?v=hdujeBDFxM4&list=
  PLLfZk-j6DDwVk59HaCj45PIcjjkXZNT6J&index=24

  Tilt http://www.youtube.com/watch?v=iFupyacdIuI&list=
  PLLfZk-j6DDwVk59HaCj45PIcjjkXZNT6J&index=25

- .MPG3

  http://www.youtube.com/watch?v=HcMyeRjIJXA&list=
  PLLfZk-j6DDwVk59HaCj45PIcjjkXZNT6J&index=26

Chapter 9: Assessment for Distance Education

Chapter 10: Intellectual Property: Ownership, Distribution, and Use

Chapter 11: Managing and Leading a Distance Education Organization

- Introduction to the Virtual School Summit
  https://vimeo.com/8974652

- Virtual Schooling: What Administrators Should Know
  https://vimeo.com/9024384

- Virtual Schooling: Legal Issues
  https://vimeo.com/9023507

- Virtual Schooling: Experiences
  https://vimeo.com/9003477

- Virtual Schooling: Funding the Virtual School
  https://vimeo.com/9001271

- Virtual Schooling: Teaching Online
  https://vimeo.com/8999696

- Virtual Schooling: Selecting Vendors
  https://vimeo.com/8997446

Chapter 12: Evaluating Teaching and Learning at a Distance

▪ South Dakota Evaluation Report—Simonson summarizes the evaluation process followed in South Dakota near the conclusion of that's State's Star Schools Project.

   https://vimeo.com/77514339

ACKNOWLEDGMENTS

Many individuals participated in the development of the ideas presented in this text. In particular, Dan Hanson, Nancy Maushak, Charles Schlosser, and Mary Anderson of the Technology Research and Evaluation Group at Iowa State University contributed a great deal to the development of *Teaching and Learning at a Distance.*

CHAPTER 1

Foundations of Distance Education

CHAPTER GOAL

The purpose of this chapter is to discuss the importance of distance education and the impact that distance education has on the improvement of education.

CHAPTER OBJECTIVES

After reading and reviewing this chapter, you should be able to

1. Explain why students demand to learn at a distance even though they may prefer to learn in the classroom with the teacher and their classmates.
2. Define *distance education*.
3. Explain Coldeway's quadrants.
4. Discuss Richard Clark's "mere vehicles" quote as it relates to distance education.
5. Explain how Jim Finn might compare stirrups to distance education.
6. Give examples of how distance education is being used in several locations of the world and in the United States.
7. Discuss telemedicine and relate the topic to distance education. Explain a vision for education and schooling in the future.
8. Define disruptive technology and relate distance education to this concept.

CHEMISTRY AT A DISTANCE? A TRUE STORY

Chemistry is a hands-on, laboratory-based course that many consider one of the most rigorous in the average high school curriculum. Many students dread taking chemistry, and in many small communities there is only one chemistry teacher in the school.

Recently, four high school chemistry teachers decided that they could improve their basic chemistry course if they collaborated and team-taught. The only problem was that their schools were about 60 miles from each other.

This did not stop them, however, because their schools were connected with a fiber-optic network that permitted full-motion video signals to be sent between the four schools. The network also carried a high-speed Internet connection that allowed easy access to the web.

Not only did the four teachers want to collaborate, but more important, they wanted their students to collaborate. To accomplish this, they decided on some basic objectives and then planned the curriculum.

The teachers decided that they would teach concepts cooperatively, act as laboratory super visors for each other's students, and serve as partners with student collaborators. They also decided upon another important goal: to have their students cooperate across schools. Finally, they decided that the chemistry projects should be authentic and deal with local, real-world issues.

Increasingly, courses such as chemistry are being taught to distant and local learners synchronously and asynchronously.

Next, the four teachers met to plan their curriculum. They identified eight modules that could be shared among the four schools. These modules were taught by one or two of the four chemistry teachers, and required collaboration by the students from the four schools. The modules included live television instruction presented by one of the teachers, collaborative work by students who communicated with each other by television and the Internet, and class assignments that dealt with various aspects of a specific chemistry concept, such as the local ecology. Stu dents investigated their portion of the problem and then shared results with their distant classmates. Each module ended with a live, interactive discussion, presentation, and sharing of information over the fiber-optic television network.

For all practical purposes, the students in the four schools became one large class, with subgroups of students who worked with classmates from their own school and also with distant friends. The teachers served as presenters some of the time, but most often as tutors who worked with subgroups of students. The Internet and e-mail were used to keep every one communicating outside of class, and even outside of school.

By any measure, the course was a huge success. Students learned chemistry; test scores showed that. They also discovered how to collaborate as real scientists with col leagues at distant locations, and they discovered the power of distance education to open up their school to resources available elsewhere.

Telecommunications technology made this possible. Their chemistry classroom became a "room with a view," connected to other chemistry classrooms and to the resources of the world available through the Internet. The course became more like real chemistry—chemistry practiced to solve actual problems outside the school involving experts from a number of areas brought together because of their expertise, without regard for geography or time.

Distance education is one of the most dramatic of the recent technology-based innovations influencing education. The scenario just described is only one of thousands of examples of how distance education is changing learning and teaching.

DISTANCE EDUCATION TODAY AND TOMORROW

In the last few years, distance education has become a major topic in education. In a recent year, more than 100 professional conferences dealt with some aspect of distance education, and almost every professional organization's publications and conferences have shown a huge increase in the number of presentations and articles related to distance education. Many educators are making grand claims about how distance education is likely to change education and training. Certainly, the concept of distance education is exciting, and recent hardware and software innovations are making telecommunications distance education systems more available, easier to use, and less costly. Distance education has entered the mainstream.

Whether distance education is a mainstream form of education has been examined for several years by the Sloan Consortium. *Digital Faculty* (Allen & Seaman, 2012; Seaman, Allen, & Seaman, 2018) is a recent annual report by the Sloan Consortium, and presents the latest data about the growth and spread of online education in higher education in the United States. The first report, *Sizing the Opportunity* (Allen & Seaman, 2003), indicated that online and/or distance education was growing rapidly and was perceived positively by faculty and administrators. The authors of this report defined online learning to be courses where most or all of the content is delivered online. Typically, these courses have no face-to-face meetings. In 2013, it was reported that distance education was significantly more popular and mainstream.

One indication that online courses are a regular activity of institutions of higher education is the role of core faculty in online instruction. There has been a long-held belief that online courses are taught by adjunct professors, rather that full-time staff. *Growing by Degrees* (Allen & Seaman, 2005) refutes this perception. It reports that about two thirds of online courses are taught by regular faculty, a percentage that is often higher than the percentage of regular courses taught by core faculty.

Another indicator of the growth of online education is the importance of this instructional approach to the long-term strategy of the institution. In 2013, approximately 70% of institutions indicated that online instruction was critical to their long-term plans, up from 49% in 2003. The only institutions that did not see online instruction as part of their long term strategies were the smallest nonprofit colleges. In 2013, enrollment in online courses had increased to about 6.7 million from 2 million in 2003. Growth has been continuous, often exceeding the expectations of organizational planners. In other words, over 30% of colleges students are enrolled in at least one online course.

Another interesting report dealing with distance education in the Midwest was released by the Sloan Consortium (Allen & Seaman, 2007). This report indicated that:

- The 11 Midwestern states represent about 15% of online enrollment, with over 460,000 students taking at least one online course in fall 2005.
- The proportion of Midwestern institutions with fully online programs rises steadily as institutional size increases, and about two thirds of the very largest institutions have fully online programs, compared to only about one sixth of the smallest institutions.
- Midwestern doctoral/research institutions have the greatest penetration of offering online programs as well as the highest overall rate (more than 90%) of having some form of online offering (either courses or full programs).
- The proportion of people who think that online learning outcomes are superior to those for face-to-face learning is still relatively small but has grown by 34% since 2003, from 10.2% to 13.7%. This is okay, since distance education should not be considered as better but as equivalent.

The Sloan Consortium reports (Allen & Seaman, 2012; Seaman, Allen & Seaman 2018) also provide excellent criteria for distinguishing between online courses, blended/

FIGURE 1–1   There are conflicting pressures on distance educators—students prefer to learn in a classroom, but demand to be permitted to learn at a distance.

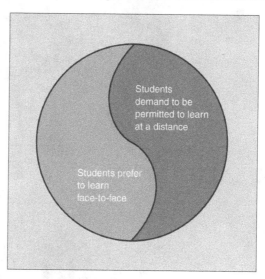

hybrid courses, and web-facilitated courses. An online course is one where most of the content is delivered online, which means at least 80% of the course content. A blended or hybrid course combines online and face-to-face delivery; thus, 30% to 79% of the course's content is delivered online. A web facilitated course uses web-based technology, but less than 30% of the content is delivered online.

In spite of the phenomenal growth of distance education two conflicting pressures confront distance educators (Figure 1–1). First, *students say their first choice is not to learn at a distance.* When asked, they say they prefer meeting with the learning group and the instructor in the classroom, the lecture hall, the seminar room, or the laboratory. Students report that they value the presence of a learning group, and that the informal interactions that occur before and after, and sometimes during, a formal class are valuable components of the total learning experience. Second, and conversely, evidence suggests that *students are increasingly demanding to be allowed to learn at a distance.* They want to be able to supplement, and even replace, conventional learning experiences with distance education experiences. Learners say this is because many other considerations besides personal preferences motivate them, especially considerations about where and when they learn (Seaman et al., 2018).

These opposing preferences pose a dilemma for the educational community. Should resources be dedicated to improving the traditional educational infrastructure of buildings, classrooms, laboratories, and offices, and should students be transported to these facilities? Or should money be used to develop modern and sophisticated telecommunications systems? The trend seems to be toward telecommunications. Because of advances in technology, effective educational experiences can be provided for learners, no matter where they are located. In other words, technologies are now available to develop cost-effective distance learning systems.

Virtual schools are becoming important in many locations (Berge & Clark, 2009). The Florida Virtual School, established in the late 1990s, offers a wide selection of courses

Compressed video systems use telephone lines and Internet connections to permit live, two-way, interactive televised instruction.

(Johnson, 2007). The Arkansas Virtual Academy is another successful example of a state-wide distance education program.

Universities are also offering virtual schools. Indiana University High School and the University of Missouri's Columbia High School are examples of university-sponsored virtual schools. The North Central Association of Colleges and Schools has accredited both schools. The Indiana and Missouri schools are financially independent of their universities. Students pay tuition for courses that are developed and taught by certified teachers. A large number of other states are following the lead of Florida, Arkansas, Indiana, and Missouri. Concepts such as the virtual school have caused the practice of distance education to dramatically change in the last decade. Traditional approaches to distance education based on the delivery of print and broadcast media technologies are no longer as relevant to the field as it is practiced in the United States as they once were.

As a matter of fact, a redefinition of distance education has occurred. Distance education is now often defined as:

> institution-based, formal education where the learning group is separated, and where interactive telecommunications systems are used to connect learners, resources, and instructors. (Schlosser & Simonson, 2010, p. 1)

This definition has also been adopted by the *Encyclopaedia Britannica* in 2009 (Simonson, 2009).

THE EFFECTIVENESS OF DISTANCE EDUCATION—IN CASE YOU WONDER

Many who begin studying distance education wonder about the effectiveness of this approach to teaching and learning, and while Chapter 3 discusses distance education research in depth, this section summarizes that research and briefly describes what we know about the effectiveness of distance teaching and distance learning. Simonson, Schlosser, and Orellana (2011) completed a review of research on distance education and concluded that "it is not different education, it is distance education" (p. 124), and "research clearly shows that distance education is an effective method for teaching and learning" (p. 139). Another indication that distance education has become a dominant trend in education and training is the publication of comprehensive references about the field. For example, Moore's (2013) *Handbook of Distance Education* is in its third edition and contains 44 chapters and more than 700 pages.

Additionally, in 2009 the United States Department of Education published a meta analysis and review of online learning studies and concluded that online learning students achieved better than traditional students because they tended to allocate more time to their studies. These studies build on and support previous research about the effectiveness of distance education.

> According to the 248 studies that were compiled by Russell (1999), there is no significant difference between distance learning and traditional classroom learning. In other words, distance learning (can be) considered as effective as face-to-face learning, and our results support this conclusion. (Dean, Stahl, Sylwester, & Peat, 2001, p. 252)

Simonson et al. (2011) reported results that are indicative of the research on the field of distance education. Most who are deeply involved in the field of distance education are unsurprised by these summaries of the research. As a matter of fact, it is very clear that instruction delivered to distant learners is effective and that learning outcomes can be successfully attained when offered to students at a distance (Anglin & Morrison, 2000; Cavanaugh, Gillan, Kromrey, Hess, & Blomeyer, 2004; Hanson, Maushak, Schlosser, Anderson, & Sorensen, 1997; Simonson, 2002; Simonson et al., 2011).

In 2012 and 1983, Clark clearly stated that the media used to deliver instruction had no significant impact on learning. Clark stated that:

> The best current evidence is that media are mere vehicles that deliver instruction but do not influence student achievement any more than the truck that delivers our groceries causes changes in nutrition ... only the content of the vehicle can influence achievement. (p. 445)

After more than a decade of criticism and attempts to refute his review of over 50 years of instructional technology research, Clark (1994, 2012) once again reviewed the research on technology used to deliver instruction and noted:

> It is likely that when different media treatments of the same informational content to the same students yield similar learning results the cause of the results can be found in a method which the two treatments share in common ... give up your enthusiasm for the belief that media attributes cause learning. (p. 28)

Since the publication of Clark's widely distributed comments, a number of researchers have attempted to find fault with his premise. They have not been successful. It is currently the consensus that "media are mere vehicles" and that we should "give up [our] enthusiasm" that the delivery media for instructional content significantly influences learning.

Unfortunately, some have misinterpreted the "no significant differences" phenomenon and assumed that instructional technology and distance education do not promote learning.

This is incorrect. Actually, the evidence is quite clear that students of all ages can learn from instruction delivered using technology, and that distance education works.

In the first years of widespread growth of distance education in the United States, Han son et al. (1997) summarized the research on distance education in a publication of the Association for Educational Communications and Technology. This widely distributed review concluded that:

> comparative research studies on achievement tend to show no significant difference between different delivery systems and between distance education and traditional education ... several recent studies indicate a significant higher achievement level in those learning at a distance ... the accepted position is that the delivery system affects no inherent difference on achievement. (p. 22)

In other words, it is not the fact that instruction is delivered in a traditional, face-to face environment or at a distance that predicts learning (Anglin & Morrison, 2000; Berge & Mrozowski, 2001; Darwazeh, 2000; Simonson, 2002; Simonson et al., 2011).

It is clear from the research literature that distance education works (e.g., Hanson et al., 1997; Simonson, 2002; Simonson et al., 2011). Why it works and how it works are important concepts to understand, however. The following conclusions about instruction delivered to distant learners are directly related to effectiveness:

- Training in effective instructional strategies is critical for teachers of distant learners.
- Distance education courses should be carefully designed and developed before instruction begins.
- Visualization of ideas and concepts is critical when designing instruction to be delivered to distant learners.
- Adequate support systems must be in place to provide the distant learner with access to resources and services.

Distance education efforts are increasingly being concentrated on K–12 education.

- Interaction between the instructor and students and among students must be possible and encouraged.
- Assessment should be designed to relate to the specific learning outcomes of the instructional experiences.

In summary, distance education can be as effective as any other category of instruction. Learning occurs and knowledge is retained. Students report that they have learned and that they think their distance learning experiences are as successful as more traditional education. The keys to successful distance education are in the design, development, and delivery of instruction, and are not related to geography or time.

WHAT IS DISTANCE EDUCATION?

It is the nature of questions that they are easier to ask than to answer. This is true of the question "What is distance education?" for at least several reasons. First, *distance* has multiple meanings, although this book advocates the definition presented earlier and in Chapter 2. *Distance* can mean geographical distance, time distance, and possibly even intellectual distance.

Second, the term *distance education* has been applied to a tremendous variety of programs serving numerous audiences via a wide variety of media. Some use print, some use telecommunications, and many use both. Finally, rapid changes in technology challenge the traditional ways in which distance education is defined.

Dan Coldeway, of South Dakota's Dakota State University, provided a framework useful in helping to define four ways in which education can be practiced. This framework, which considers the two variables of time and place, gives insight into different approaches to the practice of education and distance education. Combinations of time and place result in four approaches to education: same-time, same-place education (ST-SP); different-time, same-place education (DT-SP); same-time, different-place education (ST-DP); and differ ent-time, different-place education (DT-DP).

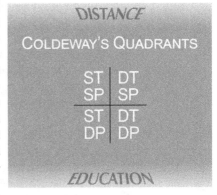

Traditional education takes place at the same time in the same place. This is typically the regular self-contained classroom that most often is teacher centered. Different-time, same-place education means that individual learning occurs in a learning center, or that multiple sections of the same classes are offered so students can attend the class in the same place at a time they choose. This is education that is available at different times to students but in the same place, such as the media center or computer laboratory.

The last two categories focus on education occurring in different places. Instruction can be delivered to different places at the same time when telecommunications systems are used. Often, television is used to connect the local classroom with the teacher and students to learners at a distance. Satellite, compressed video, fiber-optic systems, and webcasting are increasingly used for same-time, different-place education. Increasingly, web-based video systems such as Zoom are being used to deliver live instruction. This approach is also called *synchronous distance learning*. Students can also learn at different times and in different places. Coldeway has said that the purest form of distance education occurs at different times and in different places. In other words, learners choose when and where to learn and when and where to access instructional materials. Recently, World Wide Web courses have been offered to learners anywhere they have access and whenever they choose. This approach is called *asynchronous distance learning*.

FACTS ABOUT DISTANCE EDUCATION

- Eminent historian Frederick Jackson Turner ran the correspondence program of the University of Wisconsin in the late 1800s.
- The state of Iowa has a state-owned, 3,000-mile fiber-optic network, called the Iowa Communications Network, with over 1,000 high-tech classrooms for the purpose of offering distance instruction throughout the state.
- *Telemedicine* refers to medicine at a distance, and *telelaw* refers to law at a distance.
- Research on the effectiveness of distance education clearly shows that students who learn at a distance do not learn any worse, or any better, than traditional students.
- The United States Distance Learning Association is a professional organization of those involved in distance education.
- Universities such as the University of Chicago, the University of Wisconsin, and the University of Iowa championed correspondence education in the later years of the 19th century and early in the 20th century.
- Satellites, once popular ways to deliver instruction until being replaced by the Internet, orbit approximately 23,000 miles about the equator at an orbiting speed that matches the rotation of the Earth. This geosynchronous orbit makes these satellites appear to be stationary on the surface of the Earth. The location where the satellites orbit is called the Clarke Belt, after science fiction writer Arthur C. Clarke, who wrote about communication satellites in geosynchronous orbit in a story published in the 1940s.
- The foundations of the Internet were begun by the U.S. Department of Defense and by a number of research universities as a way to share scientific and technical information between scientists.
- *IP* stands for *Internet Protocol*, the rules used to send information over the Internet.
- The Internet is a packet-switched network, meaning that messages are divided into packets that are disassembled and then sent to the distant site where the packets are reassembled into the complete message.
- Star Schools is the name of a program of the U.S. Department of Education that funded the implementation of distance education in schools and colleges in the United States. The term was coined by Senator Ted Kennedy, who was opposed to the use of satellites for "star wars," so he advocated the use of satellites for education and proposed the Star Schools program. The Star Schools program provided millions of dollars for innovative distance education programs. It was terminated in 2005.

Distance Education as a Disruptive Technology

A technology or disruptive innovation is a technological innovation, product, or service that eventually overturns the existing dominant technology or product in the market. Disruptive innovations can be broadly classified into lower end and new-market disruptive innovations. A new-market disruptive innovation is often aimed at nonconsumption, whereas a lower end disruptive innovation is aimed at mainstream customers who were ignored by established companies. Sometimes, a disruptive technology comes to dominate an existing market by either filling a role in a new market that the older technology could not fill or by successively moving up-market through performance improvements until finally displacing the market incumbents. (Simonson, 2010, p. 74)

By contrast, "sustaining technology or innovation" improves product performance of established products. Sustaining technologies are often incremental." Sustaining technologies maintain a rate of improvement, give users something more or better that they value (Teets, 2002).

Thus, technological innovations might be categorized along a continuum from *sustaining* to *disruptive*. In education, a sustaining technology might be a SmartBoard, which in most applications is a way to present information dynamically and efficiently—a sustaining upgrade to the chalk board and overhead projector.

As a matter of fact, most attempts to integrate instructional technology into the traditional classroom are examples of sustaining technologies—computer data projectors, DVD players, e-books—all which "improve product performance of *established* products." Most integrated technologies sustain, and do not disrupt (Christensen, 2003).

On the other hand, distance education is certainly not a sustaining technology. Rather, distance education, virtual schooling, and e-learning are disruptive.

For example, distance education is aimed at students (older, working, remotely located learners) who are "ignored by established companies" (traditional schools). Distance education presents a different package of performance attributes that are not valued by existing customers. Distance education has come to "dominate ... by filling a role ... that the older technology could not fill" (Christensen, 2003).

Clayton Christensen (Wessel & Christensen, 2012; 2003, 2008; Christensen, Anthony, & Roth, 2004) has written extensively about the concept of disruptive technologies. Christensen's work has been widely embraced in business. His work helps explain why some established industries fail, and others spring up, seemingly from nowhere. No better example is the personal computer. Not a single minicomputer manufacturer has been a successful manufacturer of personal computers—they did not see the power of the new technology until others had captured market share. Similarly, most in education have ignored the potential of looking at the ideas behind Christensen's theory, and how disruptive technologies might transform education and training.

In Florida, there is a mandate that every public school district must establish a virtual K–8, and K–12 school (Simonson, 2008). Many have wondered why Florida legislators would pass such a sweeping law—perhaps the answer is disruptive technology. Whatever the reason for Florida to establish virtual schools, it is clear that distance education and virtual schooling are disrupting traditional education, and this may be a good thing. It might be a good idea for educators to become more cognizant of Clayton Christensen's work, and the power of disruptive technologies to change education.

MEDIA IN EDUCATION: EARLIER DEBATES

The discussion about distance education is somewhat reminiscent of a recent debate in the educational technology field referred to previously that began when Richard Clark, a researcher and theorist, published a classic article containing his now famous "mere vehicles" analogy.

Clark summarized over 6 decades of educational media research. It was obvious to him that many researchers were reporting about flawed studies involving media. Clark believed that many educators did not understand the last 60 years of research about media and learning.

Even more alarming was that many practitioners were making unrealistic claims about the impact of technology on learning. According to Clark, a large segment of the educational community felt that media-based instruction was inherently better than teaching when media were not used.

In 1983 (and 2012), Clark wrote in volume 53 of the *Review of Educational Research* that:

> the best current evidence is that media are *mere vehicles* that deliver instruction but do not influence student achievement any more than the truck that delivers our groceries causes changes in nutrition … only the content of the vehicle can influence achievement. (p. 445)

Clark's 1983 article went on to convincingly claim that instructional media were excellent for storing educational messages and for delivering them almost anywhere. However, media were not responsible for a learning effect. Learning was not enhanced because instruction was media based. Rather, the content of the instruction, the method used to pro mote learning, and the involvement of the learner in the instructional experience were what, in part, influenced learning. Although many did not, and still do not, agree with Clark, his article caused a reassessment of how educators looked at the impact of media. Clark continued to implore the education community to "give up your enthusiasm for media effects on learning," which was the theme of an additional publication on this topic (Clark, 1994, 2012). "Give up your enthusiasm" has become the new rallying cry for those who do not think there is a media effect.

Certainly, some distance educators claim that distance education is the best way to learn because it allows students to acquire knowledge when it is most relevant to them. However, most who have studied distance learning make few claims about the approach being better. Rather, they say it is a viable and important approach to learning and teaching that should be one option of many available.

A second analogy by another great technology pioneer also has relevance to distance education. In the 1960s, Jim Finn from the University of Southern California talked about the stirrup as a technological innovation that changed society. He often told a story that went like this:

> The Anglo-Saxons, a dominating enemy of Charles Martel's Franks, had the stirrup but did not truly understand its implications for warfare. The stirrup made possible the emergence of a warrior called the knight who understood that the stirrup enabled the rider not only to keep his seat, but also to deliver a blow with a lance having the combined weight of the rider and charging horse. This simple concept permitted the Franks to conquer the Anglo-Saxons and change the face of Western civilization. Martel had a vision to seize the idea and to use it. He did not invent the stirrup, but knew how to use it purposefully. (Finn, 1964, p. 24)

Finn (1964) summarized the implications of this story as follows:

> The acceptance or rejection of an invention, or the extent to which its implications are realized if it is accepted, depends quite as much upon the condition of society, and upon the imagination of its leadership, as upon the nature of the technological item itself....

> The Anglo-Saxons used the stirrup, but did not comprehend it; and for this they paid a fearful price.... It was the Franks alone—presumably led by Charles Martel's genius—who fully grasped the possibilities inherent in the stirrup and created in terms of it a new type of warfare supported by a novel structure of a society that we call feudalism.... For a thousand years feudal institutions bore the marks of their birth from the new military technologies of the eighth century. (p. 24)

What Clark strongly proposed with his "mere vehicles" and "give up your enthusiasm" arguments was that media and technology did not directly affect learning. He forcefully argued that educators should not claim that technology-based learning, such as modern distance education systems, had any inherent advantage (or disadvantage for that matter) over other methods of learning. Like Finn, Clark proposed that technologies might provide ways of accomplishing tasks that are new and not readily obvious. Finn advocated that practitioners should attempt to identify unique approaches for change by using new technologies in new ways. Finn's story explained that the stirrup not only made getting on and off a horse easier, but also made possible a new, previously unheard-of consequence—the emergence of the knight—and it was the knight who caused significant and long-lasting changes in society. Perhaps the correct application of distance education will significantly change and restructure learning and teaching on par with the societal change—called feudalism—needed to support the knight.

The implication of the arguments of these two educators is that when new technologies emerge, they often allow users to be more efficient. However, it is not technologies themselves that cause changes; rather, changes occur because of new ways of doing things that are enabled by technologies. The stirrup made riding horses easier and more efficient, but it was the knight who changed medieval society.

 STATUS OF DISTANCE EDUCATION

Worldwide Examples

Distance education has a major and varied impact worldwide. Whereas politics and economics influence how distance education is employed, a strong demand exists in the world for distance education opportunities. The examples that follow illustrate some of the factors that influence distance education and show the demand for distance learning opportunities (Amirault,& Visser, 2017; Visser, Visser, Amirault, & Simonson, 2012).

1. Anadolu University in Turkey reaches over 500,000 distance education students, which makes it one of the largest university on Earth. The university was created in 1981 during a sweeping reorganization of Turkey's higher education system. Its mission is to provide distance instruction to the citizens of Turkey. In 1983, it had almost 30,000 students in business administration and economics, making the university an immediate success. As of 2010, approximately 34% of the students that enrolled in the 2-year degree programs graduated in 2 years, and about 23% of those enrolled in 4-year programs graduated in 4 years. The vast majority of the students enrolled at Anadolu University were working adults with full or part-time jobs. Distance education offered by Anadolu University has made postsecondary education a possibility for many in Turkey who would not have access to higher education (Demiray, 2017). Professors at Anadolu publish an online journal that can be accessed at http://tojde.anadolu.edu.tr.

2. The Open University of Hong Kong opened in 1989 to serve residents of that huge metropolitan area. Recently, the university has begun to market itself to learners in China, and it has thousands of students from the mainland (Cohen, 2000). Unlike Hong Kong's eight conventional universities, the Open University accepts all applicants. It has had over 100,000 students, of which approximately 10% have graduated. Administrators from the Open University of Hong Kong plan to offer distance education throughout China and Southeast Asia (Zhang, Perris, & Yeung, 2005).

3. In sub-Saharan Africa, political instability and economic depression have caused a decline in educational standards in some countries. As the population increased in these countries, a tremendous classroom shortage emerged, and both the number of qualified teachers and the availability of instructional materials became inadequate. Distance education is seen as having the potential to contribute to national reconstruction by providing economically feasible educational opportunities to many people. Collaboration with a variety of international distance education organizations has provided expertise and support for the practice of distance education. As a result, distance education at a basic level, as it is practiced in many regions of Africa, has expanded quite sharply. However, although growth in distance education in sub-Saharan African countries is evident, it does not yet have a wide impact. Lack of funding prevents distance education institutions from reaching many potential students (Day, 2005; Visser & West, 2005; Visser, Visser, & Buendia, 2005). According to Nsomwe-a-nfunkwa (2014: 2009), the enrollment in the French Digital Campus of Kinshasa (Congo) has more than doubled from 2004 to 2008 and again to 2014.

4. China developed a national higher distance education program in the late 1970s and early 1980s in response to a growth in population and a high cost per capita for the craft like approach to regular higher education in the country. Because China could not afford to meet the higher education needs of the expanding population, a national radio and TV university system was developed. By 1985, China had over 30,000 TV classes throughout the country and employed almost 25,000 academics. One in five students studying in higher education was enrolled in a radio and TV university. This national system incorporated a centralized approach to course development, delivery, and examinations. However, despite an increase in offerings, student numbers have significantly decreased. Recently, only 1 in every 13 students in higher education was enrolled in a radio and TV university (Li, Chen,& Wang, 2009). Socioeconomic factors have caused changes in the mass market for higher education in China. The centralized approach to course development and delivery no longer meets the diverse needs of learners and does not adapt itself quickly to the new conditions. In response, China's radio and TV universities have changed from a central system of course development and delivery to a regionally responsive system that provides a wide variety of both diploma and nondiploma courses (Ding, 1994, 1995; Hurd & Xioa, 2006; Li et al., 2009; Yang, Wang, Shen, & Han, 2007).

5. Distance education has had a long history in European countries. The continuation of this tradition is evident in the vast array of programs offered by European Union countries. In some countries, open distance teaching universities offer the majority of the country's distance education programming. Spain's Universidad Nacional de Education a Distancia may be Europe's largest distance teaching university, with a current enrollment of about 130,000 students. In other countries, traditional universities deliver the majority of the courses. France, for example, has no national distance teaching university, but offers higher distance education through 22 offices within traditional universities. Recently, 34,000 students were enrolled in these programs. In

some cases, governments provide substantial distance education training opportunities that do not lead to a university degree. France is a leader in this area, providing over 350,000 students a year with opportunities at a range of levels: elementary school, high school, technical and professional qualifications, teacher training, and university-level and postgraduate courses. In addition, 250,000 students are served by proprietary distance training providers in France (Keegan, 1994). Distance instruction in the European Union uses a wide variety of media to deliver courses. These range from traditional correspondence delivery, to computer conferencing, to two way audio and video virtual classrooms (Holmberg, 1995; Keegan, 1995). Using these technologies, the established distance education and training organizations of Europe will continue to play a significant role in education in and beyond the European Union (Vrasidas, 2008).

United States

Distance educators are often asked about the quality and extent of online education in the United States. Many individuals, especially new students, want to know if instruction delivered at a distance is of high quality, and if distance education is a passing fad or a viable approach to teaching and learning. The Sloan Consortium has attempted to answer these questions. The Sloan Consortium is a collection of "institutions and organizations committed to quality online education." Their reports (Seaman, Allen & Seaman, 2018; Allen & Seaman, 2012) provide a wealth of information about the field of distance education in general, and about online instruction more specifically.

The Sloan reports used surveys to obtain information related to four fundamental questions:

1. Will students embrace online education as a delivery method?
2. Will institutions embrace online education as a delivery method?
3. Will faculty embrace online education as a delivery method?
4. Will the quality of online education match that of face-to-face instruction?

Almost 1,000 surveys (about 33% of those sent) were returned from chief academic officers from accredited degree-granting institutions of higher education in the United States. The report is interesting reading, and the results are important, if not surprising, to those in the field:

- The majority of chief academic officers believe that the learning outcomes in online courses will equal or exceed that of face-to-face courses within 3 years.
- The overall growth rate for enrollment in online courses is expected to be 20%.
- Profit institutions expect a growth rate that is faster than that of other institutions (40%).
- Private, nonprofit institutions expect to use online education less than other institutions.
- Given an option, students will enroll in online courses.
- Overall, attitudes of faculty remain conservative about the quality of online education.

Other interesting results show that over 90% of public universities offer online courses, and about half offer degree programs online. About 85% of public universities consider online education critical to their long-term academic strategies, as compared with about 50% for private institutions. Faculty at public universities are more accepting of the value of online education than their colleagues at private universities, and public universities enrolled more than 2 million students in online courses.

The Sloan Consortium reports authenticate the amazing growth of distance education, yet they also identify the very important issues that still confront the field if distance education is to continue to grow in importance.

Simonson recently compiled a number of articles that deal with distance education in states and institutions (Simonson, 2016). At the university level, it is reported that distance education enrollment is in the tens of millions, nationally. This includes enrollment in courses offered by traditional universities and those offered by distance learning universities. The U.S. military is heavily involved in distance education technology because distance education is viewed as a cost-efficient way to deliver technical training to a large number of soldiers. The development of new weapons systems and other technologies increases the demand for this type of training. The army's Interactive Teletraining Network, the navy's Video Teletraining Network, and the air force's Teleteach Expanded Delivery System, and NASA's Digital Learning Network (Simonson, 2013; Tally, 2009) all provide distance training opportunities for personnel across the United States and around the world.

A focus on education in the primary and secondary schools separates American distance education from traditional European distance education. This emphasis on kindergarten through Grade 12 (K–12) students is demonstrated by the growth of virtual schools (Berge & Clark, 2005), and in the federally funded Star Schools projects. The U.S. Department of Education began the Star Schools program "to encourage improved instruction in mathematics, science, foreign languages, literacy skills, and vocational education for underserved populations through the use of telecommunications networks" (Simonson, 1995, pp. 3–4). Funding for the Star Schools program ended in 2005.

Although these projects are not limited to K–12 programming, their primary emphasis is on K–12 students and teachers. A variety of network technologies including satellite, cable, telephone networks, fiber optics, microcomputer-based laboratories, multimedia, and electronic networking technologies have been used to deliver instructional programming to more than 6,000 schools nationwide through the Star Schools project (U.S. Department of Education, 1995).

The Star Schools project sponsored several special statewide projects that fund the development of statewide infrastructures, allowing for synchronous interaction between students and instructors. The most comprehensive is in Iowa. Currently, Iowa's 3,000-mile statewide fiber-optic network connects more than 1,000 educational sites, with more sites to be added in the next few years. Hundreds of thousands of hours of K–12 programming are provided each year, in addition to teacher professional development and higher education course opportunities. Kentucky and Mississippi have joined Iowa in developing state wide systems that promote personalized interactive instruction and learning (Gillispie, Cassis, Fujinaka, & McMahon, 2013).

South Dakota is another state that has significantly committed to distance education for K–12 students. In South Dakota, the Digital Dakota Network links every school building to a compressed video network. Over 300 sites are located throughout the state (Figure 1–2). Teachers have been trained in special month-long Distance Teaching and Learning Academies, and teachers and university faculties have designed curriculum materials, including entire courses. South Dakota educators have also conducted major research and evaluation activities to document the impact of distance education in the state (Bauck, 2001; Simonson, 2005). As the examples show, distance education has a major impact worldwide. In addition to economics and politics, the growth and impact of distance education is directly linked to the availability of new technologies. "As technology links

Iowa Communications Network Video Classrooms

FIGURE 1–2 South Dakota has the Digital Dakota Network that links hundreds of sites in the state for interactive instruction.

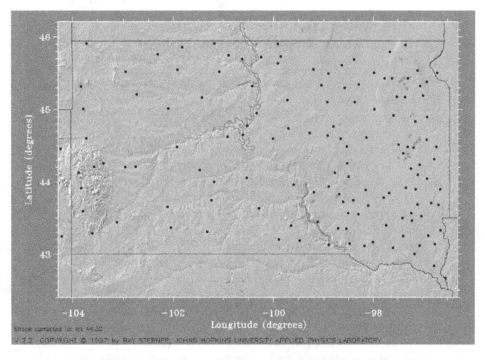

Source: Ray Sterner of the Johns Hopkins Applied Physics Laboratory, licensed by North Star Science and Technology, LLC. [Online.] Available at: www.landforms.biz. Reprinted with permission.

distant sites in an electronic web of information and new communication channels, people around the globe are pulled together" (Thach & Murphy, 1994, p. 5). This type of communication has contributed to globalization. Globalization implies that people are connected more or less contemporaneously with distant events. The new computer-mediated communications and telecommunications technologies contribute to globalization.

Other significant distance education initiatives are Network Nebraska (Decker, 2008), Western Governors University (Eastmond, 2007), Capella University (Thornton, 2007), and Walden University (Shepard, 2008). Distance educators will be challenged both by globalization and by the emerging technologies. How they take advantage of these opportunities will give new meaning to the practice of distance education.

Accreditation. Many in traditional education worry about the quality of distance education programs. Some have called distance education institutions diploma mills, especially those that are profit-generating. A *diploma mill* has the following characteristics: no classrooms, untrained or nonexistent faculties, and unqualified administrators with profit as their primary motivation (Simonson, 2004).

Legitimate institutions have expended considerable effort to demonstrate the quality of their distance education programs. One of the most important activities involves accreditation. Probably the most important form of accreditation, which involves in-depth scrutiny of a school or college's entire program by outside evaluators, comes from regional accrediting agencies, such as the North Central Association and the Southern Association of Colleges and Schools. The North Central Association and Southern Association of Colleges and Schools are examples of regional agencies that accredit institutions in their geographic areas. Generally, the same standards are applied to traditional and distance education programs. National accreditation agencies also accredit colleges.

How Much Distance Education Is Too Much Distance Education?

There may be a tendency among distance educators to advocate for an increase in the amount of instruction that is offered at a distance—to attempt to offer all courses, most programs, and many degrees at a distance. All with little or no rationale for this movement toward totality.

There was a time when distance delivered instruction was a relatively insignificant percentage of all teaching being offered. To most distance educators it has been refreshing to see virtual schooling, online learning, and e'learning move from the periphery to the mainstream, and to see learners at all levels from K-12 schools to corporate training to ask, is this offered online

Is this the right approach to take? Is distance delivered instruction of all courses at all levels the ultimate goal of the field? Alternatively, is there a "tipping point," a point of critical mass, or an edge of practicality? Is there research on how much is too much, or rather, how much is just enough?

Certainly, there is no simple formula that determines what amount of any type of instruction is too much, or not enough—mission statements, client characteristics, geographic limitations, and finances play a determining role. However, what if a group of researchers could develop a model, a rubric, or a formula to help the organization decide what is the right amount of distance education for it.

Most would agree that in almost any training or education organization there are some elements that should be delivered at a distance, and it is likely that few if any organizations should do everything online. So, somewhere between 1% and 99% is the correct amount of distance education.

As William Blake said, "You never know what enough is unless you know what is more than enough."

TELEMEDICINE

Tele means "at a distance," so in its simplest form, *telemedicine* is defined as *medicine at a distance.* The Institute of Medicine defines telemedicine as *the use of electronic information and communications technologies to provide and support health care when distance separates the participants* (Grigsby & Sanders, 1998). Grigsby and Sanders (1998) define telemedicine as *the use of telecommunications and information technology to provide health care services to persons at a distance from the provider.* Actually, there exist in the literature dozens of definitions of telemedicine, but all contain these components:

1. Separation or distance between individuals and/or resources;
2. Use of telecommunications technologies;
3. Interaction between individuals and/or resources; and
4. Medical or health care.

Also, it is implied in most definitions that telemedicine refers to health care offered by recognized, formally accredited medical organizations. Organizational affiliation differentiates telemedicine from self-diagnosis, unsanctioned medical treatment, and quackery (Nagy, L, 2017).

Background

The term *telemedicine* has become common in the medical literature during the last decade. However, most give credit for originating the term to Kenneth Byrd, who, along with several other physicians, formed a video microwave network in 1968 from Massachusetts General Hospital to Boston's Logan Airport. There were a number of other projects at about the same time, but this effort is considered the modern launching of the concept of telemedicine.

Telemedicine is a growing field within the profession of medicine. It has journals, such as the *Journal of Telemedicine* and *Telemedicine Today* and *Telemedicine and e-Health,* has a professional association (the American Telemedicine Association, http://www.atmeda.org/), and holds an annual professional meeting.

Articles dealing with various aspects of telemedicine can be found in the journals of the various subdisciplines of medicine, and scientific research is being conducted and reported with increasing frequency in prestigious journals of the profession. Finally, federal and state governments and private organizations are funding telemedicine projects totaling tens to hundreds of millions of dollars. The communications revolution is having an impact on medicine just as it is on education, training, government, business, and law (Tulu, Chatterjee, & Maheshwari, 2007). A recent meta-analysis dealing with telemedicine/telehealth indicated that there were positive effects related to clinical care, even in different patient populations (Dellifraine, 2008).

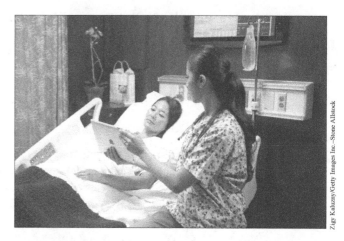

Physicians can consult with specialists using desktop video conferencing systems.

Mobile videoconferencing systems increase access to medical information anywhere it is needed.

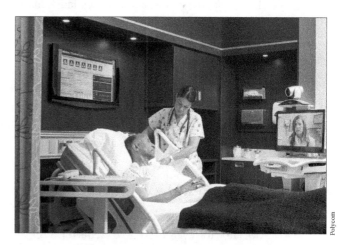

Interactive telecommunications technologies expand the specialized information available to doctors.

Applications

Kvedar, Menn, and Loughlin (1998) list four major applications for telemedicine: remote consultation, remote monitoring, remote education, and telementoring.

Remote consultation is the most common telemedicine application and what most refer to when they use the term *telemedicine.* This application implies one health care provider seeking the advice of a professional colleague or subspecialist to resolve a patient's problem.

Remote monitoring is a long-standing application where the most common use is to access a patient's vital signs at a distance using telecommunications technologies (telehome care). Total cost, cost per patient, and cost per visit were all reduced by telehomecare (Rojas & Gagnon, 2008).

Remote education is increasingly important as the geographically concentrated expertise of a medical unit is redistributed to isolated practicing professionals and professionals in training.

Telementoring involves the development of techniques to share the output of surgical tools such as endoscopes and laparoscopes with distant locations.

The Institute of Medicine (Grigsby & Sanders, 1998) organizes applications of telemedicine differently and identifies five areas of emphasis: patient care, professional education, patient education, research, and health care administration.

Impediments to Telemedicine

The Institute of Medicine identifies five concerns that prevent and slow the growth of telemedicine: professional licensure; malpractice liability; privacy, confidentiality, and security; payment policies; and regulation of medical devices.

Professional licensure issues stem from the traditional view of professional practice as involving a face-to-face encounter between clinician and patient. Telemedicine breaks the physical link and may complicate where a telemedicine practitioner should be licensed if the professional and the patient are in different states. Currently, multiple state licenses are required.

Malpractice liability is usually described as a deviation from the accepted medical standard of care. For telemedicine practitioners, the subject of malpractice presents potentially complicated legal issues, since state law generally governs liability.

Privacy, confidentiality, and security issues relate to serious questions that have been raised about current legal protections for medical privacy and confidentiality. The Hippocratic Oath requires that physicians keep silent about what they learn from patients, "counting such things to be as sacred secrets." Information and telecommunications links present new opportunities for privacy infringements.

Payment policies for telemedicine are a major barrier to the growth of telemedicine. Until 1999, telemedicine did not meet the requirements of the Health Care Financing Administration (now known as the Centers for Medicare and Medicaid Services) for in-person, face-to-face contact between providers and patients. Although most medical consultations using telemedicine have been ineligible for payment in the past, guidelines for reimbursement are still evolving. Currently, Medicare covers interactive video systems (Grigsby & Sanders, 1998), and for this reason most health care organizations are using two-way videoconferencing for their initial telemedicine initiatives.

Regulation of medical devices is of concern because the federal Food and Drug Administration (FDA), through its center, regulates some of the devices used in telemedicine.

In summary, the issues that have slowed the growth of telemedicine are important and should be addressed. However, they are not necessarily unique within the medical profession. Rather, they are issues that are resolved continuously as the health care field adopts new technologies, both medical and informational.

Limited research is reported on the medical effectiveness and cost effectiveness of telemedicine. Current research seems to support the conclusion that telemedicine is effective when practiced correctly, but that additional evaluation and assessment activities need to be conducted.

Telemedicine will continue to be a dynamic influence within the profession of medicine. The benefits of this innovation will be in two primary areas: medical benefits and cost benefits. First, telemedicine is a logical extension of the growth of the technical and technological aspects of health care. The medical benefits of an active telemedicine program are related to how professionals use the technology. A modification of a famous analogy used in educational research when applied to telemedicine summarizes the medical impact of tele-medicine. Telemedicine and information technologies are *mere vehicles* that permit the delivery of health services, but they have no greater impact on health care than, as Clark said and was discussed above, the truck that delivers our groceries has on nutrition. It is the content of the vehicle that permits effective health care, not the vehicle itself (Clark, 1983, 2012). Second, cost effectiveness is likely to be the most significant outcome of telemedi-cine. The significant costs of medical care and the increased requirements for services that are projected for the next several decades forecast a cost advantage for the organizations that understand and utilize technologies effectively. Certainly, telemedicine is only one category of technology, but it may soon be the "ears and eyes" of the health care organization.

In summary, telemedicine is a recognized subcategory of the health services profes-sion. As a technique and tool in the modern medical center it has the potential to expand and accelerate the services offered and the impact made. Other professions, such as law, are moving cautiously to adopt distance education concepts. Nova Southeastern Univer-sity's law school was recently recognized as the "nation's most wired law school." Tele communications technologies will have increasing impact on most fields of endeavor, not just education, as they improve and become more widely available.

CHARACTERISTICS OF DISTANCE EDUCATION: TWO VISIONS

Recently, a number of advances have been made in the study of learning and teaching that are providing educators with strategies for improving the educational experience. Often, these advances are considered to be in opposition to the common practices of distance edu-cation because of the misconception that teachers lecture to distant learners. This is chang-ing dramatically, however, as distance education systems attempt to provide a learning site that is a "room with a view."

The First Scenario—Distance Education in Schools

This emerging approach relies strongly on distance education and suggests a scenario for the school and classroom of the future similar to the following scenario, which implies that classrooms of the future will be rich in technology and will continue to have teachers who are responsible for the learning events that occur:

> In every community and neighborhood there are schools surrounded by playgrounds and sports fields with trees and grass. The schools themselves look modern but very familiar. The schools are open 24 hours per day, every day, all year. Each is a part of a locally con-trolled and supported district that is one of several hundred that make up a technology-rich statewide educational system. Classrooms are considered rooms with a view. Every learner and teacher possesses a high-powered multimedia computer-device that is con-nected to a worldwide network containing virtually unlimited educational resources. The network connects the learner to multisensory multimedia resources that are accessi-ble from school, home, and business. Education is learner and learning centered and technology supported. Schools are small, with about 600 to 800 students, and classes never exceed 25. In the evenings the classrooms are converted to learning laboratories that are used by the entire community. Each classroom has full-motion video links to state and national networks that permit true interactive learning. Students have desktop

video access through their computer-devices, also. The educational philosophy of this school is to promote authentic, student-centered learning activities that are cognitively situated whenever possible in real-world events. The school and its classrooms are a community resource. Outside of school, students continue to learn, even when on vacation. A robust network connects students to their teachers and to the resources needed for learning. Schools provide computer-devices and access when students need them, and the high-speed network is a free wireless canopy that covers the community.

This scenario could be considered a dream rather than a vision. However, it is based on the following widely available and generally accepted techniques and technologies. First, instruction is learner centered. The networked computer-device permits the learner to access events of instruction that can be tailored to meet individual needs. Second, multimedia instruction is routine, especially when networked computer-device and video systems are used. Interactive instruction is possible because telecommunications technologies permit the learner to contact databases, information sources, instructional experts, and other students in real-time and interactive ways. For example, individual students can use their computers to contact other students or individuals who have information they need. Also, the entire class can participate in interactive video sessions with teachers from remote sites or with groups of students from other schools. Instruction is authentic because it is not teacher centered; rather it is content and learner centered.

Businesses, including health organizations, are using videoconferencing to replace travel.

Students can easily interact with students and teachers from remote sites using videoconferencing.

The teacher orchestrates the individual learning activities of students who collaborate with classmates, with distant learners, with the teacher, and with multimedia technology available locally or from the World Wide Web. Finally, the learning environment of the future encourages collaboration without the limitations inherent in the self-contained class room.

The Second Scenario—
Distance Education in the Corporation

The corporation headquarters looks like an inviting place to work. When employees report to work they find that every office has a large flat-panel display connected to a small, nearly invisible powerful computer that is connected to a high-speed local and wide area network. Also connected to the computer is a small, high-quality video camera with microphone and speakers. The office looks modern, but familiar. It is one in a

Training of staff is cost effective when videoconferencing is used.

The office of tomorrow will have readily accessible videoconferencing systems.

cluster that constitutes the on-site work sites of a team of seven professionals. At any one time only a few of the office cubicles have someone in them, but in all cases they are easily seen on the displays in the home offices of physically missing employees. The work group is continuously connected for the sharing of video, audio, and information.

The computer network is connected to online resources that permit "just-in-time" access to information and data. Members of the team effortlessly work with colleagues in the work group without regard for their physical location, and other teams can be contacted with the click of a mouse button. Employees are provided with high-speed, wireless handheld devices that keep them connected to each other and to the resources needed to conduct business.

The criminal justice system is using videoconferencing to reduce the need to travel.

Office cubicles are located near a conference room that contains an interactive tele-communications system that can be connected to other systems using a variety of networking protocols. This room is used for training when group interaction is important. Large, flat-panel high definition displays permit easy viewing and simple, yet powerful cameras and microphones facilitate group interaction at a distance. The class room is connected to a bridge that can connect dozens of sites, including the locations of those working at home or employees who are in the field.

At home, members of the team have similar configurations of technology, although the settings are much less formal and more varied. Working at home is encouraged.

Of critical importance to the work group is access to training, which is a continuous need. Learning about new products, new ideas, and new approaches is a regular require-ment of the job. Training is modularized around single concepts and is con ducted synchronously and asynchronously by trainers who are part of the corporate training team, and by outside experts who are brought in electronically when their specific skills are needed. Learning objects are used by corporate trainers to design instructional pack-ages that are offered over the network to employees of the corporation. Training events are archived for later review.

Industries bring distance education technologies right to the worker.

Businesses will increasingly have access to seminar rooms that use videoconferencing.

Training is technologically based, highly visual, modularized around single concepts, and available on-demand. The employees of the corporation have access to trainers whenever training is needed. Trainers work in teams, and have access to a wealth of resources, including subject-matter experts from inside and outside the company. Trainers are a corporation resource who provide training at a distance to the members of the corporate community. Information and training are as important to the corporation as are products and sales.

Why scenarios? Much of this is possible because of the concept of distance education, which is the bringing of learners and the content of instruction together no matter where each is located. Interactive, real-time, on-demand, learner-centered, authentic, and learner constructed events will characterize the educational environment of the future. Ultimately, the concept of distance will disappear as insignificant, and the idea of interaction will replace it.

SUMMARY

Separation of the student and the teacher is a fundamental characteristic of distance education. More often, educators are using technology to increase the access of the distant learner to the local classroom, to improve access of all learners to resources, and to make the experience of the remote student equivalent to the experience of the local learner.

Distance education is a dramatic idea. It may change, even restructure, education, but only if it is possible to make the experience of the distant learner complete, satisfying, and acceptable. If distance education is to be a successful and mainstream approach, then it is imperative that distance education systems be designed to permit equivalent learning experiences for distant and local students. Distance education using interactive telecommunications technologies is an exciting emerging field. However, practitioners should not promote distance education as the next great technological solution to education's problems, nor make grand claims about the impact of telecommunications systems. Rather, distance education specialists should strive to understand technology and technological approaches that make the experiences of distant and local learners positive and equivalent, at least until someone's genius identifies an approach to learning using telecommunications systems to change education, just as Charles Martel's use of the stirrup changed society.

CASE STUDY

The director of training has called a meeting and you are invited. At the meeting you are informed that staff development for the sales staff—your job—will be moved to an online approach. You are to prepare a plan that supports this decision to be given to the skeptical sales staff. How will you start?

DISCUSSION QUESTIONS

1. What are Coldeway's quadrants, and which quadrant did Coldeway consider the purest form of distance education? What are the pros and cons of dividing educational events into one of Coldeway's four categories?
2. What is the fundamental characteristic of distance education? Discuss what this means. What are the various kinds of distance?
3. Learners prefer not to learn at a distance. Explain.
4. Richard Clark says media are "mere vehicles that deliver instruction but do not influence student achievement." Discuss Clark's analogy and decide if it is accurate. Are media vehicles? What does the word *mere* imply?
5. What do stirrups and distance education have in common? Discuss the concept of innovations and how they are used or not used. Has distance education changed teaching and learning?
6. Write a vision for a school 10 years from today—include a section on school security and distance education.

REFERENCES

Allen, I. E., & Seaman, J. (2003). *Sizing the opportunity: The quality and extent of online education in the United States, 2002 and 2003*. Wellesley, MA: Sloan Consortium.

Allen, I. E., & Seaman, J. (2005). *Growing by degrees: Online education in the United States, 2005*. Wellesley, MA: Sloan Consortium.

Allen, I. E., & Seaman, J. (2007). *Making the grade: Online education in the United States, 2006: Midwestern edition*. Wellesley, MA: Sloan Consortium.

Allen, I. E., & Seaman, J. (2012). *Changing course: Ten years of tracking online education in the United States*. Babson Park, MA: Babson Survey Research Group.

Amirault, R. & Visser Y. (2017). The state of distance education and e-learning around the glove. *Quarterly Review of Distance Education, 18*(2), 87–90.

Anglin, G., & Morrison, G. (2000). An analysis of distance education research: Implications for the instructional technologist. *Quarterly Review of Distance Education, 1*(3), 189–194.

Bauck, T. (2001). Distance education in South Dakota. *Tech Trends, 23*(2), 22–25.

Berge, Z. L., & Clark, T. (Eds.). (2005). *Virtual schools: Planning for success.* New York, NY: Teachers College Press.

Berge, Z., & Clark, T. (2009). Virtual schools: What every superintendent needs to know. *Distance Learning, 6*(2), 1–9.

Berge, Z., & Mrozowski, S. (2001). Review of research in distance education. *The American Journal of Distance Education, 15*(3), 5–19.

Cavanaugh, C., Gillan, K. J., Kromrey, J., Hess, J., & Blomeyer, R. (2004). *The effects of distance education on K–12 student outcomes: A meta-analysis.* Naperville, IL: Learning Point Associates.

Christensen, C. M. (2008). *Disrupting class: How disruptive innovation will change the way the world learns.* New York, NY: McGraw Hill.

Christensen, C. M., Anthony, S. D., & Roth, E. A. (2004). *Seeing what's next.* Boston, MA: Harvard Business School Press.

Christensen, C. M. (2003). *The innovator's dilemma: The revolutionary book that will change the way you do business.* New York, NY: HarperCollins.

Clark, R. E. (1983). Reconsidering research on learning from media. *Review of Educational Research, 53*(4), 445–459.

Clark, R. E. (1994). Media will never influence learning. *Educational Technology Research and Development, 42*(2), 21–29.

Clark, R. E. (2012). *Learning from media: Arguments, analysis, and evidence* (2nd ed.). Charlotte, NC: Information Age.

Cohen, D. (2000, July 14). Hong Kong's boom in distance education may be a sign of what's to come in Asia. *Chronicle of Higher Education,* p. A50.

Darwazeh, A. N. (2000). Variables affecting university academic achievement in a distance versus conventional education setting. *Quarterly Review of Distance Education, 1*(2), 157–167.

Day, B. (2005). Open and distance learning enhanced through ICTs: A toy for Africa's elite or an essential tool for sustainable development? In Y. L. Visser, L. Visser, M. Simonson, & R. Amirault (Eds.), *Trends and issues in distance education: International perspectives* (pp. 171–182). Charlotte, NC: Information Age.

Dean, P. J., Stahl, M. J., Sylwester, D. L., & Peat, J. A. (2001). Effectiveness of combined delivery modalities for distance learning and resident learning. *Quarterly Review of Distance Education, 2*(3), 247–254.

Decker, B. (2008). Constructing the 39th statewide network: The story of Network Nebraska. *Distance Learning, 5*(3), 1–10.

Dellifraine, J. (2008). Home-based telehealth: A review and meta-analysis. *Journal of Telemedicine and Telehealthcare, 14*(2), 62–66.

Demiray, U. (2017). Distance education under neoliberal globalization: The political economy of an emerging trend in education. *Distance Learning, 14*(3), 43–54.

Demiray, U. (2005). Distance education in Turkey: Experiences and issues. In Y. L. Visser, L. Visser, M. Simonson, & R. Amirault (Eds.), *Trends and issues in distance education: International perspectives* (pp. 163–170). Charlotte, NC: Information Age.

Ding, X. (1994). China's higher distance education—Its four systems and their structural characteristics at three levels. *Distance Education, 15*(2), 327–346.

Ding, X. (1995). From Fordism to new-Fordism: Industrialisation theory and distance education—A Chinese perspective. *Distance Education, 16*(2), 217–240.

Eastmond, D. (2007). Education without borders: The Western Governors University story. *Distance Learning, 4*(2), 1–14.

Falduto, V., & Ihde, R. (2007). The Arkansas Virtual High School: A learning environment approach. *Distance Learning, 4*(2), 71–79.

Finn, J. (1964). The Franks had the right idea. *NEA Journal, 53*(4), 24–27.

Gillispie, J., Cassis, J. Fujinaka, T., & McMahon, G. (2013). Meeting the shifting perspective: The Iowa Communications Network. In M. Simonson (Comp.), *Distance education: Statewide, institutional, and international applications* (pp. 3–13). Charlotte, NC: Information Age.

Grigsby, J., & Sanders, J. (1998). Telemedicine: Where it is and where it is going. *Annals of Internal Medicine, 129*(2), 123–127.

Hanson, D., Maushak, N., Schlosser, C. A., Anderson, M. L., & Sorensen, M. (1997). *Distance education: Review of the literature* (2nd ed.). Washington, DC: Association for Educational Communications and Technology.

Holmberg, B. (1995). The evolution of the character and practice of distance education. *Open Learning, 10*(2), 47–53.

Hurd, S., & Xiao, J. (2006). Open and distance language learning at the Shantou Radio and TV University, China, and the Open University, United Kingdom: A cross-cultural perspective. *Open Learning, 21*(3), 205–219.

Johnson, K. (2007). Florida Virtual School: Growing and managing a virtual giant. *Distance Learning, 4*(1), 1–6.

Keegan, D. (1994). *Distance training in the European Union* (ZIFF Papiere). Hagen, Germany: Institute for Research into Distance Education, Fern Universitat. (ERIC Document Reproduction Service No. ED381684)

Keegan, D. (1995). *Distance education technology for the new millennium: Compressed video teaching.* (ERIC Document Reproduction Service No. ED 389931)

Kvedar, J., Menn, E., & Loughlin, K. (1998). Telemedicine: Present applications and future prospects. *Urologic Clinics of North America, 25*(1), 137–149.

Li, C., Huina, C., & Nan, W. (2009). Distance education in China: The current state of e-learning. *Campus-Wide Information Systems, 26*(2), 82–89

Macwilliams, B. (2000, September 22). Turkey's old-fashioned distance education draws the largest student body on earth. *Chronicle of Higher Education,* pp. A41–42.

Moore, M. (2013). *Handbook of distance education* (3rd ed.). New York, NY: Routledge.

Nagy, L. (2017) Telehealth. *Distance Learning,* 14(2), 41-47.

Nsomwe-a-nfunkwa, B. (2015).Lack of ICT literacy for freshman students of the University of Kinshasa. *Distance Learning, 12*(4) 1–6.

Nsomwe-a-nfunkwa, B. (2009). Increasing the need for distance learning in the Democratic Republic of the Congo. *Distance Learning, 6*(1), 1–6.

Picciano, A., & Seaman, J. (2007). *K–12 online learning: A survey of U.S. school district administrators.* Needham, MA: Sloan Consortium.

Rojas, S., & Gagnon, M. (2008). A systematic review of the key indicators for assessing telehomecare cost-effectiveness. *Telemedicine and e-Health, 14*(9), 896?904.

Russell, T. L. (1999). *No significant difference phenomenon.* Raleigh, NC: North Carolina State University.

Schlosser, L. A., & Simonson, M. (2010). *Distance education: Definition and glossary of terms* (3rd ed.). Charlotte, NC: Information Age.

Seaman, J., Allen, I. E. & Seaman, J. (2018). *Grade increase: Tracking distance education in the United States.* Babson Park, MA: Babson Survey Research Group

Shepard, M. (2008). A walk around Walden Pond: Reflections on the educational technology PhD specialization, Walden University. *Distance Learning, 5*(4),1–6.

Simonson, M. (1995). Overview of the Teacher Education Alliance, Iowa Distance Education Alliance research plan. In C. Sorensen, C. Schlosser, M. Anderson, & M. Simonson (Eds.), *Encyclopedia of distance education research in Iowa* (pp. 3–6). Ames, IA: Teacher Education Alliance.

Simonson, M. (2002). In case you are asked: Effectiveness of distance education. *Quarterly Review of Distance Education, 3*(4), vii–ix.

Simonson, M. (2004). Diploma mills and distance education. *Quarterly Review of Distance Education.* 5(3), vii–viii.

Simonson, M. (2005). South Dakota's statewide distance education project: Diffusion of an innovation. In Z. Berge & T. Clark (Eds.), *Virtual schools: Planning for success.* New York, NY: Teachers College Press.

Simonson, M. (2008). Virtual schools mandated. *Distance Learning, 5*(4), 84.

Simonson, M. (2009). Distance learning: Education beyond buildings. *Encyclopaedia Britannica 2009 Book of the Year,* 231.

Simonson, M. (2010). Distance education as a disruptive technology. *Distance Learning, 7*(1), 74.

Simonson, M. (Comp.). (2016). *Distance education: Statewide, institutional, and international applications* (2nd ed.). Charlotte, NC: Information Age.

Simonson, M., Schlosser, C., & Orellana, A. (2011). Distance education research: A review of the literature. *Journal of Computing in Higher Education, 23*(2), 124–142

Tally, D. (2009). Reaching beyond the conventional classroom: NASA's digital learning network. *Distance Learning, 6*(4), 1–8.

Teets, J. (2002). www.distechs.com. Retrieved from http://www.distechs.com/index.php?page=disruptive-technology-defined

Thach, L., & Murphy, L. (1994). Collaboration in distance education: From local to international perspectives. *The American Journal of Distance Education, 8*(3), 5–21.

Thornton, N. (2007). Capella University. *Distance Learning, 4*(3), 1–8.

Tulu, B., Chatterjee, S., & Maheshwari, M. (2007). Telemedicine taxonomy. *Telemedicine and eHealth, 13*(3), 349–358.

U.S. Department of Education, Office of Planning, Evaluation, and Policy Development. (2009). *Evaluation of evidence-based practices in online learning: A meta-analysis and review of online learning studies.* Washington, DC: Author.

U.S. Department of Education. (1995). *The Star Schools program.* (Available from Star Schools, U.S. Department of Education, 555 New Jersey Avenue NW, Washington, DC 20208-5644).

Vrasidas, C. (2008). Perspectives on e-learning: Case studies from Cyprus. *Distance Learning, 5*(2), 1–8.

Visser, L., Visser, Y. L., Amirault, R., & Simonson, M. (2012). *Trends and issues in distance eduction: International perspectives* (2nd ed.). Charlotte, NC: Information Age.

Visser, L., & West, P. (2005). The promise of m-learning for distance education in South Africa and other developing nations. In Y. L. Visser, L. Visser, M. Simonson, & R. Amirault (Eds.), *Trends and issues in distance education: International perspectives* (pp. 131–136). Charlotte, NC: Information Age.

Visser-Valfrey, M., Visser, J., & Buendia, M. (2005). Thank you for (not) forgetting us: A reflection on the trials, tribulations, and take-off of distance education in Mozambique. In Y. L. Visser, L. Visser, M. Simonson, & R. Amirault (Eds.), *Trends and issues in distance education: International perspectives* (pp. 217–244). Charlotte, NC: Information Age.

Wessel, M. & Christensen C. (2012). Surviving disruption. *Harvard Business Review, 90*(12), 56–64.

Yang, F., Wang, M., Shen, R., & Han, P. (2007). Community-organizing agent: An artificial intelligent system for building learning communities among large numbers of learners. *Computers & Education, 49*(2), 131–147.

Zhang, W., Perris, K., & Yeung, L. (2005). Online tutorial support in open and distance learning: Students' perceptions. *British Journal of Educational Technology, 36*(5), 789–804.

SUGGESTED READINGS

Hanna, D. (1995). *Mainstreaming distance education.* Paper presented at the conference of the National Association of State University and Land Grant Colleges, Madison, WI.

Jurasek, K. (1993). *Distance education via compressed video* (Unpublished master's thesis). Iowa State University, Ames, IA.

Kozma, R. (1994). Will media influence learning: Reframing the debate. *Educational Technology Research and Development, 42*(2), 7–19.

Simonson, M. (2008). Virtual schools mandated. *Distance Learning, 5*(4), 84–83.

Simonson, M. (1996). *Reinventing distance education.* Paper presented at the annual convention of the U.S. Distance Learning Association, Washington, DC.

Simonson, M., & Schlosser, C. (1995). More than fiber: Distance education in Iowa. *Tech Trends, 40*(3), 13–15.

CHAPTER 2

Definitions, History, and Theories of Distance Education

CHAPTER GOAL

The purpose of this chapter is to review the definitions, history, and theories of distance education.

CHAPTER OBJECTIVES

After reading and reviewing this chapter, you should be able to

1. Discuss the reason for different definitions of distance education.
2. Describe the various definitions of distance education that have been offered.
3. List and explain the five main elements of the various definitions of distance education given by Keegan.
4. Give the emerging definition of distance education that is appropriate for the United States.
5. Outline the general history of distance education, explaining how it began with correspondence study and evolved into the use of electronic communications media.
6. Discuss the emergence of distance teaching universities.
7. Explain the various theoretical approaches to distance education, including theories of independence, industrialization, and interaction and communication.
8. Synthesize the various theories of distance education.
9. Describe the emerging theory of distance education that relates to equivalence of learning experiences.
10. Explain Fordism, neo-Fordism, and post-Fordism.

DEFINING DISTANCE EDUCATION

Distance education was defined in Chapter 1 as institution-based, formal education where the learning group is separated, and where interactive telecommunications systems are used to connect learners, resources, and instructors (Simonson, 2009, 2010). This definition has gained wide acceptance. The Association for Educational Communications and Technology has published a monograph that explains this definition (Schlosser & Simonson, 2010), and in the *2009 Encyclopaedia Britannica Book of the Year*, distance education/learning is explained and defined on page 231.

Four characteristics distinguished distance education. First, distance education was by definition carried out through institutions; it was not self-study or a nonacademic learning environment. The institutions might or might not offer traditional classroom-based instruction as well, but they were eligible for accreditation by the same agencies as those employing traditional methods.

Second, geographic separation was inherent in distance learning, and time might also separate students and teachers. Accessibility and convenience were important advantages of this mode of education. Well-designed programs could also bridge intellectual, cultural, and social differences between students.

Third, interactive telecommunications connected the learning group with each other and with the teacher. Most often, electronic communications, such as e-mail, were used, but traditional forms of communication, such as the postal system, might also play a role. Whatever the medium, interaction was essential to distance education, as it was to any education. The connections of learners, teachers, and instructional resources became less dependent on physical proximity as communications systems became more sophisticated and widely available; consequently, the Internet, cell phones, and e-mail had contributed to the rapid growth in distance education.

Finally, distance education, like any education, established a learning group, sometimes called a learning community, which was composed of students, a teacher, and instructional resources—i.e., the books, sound, video, and graphic displays that allowed the student to access the content of instruction.

Four main components comprise this definition (Figure 2–1). First is the concept that distance education is institutionally based. This is what differentiates distance education from self-study. Whereas the institution referred to in this definition could be a traditional educational school or college, increasingly there are emerging nontraditional institutions that offer education to students at a distance. Businesses, companies, and corporations are offering instruction at a distance. Many educators and trainers are advocating the accreditation of institutions that offer distance education to add credibility, improve quality, and eliminate diploma mills.

The second component of the definition of distance education is the concept of separation of the teacher and student. Most often, separation is thought of in geographic terms—teachers are in one location and students are in another. Also implied by the definition is the separation of teachers and students in time. Asynchronous distance education means that instruction is offered and students access it at separate times, or anytime it is

FIGURE 2–1   There are four components to the definition of distance education.

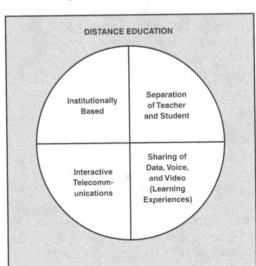

convenient to them. Finally, intellectual separation of teachers and learners is important. Obviously, teachers have an understanding of the concepts presented in a course that students do not possess. In this case, the reduction of separation is a goal of the distance education system.

Interactive telecommunications is the third component of the definition of distance education. Interaction can be synchronous or asynchronous—at the same time, or at different times. Interaction is critical, but not at the expense of content. In other words, it is important that learners be able to interact with each other, with resources of instruction, and with their teacher. However, interaction should not be the primary characteristic of instruction but should be available, commonplace, and relevant.

The phrase *telecommunications systems* implies electronic media, such as television, telephone, and the Internet, but this term need not be limited to only electronic media. *Telecommunications* is defined as "communicating at a distance." This definition includes communication with the postal system, as in correspondence study, and other nonelectronic methods for communication. Obviously, as electronic telecommunications systems improve and become more pervasive, they likely will be the mainstay of modern distance education systems. However, older, less sophisticated systems of telecommunication will continue to be important.

Finally, we examine the concept of connecting learners, resources, and instructors. This means that there are instructors who interact with learners and that resources are available that permit learning to occur. Resources should be subjected to instructional design procedures that organize them into learning experiences that promote learning, including resources that can be observed, felt, heard, or completed. A core principle of effective distance education is the concept of instructional design. It is design that allows content to become instruction. Design – instructional design – is the critical element of effective distance education.

The definition of distance education includes these four components. If one or more are missing, then the event is something different, if only slightly, than distance education.

Related Terms

E-learning—usually this term refers to distance education in the private sector, what some also call e-training.

Virtual Education/Virtual Schooling—this is used to refer to distance education in K–12 education.

On-Line Learning/On-Line Education—this is the common distance education term used in higher education.

"Distance education" is considered the overall and inclusive term, even though the four are used interchangeably, probably in error.

This definition is not the only one and certainly is not the first offered for distance education. As a matter of fact, distance education has been defined from a number of perspectives over the years. Moore (2013) writes that distance education originated in Germany and the University of Tubingen. And Rudolf Manfred Delling (1985) stated that distance education, in general, is a planned and systematic activity that comprises the choice, didactic preparation, and presentation of teaching materials as well as the supervision and support of student learning, which is achieved by bridging the physical distance between student and teacher by means of at least one appropriate technical medium.

For Hilary Perraton (1988), distance education is an educational process in which a significant proportion of the teaching is conducted by someone removed in space and/or time from the learner.

The U.S. Department of Education's Office of Educational Research and Improvement defines distance education as "the application of telecommunications and electronic devices which enable students and learners to receive instruction that originates from some distant location" (2006, p. 1). Typically, the learner may interact with the instructor or program directly, and may meet with the instructor on a periodic basis.

Grenville Rumble (1989) also offered a definition of distance education. He noted that, in any distance education process, there must be: a teacher; one or more students; a course or curriculum that the teacher is capable of teaching and the student is trying to learn; and a contract, implicit or explicit, between the student and the teacher or the institution employing the teacher that acknowledges their respective teaching/learning roles.

- Distance education is a method of education in which the learner is physically separate from the teacher. It may be used on its own, or in conjunction with other forms of education, including face to face. In distance education, learners are physically separated from the institution that sponsors the instruction.
- The teaching/learning contract requires that the student be taught, assessed, given guidance, and, where appropriate, prepared for examinations that may or may not be conducted by the institution. This must be accomplished by two-way communication. Learning may be undertaken individually or in groups; in either case, it is accomplished in the physical absence of the teacher.

For Desmond Keegan (1996), the following four definitions were central to an attempt to identify the elements of a single, unifying definition of distance education:

- The French government, as part of a law passed in 1971, defined distance education as education that either does not imply the physical presence of the teacher appointed to dispense it in the place where it is received or in which the teacher is present only on occasion or for selected tasks.
- According to Börje Holmberg (1985), distance education covers the various forms of study at all levels that are not under the continuous, immediate supervision of tutors present with their students in lecture rooms or on the same premises but which, nevertheless, benefit from the planning, guidance, and teaching of a supporting organization.
- Otto Peters (1988) emphasized the role of technology, saying that distance teaching/ education (*Fernunterricht*) is a method of imparting knowledge, skills, and attitudes. It is rationalized by the application of division of labor and organizational principles as well as by the extensive use of technical media, especially for the purpose of reproducing high-quality teaching material, which makes it possible to instruct great numbers of students at the same time wherever they live. It is an industrialized form of teaching and learning.
- For Michael Moore (2013), the related concept of "distance teaching" was defined as the family of instructional methods in which the teaching behaviors are executed apart from the learning behaviors, including those that in a contiguous situation would be performed in the learner's presence, so that communication between the teacher and the learner must be facilitated by print, electronic, mechanical, or other devices.

Keegan identified five main elements of these definitions and used them to compose a comprehensive definition of distance education.

1. The quasi-permanent separation of teacher and learner throughout the length of the learning process (this distinguishes it from conventional, face-to-face education).
2. The influence of an educational organization both in the planning and preparation of learning materials and in the provision of student support services (this distinguishes it from private study and teach-yourself programs).
3. The use of technical media—print, audio, video, or computer—to unite teacher and learner and carry the content of the course.
4. The provision of two-way communication so that the student may benefit from or even initiate dialogue (this distinguishes it from other uses of technology in education).
5. The quasi-permanent absence of the learning group throughout the length of the learning process so that people are usually taught as individuals and not in groups, with the possibility of occasional meetings for both didactic and socialization purposes.

Garrison and Shale (1987) argued that, in light of advances in distance education delivery technologies, Keegan's definition was too narrow and did not correspond to the existing reality and future possibilities. Although declining to offer a definition of distance education, Garrison and Shale offered the following three criteria they regarded as essential for characterizing the distance education process:

1. Distance education implies that the majority of educational communication between (among) teacher and student(s) occurs noncontiguously.
2. Distance education must involve two-way communication between (among) teacher and student(s) for the purpose of facilitating and supporting the educational process.
3. Distance education uses technology to mediate the necessary two-way communication.

Keegan's definition and the definitions preceding it define the traditional view of distance education. Rapid changes in society and technology are challenging these traditional definitions.

EMERGING DEFINITIONS

The contemporary period is often characterized as one of unpredictable change. Globalization, brought on by supersonic air travel, satellite television, computer communications, and societal changes, has inspired new ways of looking at distance education. Edwards (1995) uses the term *open learning* to describe a new way of looking at education in a quickly changing and diverse world. He indicates that distance education and open learning are two distinct approaches to education. Although he does not define the two, he states that distance education provides distance learning opportunities using mass-produced courseware to a mass market. In contrast, open learning places greater emphasis on the current specific needs and/or markets available by recognizing local requirements and differences instead of delivering an established curriculum. Open learning shifts from mass production and mass consumption to a focus on local and individual needs and requirements. Edwards states that this can occur outside of the traditional organization of education. This is a major difference between his description of open learning and the previous definitions of distance education.

More recently, the idea of the "virtual school" has become popular and is often used when referring to distance education in K–12 schools. *Virtual* is defined as something quasi, or pseudo. Virtual is often a potential state that at some time might become "actual." And, just to add to the confusion, *actual* is generally considered to be the opposite of *virtual*. So, it must be that a virtual school would be a potential school as compared to an actual school.

Increasingly, the popular press and the educational literature talk about distance education—teaching and learning at a distance—as virtual education that happens in a virtual school. Most definitions of distance education do not imply anything virtual or potential, or pseudo. Rather, distance education is about as real and actual as education can be. Some are advocating for the field of distance education to find better words than *virtual* to describe the process of educating using technology without the need for the instructor and the learner to be in the same location, or for them to be communicating at the same time. The Florida Virtual School has the phrase "Any time, any place, any path, any pace" to indicate its approach to teaching and learning. It is a real school. It is an institution where learning occurs because of the efforts of teachers. The phrase *virtual school* tends to be used most often in K–12 education (Simonson, 2007b).

A BRIEF HISTORY OF DISTANCE EDUCATION

Distance education seems a new idea to most educators of today. However, the concepts that form the basis of distance education are more than a century old. Certainly, distance education has experienced growth and change recently, but the long traditions of the field continue to give it direction for the future. This section offers a brief history of distance education, from correspondence study, to electronic communications, to distance teaching universities.

Correspondence Study

The roots of distance education are at least 160 years old. An advertisement in a Swedish newspaper in 1833 touted the opportunity to study "Composition through the medium of the Post." In 1840, England's newly established penny post allowed Isaac Pitman to offer shorthand instruction via correspondence. Three years later, instruction was formalized with the founding of the Phonographic Correspondence Society, precursor of Sir Isaac Pitman's Correspondence Colleges. Distance education, in the form of correspondence study, was established in Germany by Charles Toussaint and Gustav Langenscheidt, who taught language in Berlin. Correspondence study crossed the Atlantic in 1873 when Anna Eliot Ticknor founded a Boston-based society to encourage study at home. The Society to Encourage Studies at Home attracted more than 10,000 students in 24 years. Students of the classical curriculum (mostly women) corresponded monthly with teachers, who offered guided readings and frequent tests.

From 1883 to 1891, academic degrees were authorized by the state of New York through the Chautauqua College of Liberal Arts to students who completed the required summer institutes and correspondence courses. William Rainey Harper, the Yale professor who headed the program, was effusive in his support of correspondence study, and confident in the future viability of the new educational form: The student who has prepared a certain number of lessons in the correspondence school knows more of the subject treated in those lessons, and knows it better, than the student who has covered the same ground in the classroom.

The day is coming when the work done by correspondence will be greater in amount than that done in the classrooms of our academies and colleges; when the students who shall recite by correspondence will far outnumber those who make oral recitations.

In 1891, Thomas J. Foster, editor of the *Mining Herald,* a daily newspaper in eastern Pennsylvania, began offering a correspondence course in mining and the prevention of mine accidents. His business developed into the International Correspondence Schools, a commercial school whose enrollment exploded in the first 2 decades of the 20th century, from 225,000 in 1900 to more than 2 million in 1920. In 1886, H. S. Hermod of Sweden, began teaching English by correspondence. In 1898, he founded Hermod's, which would become one of the world's largest and most influential distance teaching organizations.

Correspondence study continued to develop in Britain with the founding of a number of correspondence institutions, such as Skerry's College in Edinburgh in 1878 and University Correspondence College in London in 1887. At the same time, the university extension movement in the United States and England promoted the correspondence method. Among the pioneers in the field were Illinois Wesleyan in 1877 and the University Extension Department of the University of Chicago in 1892. Illinois Wesleyan offered bachelor's, master's, and doctoral degrees as part of a program modeled on the Oxford, Cambridge, and London model. Between 1881 and 1890, 750 students were enrolled; and in 1900, nearly 500 students were seeking degrees. However, concerns about the quality of the program prompted a recommendation that it be terminated by 1906.

Correspondence study was integral to the University of Chicago. The school, founded in 1890, created a university extension as one of its five divisions, the first such division in an American university. The extension division was divided into five departments: lecture study, class study, correspondence teaching, library, and training.

The correspondence study department of the University of Chicago was successful, at least in terms of numbers. Each year, 125 instructors taught 3,000 students enrolled in 350 courses. Nevertheless, enthusiasm within the university for the program waned, partly for financial reasons.

At the University of Wisconsin, the development of the "short course" and farmers' institutes in 1885 formed the foundation for university extension. Six years later, the university announced a program of correspondence study led by eminent historian Frederick Jackson Turner. However, as at the University of Chicago, faculty interest waned. Further, public response was minimal, and the correspondence study program was discontinued in 1899. Correspondence study would have to wait another 7 years to be reborn under a new, stronger correspondence study department within the school's university extension division.

Moody Bible Institute, founded in 1886, formed a correspondence department in 1901 that continues today, with a record of over 1 million enrollments from all over the world. Correspondence study/distance education has had a significant impact on religious education that emphasizes the social context within which a student lives.

Distance education began to enrich the secondary school curriculum in the 1920s. Students in Benton Harbor, Michigan, were offered vocational courses in 1923, and 6 years later, the University of Nebraska began experimenting with correspondence courses in high schools.

In France, the Ministry of Education set up a government correspondence college in response to the impending World War II. Although the Centre National d'Enseignement par Correspondences was established for the education of children, it has since become a huge distance teaching organization for adult education.

The original target groups of distance education efforts were adults with occupational, social, and family commitments. This remains the primary target group today. Distance education provides the opportunity to widen intellectual horizons, as well as the chance to improve and update professional knowledge. Further, it stresses individuality of learning and flexibility in both the time and place of study.

Two philosophies of distance education became identifiable. The full liberalism of programs offered by Hermod's, in Sweden, emphasized the free pacing of progress through the program by the student. Other programs, such as those offered by the University of Chicago, offered a more rigid schedule of weekly lessons.

Electronic Communications

Europe experienced a steady expansion of distance education, without radical changes in structure, but with gradually more sophisticated methods and media employed. Audio recordings were used in instruction for the blind and in language teaching for all students. Laboratory kits were used in such subjects as electronics and radio engineering. Virtually all large-scale distance teaching organizations were private correspondence schools.

In the United States, advances in electronic communications technology helped determine the dominant medium of distance education. In the 1920s, at least 176 radio stations were constructed at educational institutions, although most were gone by the end of the decade. The surviving stations were mostly at land-grant colleges.

In the early 1930s, experimental television teaching programs were produced at the University of Iowa, Purdue University, and Kansas State College. However, it was not until the 1950s that college credit courses were offered via broadcast television: Western Reserve University was the first to offer a continuous series of such courses, beginning in 1951. Sunrise Semester was a well-known televised series of college courses offered by New York University on CBS from 1957 to 1982.

Satellite technology, developed in the 1960s and made cost effective in the 1980s, enabled the rapid spread of instructional television. Federally funded experiments in the United States and Canada, such as the Appalachian Education Satellite Project (1974–1975), demonstrated the feasibility of satellite-delivered instruction. However, these early experiments were loudly criticized for being poorly planned. More recent attempts at satellite-delivered distance education have been more successful. The first state educational satellite system, Learn/Alaska, was created in 1980. It offered 6 hours of instructional television daily to 100 villages, some of them accessible only by air. The privately operated TI-IN Network, of San Antonio, Texas, delivered a wide variety of courses via satellite to high schools across the United States beginning in 1985.

In the late 1980s and early 1990s, the development of fiber-optic communication systems allowed for the expansion of live, two-way, high-quality audio and video systems in education. Whereas the initial cost of fiber-optic systems may be high, the long-term savings and benefits of the technology outweigh the initial costs. Many consider fiber-optic delivery systems as the least expensive option for the high-quality, two-way audio and video required for live two-way interactive distance education. Iowa has the largest statewide fiber-optic system. Currently the Iowa Communications Network (ICN) provides full-motion, two-way interactive video, data (Internet), and voice services to over 1,000 Iowa classrooms. School districts, area education agencies, and public libraries in Iowa have classrooms connected to the fiber-optics of the ICN. The ICN also serves as the backbone for computer telecommunications, and asynchronous, Internet-based programs are being offered to distant learners. Over 100,000 hours of formal educational opportunities were offered during the first 18 months of the network's service. Recently, hundreds of thousands of hours were being offered every month (Gillispie, Cassis, Fujinaka, & McMahon 2013).

Distance education opportunities are quickly growing through the use of computer-mediated communications and the Internet. Both credit and noncredit courses have been offered over using the Internet since the mid-1980s. In most cases, a teacher organizes the course materials, readings, and assignments. The students read the material, view videos, listen to recordings, complete assignments, and participate in online discussions with other classmates. The advent of computer conferencing capabilities has had an impact on the traditional approach to the design of distance education instruction. Computer conferencing increases the potential for interaction and collaborative work among the students. This type of collaboration among students was difficult with previous forms of distance education.

In addition, computer networks are a convenient way to distribute course materials to students around the world. Many faculty members now use the convenient user interface of the World Wide Web to make course materials available to their students. The British Open University, Fern Universität of Germany, and the University of Twente in the Netherlands are some of the leading providers of online courses in Europe. In the United States, the Western Governors University, Nova Southeastern University, and the University of Phoenix have been traditional leaders in providing distance education. They, along with many other universities, now offer thousands of courses online.

Some might consider Massive Open Online Courses (MOOCs; rhymes with how cows talk, mooo-k) as the future of distance education—most do not. MOOCs are usually well designed college level courses, delivered using the Internet to anyone who wishes to enroll. MOOC courses are massive, often with enrollments in the tens of thousands. Next, they are open, meaning open access courseware is used to deliver the course, and enrollment is open to anyone who is interested. Next, MOOCs are online, fully online, and asynchronous. And last, they are courses, often a digitized version of a traditional lecture class with sessions recorded in video, audio, and posted online (Simonson, 2012). At this point, the longevity of MOOCs is questioned and considerable debate is occurring among administrators and faculty (Lombardi, 2013). In other words, the impact of MOOCs is yet to be determined.

Distance Teaching Universities

The 1962 decision that the University of South Africa would become a distance teaching university brought about a fundamental change in the way distance education was practiced in much of the world. Another landmark was the founding, in 1971, of the Open University of the United Kingdom, a degree-giving distance teaching university offering full degree programs, sophisticated courses, and the innovative use of media (Holmberg, 1986). The Open University brought heightened prestige to distance education and spurred the establishment of similar institutions in industrial nations such as West Germany, Japan, and Canada, as well as in such lesser developed nations as Sri Lanka and Pakistan.

Although the distance teaching universities shared numerous similarities, they were not identical in their mission or practice. Two of the largest and most influential, the Open University of the United Kingdom and the German Fern Universität, differ widely. The British school favors employed, part-time students of above-normal study age, and allows them to enroll without formal entrance qualifications.

The German Fern Universität, founded in 1975, offers a more rigorous program than its British counterpart. Despite strict, formal entrance requirements, it had 28,000 students in 1985. However, the dropout rate is very high, and in its first decade, only 500 students completed the full curricula for a university degree.

Holmberg (1986) offers numerous political, economic, and educational reasons for the founding of distance teaching universities, including:

▪ The need felt in many countries to increase the offerings of university education generally;

▪ A realization that adults with jobs, family responsibilities, and social commitments form a large group of prospective part-time university students;

▪ A wish to serve both individuals and society by offering study opportunities to adults, among them disadvantaged groups;

▪ The need found in many professions for further training at an advanced level;

▪ A wish to support educational innovation; and

▪ A belief in the feasibility of an economical use of educational resources by mediated teaching.

Massive Open Online Courses (MOOCs)

Massive open online courses, or MOOCs, pronounced interestingly enough as mooooks as in cow sounds, are the "talk of the town." A recent issue of the *Chronicle of Higher Education* dedicated its entire issue to the topic of MOOCs. The *New York Times* has written about MOOCs, as have many local newspapers.

Just what are MOOCs and what do they offer to the field of distance education. Simply, the name tells it all. MOOC courses are massive, often with enrollments in the tens of thousands. Next, they are open, meaning open access courseware is used to deliver the course, and enrollment is open to anyone who is interested. Next, MOOCs are online, fully online and asynchronous. And last, they are courses, often a digitized version of a traditional lecture class with sessions recorded in video, audio and posted online.

But, are MOOCs distance education, as many think? First, one needs to define distance education. Distance Learning journal has regularly applied this definition:

> Institutionally-based formal education, where the learning group is separated, and where interactive communications technologies are used to connect the instructor, learners and resources. (Simonson et al., 2012)

At first glance this definition does seem to include MOOCs as they are most often configured. MOOCs are institutionally-based, at least originally they were. The great universities of the United States, such as the Massachusetts Institute of Technology, and Stanford, offer MOOCs. Interestingly, many of the instigators of MOOCs initiatives have left their universities to offer massive online courses via private corporations.

Next, it is obvious that the learning group is separated, at least the learners and resources are geographically separated. But what about the instructors? Certainly MOOC designers and the talent featured in the videos can be considered instructors, but are these individuals actually involved in the use of the MOOC or are they "just talent?" Instructor involvement in the teaching and learning process is unclear.

Most definitely, communications technologies are used to deliver content and make the content available to learners; most often content is digitized content via the web. Often, class presentations are video recorded, documents are digitized, and self-test quizzes and exams are written and programmed, often with self-scoring.

So, are MOOCs distance education? A closer examination of the definition of distance education may be helpful. Distance education consists of distance teaching AND distance learning—two components of the education process. Do MOOCs provide both teaching and learning? Some say no, since the instructional aspects of MOOCs are programmed and offered but only as a pre-packaged self–study system.

MOOCs are usually loaded with outstanding content, and well-delivered presentations, but those who would claim that MOOCs are the future of higher education need only review the instructional films and instructional video phenomena of the 1960s and 1970s. Excellent self-study, but not education.

Educational Colonialism

Colonialism, the noun, is the policy or practice of acquiring full or partial political control over another country, occupying it with settlers, and exploiting it economically.

Education, the noun, is the process of receiving or giving systematic, formal instruction, usually at a school or university—also, an enlightening experience involving teaching and learning.

So, is there such a thing as educational colonialism, which could be defined as the policy of acquiring full or partial control over another country's educational system, occupying it will nonlocal teachers, and exploiting it educationally?

To some, distance education could be an example of educational colonialism, since the practice of teaching and learning at a distance seems to be the antithesis of local education. Yet, most readers of this journal probably think it may be possible to combine the advantages of distance education with the expectation of many that they should control their local schools, colleges and universities.

The massive open online course is a notable application of distance education. MOOCs utilize the expertise of eminent scholars and teachers, often from the most prestigious universities to offer world class education to anyone in the world, sometimes for free.

Is it possible for the field of distance education to be tailored to meet local needs? Can distance education, defined as institutionally based formal education with interactive telecommunications systems used to connect learners, instructors and resources, be a community, region, or state-based approached. Or, must distance education ultimately be a massive system?

Possibly we should be advocating a new approach to distance education—the localization of distance education. Next, another definition is needed—localization or local control. Here is what the Great Schools Partnership says about local control in education

In education, **local control** refers to (1) the governing and management of public schools by elected or appointed representatives serving on governing bodies, such as school boards or school committees, that are located in the communities served by the schools, and (2) the degree to which local leaders, institutions, and governing bodies can make independent or autonomous decisions about the governance and operation of public schools.

The concept of local control is grounded in a philosophy of government premised on the belief that the individuals and institutions closest to the students and most knowledgeable about a school—and most invested in the welfare and success of its educators, students, and communities—are best suited to making important decisions related to its operation, leadership, staffing, academics, teaching, and improvement.

Wow, an interesting situation. distance education provides the promise of teaching and learning from the best people and places to nearly anyone, anywhere. Yet, there is considerable and important relevance to the local control of education, especially in the United States. Is localized distance education possible? Perhaps it would be a good idea to study the concept of localization of distance education.

And finally, as Thomas Jefferson is purported to have said, perhaps written, an educated citizenry is a vital requisite for our survival as a free people.

THEORY AND DISTANCE EDUCATION

Most students, and many teachers, cringe at the thought of a discussion of theory. This need not be the case. This section is designed not to intimidate or to bore, but to inform. Theory is important to the study of distance education because it directly impacts the practice of the field.

Traditionally, theories of distance education have come from sources external to North America. Recently, the field in the United States has matured to the point where indigenous definitions and theories have begun to emerge.

The Need for Theory

Although forms of distance education have existed since the 1840s and attempts at theoretical explanations of distance education had been undertaken by leading scholars in the field, the need for a theory base of distance education was still largely unfulfilled in the 1970s. Holmberg (1985) stated that further theoretical considerations would contribute results that would give distance educators a firmly based theory, a touchstone against which decisions could be made with confidence. In 1986, Holmberg continued to recognize the need for theoretical considerations:

> One consequence of such understanding and explanation will be that hypotheses can be developed and submitted to falsification attempts. This will lead to insights telling us what in distance education is to be expected under what conditions and circumstances, thus paving the way for corroborated practical methodological application. (p. 3)

Moore (1994) was concerned that the progress of distance education would be hindered by the lack of attention to what he called the "macro factors." He indicated that in this area of education there was a need to describe and define the field, to discriminate between the various components of the field, and to identify the critical elements of the various forms of learning and teaching.

Keegan (1988) implied the continued need for a theory of distance education when he lamented the lack of it:

> Lack of accepted theory has weakened distance education: there has been a lack of identity, a sense of belonging to the periphery and the lack of a touchstone against which decisions on methods, on media, on financing, on student support, when they have to be made, can be made with confidence. (p. 63)

More recently, Keegan (1988) stated his ideas about what the theory should encompass. According to Keegan, a firmly based theory of distance education will be one that can provide the touchstone against which decisions—political, financial, educational, social—

when they have to be made can be made with confidence. This would replace the ad hoc response to a set of conditions that arises in some "crisis" situation of problem solving, which normally characterizes this field of education.

In a general sense, *theory* is taken to mean a set of hypotheses logically related to one another in explaining and predicting occurrences. Holmberg (1985) stated the following:

> the aim of the theoretician is to find explanatory theories; that is to say, the theories that describe certain structural properties of the world, and which permit us to deduce, with the help of initial conditions, the effects to be explained.... Theoretical, to bring explanation, on the other hand practical, to provide for application or technology. (p. 5)

Keegan (1995) added:

> A theory is something that eventually can be reduced to a phrase, a sentence or a paragraph and which, while subsuming all the practical research, gives the foundation on which the structures of need, purpose and administration can be erected. (p. 20)

In 1995 Holmberg gave a more specific definition of the concept of theory. He stated that a theory means:

> a systematic ordering of ideas about the phenomenon of our field of inquiry and an overarching logical structure of reasoned suppositions which can generate intersubjectively testable hypotheses. (p. 4)

Holmberg suggested that distance education has been characterized by a trial-and-error approach with little consideration being given to a theoretical basis for decision making. He suggested that the theoretical underpinnings of distance education are fragile. Most efforts in this field have been practical or mechanical and have concentrated on the logistics of the enterprise.

To some, distance education represents a deviation from conventional education. Holmberg claimed it was a distinct form of education. Keegan (1996) also concluded that distance education is a distinct field of education, parallel to and a complement of conventional education. Shale (1988) countered that all of what constitutes the process of education when teacher and student are able to meet face to face also constitutes the process of education when the teacher and student are physically separated.

Cropley and Kahl (1983) compared and contrasted distance education and face-to-face education in terms of psychological dimensions, and claimed neither set of principles emerged in a pure form. Peters (1988) strongly stated that:

> Anyone professionally involved in education is compelled to presume the existence of two forms of instruction which are strictly separable: traditional face-to-face teaching based on interpersonal communication and industrialized teaching, which is based on objectivized, rationalized technologically produced interaction. (p. 20)

In his landmark work *The Foundations of Distance Education,* Keegan (1996) classified theories of distance education into three groups:

- Theories of independence and autonomy
- Theories of industrialization of teaching
- Theories of interaction and communication

A fourth category seeks to explain distance education in a synthesis of existing theories of communication and diffusion, as well as philosophies of education.

Theory of Independent Study—Charles Wedemeyer

For Wedemeyer (1981), the essence of distance education was the independence of the student. This was reflected in his preference for the term *independent study* for distance education at the college or university level. Wedemeyer was critical of contemporary patterns of higher education. He thought that outdated concepts of learning and teaching were being employed, and that they failed to utilize modern technologies in ways that could alter the institution.

Wedemeyer set forth a system with 10 characteristics emphasizing learner independence and adoption of technology as a way to implement that independence. According to Wedemeyer (1981), the system should do the following:

1. Be capable of operation anyplace where there are students—or even only one student—whether or not there are teachers at the same place at the same time;
2. Place greater responsibility for learning on the student;
3. Free faculty members from custodial-type duties so that more time can be given to truly educational tasks;
4. Offer students and adults wider choices (more opportunities) in courses, formats, and methodologies;
5. Use, as appropriate, all the teaching media and methods that have been proved effective;
6. Mix media and methods so that each subject or unit within a subject is taught in the best way known;
7. Cause the redesign and development of courses to fit into an "articulated media program";
8. Preserve and enhance opportunities for adaptation to individual differences;
9. Evaluate student achievement simply, not by raising barriers concerned with the place, rate, method, or sequence of student study; and
10. Permit students to start, stop, and learn at their own pace.

Wedemeyer proposed separating teaching from learning as a way of breaking education's "space-time barriers." He suggested six characteristics of independent study systems:

1. The student and teacher are separated.
2. The normal processes of teaching and learning are carried out in writing or through some other medium.
3. Teaching is individualized.
4. Learning takes place through the student's activity.
5. Learning is made convenient for the student in his or her own environment.
6. The learner takes responsibility for the pace of his or her own progress, with freedom to start and stop at any time.

Wedemeyer noted four elements of every teaching/learning situation: a teacher, a learner or learners, a communications system or mode, and something to be taught or learned. He proposed a reorganization of these elements that would accommodate physical space and allow greater learner freedom. Key to the success of distance education, Wedemeyer believed, was the development of the relationship between student and teacher.

Theory of Independent Study and Theory of Transactional Distance—Michael Moore

Formulated in the early 1970s, Moore's theory of distance education, which he calls "independent study," is a classification method for distance education programs. Shaped in part by Moore's adult education and university extension experience, it examines two variables in educational programs: the amount of learner autonomy and the distance between teacher and learner. Transactional distance is stated to "connote the interplay among the environment, the individuals and the patterns of behaviors in a situation" (Moore, 2013, p. 68; Moore & Kearsley, 2012) states that the theory of transactional distance is a "typology of all education programs having this distinguishing characteristic of separation of teacher and learner" (p. 68). Transactional distance is relative rather than absolute, and describes the fullest range of all possible degrees of structure, dialogue, and autonomy in environments that have the special characteristic of teacher and student being spatially separate from one another (Moore, 2013).

For Moore, distance education is composed of two elements, each of which can be measured. First is the provision for two-way communication (dialog). Some systems or programs offer greater amounts of two-way communication than others. Second is the extent to which a program is responsive to the needs of the individual learner (structure). Some programs are very structured, while others are very responsive to the needs and goals of the individual student.

In the second part of this theory, Moore (2013) addresses learner autonomy. He notes that in traditional school settings, learners are very dependent on teachers for guidance, and that in most programs, conventional and distance, the teacher is active whereas the student is passive. In distance education, there is a gap between teacher and student, so the student must accept a high degree of responsibility for the conduct of the learning program. The autonomous learner needs little help from the teacher, who may be more of a respondent than a director. Some adult learners, however, require help in formulating their learning objectives, identifying sources of information, and measuring objectives.

Moore (2013) classifies distance education programs as "autonomous" (learner determined) or "nonautonomous" (teacher determined), and gauges the degree of autonomy accorded the learner by answers to the following three questions:

1. Is the selection of learning objectives in the program the responsibility of the learner or of the teacher? (autonomy in setting of objectives)
2. Is the selection and use of resource persons, of bodies and other media, the decision of the teacher or the learner? (autonomy in methods of study)
3. Are the decisions about the method of evaluation and criteria to be used made by the learner or the teacher? (autonomy in evaluation)

Theory of Industrialization of Teaching—Otto Peters

In a major treatise on education, Otto Peters of Germany developed a view of distance education as an industrialized form of teaching and learning. He examined a research base that included an extensive analysis of the distance teaching organizations of the 1960s.

This led him to propose that distance education could be analyzed by comparing it with the industrial production of goods. He stated that from many points of view, conventional, oral, group-based education was a preindustrial form of education. His statement implied that distance teaching could not have existed before the industrial era. Using economic and industrial theory, Peters (1988) proposed the following new categories (terminology) for the analysis of distance education:

- **Rationalization.** The use of methodical measures to reduce the required amount of input of power, time, and money. In distance education, ways of thinking, attitudes, and procedures can be found that only established themselves in the wake of an increased rationalization in the industrialization of production processes.
- **Division of labor.** The division of a task into simpler components or subtasks. In distance education, the tasks of conveying information, counseling, assessment, and recording performance are performed by separate individuals. To Peters, the division of labor is the main prerequisite for the advantages of distance education to become effective.
- **Mechanization.** The use of machines in a work process. Distance education, Peters noted, would be impossible without machines. Duplicating machines and transport systems are prerequisites, and later forms of distance teaching have the additional facilities of modern means of communication and electronic data processing installations.
- **Assembly line.** Commonly, a method of work in which workers remain stationary, while objects they are working on move past them. In traditional distance education programs, materials for both teacher and student are not the product of an individual. Rather, instructional materials are designed, printed, stored, distributed, and graded by specialists.
- **Mass production.** The production of goods in large quantities. Peters noted that because demand outstrips supply at colleges and universities, there has been a trend toward large-scale operations not entirely consistent with traditional forms of academic teaching. Mass production of distance education courses, however, can enhance quality. Peters believed that the large number of courses produced forced distance teaching organizations to analyze the requirements of potential distance learners far more carefully than in conventional teaching and to improve the quality of the courses.
- **Preparatory work.** Determining how workers, machines, and materials can usefully relate to each other during each phase of the production process. Peters thought that the success of distance education depended decisively on a preparatory phase. The preparatory phase concerns the development of the distance study course involving experts in the various specialist fields with qualifications often higher than those of other teachers involved in distance study.
- **Planning.** The system of decisions that determines an operation prior to it being carried out. Peters noted that planning was important in the development phase of distance education, as the contents of correspondence units, from the first to the last, must be determined in detail, adjusted in relation to each other, and represented in a predetermined number of correspondence units. The importance of planning is even greater when residential study is a component of a distance education program.
- **Organization.** Creating general or permanent arrangements for purpose-oriented activity. Peters noted the relationship between rational organization and effectiveness of the teaching method. Organization makes it possible for students to receive exactly predetermined documents at appointed times, for an appropriate university teacher to be immediately available for each assignment sent in, and for consultations to take place at

fixed locations at fixed times. Organization, Peters pointed out, was optimized in large distance education programs.

▪ **Scientific control methods.** The methods by which work processes are analyzed systematically, particularly by time studies, and in accordance with the results obtained from measurements and empirical data. The work processes are tested and controlled in their elementary details in a planned way, in order to increase productivity, all the time making the best possible use of working time and the staff available. In distance education, some institutions hire experts to apply techniques of scientific analysis to the evaluation of courses.

▪ **Formalization.** The predetermination of the phases of the manufacturing process. In distance education, all the points in the cycle, from student, to distance teaching establishment, to the academics allocated, must be determined exactly.

▪ **Standardization.** The limitations of manufacture to a restricted number of types of one product, in order to make these more suitable for their purpose, cheaper to produce, and easier to replace. In distance education, not only is the format of correspondence units standardized, so are the stationery for written communication between student and lecturer, the organizational support, and also the academic content.

▪ **Change of function.** The change of the role or job of the worker in the production process. In distance education, change of function is evident in the role of the lecturer. The original role of provider of knowledge in the form of the lecturer is split into that of study unit author and that of marker; the role of counselor is allocated to a particular person or position. Frequently, the original role of lecturer is reduced to that of a consultant whose involvement in distance teaching manifests itself in periodically recurrent contributions.

▪ **Objectification.** The loss, in the production process, of the subjective element that was used to determine work to a considerable degree. In distance education, most teaching functions are objectified as they are determined by the distance study course as well as technical means. Only in written communication with the distance learner or possibly in a consultation or the brief additional face-to-face events on campus does the teacher have some individual scope left for subjectively determined variants in teaching method.

▪ **Concentration and centralization.** Because of the large amounts of capital required for mass production and the division of labor, there has been a trend toward large industrial concerns with a concentration of capital, a centralized administration, and a market that is monopolized. Peters noted the trend toward distance education institutions serving very large numbers of students. The Open University of the United Kingdom, for instance, recently had tens of thousands of students. It is more economical to establish a small number of such institutions serving a national population, rather than a larger number of institutions serving regional populations.

Peters concluded that for distance teaching to become effective, the principle of the division of labor is a constituent element of distance teaching. The teaching process in his theory of industrialization is gradually restructured through increasing mechanization and automation. He noted that:

▪ The development of distance study courses is just as important as the preparatory work—taking place prior to the production process.

▪ The effectiveness of the teaching process particularly depends on planning and organization.

▪ Courses must be formalized and expectations of students must be standardized.

- The teaching process is largely objectified.
- The function of academics teaching at a distance has changed considerably vis-à-vis university teachers in conventional teaching.
- Distance study can only be economical with a concentration of the available resources and a centralized administration.

According to Peters, within the complex overall distance teaching activity, one area has been exposed to investigation that had been regularly omitted from traditional analysis. New concepts were used to describe new facts that merit attention. He did not deny that a theory of the industrialization of teaching had disadvantages, but in any exploration of teaching, the industrial structures characteristic of distance teaching need to be taken into account in decision making.

Theory of Interaction and Communication— Börje Holmberg

Holmberg's theory of distance education, what he calls *guided didactic conversation*, falls into the general category of communication theory. Holmberg (1985) noted that his theory had explanatory value in relating teaching effectiveness to the impact of feelings of belonging and cooperation as well as to the actual exchange of questions, answers, and arguments in mediated communication. Holmberg offers seven background assumptions for his theory:

1. The core of teaching is interaction between the teaching and learning parties; it is assumed that simulated interaction through subject-matter presentation in preproduced courses can take over part of the interaction by causing students to consider different views, approaches, and solutions and generally interact with a course.
2. Emotional involvement in the study and feelings of personal relation between the teaching and learning parties are likely to contribute to learning pleasure.
3. Learning pleasure supports student motivation.
4. Participation in decision making concerning the study is favorable to student motivation.
5. Strong student motivation facilitates learning.
6. A friendly, personal tone and easy access to the subject matter contribute to learning pleasure, support student motivation, and thus facilitate learning from the presentations of preproduced courses (i.e., from teaching in the form of one-way traffic simulating interaction, as well as from didactic communication in the form of two-way traffic between the teaching and learning parties).
7. The effectiveness of teaching is demonstrated by students' learning of what has been taught.

These assumptions, Holmberg (1986) states, are the basis of the essential teaching principles of distance education. From these assumptions he formed his theory that distance teaching will support student motivation, promote learning pleasure, and make the study relevant to the individual learner and his or her needs, creating feelings of rapport between the learner and the distance education institution (its tutors, counselors, etc.); facilitating access to course content; engaging the learner in activities, discussions, and decisions; and generally catering to helpful real and simulated communication to and from the learner.

Holmberg notes that this is admittedly a leaky theory. However, he adds, it is not devoid of explanatory power—it does, in fact, indicate essential characteristics of effective distance education.

In 1995, Holmberg significantly broadened his theory of distance education. His new comprehensive theory of distance education is divided into eight parts. This expanded theory encompasses the theory just stated previously, plus these additions:

1. Distance education serves individual learners who cannot or do not want to make use of face-to-face teaching. These learners are very heterogeneous.

2. Distance education means learners no longer have to be bound by decisions made by others about place of study, division of the year into study terms and vacations, timetables, and entry requirements. Distance education thus promotes students' freedom of choice and independence.

3. Society benefits from distance education, on the one hand, from the liberal study opportunities it affords individual learners, and, on the other hand, from the professional/occupational training it provides.

4. Distance education is an instrument for recurrent and lifelong learning and for free access to learning opportunities and equity.

5. All learning concerned with the acquisition of cognitive knowledge and cognitive skills as well as affective learning and some psychomotor learning are effectively provided for by distance education. Distance education may inspire metacognitive approaches.

6. Distance education is based on deep learning as an individual activity. Learning is guided and supported by noncontiguous means. Teaching and learning rely on mediated communication, usually based on preproduced courses.

7. Distance education is open to behaviorist, cognitive, constructivist, and other modes of learning. It has an element of industrialization with division of labor, use of mechanical devices, electronic data processing, and mass communication, usually based on preproduced courses.

8. Personal relations, study pleasure, and empathy between students and those supporting them (tutors, counselors, etc.) are central to learning in distance education. Feelings of empathy and belonging promote students' motivation to learn and influence the learning favorably. Such feelings are conveyed by students being engaged in decision making; by lucid, problem-oriented, conversation like presentations of learning matter that may be anchored in existing knowledge; by friendly, noncontiguous interaction between students and tutors, counselors, and others supporting them and by liberal organizational/administrative structures and processes.

Though it is an effective mode of training, distance education runs the risk of leading to mere fact learning and reproduction of accepted "truths." However, it can be organized and carried out in such a way that students are encouraged to search, criticize, and identify positions of their own. It thus serves conceptual learning, problem learning, and genuinely academic ends.

In sum, the previous list represents, on the one hand, a description of distance education and, on the other hand, a theory from which hypotheses are generated and that has explanatory power in that it identifies a general approach favorable to learning and to the teaching efforts conducive to learning.

Andragogy—Malcolm Knowles

Most now consider Knowles's work to be a theory of distance education; it is relevant because most often adults are involved in distance education, and andragogy deals with frameworks for programs designed for the adult learner. At its core is the idea that "the attainment of adulthood is concomitant on adults' coming to perceive themselves as self-directing individuals" (Brookfield, 1986).

Knowles spent a career formulating a theory of adult learning based on research and experience related to the characteristics of the adult learner (Knowles, 1990). The andragogical process consists of seven elements:

1. The establishment of a climate conducive to adult learning, which includes a physical environment that is conducive to the physical well-being of the adult learner, and a psychological environment that provides for a feeling of mutual respect, collaborativeness, trust, openness, and authenticity.
2. The creation of an organizational structure for participatory learning that includes planning groups where learners provide input about what is to be learned and options regarding learning activities.
3. The diagnosis of needs for learning that includes differentiating between felt needs and ascribed needs.
4. The formulation of directions for learning that includes objectives with terminal behaviors to be achieved and directions for improvement of abilities.
5. The development of a design for activities that clarifies resources and strategies to accomplish objectives.
6. The development of a plan that provides evidence when objectives are accomplished.
7. The use of quantitative and qualitative evaluation that provides a rediagnosis of needs for learning.

Knowles's andragogy suggests a number of characteristics needed in distance education systems designed for adults. For example:

▪ The physical environment of an online video-based classroom used by adults should be designed so that participants are able to see what is occurring, not just hear it.
▪ The environment should be one that promotes respect and dignity for the adult learner.
▪ Adult learners must feel supported, and when criticism is a part of discussions or presentations made by adults, it is important that clear ground rules be established so comments are not directed toward a person, but instead concentrate on content and ideas.
▪ A starting point for a course, or module of a course, should be the needs and interest of the adult learner.
▪ Course plans should include clear course descriptions, learning objectives, resources, and timelines for events.
▪ General-to-specific patterns of content presentation work best for adult learners.
▪ Active participation should be encouraged, such as by the use of work groups or study teams.

A Synthesis of Existing Theories—Hilary Perraton

Perraton's theory of distance education is composed of elements from existing theories of communication and diffusion, as well as philosophies of education. It is expressed in the form of 14 statements, or hypotheses. The first five of these statements concern the way distance teaching can be used to maximize education:

- You can use any medium to teach anything.
- Distance teaching can break the integuments of fixed staffing ratios that limited the expansion of education when teacher and student had to be in the same place at the same time.
- There are circumstances under which distance teaching can be cheaper than orthodox education, whether measured in terms of audience reached or of learning.
- The economies achievable by distance education are functions of the level of education, size of audience, choice of media, and sophistication of production.
- Distance teaching can reach audiences who would not be reached by ordinary means.

The following four statements address the need to increase dialog:

- It is possible to organize distance teaching in such a way that there is dialog.
- Where a tutor meets distance students face to face, the tutor's role is changed from that of a communicator of information to that of a facilitator of learning.
- Group discussion is an effective method of learning when distance teaching is used to bring relevant information to the group.
- In most communities, resources are available that can be used to support distance learning to its educational and economic advantage.

The final five statements deal with method:

- A multimedia program is likely to be more effective than one that relies on a single medium.
- A systems approach is helpful in planning distance education.
- Feedback is a necessary part of a distance learning system.
- To be effective, distance teaching materials should ensure that students undertake frequent and regular activities over and above reading, watching, or listening.
- In choosing between media, the key decision on which the rest depend concerns the use of face-to-face learning.

Equivalency Theory: An American Theory of Distance Education

The impact of new technologies on distance education is far-ranging. Desmond Keegan (1995) suggests that electronically linking instructor and students at various locations creates a virtual classroom. Keegan goes on to state:

> The theoretical analyses of virtual education, however, have not yet been addressed by the literature: Is it a subset of distance education or to be regarded as a separate field of educational endeavor? What are its didactic structures? What is the relationship of its cost effectiveness and of its educational effectiveness to distance education and to conventional education? (p. 21)

It is in this environment of virtual education that the equivalency theory of distance education has emerged. Some advocates of distance education have mistakenly tried to provide identical instructional situations for all students, no matter when or where they learn. Since it is more difficult to control the situations of distant learners, some have decided that all learners should participate as distant learners. This is based on the idea that learners should have identical opportunities to learn. This is a mistake. Simonson theorizes that for distance education to be successful in the United States, its appropriate application should be based on the approach

> that the more equivalent the learning experiences of distant students are to that of local students, the more equivalent will be the outcomes of the learning experience. (2009, p. 25)

In other words, equivalent, rather than identical, learning experiences should be provided to each learner whether local or distant, and the expectation should be that equivalent outcomes, rather than identical, should be expected of each learner. Thus, each learner might access different, unequal, yet equivalent instructional strategies, varying instructional resources, or individually prescribed activities that are different from what is prescribed to other students. If the distance education course is effectively designed and equivalent experiences are available, then potential learners will reach the course's instructional objectives (Simonson & Schlosser, 1999).

This theory is based on the definition of distance education as formal, institutionally based education where the learning group is separated, and where interactive telecommunications systems are used to connect learners, resources, and instructors.

Simonson and Schlosser (1995) in elaborating on this theory state:

> It should not be necessary for any group of learners to compensate for different, possibly lesser, instructional experiences. Thus, those developing distance educational systems should strive to make equivalent the learning experiences of all students no matter how they are linked to the resources or instruction they require. (pp. 71–72)

Key to this theoretical approach is the concept of equivalency. Local and distant learners have fundamentally different environments in which they learn. It is the responsibility of the distance educator to design, even overdesign, learning events that provide experiences with equivalent value for learners. Just as a triangle and a square may have the same *area* and be considered equivalent even though they are quite different geometrical shapes, the experiences of the local learner and the distant learner should have *equivalent value* even though these experiences might be quite different. In 2006, the U.S. Department of Education's Office of Postsecondary Education released an interesting report titled "Evidence of Quality in Distance Education Programs Drawn from Interviews with the Accreditation Community." In this report it was noted that a "red flag" or warning sign of ineffective distance education programs was when faculty attempted or were encouraged to directly convert regular courses into distance-delivered courses (Simonson, 2007a). Identical traditional and distance-delivered courses are not likely to be effective, rather, a variety of equivalent instructional approaches should be provided for students—local and distant—to learn from.

Another key to this approach is the concept of the learning experience. A learning experience is anything that promotes learning, including what is observed, felt, heard, or done. It is likely that different students in various locations, learning at different times, may require a different mix of learning experiences. Some will need a greater amount of observing, and others a larger dosage of doing. The goal of instructional planning is to make the sum of learning experiences for each learner equivalent. Instructional design procedures should attempt to anticipate and provide the collection of experiences that will be most suitable for each student or group of students (Schlosser & Simonson, 2010).

A Theoretical Framework for Distance Education—Desmond Keegan

Keegan (1996) suggested that the theoretician had to answer three questions before developing a theory of distance education:

1. *Is distance education an educational activity?* Keegan's answer was that although distance education institutions possess some of the characteristics of businesses, rather than of traditional schools, their educational activities are dominant. Distance education is a more industrialized form of education. The theoretical bases for distance education, Keegan pointed out, are within general education theory.

2. *Is distance education a form of conventional education?* Keegan thought that because distance education is not based on interpersonal communication and is characterized by a privatization of institutionalized learning (as is conventional education), it is a distinct form of education. Therefore, while the theoretical basis for distance education could be found within general education theory, it could not be found within the theoretical structures of oral, group-based education.

    However, Keegan considered virtual systems based on teaching face to face at a distance to be a new cognate field of study to distance education. He thought that a theoretical analysis of virtual education still needed to be addressed.

3. *Is distance education possible, or is it a contradiction in terms?* Keegan pointed out that if education requires intersubjectivity—a shared experience in which teacher and learner are united by a common zeal—then distance education is a contradiction in terms. Distance instruction is possible, but distance education is not. Again, the advent of virtual systems used in distance education challenges the traditional answer to this question.

Central to Keegan's concept of distance education is the separation of the teaching acts in time and place from the learning acts. Successful distance education, he states, requires the reintegration of the two acts:

▪ The intersubjectivity of teacher and learner, in which learning from teaching occurs, has to be artificially re-created. Over space and time, a distance system seeks to reconstruct the moment in which the teaching/learning interaction occurs. The linking of learning materials to learning is central to this process (Keegan, 1996, pp. 43–45).

▪ Reintegration of the act of teaching at a distance is attempted in two ways. First, learning materials, both print and nonprint, are designed to achieve as many of the characteristics of interpersonal communication as possible. Second, when courses are presented, reintegration of the teaching act is attempted by a variety of techniques, including communication by correspondence, telephone tutorial, online computer communication, comments on assignments by tutors or computers, and teleconferences.

The process of reintegrating the act of teaching in distance education, Keegan suggests, results in at least five changes to the normal structure of oral, group-based education:

1. The industrialization of teaching;
2. The privatization of institutional learning;
3. Change of administrative structure;
4. Different plant and buildings; and
5. Change of costing structures.

Keegan offers three hypotheses drawn from his theoretical framework:

1. Distance students have a tendency to drop out of those institutions in which structures for the reintegration of the teaching acts are not satisfactorily achieved.
2. Distance students have difficulty achieving quality of learning in those institutions in which structures for the reintegration of the teaching acts are not satisfactorily achieved.
3. The status of learning at a distance may be questioned in those institutions in which the reintegration of the teaching acts is not satisfactorily achieved.

Fordism, Neo-Fordism, Post-Fordism: A Theoretical Debate

Recently, Peters's view of distance education has received renewed attention. For examples, the recent explosion in popularity of Massive Open Online Courses has brought about a reexamination of industrialization, and the principles of Fordism. MOOCs have "struck a nerve among university executives, trustees, and faculty" (Lombardi, 2013,p. 293). Interestingly, most of those who are "nerve-struck" have never heard of Otto Peters and industrialized education. (Swan, 2010).

Peters theory of industrialized education is a point of departure and is extended and revised based on contemporary industrial transformation in a debate on the future of distance education. *Fordism* and *post-Fordism* are the terms borrowed from industrial sociology to classify the opposing views of the debate. This debate deals with changes in the practice of distance education and represents wider debates about the nature of change in the contemporary period (Edwards, 1995; McGee & Green, 2008). While not all would agree that the Fordist framework applies to distance education (Rumble, 1995a, 1995b, 1995c), it has become the mainstream theory of distance education in international literature and provides a useful analogy in debating the practice of distance education.

The term *Fordism* is derived from Henry Ford's approach to the mass production for mass consumption of automobiles early in the 20th century. *Fordism, neo-Fordism,* and *post-Fordism* are terms that represent three ways to conceptualize the production of distance education. Each of these ideal-type models suggests very different social, political, and educational outcomes. Badham and Mathews (1989) provide a clear model for understanding the three categories of distance education production.

They proposed that a firm's production process and its production strategy can be defined in terms of the three variables of product variety, process innovation, and labor responsibility, and they suggested that a production paradigm represents an exemplary model of efficient production, which guides organizational strategy.

In looking at these three variables, Fordism would be described as having low product innovation, low process variability, and low labor responsibility. Neo-Fordism would have high product innovation and high process variability, but would maintain the low labor responsibility of the Fordism definition. High product innovation, high process variability, and high labor responsibility would typify the post-Fordism model. Campion (1995) illustrated how these three different production processes relate to distance education:

- The *Fordist strategy* for distance education suggests a fully centralized, single-mode, national distance education provider, gaining greater economies of scale by offering courses to a mass market, thereby justifying a greater investment in more expensive course materials. Rationalization of this kind allows for increased administrative control and a more extreme division of labor as the production process is fragmented into an increasing number of component tasks.
- The *neo-Fordist strategy* extends the Fordist system by allowing much higher levels of flexibility and diversity, and by combining low volumes with high levels of product and process innovation. However, neo-Fordist production retains a highly centralized Fordist approach to labor organization and control. A neo-Fordist expression of distance education might well be represented by a centrally controlled, perhaps multinational, yet locally administered model of distance education. By also using self-instructional course materials for teaching on-campus students, it has the potential to massively reduce costs across the whole student population. However, and most important, a neo-Fordist manifestation of distance education bears a strong relationship to that of the Fordist route inasmuch as it has an overall despoiling effect on academic staff.
- *High levels of all three variables characterize the post-Fordist strategy:* product innovation, process variability, and labor responsibility. It is opposed to neo-Fordism and to Fordism, dispensing with a division of labor and rigid managerial control and deliberately fostering a skilled and responsible workforce. A post-Fordist model of distance education would be decentralized and retain integration between the study modes. Academic staff would, however, retain autonomous control of their administered courses, and in so doing, would be able rapidly to adjust course curriculum and delivery to the changing needs of students.

In general, Fordist distance education involves mass production for mass consumption. It encompasses centralized control, a division of work tasks associated with distance education, and the creation of management for the division of the work tasks. Courses are developed by a small core of skilled workers and delivered centrally, with a deskilling effect on the teacher. In a neo-Fordist system, course development, delivery, and administration are mixed between a centralized office and regional or local offices. This allows for more flexibility in course development and delivery. In the neo-Fordist model, the teacher is still given little responsibility beyond delivering the developed materials.

The post-Fordist approach to distance education would focus on the consumer rather than the product. Administration would be decentralized, democratic, and participatory, and the division of labor would be informal and flexible. Teachers would have a high responsibility to develop curriculum and respond to the learning needs of their students. Much of education as it developed over the past century fits the Fordist paradigm. Renner (1995) states that education became a formalized system of production that could be monitored, maintained, and controlled in the same way as the factory. The practice of distance education has also been greatly influenced by the Fordist paradigm. It has been argued that Fordism is still the dominant international paradigm in distance education.

Distance education has been influenced by the Fordist paradigm because it is the model that has been most successful in business throughout this century. Evans (1995) states that distance education can be seen as both a product and a process of modernity. Its administrative systems, distribution networks, and print production processes are characteristic of modern societies with developed mass production, consumption, and management. The Fordist approach to distance education provides cost efficiencies and quality production of materials unachievable outside of the Fordist model. In addition, global competition in distance education will favor the marketing power of large educational providers. The Fordist approach to the practice of distance education provides obvious advantages.

However, major concerns about the continuation of the Fordist paradigm in distance education have been expressed. These concerns revolve around the following themes:

▪ Mass markets for delivered instruction have changed, reducing the demand for centrally produced instruction for mass delivery.
▪ The Fordism model is unable to adapt to the needs of a fast-changing society.
▪ The focus on instructional production and the systematic use of preprogrammed curricula are incompatible with higher levels of educational quality.

With heightened competition, diversification of demand, and rapid developments in communication and information technology, the Fordist rationale, which presumes a uniform mass market to support mass production, is inappropriate. As a result, the cost effectiveness and cost efficiency of centrally developed and delivered instruction has declined. Ding (1995), in reporting on China's distance education system, indicates that the market for many of the traditional disciplines is close to saturation, while there are many demands for specific disciplines and specialties. However, Ding states that a relatively small demand exists in each specialty, such as English for foreign trade, tourist economics, manufacture of household appliances, and so on. In addition, different regions of the country report differing needs. Renner concludes that open education markets are becoming more fragmented, competitive, and specialized. A search for more efficient and flexible forms of organizational structure is an inescapable outcome.

The Fordist structure is not well suited to easily adapt to the changing needs in society. If we combine an increasingly differentiated consumer market with the power and speed of contemporary interactive computer communications technologies and add to this a more highly educated workforce, then the bureaucratic practices of the past would seem far from sustainable. This new environment requires a flexible structure in which ideas are readily tried and shared. In China, Ding found that the Fordist structure could not adapt itself to the new conditions of the market immediately and quickly. He stated that the Fordist structure could not adapt curricula to the regional needs of the country or alter the structure and content of the course to the needs of the students. The answer, according to Renner, is to place an emphasis on labor flexibility that would allow individual academics to produce and deliver quality curriculum more readily customized to student needs. It is felt that post-Fordist systems of distance education would be able to rapidly respond to the needs of society.

Renner's statement that the systematic use of preprogrammed curricula is incompatible with higher levels of educational quality suggests a controversy that goes beyond the debate on Fordism. Preprogrammed curricula used in the Fordist approach to distance education are products of instructional design based on behaviorism.

Post-Fordism is directly linked to constructivism (McGee & Green, 2008). Renner states that the relationship between constructivism and post-Fordism is intimate. The constructivist thinks that the individual gives meaning to the world through experience. Ideally, it is a process of personal and cooperative experimentation, questioning, and problem solving through which meaning can be constructed. This approach to learning is viewed as incompatible with mass production of instructional curricula developed with instructional design methods based in behaviorism that assume a more passive approach to learning. For constructivist learning to occur, teaching must remain flexible and sensitive to learner needs, from intellectual, cognitive, and psychological perspectives. Centrally devised educational courseware that dictates teaching sequences to students and deskilled tutor-grade staff discourage the customization and construction of knowledge.

For the advocates of post-Fordism, neo-Fordism is no more acceptable than Fordism. Although there is higher product innovation and process variability, labor responsibility is still low. This view of the role of labor divides the new-Fordist approach from the post-Fordist approach. The neo-Fordism division of labor leaves the teacher and the academic staff divorced from research, curriculum development, and scholarly inquiry. They simply deliver the curriculum prepared for them. Proponents of the post-Fordist paradigm have two disagreements with this approach. First, this approach again assumes a behavioral-based instructional design method for curricula development. The preceding paragraph outlined the post-Fordist's concerns about this method. Second, post-Fordists would see this approach as exploiting the worker. High product innovation and high process variability put additional demands on the worker without additional compensation. The neo-Fordism and post-Fordism approaches to distance education are fundamentally different.

The debate about Fordism is intricate, heated, and tied in with differing political, economic, aesthetic, ethical, and educational perspectives. The issues raised in this debate are important because policymakers introduce regulations, generate institutional structures, and effectively organize workplace practices on the basis of such paradigms. How students learn, and frequently what they learn, is a product of these decisions. As the role of distance education is defined in a changing society, these issues need to be given careful consideration.

There is little involvement in the Fordism/post-Fordism debate by American distance educators. In the United States, local control, small classes, rapport between teachers and students, and highly personalized instruction are hailed as important characteristics of its highly respected educational system (Simonson, 1995). This approach to education is diametrically opposed to the mass production, centralized control advocated by a Fordist approach to distance education. While Thach and Murphy (1994) suggest that there is a need for national coordination of higher distance education and that local and state control of education inhibit opportunities for collaboration at a distance among institutions, the United States' traditional approach to education is prevalent. This focus on student needs, personalized instruction, and interaction is evident in the following statement by Michael Moore (1994, 2013):

> In a typical United States course that uses teleconferencing technologies to link, let us say, six sites, the curriculum problem is how to integrate the local interests and needs, as well as the local knowledge that lies at each site, into the content to be taught. (p. 5)

 ## SUMMARY

In the rapidly changing and diverse environment in which distance education is practiced, many questions remain unanswered. In this environment it is difficult to arrive at one definition or agree on a theory of how to practice and do research in the field of distance education. New technologies, globalization, and new ideas about student learning challenge the traditional approaches to the practice of distance education. This theme of change is evident in the discussions of distance education and its definition, history, status, and theory.

Numerous definitions of distance education have been proposed. Most include the separation of teacher and learner, the influence of an educational organization, the use of media to unite teacher and learner, the opportunity for two-way communication, and the practice of individualized instruction. The traditional definitions describe distance education as taking place at a different time and in a different place, whereas recent definitions, enabled by new interactive technologies, also stress education that takes place at the same time but in a different place. The role of educational organizations in the distance education process has also been challenged. For example, open learning is a form of distance education that sometimes occurs without the influence of an educational organization. MOOCs often are not sponsored by an educational organization, thus by applying our definition, they are not distance education, but self-study. These issues will continue to be debated as distance educators seek definitions that fit a changing world.

Investigating the relatively brief history of distance education reveals both diversity and an ongoing change in its practice. Historically, diverse practices of distance education have been developed according to the resources and philosophies of the organizations providing instruction. The history also shows that advances in technology have promoted key changes in distance education. These changes have been most evident in the rapid development of electronic communications in recent decades. How the future of distance education will be shaped by the integration of its history and these new technologies is yet to be seen. Changes in society, politics, economics, and technology are impacting the status of distance education around the world. In some cases, distance education is seen as an answer to inadequate educational opportunities caused by political and/or economic instability. In other situations, established distance education providers are being required by a changing society to convert from mass instruction to a more decentralized approach to meet the diverse needs of their students. In many countries, the need for continuing education or training and access to degree programs is accelerated by the demands of a changing society. Students in rural or isolated parts of the world look to distance education for opportunities to "keep up" with the outside world. Again, technology advances are a major influence for change in distance education worldwide. The globalization of the world enabled by these new technologies will challenge distance educators to rethink the practice of distance education to take advantage of these new opportunities.

The changing and diverse environment in which distance education is practiced has inhibited the development of a single theory upon which to base practice and research. A variety of theories have been proposed to describe traditional distance education. They include theories that emphasize independence and autonomy of the learner, industrialization of teaching, and interaction and communication. These traditional theories emphasize that distance education is a fundamentally different form of education. Recent emerging theories, based on the capabilities of new interactive audio and video systems, state that distance education is not a distinct field of education. Both utilization of existing educational theory and the creation of like experiences for both the distant and local learner are emphasized. Traditional distance education theorists will need to address the changes to distance education facilitated by new technologies.

Advocates of the new theories will need to consider their impact on the traditional strengths of distance education. Specifically, the focus of the new theories on face-to-face instruction eliminates the advantage of time-independent learning that traditional theories of distance education value. The debate on these theoretical issues will only increase in the face of continued change. One indication of the impact of change in distance education theory is the Fordist/post-Fordist/neo-Fordist debate. Fordist distance education is administered centrally and involves mass production of curricula for mass consumption. Rapid changes in society have resulted in diverse market needs. The Fordist paradigm is unable to respond quickly to these needs. The post-Fordist paradigm implements a decentralized, democratic administration that focuses on the consumer. In this paradigm, teachers have a high responsibility to respond to individual needs of students. Central to the debate between Fordists and post-Fordists are changing views about how learning occurs. The Fordist approach is based in behaviorism learning theory, in which knowledge is delivered to the learner. The constructivist approach to learning, in which individuals give meaning to the world through experience, underlies the post-Fordist position. The debate on these differences will continue as distance education adapts to meet the needs of a changing society.

An environment in which technology, society, economics, politics, and theories of learning are all in transition suggests that definitions, theories, and the practice of distance education will continue to be contested. This theme of change will both challenge and motivate distance educators and researchers as they strive to understand and develop effective ways to meet the needs of learners around the world.

CASE STUDY

A large Midwestern university is considering offering MOOCs, and accepting MOOC courses for credit. In order to present the plan to accept MOOCs to faculty, the provost wants a group to prepare a "white" paper that gives the advantages of MOOCs that includes the foundations in research and theory that support MOOCs. The committee is made up of faculty, administrators, and the University comptroller.

DISCUSSION QUESTIONS

1. Why are there different definitions of distance education? Discuss and develop the definition that you feel is most appropriate.
2. Discuss Desmond Keegan's five main elements of the various definitions of distance education. Write a paragraph explaining which of the elements is most critical and which is least critical.
3. Many think that in the near future the concept of distance will become relatively unimportant. What do you think this means?
4. Correspondence study is a form of distance education that developed during World War II. Is correspondence study still important today?
5. What might be the reasons for the founding of special distance teaching universities. Why is there no national distance learning university in the United States?
6. Distance education has a long history in European countries. Why is distance learning more commonplace in Europe than in the United States?
7. Keegan writes that the lack of an accepted theory of distance education has weakened the field. Discuss the importance of theory and how theory helps the practitioner of distance education.
8. Wedemeyer has six characteristics of independent study systems. Why would Wedemeyer's perspective be important to American educators?
9. Explain the concept of the assembly line as it relates to the industrialization of teaching. Will industrialized education ever be important in American education? Explain.
10. Simonson proposed an emerging theory of distance education. What learning experiences are different for local and distant learners.

REFERENCES

Badham, R., & Mathews, J. (1989). The new production systems debate. *Labour and Industry, 2*(2), 194–246.

Brookfield, S. (1986). *Understanding and facilitating adult learning.* San Francisco, CA: Jossey-Bass.

Campion, M. (1995). The supposed demise of bureaucracy: Implications for distance education and open learning—More on the post-Fordism debate. *Distance Education, 16*(2), 192–216.

Cropley, A. J., & Kahl, T. N. (1983). Distance education and distance learning: Some psychological considerations. *Distance Education, 4*(1), 27–39.

Delling, R. M. (1985, August). *Towards a theory of distance education.* Paper presented at the ICDE Thirteenth World Conference, Melbourne, Australia.

Ding, X. (1995). From Fordism to new-Fordism: Industrialisation theory and distance education—A Chinese perspective. *Distance Education, 16*(2), 217–240.

Edwards, R. (1995). Different discourses, discourses of difference: Globalisation, distance education, and open learning. *Distance Education, 16*(2), 241–255.

Evans, T. (1995). Globalisation, post-Fordism and open and distance education. *Distance Education, 16*(2), 256–269.

Garrison, D. R., & Shale, D. (1987). Mapping the boundaries of distance education: Problems in defining the field. *The American Journal of Distance Education, 1*(1), 7–13.

Gillispie, J., Cassis, J., Fujinaka, T. & McMahon, G. (2013). *Meeting the shifting perspective; the Iowa Communications Network.* In M. Simonson (Comp.), *Distance education: Statewide, institutional, and international applications* (pp. 3–13). Charlotte, NC: Information Age.

Great Schools Partnership | 482 Congress Street, Suite 500 | Portland, ME 0410 http://edglossary.org/local-control/

Holmberg, B. (1985). *The feasibility of a theory of teaching for distance education and a proposed theory* (ZIFF Papiere 60). Hagen, West Germany: Fern Universität, Zentrales Institute fur Fernstudienforschung Arbeitsbereich. (ERIC Document Reproduction Service No. ED290013)

Holmberg, B. (1986). *Growth and structure of distance education* (3rd ed.). London, England: Croom Helm.

Holmberg, B. (1995). *The sphere of distance-education theory revisited.* (ERIC Document Reproduction Service No. ED386578)

Keegan, D. (1988). Theories of distance education: Introduction. In D. Sewart, D. Keegan, & B. Holmberg (Eds.), *Distance education: International perspectives* (pp. 63–67). New York, NY: Routledge.

Keegan, D. (1995). *Distance education technology for the new millennium: Compressed video teaching.* (ERIC Document Reproduction Service No. ED389931)

Keegan, D. (1996). *The foundations of distance education* (3rd ed.). London, England: Croom Helm.

Knowles, M. (1990). *The adult learner: A neglected species* (4th ed.). Houston, TX: Gulf.

Lombardi, M. (2013). The inside story: Campus decision making in the wake of the latest MOOC tsunami. *Journal of Online Teaching and Learning, 9*(2), 239–247.

McGee, P., & Green, M. (2008). Lifelong learning and systems: A post-Fordist analysis. *Journal of Online Learning and Teaching, 4*(2), 146–157.

Moore, M. & Kearsley, G. (2012). *Distance education: A systems view* (3rd ed.). New York, NY: Cenage.

Moore, M. (1994). Autonomy and interdependence. *The American Journal of Distance Education, 8*(2), 1–5.

Moore, M. G. (Ed.). (2013). The theory of transactional distance. In *Handbook of distance education* (3rd ed., pp. 66–85). New York, NY: Routledge.

Perraton, H. (1988). A theory for distance education. In D. Sewart, D. Keegan, & B. Holmberg (Eds.), *Distance education: International perspectives* (pp. 34–45). New York, NY: Routledge.

Peters, O. (1988). Distance teaching and industrial production: A comparative interpretation in outline. In D. Sewart, D. Keegan, & B. Holmberg (Eds.), *Distance education: International perspectives* (pp. 95–113). New York, NY: Routledge.

Renner, W. (1995). Post-Fordist visions and technological solutions: Education technology and the labour process. *Distance Education, 16*(2), 285–301.

Rumble, G. (1989). On defining distance education. *The American Journal of Distance Education, 3*(2), 8–21.

Rumble, G. (1995a). Labour market theories and distance education I: Industrialisation and distance education. *Open Learning, 10*(1), 10–21.

Rumble, G. (1995b). Labour market theories and distance education II: How Fordist is distance education? *Open Learning, 10*(2), 12–28.

Rumble, G. (1995c). Labour market theories and distance education III: Post-Fordism the way forward? *Open Learning, 10*(3), 47–52.

Schlosser, L. A., & Simonson, M. (2010). *Distance education: Definition and glossary of terms* (3rd. ed.). Charlotte, NC: Information Age.

Shale, D. (1988). Toward a reconceptualization of distance education. *The American Journal of Distance Education, 2*(3), 25–35.

Simonson, M. (1995). Overview of the Teacher Education Alliance, Iowa Distance Education Alliance research plan. In C. Sorensen, C. A. Schlosser, M. L. Anderson, & M. Simonson (Eds.), *Encyclopedia of distance education research in Iowa* (pp. 3–6). Ames, IA: Teacher Education Alliance.

Simonson, M. (2007a). What the accreditation community is saying about quality in distance education. *Distance Learning, 4*(2), 104.

Simonson, M. (2007b). Virtual schools. *Distance Learning, 4*(1), 76.

Simonson, M. (2009). Distance learning. In *The 2009 book of the year* (p. 231). Chicago, IL: Encyclopaedia Britannica.

Simonson, M. (2012). MOOC madness. *Distance Learning, 9*(4), 103-104.

Simonson, M., & Schlosser, C. (1995). More than fiber: Distance education in Iowa. *Tech Trends, 40*(3), 13–15.

Simonson, M., & Schlosser, C. (1999). Theory and distance education: A new discussion. *The American Journal of Distance Education, 13*(1), 60–75.

Swan, K. (2010). Teaching and learning in post-industrial distance education. In M. Cleveland-Innes & D. Garrison (Eds.), *An introduction to distance education* (pp. 100–110). New York, NY: Taylor & Francis.

Thach, L., & Murphy, L. (1994). Collaboration in distance education: From local to international perspectives. *The American Journal of Distance Education, 8*(3), 5–21.

U.S. Department of Education. (2006). Evidence of quality in distance education programs drawn from interviews with the accreditation community. Retrieved from http://www.itcnetwork.org/Accreditation-EvidenceofQualityinDEPrograms.pdf

Wedemeyer, C. (1981). *Learning at the backdoor.* Charlotte, NC: Information Age.

CHAPTER 3

Research and Distance Education

CHAPTER GOAL

The purpose of this chapter is to summarize the research on distance education.

CHAPTER OBJECTIVES

After reading and reviewing this chapter, you should be able to

1. Explain research dealing with learning outcomes in distance education environments.
2. Explain research on learner perceptions concerning distance education.
3. Explain research on learner attributes and other variables in distance education situations.
4. Describe research related to interaction in distance education.
5. Summarize research on distance education.

DISTANCE EDUCATION RESEARCH: SETTING A FOUNDATION

Three quotes are central to the development and growth of the field of distance education. These statements represented the themes of classic articles written by leaders in education and remain today as guides for the field (Simonson, 2009).

The first was by James Finn, one of the founders of the modern educational technology field. In 1953, in the introductory issue of *Audio-Visual Communication Review*, he wrote:

> Finally, the most fundamental and most important characteristic of a profession is that the skills involved are founded upon a body of intellectual theory and research. Furthermore, this systematic theory is constantly being expanded by research and thinking within the profession. As Whitehead says, "the practice of a profession cannot be disjoined from its theoretical understanding and *vice versa*.... The antithesis to a profession is an avocation based upon customary activities and modified by the trial and

error of individual practice. Such an avocation is a Craft ..." (Smith et al., 1951, p. 557). The difference between the bricklayer and the architect lies right here. (p. 8)

The second quote is by Campbell and Stanley, who, in their classic 1963 monograph, described the experiment

> as the only means for settling disputes regarding educational practice, as the only way of verifying educational improvements, and as the only way of establishing a cumulative tradition in which improvements can be introduced without the danger of a faddish discard of old wisdom in favor of inferior novelties. (p. 2)

The final quote is the controversial statement from the *Review of Educational Research* made by Richard Clark in 1983 and 2012 and quoted often in this book:

> The best current evidence is that media are mere vehicles that deliver instruction but do not influence student achievement any more than the truck that delivers our groceries causes changes in nutrition ... only the content of the vehicle can influence achievement. (p. 445)

Finn attempted to encourage those in the audio-visual field to take a more professional view of themselves and their discipline by basing decisions on theory supported by research. Campbell and Stanley formalized what previously had been unclear to many—the need for the rigorous application of the scientific method to the study of education. Twenty years later in 1983, Richard Clark identified why Campbell and Stanley's admonition was so important. His article documented the failure of many educational researchers to "verify educational improvements, as demanded by Campbell and Stanley" (p. 2). Clark's article was not popular. However, it clearly and precisely showed how researchers had violated basic guidelines for rigorous research, which had led many educators to adopt "inferior novelties" at the expense of scientifically validated "wisdom."

Each of these scholars had a message of critical importance to distance education—scientific inquiry, conducted with rigorous attention to correct procedures, is the key to success of our field. Research and theory are at the foundation of credibility and quality.

THE FOCUS OF DISTANCE EDUCATION RESEARCH

Emerging technologies have forced a redefinition of distance education. At the same time, the distance education research agenda has also evolved. The focus has shifted to a more learner-centered approach. Researchers are not merely looking at achievement but are examining learner attributes and perceptions as well as interaction patterns and how these contribute to the overall learning environment. Although there is continued interest in the technology, the focus is not on which medium is best, but on what attributes of the medium can contribute to a positive, equivalent learning experience. This chapter will provide a review of distance education research literature. In his 1987 landmark article "The Development of Distance Education Research," Börje Holmberg, a leading distance education theorist and researcher, suggested that the structure of distance education research should include:

- Philosophy and theory of distance education
- Distance students and their milieu, conditions, and study motivations
- Subject-matter presentation

- Communication and interaction between students and their supporting organization (tutors, counselors, administrators, other students)
- Administration and organization
- Economics
- Systems (comparative distance education, typologies, evaluation, etc.)
- History of distance education

Recently, a number of researchers have reviewed the literature on distance education and provided support for the effectiveness of instruction delivered to distant learners and guidelines for teaching and learning at a distance (Howell & Baker, 2006; Orellana, Hudgins, & Simonson, 2009; Simonson, Schlosser & Orellana, 2011; Sorensen & Baylen, 2004; Tallent-Runnels, Cooper, Lan, Thomas, & Busby, 2005). Research dealing with various aspects of distance education, once characterized as anecdotal, is now more likely to be theory based and methodologically sound. Thus, research results are beginning to have a positive impact on the practice of distance education (Simonson, 2006). For example, Hirumi (2005) has examined a significant portion of the distance education literature and has analyzed e-learning guidelines "in search of quality" (p. 309). Hirumi found that there are significant differences in how industry and education view quality and approaches for e-learning. Education guidelines focus on the quality of e-learning courses and programs, but industry develops standards in order to promote reusability and interoperability of learning objects (Hirumi, 2005). Hirumi analyzed six sets of guidelines, including:

1. The Council of Regional Accrediting Commissions (C-RAC, 2000). *Statement of the regional accrediting commissions on the evaluation of electronically offered degree and certificate programs* (www.wiche.edu/telecom/Guidelines.htm).
2. The Institute for Higher Education Policy (IHEP, 2000). *Quality on the line: Benchmarks for success in Internet-based distance education* (www.ihep.com/quality.pdf).
3. The American Council on Education (ACE, 1997). *Guiding principles for distance learning in learning society* (www.acenet.edu/calec/dist_learning/ dl_principlesIntro.cfm).
4. The American Distance Education Consortium (ADEC, n.d.a., n.d.b). *Guiding principles for distance learning* and *Guiding principles for distance teaching and learning* (www.adec.edu/admin/papers/distance-teaching_principles.html).
5. The American Federation of Teachers (AFT, 2000). *Distance education: Guidelines for good practice* (www.aft.org/higher_ed/downloadable/distance.pdf).
6. Open and Distance Learning Quality Council (ODLQC, 2001). *Standards in open and distance education* (www.odlqc.org.uk/st-int.htm).

These sets of guidelines offer a basis for development of quality distance education courses and programs (Hirumi, 2005). Also of importance is a recent publication by Lou, Bernard, and Arbrami (2006). They reported that "218 independent findings from 103 studies representing 25,320 students were analyzed in the undergraduate dataset in this meta-analysis. On average, undergraduate students achieved similarly, whether they learned in [distance education] courses or in the traditional classrooms" (p. 161). Lou et al. went on to say "there is consistent and reliable evidence that undergraduate students achieved equally, whether they learned at the remote site or the host site," and "In synchronous instructor-directed undergraduate DE, when media are used to deliver the same instruction simultaneously by the same instructor and with the same course activities and materials, there is little reason to expect undergraduate students to learn differently in the remote sites than at the host site" (p. 162).

Trends in Distance Education Research

In 2016, Zasacki-Richter and Naidu identified trends in distance education research over the last 35 years. The first theme of research dealt with the consolidation of distance education institutions. Next there was research focusing on quality assurance and student support, and finally the research emphasized the virtual university and online learning. These phases of research show a maturation of distance education. They ended their review by emphasizing that online technologies will play an important role in education and training.

LEARNING OUTCOMES

It is likely that when different media treatments of the same informational content to the same students yield similar learning results, the cause of the results can be found in a method which the two treatments share in common ??*give up your enthusiasm* for the belief that media attributes cause learning. (Clark, 1994, 2012, p. 28)

Hundreds of media comparison studies indicate, unequivocally, that no inherent significant difference exists in the achievement effectiveness of media (Clark, 1983, 2012). These results support Clark's position summarized in the previous quote: The specific medium does not matter. That being the case, the focus of future research should be on instruction itself since it is the truly critical factor in determining student achievement (Whittington, 1987).

Unfortunately, much of the research in distance education is still of the media comparison type. This is to be expected given the rapid development of distance education technology, especially in the area of two-way interactive video systems. With each technological advance, the temptation is to conduct media comparison research on the off chance that the new technology might truly bring about higher student achievement.

A Recent Summary of the Research

Evaluation of Evidence-Based Practices in Online Learning: A Meta-Analysis and Review of Online Learning Studies (U.S. Department of Education, 2009) is must reading for anyone involved in education generally, and distance education specifically. This report is a comprehensive review of 51 studies that:

- contrasted an online to a face-to-face condition,
- measured student learning outcomes,
- used a rigorous research design, and
- provided adequate information to calculate an effect size (p. ix).

The report's most quoted conclusion is printed in italics in its abstract and states,

> The meta-analysis found that, on average, students in online learning conditions performed better than those receiving face-to-face instruction. (p. ix)

The 70-page report is well-written, informative, and scholarly. It is an important document that attempts to provide a state-of-the-research report on the effectiveness of online/distance education. Unfortunately, unless carefully read, the report can be misleading.

On page 51, the report's authors, staffers from SRI International's Center for Technology in Learning under contract to the U.S. Department of Education (USDE), clearly state what *should be* the most quoted outcome of this meta-analysis where they write:

> Clark (1983) has cautioned against interpreting studies of instruction in different media as demonstrating an effect for a given medium inasmuch as conditions may vary with respect to a whole set of instructor and content variables. That caution applies well to the findings of this meta-analysis, which should not be construed as demonstrating that online learning is superior as a medium. Rather, it is the combination of elements in the treatment conditions, which are likely to include additional learning time and materials as well as additional opportunities for collaboration that has proven effective. (p. 51)

Learning Time, Materials, and Collaboration—The Big 3. Apparently online students spent more time, had access to more materials, and collaborated differently than did the traditionally taught comparison students—no wonder online students tended to achieve better. The "time studying" phenomenon is apparently pervasive. The *Chronicle of Higher Education* recently summarized the results of the 2012 National Survey of Student Engagement (NSSE) and reported that students taking online courses spent slightly more time on their course work than did students with no online courses (Berrett & Sander, 2013).

What we do not know from either the USDE or NSSE reports is *why* some students spent more time, accessed different materials, and had more collaboration opportunities. It is somewhat unfortunate that these important outcomes were not stressed instead of the misleading conclusion that "*students in online learning conditions performed better*" (U.S. Department of Education, 2009, p. ix). Certainly, research on student engagement in distance education is needed.

Many will remember the meta-analyses of the 1980s that also misled a generation of educators into thinking that computer-based instruction was superior to classroom instruction (Kulik, Bangert, & Williams, 1983; Kulik, Kulik, & Cohen, 1979, 1980). The "Kulik" studies, as they were called, concluded that students using computer-based-instruction achieved better than students who were traditionally taught. More critical analyses revealed that the most of the studies included in the Kulik studies were methodologically flawed (Clark, 1983). Unfortunately, a whole generation of educators implemented computer-based instruction, and then waited for positive effects that never materialized.

Certainly, the USDE Report is important. It represents a review of the best studies available. The Study's authors made every attempt to be methodologically and conceptually rigorous—perhaps the author of the abstract was a marketing adviser rather than a researcher. At any rate, this report should be read and analyzed by all distance educators.

And finally, as George Washington said over 230 years ago, "facts are stubborn things: and whatever may be our wishes, our inclinations, or the dictates of our passions, they cannot alter the state of facts and evidence."

Research Reported

Mary K. Tallent-Rennels and a team of other scholars published an interesting review that summarized the research on online teaching and learning (Tallent-Rennels et al., 2006). The review was organized into four primary categories:

FIGURE 3–1 On average, distant and traditional learners achieve about the same.

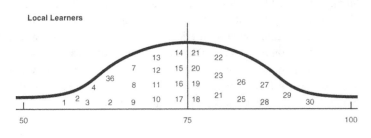

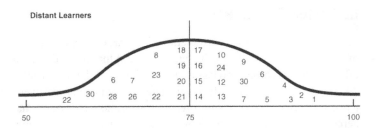

- Course environment
- Learner outcomes
- Learner characteristics
- Institutional and administrative characteristics

This review examined 68 published papers and drew a number of interesting conclusions. First, they identified the failure of authors to use standardized terms and to clarify the definitions of key ideas, in this case the types of courses taught—traditional, blended, and online. Tallent-Runnels and her coauthors suggest that these three terms be used when research is conducted and reported.

The review also found that there did not seem to be a comprehensive theory guiding the design of courses taught online and used when research is conducted. This is a critical weakness of the field.

The article goes on to identify conceptual and methodological problems with the research dealing with online teaching and learning. Apparently, the problems of early research on distance education have not yet been corrected—problems related to lack of a theory base, the ad hoc nature of studies, and the difficulty of generalizing results from one study to other similar situations.

One important conclusion reported in this review is the research finding that students have positive attitudes about online learning, and that computer anxiety is not a problem for most students. Well-designed online courses were reported to produce more positive learning outcomes and to be related to overall student satisfaction. Design and quality are important.

Ronsisvalle and Watkins (2005) reviewed the literature dealing with K–12 student success in online learning. They reported that online K–12 learning is growing and "here to stay." They reported that completion rates of online students in virtual K–12 schools were increasing; most online students received grades of B or better; and that student, teacher, parent, and administrator levels of satisfaction with online instruction was high (Ronisvalle & Watkins, 2005).

In 2004, Allen et al. conducted a meta-analysis of the effectiveness of distance learning and reported that students in distance education classes performed slightly better than did traditionally taught students. They concluded that "the current findings suggest that distance education technologies do not necessarily create a less effective learning environment and, in some instances, may enhance effectiveness" (p. 415).

It seems quite apparent, that well designed, competently taught distance education classes are as effective as more traditionally taught and designed classes. Distance education works well if designed well, and taught well.

LEARNER PERCEPTIONS

Perception, the way in which something is regarded or understood, has long been a concern of distance educators. It was a general thought that distance education was somehow less effective, less credible, and less important than traditional education (Tallent-Runnels et al. 2006). Thus, studies of student satisfaction in online courses were numerous in early distance education research; more recently, satisfaction research has evolved from general perceptions of distance education to more targeted research about specific courses and approaches.

Sun, Tsai, Finger, Chen, and Yeh (2008) attempted to determine the critical factors influencing student perceptions and satisfaction. Results revealed that the instructor's attitudes toward distance education, course quality, perceptions of content usefulness, course flexibility, and student computer anxiety were the most important factors affecting perceptions and satisfaction. Two hundred and ninety-five surveys were returned. A relatively low return rate of 46% was a concern identified by the research team who conducted post hoc analyses of nonrespondents to give greater confidence in the generalizability of results. The finding that "course quality" was one of the most important factors influencing satisfaction is important.

The results of a similar study conducted by Ozkan and Koseler (2009) supported the Sun et al. (2008) findings. The quality of the instructor, system quality, and content quality were found to be related to student satisfaction.

Selim (2007) reported that instructor attitudes toward the technology, instructor teaching style, student computer competency, use of interactive collaboration, course content, and effectiveness of the technology system were critical success factors for distance education courses. There results were obtained from surveys completed by over 500 college-age students.

LEARNER ATTRIBUTES

Sense of community has become an important research area in distance education (Carabajal, LaPointe, & Gunawardena, 2007; Ouzts, 2006). Ouzts (2006) found that student perceptions of community related to increased satisfaction toward online learning.

Wang, Foucar-Szocki, and Griffin (2003) found that the dropout rate for distance education courses they studied was about 26%. Laube (1992) examined the relationship between academic and social integration variables and the persistence of students in a secondary distance education program. Students were divided into two groups based on persistence. Completers/persisters were those who completed or still persisted in coursework

1 year after enrollment, whereas dropouts/nonstarters had dropped out during the same time.

Out of 351 surveys mailed, 181 surveys were returned, 124 in the completer/persister group and 57 in the dropout/nonstarter group. The nonreturned surveys were comprised of 44 completer/persisters and 126 dropout/nonstarters. Two variables showed important differences between the groups. Completers/persisters were more likely than dropouts/nonstarters (1) to have higher educational goals and (2) to study more than 10 hours a week.

Three variables related to social integration were studied: self-initiated contact with the school, student attitudes toward their tutors, and student attitudes toward missing peer socialization. The two groups differed significantly only in their attitudes toward their tutors, with completers/persisters indicating a more positive attitude. Both groups indicated a positive attitude toward their tutors, but a large percentage of dropouts/nonstarters selected "undecided" as a response, which contributed to the significant results obtained. Stone (1992) examined the relationship of contact with a tutor and locus of control to course completion rates for students enrolled in print-based, distance training courses. One group received weekly phone calls from the training staff, whereas the second group received only minimal feedback. Results did not show any important difference between the two groups in course completion rates. However, Stone did find that students with relatively external loci of control completed their coursework at significantly faster rates when exposed to regular telephone cues from their tutors.

Sun et al. (2008) reported that learner computer anxiety, perceptions of course quality, flexibility, ease of use, and usefulness of content were characteristics of students that were related to satisfaction. Whether satisfaction was related to learning was not investigated in this study (Sun et al., 2008) but measuring satisfaction has long been a research outcome, and is related to retention (Levy, 2007).

Tallent-Runnels et.al (2006) reported in a review of the research that:

- Web-based learning environments take into account the cognitive style of learners.
- Learners favor their ability to control their learning environment, and think this control is more than a convenience but influences satisfaction and engagement.
- Learning style relates to use of online teaching and learning tools.
- And, ultimately, Tallent-Runnels et al. (2006) reported that one approach is not best for everyone so a variety of approaches should be considered by instructional designers.

Selim (2007) reported that the learner characteristics of computer competence, degree of collaboration in the class, and opinions about course content and design are critical learning factors. Selim's (2007 results support those of Sun et al. (2008).

INTERACTION

Interaction is one of the most discussed topics in distance education (Anderson & Kuskis, 2007; Moore, 2007; Sammons, 2007). Mahle (2007) reviewed literature on interaction in distance education and concluded that interaction is a primary component of any effective distance education program. Wanstreet (2006) reviewed the literature dealing with interaction in online learning and reported on the various definitions of interaction, including an instructional exchange, computer-mediated communication, and social/psychological connections.

Researchers have attempted to determine what types and amounts of interaction in online classes is most effective. Bernard et.al (2009) has provided important information about interaction. In the meta-analysis of 74 studies dealing with interaction it was reported that overall the strength of interactive treatments was associated with increased achievement outcomes. More specifically, it was reported that student-to-student, and student-to-content interactions had greater impact than student to teacher interaction.

Orellana (2006) reported on an interesting study that related class size to interaction. This study reported that the optimal class size for an online college course taught by a single instructor was approximately 20. However, it was reported that for optimal levels of interaction, as defined by Orellana, a class size of about 16 was best. Online instructors indicated that smaller class sizes (15 students) would produce more and higher level interaction (Orellana, 2006). It was also found that classes can be too small and too large for optimum levels of interaction.

Research regarding interaction and distance education technologies indicates that different technologies allow differing degrees of interaction. However, similar to comparison studies examining achievement, research comparing differing amounts of interaction showed that interaction had little effect on achievement (Anderson & Kuskis, 2007; Beare, 1989; Souder, 1993). Those students who had little or no interaction as part of a course did not seem to miss it (May, 1993).

One recurring, and difficult to answer, question about distance education is the time commitment expected of the student in an online course. Traditionally, student time in a class has been measured by face-to-face class sessions. For example, a three semester credit, college course, meets three times a week for the 15 weeks of the semester. Class sessions are normally 50 minutes long. Thus, a traditional course syllabus would list the topics covered in each of the 45, or so, class sessions in the semester. It is also typical for students to be expected to allocate a couple of hours outside of class studying and completing assignments for every face-to-face session. Thus, for typical three semester credit college-level classes a student would be expected to go to class 45 hours and study 2 hours for each class session; 90 hours.

Some call this the Carnegie Unit, or more appropriately at the college level, the course unit (Berrett, 2012). One Carnegie/Course unit (one semester credit) requires the typical student to attend class, study, read, view, write, produce, and discuss for approximately 45 hours for one semester credit. (These are usually 50-minute hours, so for one credit the expectation is for a student to allocate about 2,250 minutes).

Distance educators have adopted the same formula. When distance education courses are planned, the designer attempts to produce teaching and learning experiences that in general requires the student to devote 2,250 minutes of study for each semester credit (Lipka, 2010; Orellana et al., 2009; Simonson, 2008). Certainly a little math is required, but this formula will work, especially when courses are designed by experienced distance educators.

BARRIERS TO DISTANCE EDUCATION

Berge and Muilenburg (2000) reviewed the literature and identified 64 potential barriers to the implementation of distance education. They surveyed several thousand persons involved in distance education, instructional technology, and training. Of those responding, 1,150 were teachers or trainers, 648 were managers, 167 were administrators in higher education, and the remaining responders were researchers and students.

When the data were analyzed, the strongest barriers to distance education were identified. Their rank order is:

1. Increased time commitment
2. Lack of money to implement distance education programs
3. Organizational resistance to change
4. Lack of shared vision for distance education in the organization
5. Lack of support staff to help course development
6. Lack of strategic planning for distance education
7. Slow pace of implementation
8. Faculty compensation/incentives
9. Difficulty keeping up with technological changes
10. Lack of technology-enhanced classrooms, labs, or infrastructure

Additionally, Berge and Muilenburg identified the least important barriers to implementation. They were (in rank order):

54. Competition with on-campus courses
55. Lack of personal technological expertise
56. Lack of acceptable use policy
57. Lack of transferability of credits
58. Problems with vast distances and time zones
59. Technology fee
60. Tuition rate
61. Local, state, or federal regulations
62. Ethical issues
63. Existing union contracts
64. Lack of parental involvement

Berge and Muilenburg concluded by identifying the need for cultural change within organizations involved or contemplating involvement with distance education. Five of the top barriers related directly to organizational culture are as follows:

▪ Organizational resistance to change
▪ Lack of shared vision for distance education in the organization
▪ Lack of strategic planning for distance education
▪ Slow pace of implementation
▪ Difficulty keeping up with technological change

In South Dakota (Simonson, 2001), a recent series of focus groups of teachers revealed the following reasons why they were reluctant to be involved in distance education:

▪ Fear
▪ Training
▪ Time
▪ Changes needed

These same groups indicated that the impediments to implementing distance education in schools were as follows:

- Need for training
- Need for and lack of support
- Time needed
- Fear of the process
- Scheduling problems
- Technical problems

In 2009, Chen reported that the three primary barriers that prevent institutions from offering distance education are program development costs, faculty workload concerns, and the need for faculty rewards for offering courses at a distance. Effective incorporation of new technologies was considered to be one way to reduce barriers.

TELEMEDICINE/TELEHEALTH

Distance education is becoming increasingly important in the professions of medicine and law. For example, the American Telemedicine Association (ATA) has regularly collected research information about the impact of telemedicine/telehealth. PubMed is a database of medical research at the National Library of Medicine. PubMed reported in 2013 that more than 12,000 publications dealing with telemedicine and telehealth were published.

ATA reports research in three categories: cost effectiveness, quality of care, and patient satisfaction (ATA, 2013).

Cost Effectiveness of Telemedicine

Research results report that in general telemedicine saves patients, providers, and payers money when compared to traditional approaches. One study reported by ATA (ATA, 2013; Cryer, Shannon, Van Amsterdam, & Leff, 2012) found that lower medical and pharmacy costs were reported, more efficient service and lower hospital admissions and readmissions resulted in a group that practiced telemedicine.

Another study reported that patients had better or comparable clinical outcomes while achieving a savings of 19% as a result of shorter length of stay and need for fewer lab and diagnostic tests. Another study reported by the ATA (2013) showed spending reductions of approximately 7.7-13.3%.

Another study reported a 25% reduction in the numbers of bed days of care and a 19% reduction of hospital admissions while maintaining a high level of patient satisfaction (ATA, 2013). It was concluded that telemedicine can be cost effective and high quality method of health care in many situations.

Telemedicine and Quality of Care

ATA (2013) reviewed a number of studies and concluded that the results demonstrated that there is no difference in the ability of the provider "to obtain clinical information, make an accurate diagnosis, and develop a treatment plan that produces the same desired clinical outcomes as compared to in-person care, when used appropriately" (p. 3.). The

ATA 2013 report concluded that quality of care is as likely to be high in telemedicine situations as it is for traditional methods.

Patient Satisfaction With Telemedicine

ATA's 2013 summary of the research reported that patient satisfaction about the use of telemedicine access to care and use of technologies to connect to health care providers was very high. Satisfaction rates of 98% were common. A number of studies reported that patient satisfaction was as high in telemedicine situations as it is for traditional patient-provider interactions. Certainly, telemedicine/telehealth are areas in need of continued research.

MYTHS REGARDING DISTANCE EDUCATION RESEARCH

A myth is an invented story, and it does not always begin with "Once upon a time." In any field, including distance education, ideas and approaches quickly emerge that seem to gain a life of their own, even though there is little, if any, factual support for them. The myth of the media effect has been discussed for decades, making the rounds every time a new instructional technology is introduced. It implies that merely using media for instruction somehow has an impact on learning. This myth has been widely discussed and soundly rebuked (Clark, 1983). Three more myths about distance education deserve the same fate.

Myth 1: The more interaction there is in a distance education class, the better. This myth is also easy to trace to its roots. Early research on distance education demonstrated clearly that the *provision* for interaction was critical. In other words, some early forms of distance education were one way, or had interaction that was so delayed that students had little if any feeling of involvement with their instructors. Students need to be able to interact with their teacher, at least to ask questions.

Interaction is *needed and should be available.* However, interaction is not the "end all and be all" of learning. It is only necessary to look at a few research studies, such as Bernard et al. (2009) to discover that interaction is not a magic potion that miraculously improves distance learning. Interaction is important, and the potential for all involved in teaching and training to be able to confer is essential.

However, forced interaction can be as strong a detriment to effective learning as is its absence. Student to student, student to content have been reported to be the most important categories of interaction with student to instructor interaction of less impact, but still important.

Myth 2: Instructor training is required for anyone planning to teach at a distance. Naturally, the more training a person has, the more likely it is that he or she will learn, assuming education works. Instructor and student training to be effective in online environments has been reported to be important (Paechter, Maier, & Macher, 2010; Sun et al., 2008). However, training in how to teach distant learners is only one of a collection of interrelated competencies needed by an effective teacher.

By far the most important competency of any teacher is content knowledge. Understanding a subject and the ability to break down the topic into meaningful and manageable concepts is fundamental for any effective teacher. In some distance education systems, the course delivery specialist may not need to know much about content, notably the industrialized systems of Europe where an assembly-line approach and division of labor are typical, and where different people prepare courses and course content. If there is only one person, the teacher, who is responsible for the entire process—from course design and course delivery to course evaluation—then knowledge of content is essential.

Myth 3: Using instructional technology in teaching is e-learning, and this is the same as distance education. A report by Zemsky and Massy titled *Thwarted Innovation: What Happened to e-Learning and Why* (2004) presents this myth. *Thwarted Innovation* presents research that exposes the failures of e-learning. A careful reading of this monograph shows that the idea of e-learning discussed is really a review of the use of technology in education. Distance education should not be confused with e-learning, and *e-learning* is considered an outdated term by some (Cole, 2004).

The definition of distance education presented in Chapters 1 and 2 clarifies what is meant by distance education. When research on the field is conducted, a clearness of definitions of terms is critical.

SUMMARY

Although it is always perilous to summarize research in a few sentences, it is also the obligation of those who have studied the literature extensively to provide others with their best estimates of what has been reported. It is probably more perilous to provide a top 22 list of research findings, but that is what follows. This list of what some might call best practices are supported by the research literature. However, each should continue to be investigated.

Best Practices in Distance Education: A Summary of Findings Reported in This Chapter

A careful and comprehensive review of the research on the theory and practice of distance education reveals 22 practices and approaches that seem clearly supported by the literature. We will call these Top Twenty Best Practices.

1. Distance education works; the literature clearly indicates that students learning in some type of distance learning environment will learn as much and as effectively as students learning in traditional, face-to-face environments. Advocates who say distance education students learning more are as suspect as those who assert that distance education students learning less.

2. Student retention in distance education courses and programs is often lower than in traditional environments.

3. Instructor attitude toward teaching and learning at a distance is an important component of effectiveness.

4. Course quality is critical—quality is strongly related to student satisfaction.

5. A student's computer anxiety must be low or effectiveness suffers.

6. Course flexibility is an important characteristic of an effective distance delivered course.

7. Learning communities are important in distance education—instructors should encourage, even facilitate the development of learning communities.

8. Interaction in distance education is important—student to student and student to content interaction are most important, followed by student to instructor and instructor to student interaction.

9. Learner control and involvement in distance delivered instruction is important, not just a convenience.

10. Training of students and instructors learning and teaching at a distance is related to effectiveness and satisfaction.

11. Technical support for students and instructors is critical.

12. Distance education can be advocated because of the convenience afforded and the autonomy provided to learners.

13. Instructor expertise in distance education and instructor support are strong predictors of student learning and satisfaction.

14. Quality instruction delivered at a distance should be equivalent not identical to instruction delivered traditionally in a classroom when learning and satisfaction are measured.

15. Computer competency is related to student success in distance education.

16. Retention is related to student satisfaction in distance education courses and programs.

17. Frequency and quality of interaction is a key to effectiveness in distance education.

18. What works effectively in traditional education is a starting point for what works in distance education; equivalency should be the goal.

19. Class size for one instructor in a distance education class should be about 20 students, plus or minus five, if effectiveness and satisfaction are outcome measures.

20. A one semester credit, college-level course delivered at a distance should require approximately 2,250 minutes of time (45, 50-minute hours) for the typical student—studying, reading, viewing, listening, writing, interacting, and producing.

21. Telemedicine/telehealth practices reduce healthcare costs significantly, and produces a high level of patient satisfaction.

22. Online students report they spend more time on their coursework than traditionally taught students.

The research clearly shows that distance education is an effective method for teaching and learning. Future research needs to focus on different populations, particularly K–12 students; psychological and social attributes of the learner; the impact of distance education on the organization; and the contributions of different media attributes to learning outcomes.

One striking summary of distance education research is summarized by the statement that "it is not different education, it is distance education," which implies that what we know about best practices in education is directly applicable to distance education.

CASE STUDY

The dean of the school of nursing in your southern university has called a meeting to discuss converting the Bachelor of Science in nursing from a traditional face-to-face delivery system to a blended and/or online delivery method. You were invited because you are an expert in distance education who recently graduated and who knows the research. The dean is likely to ask you to explain best practices in distance education and to propose general guidelines for the development of courses in the BS in nursing degree program.

DISCUSSION QUESTIONS

1. If only one conclusion could be made from the research about leaning at a distance, what would it be?
2. What is the trend of learner perceptions about learning at a distance?
3. Why is the recent meta-analysis report from the U.S. Department of Education important, and why might the results be suspect?

REFERENCES

Allen, M., Mabry, E., Mattrey, M., Bourhis, J., Titsworth, S., & Burrell, N. (2004). Evaluating the effectiveness of distance learning: A comparison using meta-analysis. *Journal of Communication, 54*(3), 402–420.

American Telemedicine Association. (2013). *Examples of research outcomes: Telemedicine's impact on healthcare cost and quality.* Washington, DC: American Telemedicine Association.

Anderson, T., & Kuskis, A. (2007). Modes of interaction. In M. G. Moore (Ed.), *Handbook of distance education* (pp. 295–309). Mahwah, NJ: Erlbaum.

Beare, P. L. (1989). The comparative effectiveness of videotape, audiotape, and telelecture in delivering continuing teacher education. *The American Journal of Distance Education, 3*(2), 57–66.

Berge, Z. L., & Muilenburg, L. Y. (2000). Barriers to distance education as perceived by managers and administrators: Results of a survey. In M. Clay (Ed.), *Distance learning administration annual 2000.* Baltimore, MD: University of Maryland–Baltimore.

Bernard, R., Abrami, P., Borokhovski, E. Wade, C. Tamim, R. Surkes, M., & Bethel, E. (2009). A meta-analysis of three types of interaction treatments in distance education. *Review of Educational Research, 79*(3), 1243–1289.

Berrett, D. (2012). Carnegie teaching foundation, inventor of the credit hour, seeks to change it. *The Chronicle of Higher Education, 59*(12), A25.

Berrett, D., & Sander, L. (2013). Many students don't practice vital quantitative skills in their coursework, survey finds. *The Chronicle of Higher Education, 60*(12), A12–13.

Campbell, D., & Stanley, J. (1963). *Experimental and quasi-experimental designs for research.* Boston, MA: Houghton Mifflin.

Carabajal, K., LaPointe, D., & Gunawardena, C. (2007). Group development in online distance learning groups. In M. Moore (Ed.), *Handbook of distance education* (pp. 137–148). Mahwah, NJ: Erlbaum.

Chen B. (2009). Barriers to adoption of technology-mediated distance education in higher-education institutions. *Quarterly Review of Distance Education, 10*(4), 333–338.

Clark, R. E. (2012). *Learning from media: Arguments, analysis, and evidence* (2nd ed.). Charlotte, NC: Information Age.

Clark, R. E. (1983). Reconsidering research on learning from media. *Review of Educational Research, 53*(4), 445–459.

Clark, R. E. (1994). Media will never influence learning. *Educational Technology Research and Development, 42*(2), 21–29.

Cole, A. (2004). E-learning outdated. *Educational Technology, 44*(2), 61.

Cryer, L., Shannon, S. B., Van Amsterdam, M., & Leff, B. (2012). Costs for "hospital at home" patients were 19 percent lower, with equal or better outcomes compared to similar inpatients. *Health Affairs, 31,* 61237-124.

Finn, J. (1953). Professionalizing the audiovisual field. *Audio-Visual Communication Review, 1*(1), 6–17.

Hirumi, A. (2005). In search of quality: An analysis of e-learning guidelines and specifications. *Quarterly Review of Distance Education, 6*(4), 209–330.

Holmberg, B. (1987). The development of distance education research. *The American Journal of Distance Education, 1*(3), 16–23.

Howell, S., & Baker, K. (2006). Good (best) practices for electronically offered degree and certificate programs: A ten-year retrospect. *Distance Learning, 3*(1), 41–47.

Kulik, C., Kulik, J., & Cohen, P. (1979). Research on audio-tutorial instruction: A meta-analysis of comparative studies. *Research in Higher Education, 11*(4), 321–341.

Kulik, J. A., Bangert, R. L., & Williams, G. W. (1983). Effects of computer-based teaching on secondary school students. *Journal of Educational Psychology, 75*(1), 19–26.

Kulik, J. A., Kulik, C.-L., & Cohen, P. A. (1980). Instructional technology and college teaching. *Teaching of Psychology, 7*(4), 199–205.

Laube, M. R. (1992). Academic and social integration variables and secondary student persistence in distance education. *Research in Distance Education, 4*(1), 2–5.

Levy, Y. (2007). Comparing dropouts and persistence in e-learning courses. *Computers & Education, 48,* 185–204.

Lipka, S. (2010). Academic credit: A currency with no set value—Colleges resist regulators calls for consistency. *The Chronicle of Higher Education, 57*(9), A1, A15–17.

Lou, Y., Bernard, R., & Abrami, P. C. (2006). Undergraduate distance education: A theory-based meta-analysis of the literature. *Educational Technology Research and Development, 54*(2), 141–176.

Mahle, M. (2007). Interactivity in distance education. *Distance Learning, 4*(1), 47–51.

May, S. (1993). Collaborative learning: More is not necessarily better. *The American Journal of Distance Education, 7*(3), 39–50.

Moore, M. (Ed.). (2007). A theory of transactional distance. In *Handbook of distance education* (pp. 89–105). Mahwah, NJ: Erlbaum.

Orellana, A. (2006). Class size and interaction in online courses. *Quarterly Review of Distance Education, 7*(3), 229–248.

Orellana, A., Hudgins, T., & Simonson, M. (2009). *The perfect online course.* Charlotte, NC: Information Age.

Ouzts, K. (2006). Sense of community in online courses. *Quarterly Review of Distance Education, 7*(3), 285–296.

Ozkan, S., & Koseler, R. (2009). Multi-dimensional students' evaluation of e-learning systems in the higher education context: An empirical investigation. *Computers & Education, 53,* 1285–1296.

Paechter, M., Maier, B., & Macher, D. (2010). Students' expectations of, and experiences in e-learning: Their relation to learning achievements and course satisfaction. *Computers & Education, 54,* 222–229.

Ronsisvalle, T., & Watkins, R. (2005). Student success in online K–12 education. *Quarterly Review of Distance Education, 6*(2), 117–124.

Sammons, M. (2007). Collaborative interaction. In M. Moore (Ed.), *Handbook of distance education* (pp. 311–321). Mahwah, NJ: Erlbaum.

Selim, H. M. (2007). Critical success factors for e-learning acceptance: Confirmatory factor models. *Computers & Education, 49,* 396–413.

Simonson, M., Schlosser, C., & Orellana, A. (2011). Distance education research: A review of the literature. *Journal of Computing in Higher Education, 23*(2), 124–142.

Simonson, M. (2001). *Connecting the schools: Final evaluation report.* North Miami Beach, FL: Nova Southeastern University. Retrieved from http://www.tresystems.com/projects/sdakota.cfgm

Simonson, M. (2006). Teaching courses online. *Quarterly Review of Distance Education, 7*(4), vii–viii.

Simonson, M. (2008). Designing the "perfect" online course. *Distance Learning, 5*(3), 92–91.
Simonson, M. (2009). Scientific rigor. *Quarterly Review of Distance Education, 10*(4), vii–viii.

Smith, B. O., Benne, K. D., Stanley, W. O., & Anderson, A. W. (1951). *Readings in the social aspects of education.* Danville, IL: Interstate.

Sorensen, C. K., & Baylen, D. M. (2004). Learning online: Adapting the seven principles of good practice to a web-based instructional environment. *Distance Learning, 1*(1), 7–17.

Souder, W. E. (1993). The effectiveness of traditional vs. satellite delivery in three management of technology master's degree programs. *The American Journal of Distance Education, 7*(1), 37–53.

Sun, P., Tsai, R., Finger, G., Chen, Y., & Yeh, D. (2008). What drives a successful e-learning? An empirical investigation of the critical factors influencing learner satisfaction. *Computers & Education, 50,* 1183–1202.

Tallent-Runnels, M. K., Cooper, S., Lan, W. Y., Thomas, J. A., & Busby, C. (2005). How to teach online: What the research says. *Distance Learning, 2*(1), 21–34.

Tallent-Runnels, M. K., Thomas, J. A., Lan, W., Cooper, S., Ahern, T. C., Shaw, S. M., & Liu, X. (2006). Teaching courses online: A review of the research. *Review of Educational Research, 76*(1), 93–135.

U.S. Department of Education, Office of Planning, Evaluation and Policy Development. (2009). *Evaluation of evidence-based practices in online learning: A meta-analysis and review of online learning studies.* Retrieved from www.ed.gov/about/offices/list/opepd?ppss?reports.html

Wang, G., Foucar-Szocki, D., & Griffin, O. (2003). *Departure, abandonment, and dropout in e-learning: Dilemma and solutions.* Sarasota Springs, NY: Maisie Center e-Learning Consortium.

Wanstreet, C. (2006). Interaction in online learning environments: A review of the literature. *Quarterly Review of Distance Education, 7*(4), 399–411.

Whittington, N. (1987). Is instructional television educationally effective? A research review. *The American Journal of Distance Education, 1*(1), 47–57.

Zemsky, R., & Massy, W. F. (2004). *Thwarted innovation: What happened to e-learning and why.* Philadelphia, PA: The Learning Alliance at the University of Pennsylvania.

Zawacki-Richter, O., & Naidu, S. (2016). Mapping research trends from 35 years of publications in *Distance Education. Distance Education, 37*(3), 245–269. doi:10.1080/01587919.2016.1185079

Technologies, the Internet, and Distance Education

CHAPTER GOAL

The purpose of this chapter is to discuss the technologies used for distance education systems and distance education classrooms.

CHAPTER OBJECTIVES

After reading and reviewing this chapter, you should be able to

1. Describe systems for categorizing media used for distance education.
2. Explain the technologies used to connect teachers and learners for distance education, including correspondence, audio, video, and desktop systems.
3. Explain the configuration of a modern distance education classroom.
4. Understand the Internet and the World Wide Web and the relationship of both to the growth of distance education.

A TRUE STORY

In the 1980s, the southeast African nation of Zimbabwe was founded from the British Commonwealth country of Rhodesia after a long and painful process. Before the founding of Zimbabwe the educational system of Rhodesia enrolled less than 500,000 learners, and most were located in the major cities and towns of the country. One of the first acts of the new government was to offer free and universal education to the nation's children, no matter where they were located. This meant that the enrollment in the country's schools increased tenfold overnight.

The teacher education faculty at the University of Zimbabwe in Harare and at other institutions of teacher training had to face the immediate problem of preparing the thousands of teachers needed by the many new and enlarged schools of the country. The approach selected was partly ingenious and partly based on necessity.

It was decided that teachers in training should attend one of the institutions of higher education for their first year of preparation. For their second and third years, these teacher education students were assigned to a school where they taught classes of students.

College students functioned as regular educators with two exceptions. First, they were under the guidance of a more experienced colleague, and second, they continued their teacher education and higher education coursework at a distance. In other words, they enrolled in a full curriculum of coursework while they also functioned as novice teachers. Their coursework was delivered to them from a distant higher education institution. For their fourth year, they returned to the university or college and completed their degrees.

In Zimbabwe, distance education became the primary technique for preparing the thousands of teachers needed to staff the new country's schools. Interestingly, the technology used to connect professors, such as those of the faculty of education at the University of Zimbabwe, and students located in the many cities, towns, and villages of the country was the postal system. Students received written assignments and printed resources from the university. They used, studied, and interacted with these materials to complete assignments, which then were returned to the faculty of education for evaluation. Follow-up assignments and materials were then posted back to students. This process continued until the second and third years of the bachelor's degree were completed. Periodic visits to the campus occurred, but the majority of the learning events and activities took place at a distance.

This system, born of the necessity of educating millions of students, used the most appropriate technology available—the postal system. Certainly, a major social, political, and ultimately educational problem was solved, even though the approach was not high-tech. However, it was efficient and effective. Whatever technology is used, the purpose is to promote communication.

A MODEL OF COMMUNICATION

Communication occurs when two or more individuals wish to share ideas. Communication in a distance education environment happens when learners interact with one another and with their instructor. Communication, including communication for distance education, is possible because individuals have overlapping fields of experience. In other words, they have things in common, such as language and culture (Figure 4–1).

Communication must be based on what the senders of messages—distance educators—have in common with the receivers of messages—distant learners. Effective instructional messages are designed according to the situation, experiences, and competencies of learners. In order to communicate, instructional ideas are encoded into some transmittable form, such as spoken words, pictures, or writing. The instructional message is then sent to the learner over a channel. If the receiver of the message is nearby, such as in the same classroom, the sender—the teacher—may speak or show pictures in order to communicate. If the learner is at a distance, then the instructional message will need to be sent over a wire (e.g., the telephone), hand-delivered (e.g., the mail), or broadcast through the air (e.g., television). In other words, media are used to communicate to distant learners. In fact, media extend the senses, so instructional messages can be sent over long distances or stored for learning at different times.

When the distant learner receives the message, it must be decoded. This means the words spoken must be heard and defined, or the pictures shown must be seen and understood. If communication is successful, the receiver—the learner—will have the same idea or understanding as the sender—the teacher.

Effective communication requires an active audience. The response of the learners who receive messages is called *feedback*. Feedback allows the sender and receiver, the

FIGURE 4–1   A model of communication.

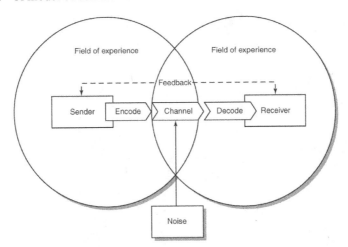

teacher and learner, to determine if the message was understood correctly. Feedback in distance education systems is often referred to as *interaction.* Feedback permits those involved in communication in a distance education system to evaluate the process.

Noise is also part of the communication process. Any disturbance that interferes with or distorts the transmission of a message is called *noise.* Audible static is one form of noise. Classroom distractions are noise, as is ambiguous or unfamiliar information.

The model of communication has been widely used to describe the interaction between message designers and audiences—teachers and learners. It is also quite relevant for distance education. Specifically, instruction must be designed in a way that capitalizes on what learners already know and what they have already experienced—their fields of experience. Then messages should be encoded so they can be effectively transmitted to distant learners.

Channels of communication, the media that connect the teacher and the distant learner, should be appropriate for the learner and the instruction. In other words, the media used to connect the learner, teacher, and learning resources must be capable of conveying all necessary information.

When instruction is designed and when feedback and interaction are planned, efforts should be made to minimize anything that might interfere with the communication process (e.g., noise). One way this can be accomplished is by sending information through multiple channels.

Models of communication provide a general orientation to the process of distance education. The model described in Figure 4–1 contains the elements to be considered when instructional messages are communicated.

THE CONE OF EXPERIENCE

One long-standing method of categorizing the ability of media to convey information is the cone of experience, introduced by Edgar Dale (1946). An adapted *cone of experience* helps organize the media used in distance education systems (Figure 4–2).

FIGURE 4–2   Cone of experience.

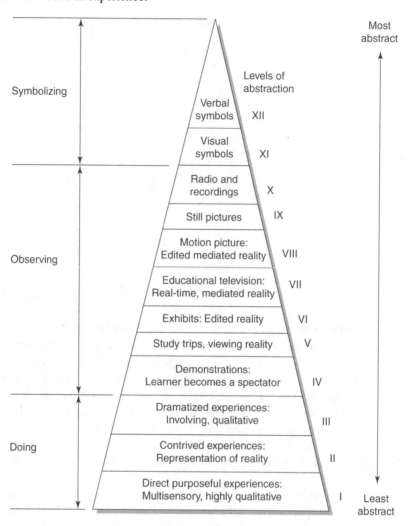

Children respond to direct, purposeful experiences, not only because they are young, but also because they are learning many new things for the first time. Real experiences have the greatest impact on them because they have fewer previous experiences to look back on and refer to than do older learners. Real experiences provide the foundation for learning.

As learners grow older and have more experiences, it is possible for them to understand events that are less realistic and more abstract. Dale first stated this basic idea when he introduced his cone of experience. Dale proposed that for students to function and learn from experiences presented abstractly (those at the higher levels of the cone), it was necessary for them to have sufficient and related experiences that were more realistic (those at the lower levels). Learners need to have direct, purposeful experiences to draw upon in order to successfully learn from events that are more abstract. For example, if children are to look at pictures of flowers and know what they are, they must have first seen, smelled, and touched real flowers.

Media permit the educator to bring sights and sounds of the real world into the learning environment—the classroom. However, when new information is presented, it is important that it be as realistic as possible. Similarly, when younger learners are involved, more realistic instruction is needed.

Still, one misunderstanding about the cone of experience is the belief that "more realistic" is always better. This is definitely not true. More realistic forms of learning are considerably less efficient in terms of uses of resources, and they are often less effective because of the many distractions of realistic instruction.

The critical job of the educator, especially the designer of distance education materials, is to be only as realistic as needed in order for learning to effectively occur. If instruction is too realistic, it can be inefficient. It may cost too much, it may have too much irrelevant information, or it may be difficult to use. Similarly, learning experiences that are too abstract may be inexpensive, but may not contain enough relevant information and may not be understood. To clarify the conflict between realistic and abstract experiences, Dale told a story about the life of a Greek sponge fisherman. The most realistic way to learn

about the fisherman's life was to go to Greece and work on a sponge boat. This approach to learning would be very realistic, effective, and authentic. It would also take a long time and cost a great deal, both in money and in learning time. An abstract way to learn about the life of a sponge fisherman would be to read about it in a book. This would take only a few hours and would cost little, even though the experience would not be overly authentic. Today, most would opt for something that is in the middle of Dale's cone, such as a 28-minute video on cable television's Discovery Channel titled "A Day in the Life of a Greek Sponge Fisherman."

A TAXONOMY OF DISTANCE EDUCATION TECHNOLOGIES

In distance education, it is imperative that educators think about how communication will occur and how to apply experiences that will promote effective and efficient learning. Most likely, a variety of techniques will be needed to provide equivalent learning experiences for all students (Figure 4–3):

- Correspondence study
- Prerecorded media
- Two-way audio
- Two-way audio with visuals
- One-way live video
- Two-way audio, one-way video

FIGURE 4–3   Distance education technologies.

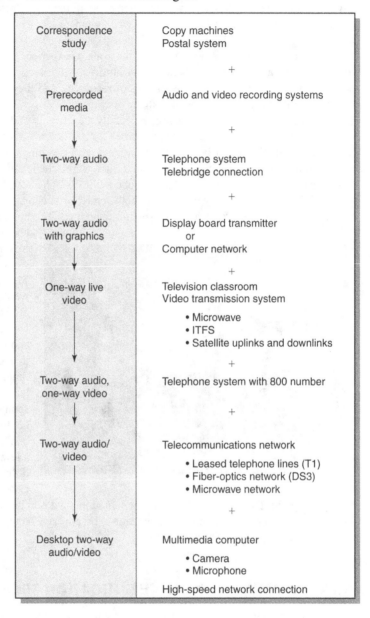

- Two-way audio/video
- Desktop two-way audio/video

Correspondence Study

The simplest and longest-lived form of distance education is generally considered cor-respondence study. This approach to distance education uses some kind of mail system, such as regular post office mail or electronic mail, to connect the teacher and the learner asynchronously (Figure 4–4).

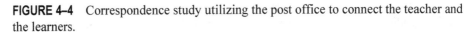

FIGURE 4–4 Correspondence study utilizing the post office to connect the teacher and the learners.

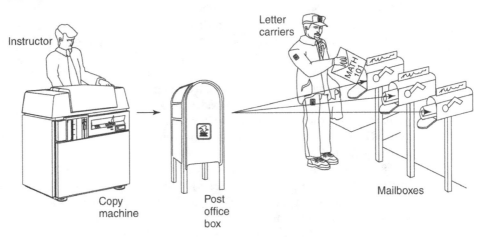

Usually, lessons, readings, and assignments are sent to the student, who then completes the lessons, studies the readings, and works on the assignments, which are mailed to the instructor for grading. For a college-level course worth three credits, there are often 10 to 12 collections of content to be completed. Each is finished in turn, and when all are completed satisfactorily, the student receives a grade.

Sophisticated forms of correspondence study have used techniques of programmed instruction to deliver information. Linear-programmed instruction is most common, but for a period of time, a number of correspondence study organizations attempted to develop print-based branched programmed instruction.

Programmed instruction normally has a block of content, followed by questions to be answered. Depending on the answers students give, they move to the next block of text (linear programmed instruction) or to another section of the programmed text (branched programmed instruction). Sometimes remedial loops of instruction are provided to help students through difficult content, or content that supposedly had been covered in previous courses or blocks of instruction. Advanced students do not need to study remedial loops. In this manner, the rate and route of instruction are varied for students of correspondence courses. Correspondence study is relatively inexpensive, can be completed almost anywhere, and has been shown to be effective. Correspondence study has been used by millions of learners of all ages since the 19th century.

Prerecorded Media

The next logical step in the development of distance education technologies, both historically and conceptually, was the incorporation of media other than print media into correspondence study systems. First, pictures and other graphics were added to correspondence study texts. Then, audiotapes and finally CDs/DVDs even videotapes were added to the collection of materials sent to distant learners. Usually, the correspondence study guide would direct the learner to look at, listen to, or view various media, in addition to assigning more traditional readings.

One interesting approach used by distance educators was borrowed from advocates of individualized instruction. This approach used audiotapes to guide the distant learner through a series of learning events, very similar to how a tutor would direct learning. This audio-tutorial approach was quite popular for a number of years, and it is still used by commercial organizations that present self-help materials for individual study.

MPG Files (Podcasting).   An .mpg audio file, often called an educational podcast, is usually a prerecorded single-concept lesson, normally audio only, but sometimes with accompanying still or motion visuals (Simonson, 2007a). Essex (2006) says a podcast is a digital "radio show"—an audio program that can be downloaded from the web. Podcasts have become a huge new information and entertainment option for Internet users. It is estimated that millions of people downloaded a podcast in the last year, and in the next few years, the podcast audience is expected to expand exponentially. The podcast has been incorporated into the culture to the degree that the word "podcast" was chosen as the *New Oxford American Dictionary*'s 2005 Word of the Year (*New Oxford American Dictionary*, 2005).

Podcasting is not a new idea. It has been around at least since the audio tutorial movement and the Sony Walkman. A podcast is really a single-concept event that is explained by an audio file, or an audio file supplemented by still pictures or video. The most widespread and current example of a type of a podcast is a song, usually 3 to 5 minutes long, available in an electronic file format, such as .mpg3 that also might be available as a music video (.mpg4) with singers, dancers, and actors in addition to the song. Luther Vandross's tune "Always and Forever" is a wonderful 4-minute, 54-second example. The tune is also available as a music video showing Vandross singing the song.

Individual songs work well as podcasts because most modern tunes have the characteristics of an effective single-concept event—what many now are calling a podcast, which really is a learning object that is stored in an .mpg format. The characteristics of an *effective* podcast are as follows:

- A podcast is a single idea that can be explained verbally, or if necessary with audio and appropriate still or motion pictures (not a face talking).
- A podcast is a recorded event that is 3 to 10 minutes long.
- A podcast is often part of a series, with each single event related to others.
- A podcast is a learning object available in an electronic format that is easily played, most often as an .mpg3 file, or .mpg4 for video podcasts.
- A podcast is stored on a website or other Internet location for easy access.
- A podcast is current and changed or updated frequently.

A recording of a lecture is a poor example of a podcast. Rather, it is best to "chunk" a 50-minute class into five or six single-concept blocks, each as a separate learning object. Effective lecturers do this already; they break up their class session into related topics. These topics can become podcasts when they are recorded electronically in an .mpg file format, especially if they are supplemented with related examples and recorded in a proper location without distracting background noises. Essex (2006) identified six tips for better podcasts:

1. Listen. Few of us have access to recording studios for our podcasts, but the environment that you are recording in should be as quiet as possible. Turn off that fan, close the windows, tell your cubicle neighbor to turn off the radio, and so on. Close the door and put a "Don't Knock" sign on it.

2. Rehearse first, but record the rehearsal as well. Oftentimes, delivery during the rehearsal take is more lively and spontaneous than the "final" version. You may want to edit together the best parts of both attempts.

3. Provide the URLs for resources on a website or, even better, on a companion blog site, rather than tediously spelling out every underscore, dash, and dot verbally.
4. Keep it short. While there are podcasts that last for an hour or more, that is asking a lot of your audience? If you have more content to cover than that time will allow, give the listeners the option to download the show in multiple segments.
5. Don't go it alone. Find a colleague with an engaging personality, sense of humor, and clear speaking voice to join you during your recording sessions. Dialogue is more interesting to listen to than monologue, and it also takes some of the pressure off. It's also good to provide multiple perspectives on issues when possible. Invite guests who are experts or at least experienced in the topic at hand.
6. Get feedback from your listeners. In order to ensure that you are meeting your audience's information needs, you should provide them with multiple methods of providing feedback on the show. Have them tweet you.

Podcasts are a reincarnation or reinvention of what the mastery learning movement of the 1960s called single-concept files or single-concept films. They were effective then, and can be effective today (Simonson, 2007a).

Two-Way Audio

Correspondence study filled a terrific void for those who wanted to learn when they could and wherever they were located. However, many wanted direct, live communication with the teacher, especially for those in precollege schools.

The first widely used live, synchronous form of distance education employed two-way audio, with either a telephone hookup, a radio broadcast with telephone call-in, or short-wave radio transmissions (Figure 4–5). In all cases, the distant learner and the instructor are interacting with some form of live, two-way audio connection. Teachers lecture, ask questions, and lead discussions. Learners listen, answer, and participate. Often, print and non-print materials are sent to distant learners, similar to correspondence study.

The key to this approach is the participation of the teacher and learners in a class session at a regularly scheduled time, or a set period of time, over a predetermined number of weeks or months, such as a semester. For example, a high school class in French might be offered by telephone, radio station broadcast, or short-wave signal every weekday from 10:00 A.M. until 10:50 A.M. for 9 weeks. Students would tune in at home, assignments would be made, and activities completed. In other words, this form of distance education models the traditional classroom—except the teacher

FIGURE 4-5 Two-way audio—audioconferencing.

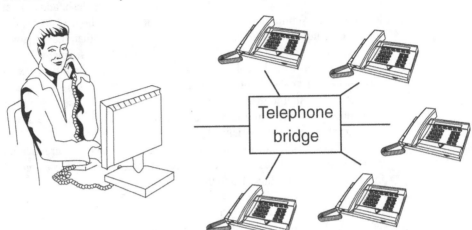

and learners can only hear one another, they cannot see each other. Obviously, this is a dated approach, rarely used today, but in its time was highly successful.

Two-Way Audio With Visuals

Recently, an embellishment of the two-way audio form of distance education has incorporated electronic methods of sending graphics information synchronously to distant learners. Two general approaches are used. The first incorporates a special display board that looks like a chalkboard but that actually transmits whatever is drawn on it to a similar display board at a distant site. Since the electronic boards are connected to one another, whatever the students at the distant site draw is also seen by the instructor.

The main disadvantage of this approach is the limited visual capability of the system and the difficulty in connecting more than two locations. A modification of this approach uses personal computers that are connected to one another, either through a central bridge computer or by using special software. For these systems, the instructor sends graphics, visuals, pictures, and even short video clips to desktop computers located at distant sites. Members of the class are connected by telephone or some other two-way audio system most often over the Internet, so they can discuss the visual information being sent via the computer.

This approach is relatively inexpensive and permits the visualization of the teleclass. The major problem is the availability the right computers and software at distant learning sites.

One-Way Live Video

This approach is often referred to as broadcast distance education, popularized in the 1950s by programs such as "Sunrise Semester," which was broadcast over commercial television stations. Presently, most broadcast television approaches to distance education are offered by public television stations or are broadcast in the early morning hours by commercial stations (Figure 4–6).

FIGURE 4–6   Satellite transmission—one-way audio, one-way video.

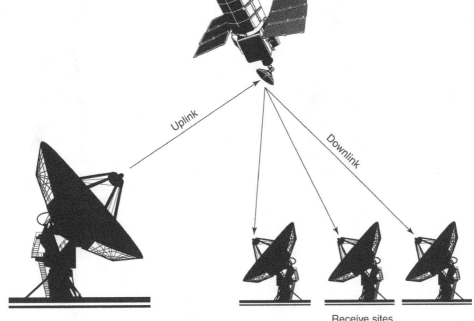

Receive sites

Programs are broadcast in installments over a 12- to 15-week period. Often, each program is about 60 minutes in length and is accompanied by packets of printed materials and readings. Sometimes, instructors are available for telephone office hours, but most commonly students watch the programs on television and respond to assignments that are described in the course packet. Completion of the assignments depends on viewing each television program, which is often broadcast several times. For those students who miss a broadcast, videorecorded versions are available, or students can record the program with their own system.

One advantage of this approach is the relatively high quality of the video broadcasts. Public television stations offer excellent productions of important historical, political, and social events. Educational institutions use these broadcasts as the basis for high school and college courses related to the topics of the television shows. The *Civil War* series and the *Lewis and Clark* series are examples of public television programming that was modified into distance education courses.

Two-Way Audio, One-Way Video

About 2 decades ago, a number of organizations began to use live television to broadcast high school and college courses. Initially, this approach used microwave transmission systems, instructional television fixed service, or community cable television networks (Figures 4–7 and 4–8).

Next, satellite communications systems became widely available (Figure 4–9). In these systems, the courses are offered synchronously (e.g., live) to students in as few as two to as

FIGURE 4–7 Instructional television fixed service—two-way audio, one-way video.

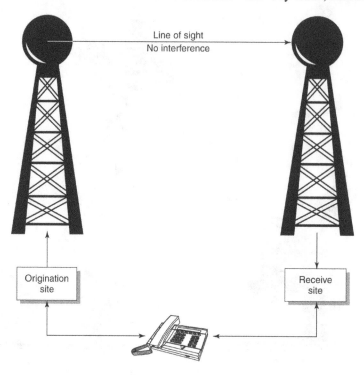

FIGURE 4–8 Cable delivery system (CATV)—two-way audio, one-way video.

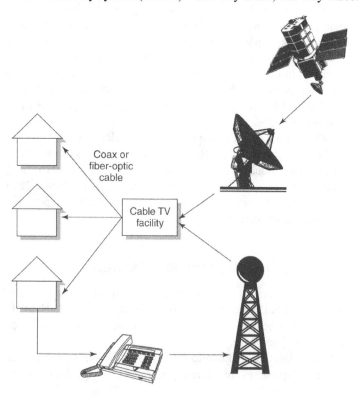

FIGURE 4–9 Satellite transmission—two-way audio, one-way video.

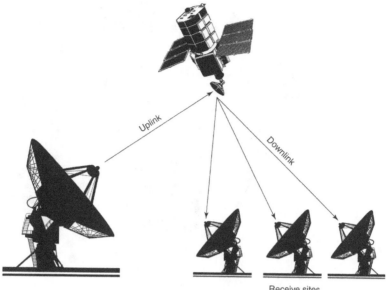

many as hundreds of locations. Students were able to interact with the instructor and with each other with something as simple as a toll-free telephone number to call, or by using a web-based chat room, to ask questions both during class and after class. Normally, students have a packet of instructional materials, including interactive study guides that they use and complete during the class presentation. Interaction between instructor and students is stressed in these kinds of courses, even ones where hundreds of students are enrolled.

In the last decade as satellite uplinks and downlinks have been replaced by Internet based teleconferences. Teleconferences, often called webinars, are short courses on specialty topics such as copyright, classroom discipline, sexual harassment, due process, or funding strategies that are offered by an organization to individuals or small groups spread throughout a wide geographic area.

A number of educational organizations have used Internet delivery to offer entire high school and college curricula. For example, United Streaming is an archived video streaming service created by Discovery Education that contains thousands of full-length videos and tens of thousands of video clips for K–12 education (Discovery Education, 2013).

Two-Way Audio/Video

Recently, especially in the United States, distance education is being widely practiced using live, synchronous television employing one of several technologies. A prevalent technology is called *compressed video* (Figure 4–10). This approach, commonly applied in corporate training, uses regular telephone lines to send and receive audio and video signals. The approach is called *compressed video* because fewer than the normal number of 30 video frames per second are transmitted between the sites. In the compressed video form, usually 15 video frames per second are transmitted using what is called a T1 connection. This level of quality is acceptable for most instruction, except when some kind of rapid motion or movement is part of instruction. As the Internet has become more robust, the use

FIGURE 4–10   Two-way audio/video—compressed videoconferencing system.

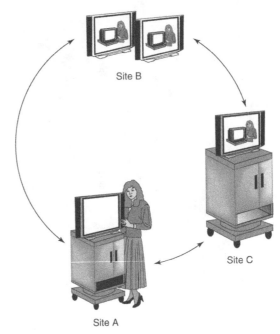

of regular telephone lines for videoconferences has decreased and the Internet is used with connectivity provided by Internet service providers such as cable companies, telephone companies, and wireless cellular companies.

Compressed video systems are often used in teleconferences for corporate training. Many schools and colleges installed compressed video networks. For this approach, a special classroom is needed that has video and audio equipment to capture the sights and sounds of instruction. The video and audio signals are manipulated by a device called a CODEC (coder/decoder) that removes redundant information for transmission to the distant site. At the receive site another CODEC converts the compressed information back into video and audio signals. Camera control information is also transmitted between sites, so it is possible for the instructor to pan, tilt, and zoom cameras.

One major advantage of compressed video systems is their portability. Many systems are installed in movable carts that can be set up in almost any classroom, laboratory, clinic,

FIGURE 4–11   Digital Dakota Network layout.

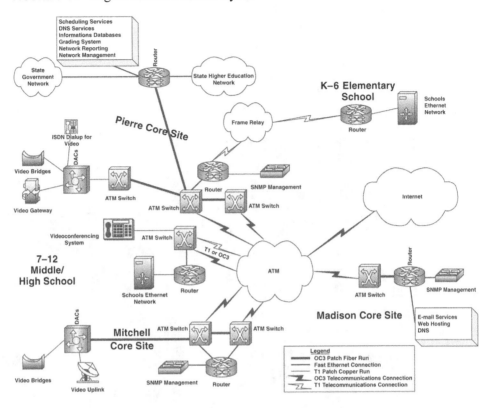

or training site where there is an Internet connection. Recently, the size of the classroom systems has been reduced significantly. The best-selling systems are called "set-top" systems because they can be set on top of a high definition television monitor. Set-top systems contain a camera, microphone, and the electronics necessary to compress and decompress outgoing and incoming transmissions. Set-top systems cost less than 25% of traditional compressed video systems, yet are of similar quality. The Digital Dakota Network (DDN) in South Dakota was designed as a compressed video network to link hundreds of educational sites for live, two-way video and audio instruction (Figure 4–11). The DDN uses traditional "roll-around" and "set-top" systems.

A second, more technically sophisticated approach to two-way audio/video instruction uses fiber-optic backbone to connect sites. Fiber-optic cable is the telecommunications medium of choice for new and updated telephone, video, and computer networking. Fiber's cost inhibits its installation in all situations, but fiber's high capacity makes it possible for one fiber (sometimes called a DS-3 connection) to carry full-motion video signals, in addition to high-quality audio signals and almost unlimited amounts of other voice and data information. One exemplary use of fiber-optics for distance education is Iowa's publicly owned Iowa Communications Network.

An Example: Two-Way Audio/Video in Iowa.   In Iowa, distance education has been redefined on a statewide basis. Iowa's approach to distance education was based on the concept that live, two-way interaction is fundamental to effective learning. The Iowa Communications Network (ICN) makes high-quality interaction possible in the state. The ICN is a statewide, two-way, full-motion interactive fiber-optic telecommunications net-

work with hundreds, now thousands, of connected classrooms. It is designed to be used by teachers and students in learning situations where they can and expect to see and hear each other. Distant and local students function together and learn from and with one another.

A key to Iowa's successful distance education system is the concept of sharing. Iowa's vision for distance education was built around the development of partnerships of schools that share courses and activities. For example, a physics class originating in Jefferson, a small town in west central Iowa, may have students in Sac City and Rockwell City, schools in two other counties. French students in Sac City have distant classmates in Jefferson and Rockwell City, and a calculus class that originates in Rockwell City is shared with students in Sac City and Jefferson. All three schools provide courses to partner schools and receive instruction from neighbors. Classes are small, with enrollments of about 20 to 25 or less, and are taught by teachers prepared in the skills needed by distance educators.

The use of fiber-optic technology, because of its extensive capacities and flexibility of use, provides unique opportunities for augmenting the instructional process beyond what is possible with other distance delivery technologies. The Iowa approach demonstrates the use of a system that emphasizes:

- Local control of the distance education curriculum
- Active involvement by educators from local school districts
- Interactive instruction
- Statewide alliances and regional partnerships
- Preservice, in-service, and staff development activities to support teachers
- Implementation using existing organizations and expertise
- Research-based instructional decision making

The Iowa Communications Network.   Central to distance education in Iowa is the Iowa Communications Network. The ICN is a statewide, two-way, full-motion interactive fiber-optic telecommunications network with hundreds of locations in each of Iowa's 99 counties (Gillispie, 2008). The ICN links colleges, universities, and secondary schools throughout the state and was constructed entirely with state and local funds. Part 1 of the Iowa Communications Network connected Iowa Public Television, Iowa's 3 public universities, and Iowa's 15 community colleges to the network. Part 2 connected at least one site in each of Iowa's 99 counties. Most Part 2 sites were high schools. Part 3 of the system is constantly growing as new sites are added. Currently it connects hundreds of schools, libraries, armories, area education agencies, and hospitals.

The plan for the ICN was completed and adopted by the Iowa legislature in 1987. Construction of Parts 1 and 2 of the network was completed during 1993. In addition to the capability of transmitting up to 48 simultaneous video channels, the ICN carries data and voice traffic; as demand increases, the system can be easily expanded without the need for

"opening the trench" to lay more fiber. Today, the ICN is used as the primary way for schools and government agencies to connect to the Internet.

In Iowa and South Dakota, and in many other states and regions, traditional education works. Educators in these two states adopted distance education, but wanted to preserve what the literature stated about effective education. The fiber-optics-based Iowa Communications Network and the compressed video Digital Dakota Network permit quality, research-based distance education since both are live, two-way audio/video networks.

Desktop Two-Way Audio/Video

One disadvantage of the video telecommunications systems described previously in this chapter is their cost and their cumbersomeness. In order to provide video-based distance education, special electronic devices are needed, satellite or telephone network time must be reserved, and equipped classrooms are required. Desktop systems often reduce the need for special high-cost equipment or special networking. Desktop systems use personal computers and the Internet to connect local and distant learners (Figure 4–12). Today, the Internet has the capacity to connect personal computers for the sharing of video and audio information. Streaming video is becoming more widely used in traditional as well as distance education classes. Mullins-Dove (2006) describes streaming video as using the Internet to allow video and audio content to play, or stream, as it is downloaded from a remote source. A key characteristic of streaming is that there is no physical file on the viewer's computer (Reed, 2001).

Early systems such as Skype are free and use very inexpensive video cameras. These systems permitted two sites to connect and to share video and audio. Multiple sites can also be connected.

Now higher quality cameras and even complete classrooms can be connected to a personal computer for transmission of instruction to distant learners. One popular system in widespread use today is Zoom, which for a single user is free, and for multiple licenses is relatively inexpensive.

FIGURE 4–12 Computer conferencing—desktop two-way audio/video.

A Look at Best Practice Issues

Wireless Canopies

A canopy is a roof-like covering, and *wireless* means no wires, so one would assume that a wireless canopy is a roof-like covering with no wires.

Well, most of us know that *wireless canopy* is used to refer to a "hot zone," or a wireless network area. Thus, a wireless canopy is a location where one can obtain access to the Internet through a high-speed connection using a computer's wireless networking card, or even a smartphone or tablet.

Increasingly, the wireless canopy is becoming used for global, more extensive network areas, such as a school campus, a neighborhood, or even an entire community. In many towns there are initiatives to establish, or at least begin planning for, citywide Internet access, usually wireless access.

These initiatives are very reminiscent of the days when community cable television (CCTV) franchises were awarded. In the 1960s and 1970s, city councils were approached by cable TV companies asking to be awarded a monopolistic franchise to offer cable TV at a reasonable price throughout the city. Franchise agreements were drawn up and signed, and cable TV commissions were established to monitor the activities of the private company that was awarded the cable TV franchise.

Savvy communities obtained one or more local access channels on the cable network, and some even negotiated for state-of-the-art production studios where programming could be created, edited, and delivered. In many cases, unfortunately, the awarding of the CCTV franchise was an opportunity lost. Many cities and towns did not aggressively pursue the potential of a citywide television network, and today cable TV is not often used for distance education, but is perceived as an entertainment system.

Today, another opportunity is waiting. For many, Internet access is a necessity, and in the last few years has become almost a necessity for almost everyone. Cities have utilities that offer essential services if those services are not offered economically by the private sector. Water, electricity, and trash collection, for example, are often city services, or at least city controlled.

Traditionally, access to information has been considered a public necessity, ever since Carnegie libraries were established in almost very town and city. The public library has always been free and open. In the last few years, Internet access has become an essential service. Certainly, there should be debate about whether the connection to the Internet is supplied by a public utility or a private provider.

The image of a city sitting under the canopy of a wireless Internet network is a vision most want to see—it is the vision of a city with universal access to the power of the Internet at a reasonable cost for everyone.

Historically, the primary problem with desktop video-conferencing using the Internet is the poor quality of the video and the limited capacity of the Internet to carry video signals. Since the Internet is a "packet-switched" network, a video signal is broken into packets that are disassembled and then sent to the distant site where the packets are reassembled into a signal. Previously, this approach was a limiting factor when live, interactive video was sent. Video streaming is a growing subset of this category of distance education. Video streaming is usually defined as the progressive downloading of a video file (Mallory, 2001). A storage space (buffer) that is much smaller than the video file is identified on the computer's hard drive. The video file begins to download into the file location and the file begins to display on the computer screen. The file continues to download from the origination site somewhere on the Internet to the buffer and onto the local computer screen. Often the video file is a prerecorded event, but live video can be streamed, also.

Three popular video file types are Apple QuickTime (.mov files), Microsoft Windows Media Player (.wmv files), and .mpg4 files. QuickTime's .mov files are very popular for standard movie downloads, but are not used as much for streamed video and audio. A commonly used strategy is to store video segments on a CD or DVD and ship them to the distant learner to use as part of a course or lesson. CDs can store approximately 650 megabytes (approximately 1 hour of video), and DVDs can store about 1.6 gigabytes or about 2 hours of video.

Desktop videoconferencing is a critical area for growth in distance education. Increasingly, the Internet will be used to connect learners for sharing of video, in addition to data (text and graphics). Before this happens, however, advances in compression standards, network protocols, and transmission media will need to be made.

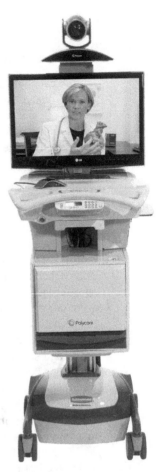

Special "distance learning" systems can be wheeled into any conference room, classroom, office, or work area.

DISTANCE EDUCATION CLASSROOMS

Two-Way Video/Audio Classrooms

Video-based distance education used to require a classroom or studio that was equipped with the technology needed for recording and displaying video and listening to sound. Initially, studios were used as distance education classrooms. Then, as distance education became more widespread, regular classrooms were converted into distance education receive and send sites (Figure 4–13). Today it is common to see in-home offices and business cubicles as send and receive sites.

Video classrooms have recording, instruction, and display equipment. Recording equipment includes video cameras—three—one that shows the instructor, one for the stu-

FIGURE 4-13 Distance learning classroom—teaching site, view from rear.

dents, and often an overhead camera mounted above the instructor console to display printed graphics materials. A switching system is needed to permit the instructor to switch between cameras and instructional equipment, such as a computer. Several companies offer devices that attach to video cameras and cause them to follow the action in the classroom. For example, when its activation button is pushed, the student camera automatically pans and zooms to the appropriate microphone location to show the student who is talking. Also, the instructor camera has sensing devices that, when activated, automatically direct the camera to follow the instructor's movements in the classroom.

Additionally, audio equipment is needed. Audio tends to cause more problems than video in distance education classrooms. Early classrooms used voice-activated microphones, but currently push-to-talk microphones are the most common.

Display equipment includes large HDTV monitors and audio speakers. Most often three display monitors are mounted in a classroom—two in the front of the room for students to view and one in the rear for the instructor. Audio speakers are connected to a volume control. Sometimes class-rooms are connected to a control room where technicians can monitor action and even control the recording and display equipment. Increasingly, however, classrooms are controlled by the teacher and students. In other words, the teacher is responsible for equipment operation and use, or students in the class are assigned these responsibilities. Many consider this approach to distance education as an extension of traditional education by linking distant sites to regular classrooms.

Classroom Technologies for Online Instruction

The key to success in an online classroom is not which technologies are used, but how they are used and what information is communicated using the technologies.

Selecting Appropriate Technologies for Online Instruction

Step #1: Assess Available Instructional Technologies. Instructional technologies can be organized into two categories: telecommunications technologies and instructional technologies. Since *telecommunications* means to communicate at a distance, telecommunications technologies are electronic methods used to connect the instructor, students, and resources. Obviously, this chapter discusses online technologies, which means a computer and network.

However, embedded within computers and networks are capabilities permitting the delivery of instruction using a variety of media. Instructional media are ways that messages are stored, and most online applications include verbal symbols (words spoken and written), visual symbols (line drawings and graphics), pictures, motion pictures, real-time video, and recorded/ edited video.

This list is similar to the one proposed by Edgar Dale, discussed earlier in this chapter. The bottom levels of Dale's cone listed realistic experiences, such as actually doing something in the real world, like going to Greece. Realistic experiences are the most difficult to make available to students. It takes a great deal of time and extensive resources to always provide totally authentic, real-world learning experiences.

Dale implied when discussing his cone that the tension between efficiency (abstract experiences) and effectiveness

(realistic experiences) is at the core of instructional design. The professor should pick learning experiences that are no more realistic than necessary in order for outcomes to be achieved. Overly abstract learning experiences require the student to compensate or to learn less effectively. Overly realistic experiences waste resources. When the professor who is designing online instruction selects the correct media, it maximizes efficiency and makes available more resources for other learning experiences.

Assessing available technologies often requires that the instructor determine the level of lowest common technologies. This means that the sophistication of the computer and software of all learners and the instructor should be determined. Also, this means that the capabilities of the telecommunications technologies must be identified. Often, lowest common technologies is determined by having students complete a survey in which they clearly identify the technologies that are available to them.

Step #2: Determine the Learning Outcomes.   Learning outcomes are those observable, measurable behaviors that are a consequence of online instruction. When learning activities are designed, it is important that some expectations for students be identified in order to guide the selection of appropriate technologies.

Since online environments should be media rich and strive for authenticity, it is critical that many technologies be used. It is also important that students demonstrate learning outcomes by using a variety of technology-based activities. Students may be expected to take a test to demonstrate their competence, but more likely they will be expected to offer some kind of real-world project that gives an authentic assessment of what they learned. Rubrics, which simply are predetermined strategies for how assignments are to be graded, should be available for students to use to guide the development of the outcome materials they produce.

One strategy used by developers of online instruction is to collect student projects and use these materials as models for subsequent students. If this strategy is used, a thoughtful and comprehensive critique of the student projects should be included so mistakes are identified and not repeated. Some developers of instruction advocate that students should begin with existing materials produced previously and redesign them to eliminate weaknesses, build on strengths, and add new concepts.

Specifically, text (words) used in a lesson could be analyzed and replaced with graphics or word pictures that are combinations of text and graphics that represent teaching concepts. Still pictures could be modified and upgraded to animations, and synchronous chats could be made more effective by including a threaded discussion strategy that involves asking questions, collecting answers, asking follow-up questions, and selecting the most appropriate final responses. Traditionalists identify learning outcomes in terms of behavioral objectives with specific conditions under which learning will occur, a precise behavior to be demonstrated that indicates learning, and an exact standard to measure competence. Recently, learner-identified objectives have become popular: the student is expected at some point during the instructional event to identify what changes he or she feels are important indicators of learning. Whatever approach is used, it is critical that outcomes of instructional events be clearly identified at some point.

Step #3: Identify Learning Experiences and Match Each to the Most Appropriate Available Technology.   Usually, the content of a course is divided into modules or units. Traditionally, a module requires about 3 hours of face-to-face instruction and 6 hours of student study or preparation, and a three-credit college course would have 12 to 15 modules. In an online course, the classical approach of organizing content around teaching and study time is no longer relevant. One approach would be to simply convert a classroom-centered course's content into online modules. For totally new courses, this approach will obviously not work.

An alternative approach is to organize a course around themes or ideas that directly relate to student activities or learning activities. For example, a course in history about the Reconstruction period following the American Civil War might have 12 modules, each with 5 learning activities, for a total of 60. The learning activities would be content-centered experiences such as reading assignments, PowerPoint presentations, and audio recordings, or learner-centered experiences, such as threaded discussions on specific topics, research assignments utilizing web search engines, or self-tests.

One example for a module dealing with a topic such as the economic redevelopment of the South in the first 5 years after the end of the Civil War might begin with a reading assignment from the textbook about the economic conditions in the South. This reading assignment would include a web-based assignment. The reading would be followed by participation in an online discussion with a small group of classmates. The purpose of this discussion would be to identify the five impediments to effective economic development. When the group agreed to the list, it would be posted to the course's bulletin board for grading by the instructor. The third learning experience in this module would be a review of a prerecorded PowerPoint presentation (a minilecture, if you will) with audio that was prepared by the instructor that discusses what actually happened economically in the South after the Civil War. Finally, the student would be expected to write a two-page critique of the period of economic development according to a rubric posted on the web. This assignment would be submitted electronically to the course's instructor for grading.

Subsequent modules in this course would be designed similarly. At several points during the course, benchmark projects would be required of students, such as an individual online chat with the instructor, or the submission of a major project that synthesized work completed for module assignments.

Once the course's content is organized into modules, the next design requirement is to match learning experiences to technology-delivery strategies. The reading assignments could be delivered using the textbook, or posted as files to be downloaded, or even read directly from the computer monitor.

PowerPoint presentations could be handled the same way, and used directly from the computer or downloaded and studied later. E-mail attachments could be used for assignment submission and chat rooms or e-mail could provide ways to hold threaded discussions.

In this example, the instructional media are relatively simple ones. What is sophisticated is the design and organization of the activities and content facilitated and delivered by the media.

Step #4: Preparing the Learning Experiences for Online Delivery.   Basically, there are four strategies for organizing instruction for online delivery. They are (1) linear programmed instruction, (2) branched programmed instruction, (3) hyperprogrammed instruction, and (4) student-programmed instruction. Often a combination of these strategies are used in a single course.

In each case, the content of the course is subdivided into modules. The modules consist of topics that relate to one another or have some sense of unity or consistency, such as the economic condition of the South after the Civil War. The modules themselves, and the learning activities within the modules, are organized according to one of the four delivery strategies.

Linear programmed instruction, a long-standing approach to individualized instruction, requires that all content be organized into concepts that are presented in blocks or chunks. Students review content, take a self-test, and if successful move to the next chunk/block of information. This happens sequentially until the content blocks are completed. Students move in the same order through the sequence of concepts. The teacher determines the order of the concepts/chunks.

Branched programmed instruction is similar, except the self-tests are more sophisticated so students can branch ahead if they are exceptionally proficient or move to remediation if they are floundering. Similar to linear programmed instruction, the order and sequence of instruction, including branches, is instructor determined. Hyperprogrammed instruction, widely advocated for web-based online instruction, also organizes content into modules and concepts, but permits students to move through the learning activities at their own rate and pace, in a route they determine themselves. This approach is popular when courses are taught asynchronously. In other words, learning experiences are identified and mediated, and students use them until either an instructor- or student-determined outcome is met. Often, each module has a terminal, or final, activity that must be completed to indicate that the student has mastered the content of this module.

Finally, the student-programmed approach uses an extremely loose structure where only the framework of the content is provided to online learners who are expected to provide the structure, outcomes, and sequence of learning activities.

For example, students who enroll in a course on the *Period of Reconstruction* would be required to organize and sequence the modules and activities, and during the course to identify personal outcomes and activities to be accomplished.

When teachers attempt to make instruction equal for all students they will fail. Rather, the teacher of online instruction should provide a wide collection of activities that make possible equivalent learning experiences for students using an approach that recognizes the fundamental differences between learners, distant and local. Equivalency is more difficult but promises to be more effective.

THE INTERNET—WHY DOES IT MATTER?

As a foundation for current approaches to distance education, it is helpful to understand what the Internet is and how it works. The Internet is not a single, clearly defined entity, but a meta-network of interconnected networks that share a common language, TCP-IP (transmission control protocol/Internet protocol). (A protocol is an electronic language that computers use to communicate with one another and exchange data. Protocols are roughly analogous to the languages humans use to communicate and share information.) These networks are in a constant state of evolution, with thousands of vendors making changes on an almost daily basis.

The Internet has no international headquarters or mailing address, no chief executive officer or board of directors, no stockholders to whom it must be accountable, and no toll-free telephone number to call for assistance or information. This is not to say that the Internet is an anarchy, although some cynical observers might disagree. Much of the planning and coordination responsibility is assumed by the Internet Society, an international, nonprofit organization established for the purposes of "global cooperation and coordination for the Internet and its internetworking technologies and applications." Founded in 1991, the society facilitates the development and implementation of Internet standards and policies and holds oversight responsibilities over several important boards and task forces that address Internet issues. Membership in the Internet Society is free and open to all interested persons anywhere in the world, including the readers of this book.

Although some national governments restrict access and practice censorship, in general the existing oversight bodies are concerned with technical and network management matters rather than what information is placed on the Internet, who puts it there, and who has access to it. This is an important issue for students and teachers using the Internet for educational purposes, because no quality-control mechanism exists to ensure that information found on the Internet is accurate and unbiased, and that it may be freely viewed by the young and innocent.

Architecture of the Internet

How is it that a fifth-grade class in Cambridge, Ohio, can participate in online interaction with counterparts in Cape Town, South Africa, and Folkestone, England? A brief look at the architecture of the Internet will help us understand the answer to that question. It will also help illustrate the enormous potential of the Internet for distance education, as well as its limitations.

Figure 4–14 is a graphic representation of the structure of the Internet. The model consists of four basic tiers of services.

FIGURE 4–14   Graphic representation of the structure of the Internet in the United States.

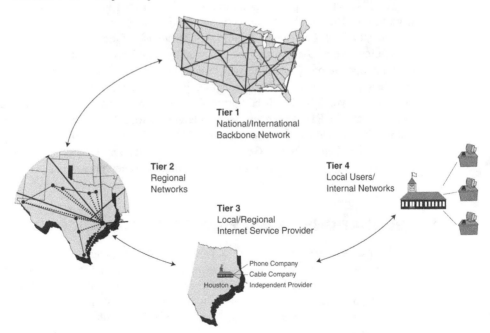

Tier 1
National/International
Backbone Network

Tier 2
Regional
Networks

Tier 4
Local Users/
Internal Networks

Tier 3
Local/Regional
Internet Service Provider

Phone Company
Cable Company
Independent Provider

Houston

Tier 1: Backbone Networks and Internet Exchange Points.   The essential framework is provided by a worldwide configuration of extremely high-bandwidth networks called *backbones.* Backbones may be regional, national, or international in coverage, and are typically operated by major telecommunications carriers such as AT&T, Sprint, and Qwest on a for-profit basis. Backbones meet and transfer data at junctions called Internet exchange points (IXs). The vast majority were located in North America, Europe, Australia, and eastern Asia, but the numbers were growing rapidly in less industrialized regions.

Tier 2: Regional Networks.   Regional networks operate backbones on a smaller scale, in the United States typically within a state or among adjacent states, connecting to one or more national or international backbones.

Tier 3: Internet Service Providers.   This is perhaps the most important component for distance educators. The individual Internet service providers (ISPs) are connected to regional networks and provide access to the Internet at the local level. These are the companies that provide Internet access to schools, businesses, private homes, and other community entities such as libraries, churches, and government offices, if not available through other networks. Internet service providers have been largely responsible for the worldwide Internet boom, because they have made the Internet available to almost everyone in their local communities.

Tier 4: Organizational and Home Networks.   These are the local area networks that interconnect computers within an organization, such as a school, college, government agency, or company, and provide Internet access to individuals within those entities. Many persons have installed wireless networks in their homes to extend Internet access to multiple computers and devices via one high-speed connection.

Are the Terms "Internet" and "World Wide Web" Interchangeable?

This is another important point to clarify. The answer is "No." The Internet is the network itself. The World Wide Web, accessed through web browsers such as Internet Explorer, Firefox, Chrome, and Safari is just one use of the network. While many e-mail applications are web-based and are accessed through browsers, others, such as Microsoft Outlook, operate on a "client-server" basis. They are on the Internet but outside the web, and users must open client software on their desktops to access their mail. File-transfer protocol (FTP), which is often used to transfer files between a server and a user's desktop, is another example. FTP servers are accessible via the web (by entering "ftp://" and the server address in the address window instead of "http://") but are more commonly accessed through FTP client software. Generally speaking, if the application is accessed through a desktop icon other than a web browser, it is on the Internet but not on the web.

FOUNDATIONS OF INTERNET-BASED DISTANCE EDUCATION

The Internet and the personal computer in general have changed the way we think about teaching and learning. To teach and learn effectively in an online environment, we must understand the concepts of *student-centered learning* and *distributed learning.* These terms will be essential to our discussions in this chapter about web-based tools that are available for educational purposes and how they are, or should be, used.

Student-Centered Learning

The model of teaching employed during the instructional television era of distance education essentially replicated the model found in the conventional classroom. Teachers and the textbook were the two primary sources of course content. Teachers lectured and demonstrated. Students listened and took notes, and then repeated the same information back to the teachers on exams. This "teacher-centered" model continues today in many courses delivered to distant learners via today's synchronous, video-based technologies. MOOCs, Massive Open Online Courses, are a recent approach for offering instruction over the Internet, and many, even most, MOOCs are presentations of prerecorded lectures by master teachers. With computer- and Internet-based technologies, however, have come exciting new opportunities for providing learning experiences to students. This philosophy of education has become popularly known as *student-centered learning,* because it so strongly promotes active learning, collaboration, mastery of course material, and student control over the learning process. Barr and Tagg (1995) discussed the differences between teacher-centered and learner-centered instructional models. See Table 4-1 for a summary of the transformations that have the strongest implications for Internet-based distance education.

Oblinger (1999) also observed these transitions, but from a slightly different perspective:

TABLE 4–1 Characteristics of the Transition From an Instructor-Based to a Learner-Based Instructional Model

Instructor-Centered Model	Learner-Centered Model
Mission and Purposes	
Provide/deliver instruction	Produce learning
Transfer knowledge from faculty to students	Elicit student discovery and construction of knowledge
Offer courses and programs	Create powerful learning environments
Teaching/Learning Structures	
Time held constant, learning varies	Learning held constant, time varies
50-minute lecture, 3-unit course	Learning environments
Covering material	Specified learning results
Success determined by accumulated credit hours	Success determined by demonstrated knowledge and skills
Learning Theory	
Learning is teacher centered and controlled	Learning is student centered and controlled
"Live" teacher, "live" students required	"Active" learner required, but not "live" teacher
Classroom and learning are competitive	Learning environments are cooperative, individualistic, collaborative, and supportive
Nature of Roles	
Faculty are primarily lecturers	Faculty are primarily designers of learning methods and environments
Faculty and students act independently	Faculty and students work in terms with each other

Source: Adapted from Barr and Tagg (1995).

- From lecturing to coaching
- From taking attendance to logging on
- From distribution requirements to connected learning
- From credit hours to performance standards
- From competing to collaborating
- From library collections to network connections
- From passive learning to active learning
- From textbooks to customized materials

We will see evidence of these transformations throughout this chapter. Successful faculty in online learning environments are able to "think out of the box" and set aside the traditional teacher-centered instructional model. It is in this context that we discuss Internet-based learning.

Distance Learning Versus Distributed Learning

The concept of *distributed learning* illustrates how the learner-centered educational model is being implemented in today's schools and colleges. Not all online learning necessarily is distance learning. Much Internet-based learning activity involves students and teachers who continue to meet at least part time in conventional classroom settings. One of the earliest definitions was offered by Saltzberg and Polyson (1995):

Distributed learning is not just a new term to replace the other DL, distance learning. Rather, it comes from the concept of distributed resources. Distributed learning is an instructional model that allows instructor, students, and content to be located in different, noncentralized locations so that instruction and learning occur independent of place and time. The distributed learning model can be used in combination with traditional classroom-based courses, with traditional distance learning courses, or it can be used to create wholly virtual classrooms. (p. 10)

Distributed learning thus is a broader term that can be, and in fact most often is, associated with face-to-face instruction that incorporates some form of technology-based learning experience, either inside or outside the classroom. In other words, students do not need to be at a distance from their instructor to benefit from distributed learning. While the primary focus of this book is distance teaching and learning in which students and their teachers are geographically separated, many distributed learning experiences may involve only resources that are at a distance, or that occur at a different time and/or place than the conventional class meeting

For example, learning materials can be located on a server anywhere in the world and accessed either by the classroom teacher as part of her presentation or independently by the students in some interactive setting. Course discussions can take place online and outside the classroom. A class activity could involve tracking a scientific expedition in real time, including interaction with the explorers and live video transmitted through the World Wide Web. High-speed networking now enables music students in Ohio to perform ensemble works with students in Pennsylvania, Texas, and Colorado. Likewise, a medical school professor in California can demonstrate unusual surgical procedures to students in Georgia and Massachusetts, complete with sophisticated graphics and audio for real-time discussion. The states identified here are for example purposes only; the participants could be almost anywhere.

Distributed learning is also represented by what are called *hybrid* or *blended* courses, in which online activities substitute for a portion of actual seat time in an otherwise conventional face-to-face course. A Sloan Consortium analysis of data collected over the period 2003–2012 found that almost 75% of higher education institutions surveyed offered blended courses, and many course sections were taught in a blended format (Allen & Seaman, 2012). Blackinton (2013) reported on a hybrid physical therapy doctoral program that incorporated the distributed learning approach.

Advantages and Limitations of Online Learning

The advantages of online learning compared with conventional face-to-face teaching are numerous.

- Unless access is deliberately restricted, courses or online course materials could be available to any qualified individual in the world with a properly equipped computer and an Internet connection. Students can participate from school, home, office, or community locations.
- Asynchronous course components are available 24 hours a day, at the learner's convenience, and are time-zone independent.
- Students can work at their own pace.
- Course materials and activities available through the web are distributable across multiple computer platforms; it makes no difference if users are using Windows or OS operating systems on laptops, smartphones or tablets.
- The technology is relatively easy for students to use.
- Learning materials are available across the entire World Wide Web.
- Online course materials, once developed, are easy to update, providing students access to current information.
- The Internet can provide a student-centered learning environment, if the materials and methods are designed to take advantage of the interactivity and resources the Internet provides.
- The Internet promotes active learning and facilitates student's intellectual involvement with the course content.
- A well-conceived online course provides a variety of learning experiences and accommodates different learning styles.
- Students become skilled at using Internet resources, a factor that may improve employment options upon graduation.
- When personal identities remain concealed, all students, regardless of gender, ethnicity, appearance, or disabling condition, can be on equal ground.
- Corporate training programs conducted via the Internet can yield significant savings in employee time and travel costs, and training can be conducted on a "just in time" basis.

The limitations of Internet course delivery may also be substantial:

- The Digital Divide is real, especially in rural and lower socioeconomic regions, contributing to a "haves and have-nots" situation. Even where the Internet is available, many potential students do not have ready access to powerful, modern computers, and if they do, they may not know how to use Internet resources.
- Online courses may emphasize the technology rather than the content and learning opportunities.
- Well-designed Internet-based courses may be labor intensive to develop, requiring time and personnel resources not available to many instructors.

■ Some instructors have difficulty adjusting to the learner-centered model of instruction and do little more than "shovel" their teacher-centered, lecture-based courses into an online format.

■ Although today's students as a whole are more technologically literate than ever before, many are technophobes who find the Internet confusing and intimidating

■ Some topics may not adapt well to delivery online.

■ Bandwidth limitations make it difficult to present advanced technologies, such as streamed video, multimedia, and memory-intensive graphics, over the web.

■ Online courses require students to take more responsibility for their own learning, a task that some find challenging.

■ Although responses to student questions may be instantaneous in the conventional classroom, feedback may be delayed by hours or even days in an online learning situation.

■ The support infrastructure, providing training and technical assistance to both students and instructor, is often minimal or nonexistent. Instructional design support during the conceptualization and development of a course is also frequently unavailable. These factors are major barriers that discourage many faculty from teaching online.

TECHNOLOGIES OF INTERNET-BASED DISTANCE EDUCATION

The Internet has its roots in the Advanced Research Projects Agency Network (ARPA-NET), a network created in 1969 to link the computing systems of military and other government agencies to those of their research partners around the United States, including universities and corporate contractors. As the ARPANET grew, important technologies such as TCP-IP, tools for electronic mail and online discussion forums, and Ethernet were developed to enhance its capabilities. In 1985, the National Science Foundation (NSF) established the NSFNET, a high-speed data transmission network that interconnected a series of NSF-funded supercomputers across the United States, and invited other networks running the TCP-IP protocol to connect to it, including the ARPANET participants. This NSFNET national backbone and its affiliated networks became known as the Internet, and 1985 is regarded by many as the Internet's birth year. The ARPANET was absorbed into the Internet and ceased to exist in 1989.

A simultaneous but separate development was the evolution of the Because It's Time Network (BITNET), founded as a general-purpose academic network in 1981 by the City University of New York and Yale University. BITNET ultimately grew to include about 600 educational institutions in the United States and was affiliated with networks in Canada, Europe, and other parts of the world. BITNET used a different protocol (RSCS/NJE) and therefore technically was not part of the Internet, but it interconnected with the Internet through "gateways" that functioned as translators between the two protocols.

Mention of BITNET in this chapter is important for two reasons. First, BITNET was the first computer network available for widespread academic use. Hundreds of thousands of college faculty members and students became acquainted with international computing networks and their capabilities through BITNET. The first acknowledged online instruction was delivered via BITNET in 1981. Second, BITNET mainframes hosted the LIST-SERV mailing list management software that enabled both BITNET and Internet users to participate in online, asynchronous group discussions on thousands of topics. The term *list-serv* has found its way into the vocabularies of most educators and students as a euphemism for an online, asynchronous discussion forum, even though other list management software products exist and the LISTSERV user's guide specifically requests that the term not be used in a generic sense. BITNET ceased operations in 1996, as its functions also became absorbed into the Internet.

The Internet itself continued to expand through the last half of the 1980s and into the early 1990s, but for educators its primary functions remained electronic mail and online discussion groups, file transfers (using file transfer protocol, or FTP software), and remote access to computers ("remote login," commonly through Telnet software). It is important to understand that many higher education faculty members were engaged in online instruction during this period, including completely online courses, using electronic mail, mailing lists, and files stored on FTP servers. Even before the introduction of the concept of the World Wide Web, this was a rich period in American distance education. (Library and web searches on the terms *computer-mediated communication* and *asynchronous learning networks* will yield a wealth of interesting resources on pre-web online learning.) Use of the Internet at the K–12 level was minimal at this time, primarily because of access issues and the general lack of computing resources, although some schools were engaged in innovative e-mail exchange programs with other schools all over the globe.

The World Wide Web itself was conceived by Tim Berners-Lee of the European Center for Particle Research (CERN) as a means of sharing data among scientists and was first used in 1989. It did not become the subject of a standard desktop application until 4 years later, when the National Center for Supercomputing Applications (NCSA) at the University of Illinois unveiled Mosaic as an all-purpose World Wide Web "browser." Within a year, more than 2 million persons around the world had downloaded Mosaic, and when Netscape appeared as the next-generation web browser in late 1994, interest in the web spread more dramatically. As access grew, the number of websites online increased exponentially—from just 130 in June 1993 to 23,500 by June 1995 and 100,000 by January 1996 to hundreds of millions today. The World Wide Web brought the "point and click" technology of the desktop computer to the Internet. Although such objects as graphics, photographs, and audio and video files were accessible through FTP and other applications (including a technology called Gopher that was very popular in the early- to mid-1990s), the web was the first Internet application to integrate them into a single screen along with text. The use of multifont text also became possible. Perhaps the most dynamic feature of the web was hypertext, the ability to link words, phrases, graphics, and other on-screen objects with other files located on the same server or on someone else's server on the other side of the world. As a result, web page developers, including teachers, could easily organize information from multiple sources and make any of it accessible to users with a single click of a mouse.

The potential for commercialization of the Internet led to a radical change in the network's architecture, as the National Science Foundation decided that the federal government should not continue to fund the backbone infrastructure in competition with private telecommunications carriers. A new structure was put in place by April 1995, and the NSFNET was retired. The transition to commercial backbone operators was seamless and unnoticed by most Internet users. With the privatization of the Internet, commercial use of the network mushroomed, as reflected in the extraordinary growth in the number of websites and individual pages after mid-1995. Internet service providers were established to serve virtually every community in the industrialized world. Most commercial entities developed websites for customer sales and support. And a whole new industry of vendors emerged to support Internet users. Thousands of these evolved to offer products and services to educators engaged in Internet-based distance education.

WEB 2.0

As the 21st century progressed, it became more and more evident that course management systems, and indeed the World Wide Web itself in its first decade of widespread public use, reflected the teacher-centered instructional paradigm (Brown, 2007). The web presented information with very little interactivity and user involvement beyond pointing, clicking, and reading. Course management systems (CMSs) were largely places for faculty to place lecture notes and other materials for student study, and for students to obtain those materials, take online quizzes, and check their grades, and were *very* instructor centered. Outside of opportunities for online discussions, which are rarely utilized effectively by "rank-and-file" faculty, CMSs were not locations that facilitated the high levels of student intellectual engagement—with content, with their instructors, and with each other—that hallmark the learner-centered instructional paradigm.

Beginning in the early 2000s, however, a new generation of web applications emerged, tools that are highly participatory and promote collaboration, networking, sharing, and the widespread generation of content, and the editing and mixing of content from diverse sources for new purposes through a model called the *mash-up*, by both groups and individuals. The term *Web 2.0* was coined by O'Reilly Media in 2003 (O'Reilly, 2005) and is now widely used in a collective sense to describe these technologies. Web 2.0 applications are not limited to education—in fact, Web 2.0 exists primarily outside the education sphere—but these technologies have extraordinary potential for education and the kinds of learner-engaging functions that should be incorporated into the next generation of course management systems. They represent the very essence of learner-centered instruction. According to Maloney (2007),

> what we can see in the web's evolution is a new focus on innovation, creation, and collaboration, and an emphasis on collective knowledge over static information delivery, knowledge management over content management, and social interaction over isolated surfing. The jargon-laden stars of the second-generation web—wikis, blogs, social networking, and so on—all encourage a more active, participatory role for users.

Web 2.0 technologies include, but certainly are not limited to, the following areas.

Blogging. Web logging, or blogging, is a form of online reporting and journaling that gives anyone an opportunity to publish on the Internet. Blogs can be open to the public or restricted to groups of readers determined by the blogger. Blogs can be excellent tools for student reflections about course content or reporting activities in a student teaching experience, for example. See Blogger.com for an example of a blogging site freely available for personal or academic use.

Wikis. A wiki is usually thought to be a space designed to be created and edited by groups of persons. The term derives from the Hawaiian word *wiki*, which means "quick." A wiki can be an excellent tool for collaborative online writing assignments and group activities compiling information in a single online resource. The best known is Wikipedia, a free online encyclopedia being written by tens of thousands of active contributors all over the world. Wiki applications, including Wiki-Site, the same engine that drives Wikipedia, are available at little or no cost to educational institutions.

Podcasting. Podcasting, which derived from the Apple product iPod and the term *broadcasting,* is the process of recording and storing audio and/or video content on the Internet for downloading and playback using iPods, MP3 players, computers, and other electronic gear that plays back audio and/or video files. College professors are now finding podcasting a convenient way to provide lectures, parts of lectures, and other course-content-related recordings to students. This concept is hardly new. We were doing this in the 1980s when the Sony Walkman came into vogue as a portable audiocassette player. Now, though, the web provides a convenient medium for the distribution of audio content by just about anyone, including students and faculty. Audio recordings are easy to make and simple to edit, and they can easily be uploaded into course management systems.

Other Forms of Content Creation.   Until the early 2000s, only webmasters and others authorized to build websites could put information on the web. No more. One of the defining characteristics of Web 2.0 is that literally anyone can generate "content" and place it on the web without knowledge of web page design tools and methods. Blogs and wikis are examples of web user content generation. YouTube, founded in February 2005 as a place where anyone can upload a video file for viewing by the masses, has become one of the most frequently visited sites on the web. Today, tens of thousands of video files *per day* were being uploaded into YouTube, and millions videos *per day* were being viewed by persons all over the world. No figures are available for how many of these uploaders are students, but a safe estimate is "plenty." Likewise, many faculty are uploading video-based lecture recordings and other course materials for convenient viewing by students. Blackinton (2013) reported that for the doctoral program in Physical Therapy videos were stored on YouTube. With video recording capabilities built into many digital cameras and even cell phones, and with most computers sold today pre-equipped with simple video editing tools, possibilities for video-based student learning activities, posted to the web, seem endless.

Social Bookmarking.   Social bookmarking was described by Alexander (2006) as "classic social software … a rare case of people connecting through shared metadata" (p. 36). As such, social bookmarking epitomizes the collaborative and sharing aspects of Web 2.0. Most of us save lists of our frequently visited websites as favorites or bookmarks in our web browsers. In social bookmarking sites people post their bookmarks for viewing by others. Through a sophisticated system of meta-tagging, or assignment of descriptive information, anyone is able to search for bookmarks on specific subjects and identify sites that others have found valuable. In a sense, social bookmarking is like Google or Yahoo! on steroids, because the sites located have already been prescreened and found to be useful by others with similar interests. Social bookmarking sites have high potential for students searching for web resources for class assignments. Moreover, once other users have been identified as posting a significant number of helpful sites, bookmarks posted on other topics by those users can be reviewed to identify "kindred spirits" with common interests. The sites provide contact information for purposes of social communication.

Social Networking.   Most college students need no introduction to social networking. Some estimate that 90% of precollege Americans ages 12 to 17 were active on social networking sites in the last year. Social networking sites promote the development of online communities through posting of personal information, journals, photos, likes and dislikes, and provide communication channels for persons with similar interests to meet virtually. Considerable research is needed on the relationship between social networking and distance education (Simonson, 2008a, 2008b).

A Look at Best Practices—Web 2.0

We all know what it means to be a friend. We learn early in life that as Emerson said, "the only way to have a friend is to be one." A friend is a person admired, respected, whose company is enjoyed.

The idea of friends has recently changed, however, at least in social networking applications. According to Boyd and Ellison (2007), social networks are web-based services that allow persons to construct a public or semipublic profile within a system, to articulate a list of other users with whom they share connections, and view and move through a list of links made by themselves and others. Most often these locations are called "social networking sites." Social network sites such as Facebook have attracted millions of participants who blog, share messages, post photos and videos, and list their friends, all in personally constructed profiles.

To participate in a social network site a user constructs a profile and by this act the social networker becomes real in a virtual world. They "type oneself into being" as Suden (2003) stated. One characteristic of most social networking site is the listing of friends; friending. Social networkers name those they want to list as friends, and in most cases the request to be a friend requires an affirmative response. Some sites even allow top eight or top ten lists of friends; as Boyd (2006) said, "in a culture where it is socially awkward to reject someone's Friendship, ranking them provides endless drama and social awkwardness" (p. 11).

Many who study the phenomena of social networking refer to the idea of Web 2.0, a trend in the use of the Internet and web that is based on collaboration and information sharing. Web 2.0 is not a new network, nor a thing. Web 2.0 is an idea in people's heads, based on the interaction between the user and provider. Examples are eBay, Wikipedia, Skype, and Craigslist.

So, what does this all mean? Certainly it is nice to have friends, even virtual ones, and social networks seem to have reached the point of "critical mass" and are here to stay, at least until a new innovative use of the web evolves.

Social networking is an important approach available to distance educators. At the least, a modest understanding of social networking is a must for distance educators. The taxonomy of social networking for distance learning might look like this:

Level 1: Learning about social networks—definitions, history, background, and examples.
Level 2: Designing for social networks—profiling, blogging, wiking, and friending.
Level 3: Studying social networks—ethics, uses, misuses, policing, supporting.
Level 4: Learning from and with social networks—social networks for teaching and learning, science, research, and theory building.

Virtual Worlds.   Virtual reality is hardly a new concept. Virtual reality in the form of computer-generated simulations dates back to the mid-1950s and has long been used for corporate, health science, and military training purposes. Projects, such as Second Life and Active Worlds, have brought these technologies to the World Wide Web and made them accessible to much broader populations, including educators. While the instinct among some has been to put classroom lectures into virtual worlds so they can be experienced by students via 3-D animation, virtual worlds appear to have (as they have for several pre-web decades) exciting potential for placing students in real-life applications of course content, for example, in problem-solving situations, and especially experiences in other places and times that would otherwise be inaccessible, such as visiting Mars, traveling through the human body's circulation system, or witnessing rituals at Stonehenge. Limitations at this time include the need for significant bandwidth at the user's end and the skills, time, and effort needed to plan and develop the animations. It is likely, however, that virtual worlds represent the standard learning environments of some point in our future.

PEDAGOGIES OF INTERNET-BASED DISTANCE EDUCATION

In their widely read, if criticized, report entitled *Thwarted Innovation: What Happened to E-Learning and Why,* Zemsky and Massy (2004) concluded that online learning was a good thing but had fallen way short of its promise (Simonson, 2004).

E-Learning Adoption Cycles

While their research was questioned, Zemsky and Massy's thoughts on e-learning adoption cycles are relevant. They noted that technology applications in both on- and off-campus instruction follow four distinct adoption cycles, each requiring pedagogical and cultural changes within the educational organization (Zemsky & Massy, 2004, p. 11). Any or all of these cycles may be operating simultaneously in different parts of the same campus.

- **Cycle 1—Enhancements to traditional course/program configurations.** In this cycle, faculty introduce basic-level technologies into their courses, such as e-mail, web resources, and PowerPoint slides, without fundamentally altering their instructional strategies.
- **Cycle 2—Course management systems.** Here, faculty use some of the basic tools a CMS offers and shift resources and course activities to an online format. Some use these tools completely in lieu of face-to-face class meetings. (Zemsky and Massy noted that more than 80% of all online course enrollments at the institutions they studied consisted of on-campus students.)
- **Cycle 3—Imported course objects.** This cycle involves embedding electronic learning objects within a course to further promote student understanding of the course material. These objects could range from photographic slides and audio and video files to complex 3-D animations and simulations.
- **Cycle 4—New course/program configurations.** In this cycle, courses are reconceptualized and redesigned to take advantage of the power of technology and the Internet in enhancing learning and increasing student engagement. "The new configurations focus on active learning and combine face-to-face, virtual, synchronous, and asynchronous interaction in novel ways. They also require professors and students to accept new roles—with each other and with the technology and support staff" (Zemsky & Massy, 2004, p. 11). Use of Web 2.0 applications is most likely to occur in a course in Cycle 4.

Zemsky and Massy (2004) felt that faculty in general were well into the first two cycles but that this interest has not expanded to Cycles 3 and 4. Specifically in the case of distance education, they observed

> good use of the presentation enhancement tools represented by PowerPoint; heavy reliance on the kind of course infrastructure that a good course management system provides; computerized assessments; and threaded discussions. At best, it would include the importation and use of elementary learning objects; in reality, it has prompted almost no development of new course/program configuration beyond taking advantage of the web's capacity to promote self-paced and just-in-time learning. (p. 12)

Other obvious reasons for the failure of educational organizations to realize the potential of online learning were not discussed in this report. These "barriers" are long-standing and are firmly entrenched in institutional culture, and they have powerful effects. Many teachers simply do not have the time or the instructional design skills for, let alone the interest in, completely redesigning their courses per Cycle 4. Campus reward systems governing promotion discourage instructional innovation by younger teachers. Instructor training is minimal to nonexistent and typically focuses upon basic PowerPoint and CMS "how-to" tutorials rather than the pedagogies of teaching online. Most educational institutions do not employ trained, professional *instructional* technology designers whose functions are to assist teachers and trainers in online course development and the creation of learning objects.

Fundamentals of Teaching Online

What advice can we offer to instructors who teach online? What kinds of processes can teachers and trainers follow to advance their online courses to Cycles 3 and 4? Here are some suggestions that are intended to supplement Chapter 5 and 7 on instructional design and teaching in a distance education environment, respectively.

Avoid "Dumping" a Face-to-Face Course Onto the Web.   Some teachers and trainers do little more than transfer course handouts and selected discussion topics to the CMS. The term *shovelware* has evolved to describe this practice: Shovel the course onto the web and say you are teaching online, but don't think about it much. Online activities for students should have specific pedagogical or course management purposes.

Organize the Course and Make the Organization and Requirements Clear to Students. Many students have never before studied in an online educational environment. If they have, chances are good that it was not a positive experience. Instructors of online courses must make the course organization, calendar, activities, and expectations as clear as possible. Students need this kind of structure and detail to help them stay organized and on task. A detailed syllabus is a good starting point.

The calendar tools provided in CMSs generally are adequate for showing students the big picture, but instructors should also provide more detailed information on a topic-by-topic basis, or week-by-week or even day-by-day in more time-compressed classes, to guide students and keep them on track. Each "weekly schedule" page should include (1) inclusive dates; (2) topics; (3) learning outcomes; (4) identification of readings and other preparatory activities; (5) schedule of activities, including quizzes or exams; (6) topics and/or specific questions to be discussed in the online forums; (7) identification of assignment(s) and due dates; and (8) any other relevant information. Let students know exactly what is expected of them, and when.

Detailed assignment instructions are imperative. Each component of an instructor's grading scheme should have its own document easily locatable within the course site. The instructions could include any of the following, as appropriate. Certainly not all these components may be necessary for all assignments.

▪ Stated purpose of the assignment.
▪ Identification of the intended audience for the assignment (e.g., "Write the proposed business plan as if it would be read by a senior executive within the company. Your instructor will assume that role during grading.").
▪ Examples of acceptable and unacceptable topics.
▪ Hyperlinks to relevant online resources.
▪ Caveats (e.g., "The proposed business plan must be realistic within the current budget climate. Do not propose eight new positions without explaining how the funds for these positions would be generated.").
▪ Identification of the required components of the assignment (e.g., "The proposal should include the following: introduction and justification of need, project goals, proposed budget, and timeline ?").
▪ Grading criteria, including areas of special emphasis.
▪ Due date.
▪ Point value.
▪ Instructions for submitting the assignment, such as in the CMS drop-box or as an e-mail attachment sent directly to the instructor.
▪ Any other special instructions or information (e.g., "Your paper will be posted on the course website.").

Keep Students Informed Constantly.   The announcements tool in a CMS is an excellent means for instructors to get new information to students. Use announcements to introduce new topics, remind about deadlines, announce schedule changes, and provide a wide variety of other timely information. Many online instructors prefer to send direct e-mail to their students for these purposes in the form of weekly updates/introductions to new topics. Regular contact is essential.

Think About Course Outcomes.   This is the first step in truly transforming a course. What knowledge, skills, and feelings does the instructor really want the students to gain in the course? In what ways do students need to be prepared for subsequent courses or for application of the course content in the real world (the real bottom line)? These are the course outcomes. Bloom's (1969) taxonomy of educational objectives is extremely useful in this process. Course activities then need to be structured to enable students to achieve those outcomes. In almost every discipline, activities can be conducted in an online environment to facilitate student learning at each of these levels. It is imperative to activate higher order thinking skills.

Test Applications, Not Rote Memory.   Student assessment must be designed to reflect the specific behaviors identified in the course outcomes. While it is possible to design multiple-choice quiz items that assess students at the analysis, synthesis, and evaluation levels of Bloom's taxonomy, these are not likely to be typical applications of the course material in the real world. Assessing students in a manner consistent with the behaviors identified in course outcomes also helps combat student academic dishonesty. Techniques such as question pools and randomization are used within CMSs to minimize cheating, but creative students can devise many ingenious ways to beat the system. Avoiding objective online testing altogether may be the best strategy.

Integrate the Power of the Web Into the Course.   This is essential for purposes of student intellectual engagement—with course content, with each other, and with the instructor and other resource persons involved in the course. The web offers powerful opportunities for resource utilization, collaboration, and communication. Many highly valuable primary sources are now available online.

For example, in the early- to mid-1990s, an agricultural economics professor at a land-grant university in the Midwest was involved with extensive economic development projects in the newly independent nations in Eastern Europe that had been Soviet republics. In the process, he collected an enormous volume of documents and videotaped interviews with numerous local, regional, and national officials of those countries, which he then had digitized with dubbed translations. As the number of websites exploded later in the decade, he identified hundreds of related sites, from United Nations and World Bank resources to countless local and national sites describing conditions in those areas related to agriculture and local economic drivers such as tourism. He then organized this information by selected country and community on his course website and asked his students to study the resources and create economic development plans based upon the information available. This was truly learning at the higher cognitive levels. The real-world learning experience was emphasized when local officials in those communities assisted in the assessment of the plans for grading purposes.

In particular, the power of the web can be employed through the use of Web 2.0 applications. These tools are all about student engagement and higher order learning.

Apply Adult Learning Principles.   If students enrolled in a course are working adults, the course design should incorporate the basic principles of adult learning. Adults are more self-directed and have specific reasons for taking the course. Many have their own learning goals in mind and expect the instructor to help them achieve those goals. Activities and assignments should be relevant to the students' immediate needs, rather than the deferred needs of traditional college-age students, and should contain options for customization. Online discussions should build on the students' personal and professional experiences. Adult students can learn as much or more from each other as from the instructor. They have many commitments in their lives in addition to the course, involving work, family, church, and community. Therefore, the instructor may need to exercise more flexibility regarding timelines and deadlines than with a class of traditional college-age sophomores. These are but a few examples.

Extend Course Readings Beyond the Text (or to Replace the Text).   Many instructors are conditioned by their own college experiences and years of practice to allow the textbook to dictate the course content and to organize course activities around the textbook. This is fine if the instructor wrote the textbook for the course, perhaps not so otherwise. The step of selection of course readings occurs about in the middle of a course development model, not at the beginning. Nowhere is it written that a course has to have a textbook. The web is positively rich with outstanding primary sources that can be used effectively to promote outcomes achievement. There is a plethora of online resources used by the agricultural economics professor identified earlier to supplement his personal collection of documents and media. In addition, more than 10,000 professional journals and other periodical publications are now available online and in full text. Almost every profession has online newsletters available free or at low cost that allow students and faculty to stay abreast of current developments. These resources are what professionals in the field use; students need to be acclimated to using them at the beginning of their respective careers.

Train Students to Use the Course Website.   Students cannot use course web tools effectively if they do not know how. Certainly, in recent years course tools have become very intuitive, However, it is essential that training be provided at the beginning of the course, through online tutorials in the case of online courses and in a face-to-face setting if available. Instructors should consistently monitor to detect if students are having difficulty navigating the course website and using its components.

FUTURE OF ONLINE EDUCATION

When the chapters for the first edition of this book were written in 1998, course management systems were new on the market and not widely used. Little attention was paid to CMSs in this edition. The web was just beginning to be exploited as a means of commerce. Few homes had broadband Internet access. Virtual schools were just starting to appear. So much has changed in such a relatively short period of time that both the fourth and fifth editions of this chapter required significant updates. And we are already seeing nationally distributed reports about the *failure* of online learning. So, it is with some trepidation that we discuss the future of Internet-based distance education. Here are four trends to watch (Benson & Whitworth, 2014).

Growth of Virtual Schools and Universities

While many teachers incorporate technology into their daily activities, and despite the emergence of a new, student-centered approach, most education today still follows fundamentally the same instructional model as it has for the past 200 years. Students sit in a classroom, teachers stand in the front and control the learning activities, students listen and take notes, and periodically some form of in-class assessment is conducted. How long will this model persist? Is this the way students will be learning in the year 2100? Probably not, although the historically glacial pace of educational change may produce doubts in some. The growth of virtual schools and colleges gives us a glimpse into a possible educational model of the future.

K–12 Initiatives.   Virtual schools at the K–12 level are now seeing significant growth. In fact, the state of Florida has mandated that every school district in the state must have a virtual K–8 and 9–12 virtual school (Simonson, 2008c). Enrollments and program quality will be the subject of much public (and undoubtedly legislative) interest and scrutiny in the years to come. In 2006, the Michigan legislature approved a requirement for all high school students in the state to take an online course as a graduation requirement (Michigan Department of Education, 2007). Dozens of states have established statewide virtual schools to reach their K–12 populations. "Cyber" schools are also being operated by universities, school districts, consortia, and private companies. The state of Ohio alone has dozens of virtual schools operating.

Virtual schools can have many benefits for students, districts, and states. They can supplement existing curricula, promote course sharing among schools, and reach students who cannot (for physical reasons or incarceration) or do not (by choice) attend school in person. Virtual schools enable districts and states to provide advanced placement courses and enrichment courses to rural schools and those in other smaller, less affluent locations. Home-schooled students, in particular, stand to benefit from courses and curricula offered online. The We///b can help overcome two of the limitations of homeschooling—the lack of interaction with other students and, as with many alternative schools, limited access to high-quality learning materials.

Higher Education Initiatives.   At the postsecondary level, interest in establishing virtual colleges and universities was stimulated by the creation in 1996 of the Western Governor's University, a collaboration of 13 western states, and by the dawn of the 21st century had spread across the country. Recently there has been a semistandardization of terms. Online learning refers to distance education in higher education, virtual schooling refers to K–12 distance education, and e-learning refers to distance education in the private, corporate sector. According to the Sloan Consortium report, most higher education institutions consider distance education to be important or very important to their future (Allen & Seaman, 2012).

Development of Standards and Learning Objects

When a consumer buys a DVD of a recent movie release, does she wonder if it will play on her home DVD player? When she buys a conventional 60-watt light bulb, or even one of the newer LED bulbs, is she afraid that it won't screw into her table lamp? When she buys gasoline at a gas station, is she concerned that it won't fuel her car? Unless the products themselves are defective, the answer is "No," because the world has established technical standards for such things. Most countries in the world have national standards institutes that work closely with the International Organization for Standardization (www.iso.org/) to ensure worldwide compatibility to the greatest degree possible.

Enter the matters of learning objects and learning management. If an instructor developed an online course using one type of course management system and the institution then licensed a different system, the course would not easily port over to the new platform. The manner of tracking student performance is not consistent from one CMS or student assessment software product to another. We currently have no easy way of identifying existing courseware to meet a specific learning need. The Masie Center (2002) has captured the nature of the problem:

> As we have seen historically with battles over such things as railway track gauge, telephone dial tones, video tape formats, e-mail protocols, and the platform battles between Microsoft, Apple, Sun, HP, and others, companies often start out with proprietary technology that will not work well with others. However, these technologies often do not meet the needs of end-users, and thus, the market typically drives the various leaders from business, academic, and government to work together to develop common "standards." This allows a variety of products to coexist. This convergence of technologies is very important for the consumers of these technologies because products that adhere to standards will provide consumers with wider product choices and a better chance that the products in which they invest will avoid quick obsolescence. Likewise, common standards for things such as content meta-data, content packaging, question and test interoperability, learner profiles, run-time interaction, etc., are requisite for the success of the knowledge economy and for the future of learning. (p. 7)

The Masie Center (2002, p. 8) identified five "abilities" that e-learning standards should enable:

1. Interoperability—can the system work with any other system?
2. Reusability—can courseware (learning objects, or "chunks") be reused?
3. Manageability—can a system track the appropriate information about the learner and the content?
4. Accessibility—can a learner access the appropriate content at the appropriate time?
5. Durability—will the technology evolve with the standards to avoid obsolescence?

This, very briefly stated, is the background for a number of collaborative efforts to develop standards for e-learning. The general process followed is that a designated organization conducts research and development activities and generates "specifications" that are a preliminary form of standards. The specifications are then put through extensive testing and continued development until they are accepted by the developer and user communities, at which time they become standards.

The Advanced Distributed Learning initiative, sponsored by the Department of Defense, took on a coordination role for developing e-learning standards in the United States, working with several organizations that develop specifications. Advanced Distributed Learning was responsible for conducting the testing, review, negotiation, and further development activities that transform specifications into standards. Accepted standards collectively form the Sharable Content Object Reference Model (SCORM) for product developers and users that ensures conformance with the five "abilities" just listed. When vendors describe their products as "SCORM-compliant," they are referring to this.

The IMS Global Learning Consortium is the organization with its focus upon developing specifications for distributed learning and CMSs. Originally oriented toward higher education only, IMS addresses a multitude of distributed learning contexts, including K–12 and corporate and government training. IMS specifications currently in various stages of development cover the following areas: accessibility, competency definitions, content packaging, digital repositories, enterprise, learner information, learning design, meta-data, question and test interoperability, simple sequencing, and vocabulary definition exchange. The value of having technical standards in each of these areas should be self-evident.

The specifications for digital repositories are particularly important as they relate to learning objects. The definitions of learning objects vary considerably from one source to another. The simple explanation is that a learning object is an object used for the purposes of learning. Some authorities consider the "old" media such as overhead transparencies and videotapes to be learning objects. Others say that learning objects have to be in digital format. To be truly useful in a standards-based context, learning objects must be digital and have certain characteristics that give them added value. One is that learning objects are meta-tagged; they carry coding containing descriptors that enable the objects to be identified during searches. Another is that learning objects should be reusable. In other words, they should be indexed in a digital repository that adheres to IMS specifications, so that they can be accessed by any instructor, anywhere, at any time.

Only a few such repositories exist at this time. For example, one of these repositories is the Multimedia Educational Resource for Teaching and Online Learning (MERLOT). Others are beginning to appear under the "open courseware" concept, the publication on the web of course materials developed by higher education institutions and shared with others. Some consider videos on Youtube as simple examples of open courseware. As digital asset management technology evolves, we can expect to see many more. These will greatly expand the number and range of instructional resources available to instructors teaching online.

Potential Impact of Open Source

Open source software is intended to be freely shared and can be improved upon and redistributed to others. The code in which the software is written is free and available to anyone to do just about anything with it, as long as the uses are consistent with a 10-part definition maintained by the Open Source Initiative (OSI). Open source does not mean "unlicensed." Open source software typically has a license, but the terms of the license should comply with the OSI definition before the software is truly open source. Nor does *open source* mean "free." The code may be free, but the costs involved in implementing the application within an organization (e.g., hardware and personnel) can be significant.

The concept of open source is relevant to this chapter because a number of initiatives have evolved to create open source CMSs that can be licensed by educational institutions. This option is appealing to many campuses that already have technical support staffs in place that can manage open source software applications. For example, the Australian open source CMS product called Moodle has become so widely adopted that it is now available in 75 languages and has produced a worldwide grassroots network for development and peer support numbering hundreds of thousands of persons. In the United States, the Sakai Project, a collaboration among Stanford University, the Massachusetts Institute of Technology, Indiana University, the University of Michigan, and a group of partners, has consolidated the individual efforts of the four institutions to develop an open source, standards-based CMS that interoperates with other campus systems and emphasizes pedagogy over course management (Simonson, 2007).

SUMMARY

The technologies used for distance education fall into two categories: *telecommunications* technologies that connect instructors to distant learners and *classroom technologies* that record, present, and display instructional information.

Most often, teachers and students use classrooms that have been designed and installed by others. However, the effective utilization of distance education classrooms requires a new set of skills for most educators and learners. Teaching with technology to learners who are not physically located in the same site where instruction is taking place requires a different set of skills and competencies than traditional education. Technologies are tools that must be mastered to be effective.

CASE STUDY

The dean of a school of education has asked a group of faculty to develop a plan for increasing the number of classes offered in the teacher education program. Part of this plan is a description of the technologies that will be needed (hardware, software, and connectivity) by students learning at a distance, and by faculty in the school. What would be needed?

A New Technology—Drones

Another True Story

Two months ago, one College purchased a drone. The drone system consisted of the aircraft itself, a controller that is connected to a smart phone or tablet, and a high definition camera. According to the manual, it will fly to an altitude of 500 yards in a radius of half a mile. The drone apparently has a very powerful computer system that automates almost everything, including obstacle avoidance (a very important function).

What educational purpose is there for drones—by the way, this drone was quickly nicknamed "lightening"?

Lightening is more than a toy, although it certainly is fun to fly. The College purchased the drone because the claim was made that it was a new type of educational technology—maybe distance education technology.

Januszewski and Molenda (2008) define educational technology as "the study and ethical practice of facilitating learning and improving performance by creating, using, and managing appropriate technological processes and resources." Earlier definitions include the word systems and systematic approach.

Certainly, the drone named Lightening is a system, and a relatively complex one, and since drones fly, they are a distance technology. The question to be asked:

> "is drone technology an educational tool of the instructional designer and the distance educator?"

This book defines distance education as "institutionally based, formal education where the learning group is separated and where interactive telecommunications systems are used to connect learners, resources, and instructors." Neither the definition of educational technology nor the definition of distance education say anything about drones.

Drone systems are in the news a lot today—most often in stories about the military. Other uses are increasing, also, such as aerial videos of storm damage in Puerto Rico, and high level views of houses being repaired on shows on the HGTV network. What is less apparent are the educational applications of drones—if there are any.

In the fields of educational technology and distance education, there is a tendency to embrace new technological tools as important, and in some cases even necessary—even drones. Learning about the hardware and the system that makes the machine function are the fun parts of being an instructional technologist and distant educator. When new technologies are introduced, it is the role of the professional, not the vendor, to determine the importance of the new tools to the field.

Telehealth is another "new technology" that has been much discussed. What is interesting is that many in the health professions are "luke warm" on their role in determining the appropriate applications of telehealth. Like many professionals, health professionals are interested in health, and not "tele."

Vendors can be crafty. They sometimes "manufacture" uses of their products, and hope it works out. Who should decide if a new product or technology innovation is important? Vendors or professionals? New technologies, if adopted by distance educators, should first be evaluated to determine if they contribute to the instructional process.

Finally, as Thoreau said "Beware of enterprises that require new clothes." In the meantime, let's all go fly our drones.

DISCUSSION QUESTIONS

1. According to Dale's cone of experience, which is the most realistic, a video of a museum, or a field trip to the museum. What would make one experience more appropriate than the other?
2. Define noise and explain how noise influences the communication process. Put noise in the context of an online course.
3. Should traditional classrooms also be equipped to be distance classrooms? Why?
4. What are the most significant advantages of Internet-based instruction? Why?
5. Explain how an online course can be structured to be student centered. Give specific strategies.
6. What is one significant trend in online learning? Why?

REFERENCES

Alexander, B. (2006). Web 2.0: A new wave of innovation for teaching and learning? *EDUCAUSE Review, 41*(2), 32–42. Retrieved from http://www.educause.edu/apps/er/erm/erm06/erm062.asp Allen, I. E., & Seaman, J. (2012). *Changing course: Ten years of tracking online education in the United States*. Babson Park, MA: Babson Survey Research Group.

Allen, I. E., & Seaman, J. (2013). *Changing course: Ten years of tracking online education in the United States.* Needham, MA: Sloan Consortium.

Barr, R. B., & Tagg, J. (1995). From teaching to learning: A new paradigm for undergraduate education. *Change, 27*(6), 13–25.

Benson, A. D., & Whitworth, A. (2014). *Research on course management systems in higher education.* Charlotte, NC: Information Age.

Blackinton, M. (2013, November). Teaching a "hands-on" profession in an online classroom. *PT in Motion, 20,* 16–23.

Bloom, B. S. (2007). *Taxonomy of educational objectives: The classification of educational goals.* London, England: Longman Group.

Boyd, D. (2006). Friends, friendsters, and Myspace Top 8: Writing community into being on social network sites. *First Monday, 11*(12).

Boyd, D. M., & Ellison, N. B. (2007). Social network sites: Definition, history, and scholarship. *Journal of Computer-Mediated Communication, 13*(1), article 11. Retrieved from http://jcmc.indiana.edu/vol13/issue1/boyd.ellison.gtml

Brown, M. (2007). Mashing up the once and future CMS. *EDUCAUSE Review, 42*(4), 8–9. Retrieved from http://www.educause.edu/apper/erm0/erm0725.asp

Dale, E. (1946). *Audiovisual methods in teaching.* Hinsdale, IL: Dryden. Discovery Education. (2006). About United Streaming. Retrieved from http://www.unitedstreaming.com/publicPages/aboutUs.cfm

Essex, C. (2006). Podcasting: A new delivery method for faculty development. *Distance Learning, 3*(2), 39–43

Gillispie, J. (2008). Meeting the shifting perspective: The Iowa Communications Network. *Distance Learning.*

Januszewski, A. & Molenda M. (2008*). Educational technology: A definition with commentary.* New York: Lawrence Erlbaum Associates.

Maise Center. (2002). *Making sense of learning specifications & standards: A decision-maker's guide to their adoption.* Saratoga Springs, NY: Author.

Mallory, J. (2001). Creating streamed instruction for the deaf and hard-of-hearing online learner. *DEOSNEWS, 11*(8), 1–6.

Mullins-Dove, T. (2006). Streaming video and distance education. *Distance Learning, 3*(4), 63–71.

New Oxford American Dictionary announces word of the year: 'Podcast'. (2005, December 6). Mac-Daily News. Retrieved December 7, 2006, from http://macdailyNews.com

Oblinger, D. G. (1999). Hype, hyperarchy, and higher education. *Business Officer, 33*(4), 22–24, 27– 31.

O'Reilly, T. (2005). *What is web 2.0? Design patterns and business models for the next generation of software.* Retrieved from http://www.oriellynet.com/pub/a/oreilly/tim/news/2005/09/30/what-is-web-20.html

Reed, R. (2001, August). Streaming technology: An effective tool for e-learning experiences. *National Association of Media and Technology Centers Bulletin,* 1–3.

Saltzberg, S., & Polyson, S. (1995). Distributed learning on the World Wide Web. *Syllabus, 9*(1), 10– 12.

Shakespeare, *Hamlet,* Act II, Scene ii, line 211.

Simonson, M. (2004). Thwarted innovation or thwarted research. *Quarterly Review of Distance Education,* 5(4), vii–ix.

Simonson, M. (2007a). Podcasting: Or, seeds floated down from the sky. *Distance Learning, 4*(2), 104.

Simonson, M. (2007b). Course management systems. *Quarterly Review of Distance Education,* 8(1), vii–ix.

Simonson, M. (2008a). Will you be my friend? *Distance Learning,* 5(2), 99–100.

Simonson, M. (2008b). Social networking for distance education: Where's the research. *Quarterly Review of Distance Education, 9*(2), vii.

Simonson, M. (2008c). Virtual schools mandated. *Distance Learning,* 5(4), 84–83.

Sundén, J. (2003). *Material virtualities.* New York, NY: Peter Lang.

Zemsky, R., & Massey, W. F. (2004). *Thwarted innovation: What happened to e-learning and why.* Philadelphia, PA: The Learning Alliance, University of Pennsylvania.

Best Practices

Podcasting ... or "Seeds Floated Down From the Sky"

Bud-like seeds floated down from the sky, from space actually—they were not noticed at first but soon the seeds grew into pods, plantlike oblong objects that when ripe disgorged a terrible creature, a creature that killed and eliminated humans and replaced them with exact physical replicas that were identical in appearance but lacking in any emotion—podpeople.

> This sentence could be the plot-line to one of the four motion pictures made over the last 50 years based on Jack Finney's 1955 book *The Body Snatchers.* The film most remember was released in 1979 starring Donald Sutherland who was one of the last on earth to remain free of will and independent of the pod menace.

Another explanation of this sentence might be a teacher's lament about the students in class constantly putting the tiny "bugs" in their ears to listen to the tens of thousands of rap tunes on their personal iPod, hidden in a back-pack.

The iPod, iPad, tablet, and smartphone have become the icons of the first decade of the 21st century, and podcasting has become one of the most talked about applications in distance education. Podcasting and iPods are written about in the popular press, in journals, and even in the prestigious *Chronicle of Higher Education.* The *Chronicle* recently published a long article with the unfortunate title "How to Podcast Campus Lectures."

Podcasting is not a new idea. It has been around at least since the audio tutorial movement and the Sony Walkman. A podcast is really a single concept event that is explained by an audio file, or an audio file supplemented by still pictures or video. The most widespread and current example of a type of a podcast is a song, usually 3 to 5 minutes long available in an electronic file format, such as .mpg3 or .mpg4, that also might be available as a music video with singers, dancers, and actors in addition to the song. Luther Vandross' tune, "Always and Forever" is a wonderful 4-minute 54-second example. The tune is also available as a music video showing Vandross singing the song.

Individual songs work well as podcasts because most modern tunes have the characteristics of an effective single concept event—what many now are calling a podcast, which really is a learning object that is stored in an .mpg format. The characteristics of an *effective* podcast are as follows:

- A podcast is a single idea that can be explained verbally, or if necessary with audio and appropriate still or motion pictures (not a face talking)
- A podcast is a recorded event that is 3–10 minutes long
- A podcast is part of a series with each single event related to others
- A podcast is a learning object available in an electronic format that is easily played, most often as an mpg3 file
- A podcast is stored on a website or other Internet location for easy access
- A podcast is current and changed or updated frequently

In spite of what the *Chronicle* says, a recording of a lecture is a poor example of a podcast. Rather, it is best to "chunk" the class into five or six single concept blocks, each as a separate learning object. Effective lecturers do this already; they break up their class session into related topics. These topics can become podcasts when they are recorded electronically in an .mpg file format, especially if they are supplemented with related examples and recorded in a proper location without distracting background noises. Podcasts are a reincarnation or reinvention of what the masterly learning movement of the 1960s called single concept files or single concept films. They were effective then, and can be effective today.

And finally, let's call them something other than podcasts. MPGcast doesn't have the same cachet as podcast, but then MPGcast doesn't remind everyone of Donald Sutherland pointing his finger at the last normal person, either.

Fenney, J. (1955). *The body snatchers*. New York, NY: Dell.

Read, B. (2007, January 26). How to podcast campus lectures. *Chronicle of Higher Education*, A32–A35.

And Finally, MOOC Madness

"Though this be madness, yet there is method in't"
—Shakespeare (*Hamlet* (Act II, Scene ii, line 211)

Massive Open Online Courses, or MOOCs, pronounced interestingly enough as moooooks as in cow sounds, are the "talk of the town." The October 5, 2012 Section B of the *Chronicle of Higher Education* dedicated its entire issue to the topic of MOOCs. The *New York Times* has written about MOOCs, and South Florida's own *Sun Sentinel* has opined on the topic of MOOCS.

Just what are MOOCs and what do they offer to the field of distance education. Simply, the name tells it all. MOOC courses are massive, often with enrollments in the tens of thousands. Next, they are open, meaning open access courseware is used to deliver the course, and enrollment is open to anyone who is interested. Next, MOOCs are online, fully online and asynchronous. And last, they are courses, often a digitized version of a traditional lecture class with sessions recorded in video, audio, and posted online.

But, are MOOCs distance education, as many think? First, one needs to define distance education. Distance education is defined as follows:

> Institutionally based formal education, where the learning group is separated, and where interactive communications technologies are used to connect the instructor, learners and resources).

At first glance this definition does seem to include MOOCs as they are most often configured. MOOCs are institutionally based, at least originally they were. The great universities of the United States, such as the Massachusetts Institute of Technology, and Stanford, offer MOOCs. Interestingly, many of the instigators of MOOCs initiatives have left their universities to offer massive online courses via private corporations.

Next, it is obvious that the learning group is separated, at least the learners and resources are geographically separated. But what about the instructors? Certainly MOOC designers and the talent featured in the videos can be considered instructors, but are these individuals actually involved in the use of the MOOC or are they "just talent?" Instructor involvement in the teaching and learning process is unclear.

Most definitely, communications technologies are used to deliver content and make the content available to learners; most often content is digitized content via the web. Often, class presentations are video recorded, documents are digitized, and self-test quizzes and exams are written and programmed, often with self-scoring. Great stuff, but ...?

So, are MOOCs distance education? A closer examination of the definition of distance education may be helpful. Distance education consists of distance teaching AND distance learning—two components of the education process. Do MOOCs provide both teaching and learning? Some say no, since the instructional aspects of MOOCs are programmed and offered but only as a prepackaged self–study system. MOOCs are usually loaded with outstanding content, and well-delivered presentations, but those who would claim that MOOCs are the future of higher education need only review the instructional films and instructional video phenomena of the 1960s and 1970s. Excellent self-study, but not education.

And finally, there is much to be learned from the study of MOOCs. As Shakespeare wrote in Hamlet "there is method in't."

Teaching and Learning at a Distance

CHAPTER 5

Instructional Design for Distance Education

CHAPTER GOAL

The purpose of this chapter is to present a process for designing instruction at a distance.

CHAPTER OBJECTIVES

After reading and reviewing this chapter, you should be able to

1. Explain why it is important to plan ahead when teaching at a distance.
2. Describe a systematic design process for instructional design.
3. Describe the types of learner information to be collected for planning.
4. Explain the decisions about content that need to be made.
5. Explain why it is important to examine teaching strategies and media.
6. Discuss how technology and resources influence the distance learning environment.
7. Discuss the literature dealing with "best practices."
8. Design a course using the Unit-Module-Topic model.
9. Describe the process for assessment of learning.

"SIGNAL FIRES?"

In one of the greatest Greek tragedies, *Agamemnon,* Aeschylus begins his drama with word of beacon fires carrying news of the fall of Troy and the return of the king—news that set in motion Clytemnestra's plan to kill her husband in long-delayed revenge for his slaying of their daughter. These signal fires would have required a series of line-of-sight beacons stretching 500 miles around the Aegean Sea. Line-of-sight communication, as signal fires would require, has a long history. Most broadcast television applications require line of sight; even communications satellites orbiting in the Clarke Belt thousands of miles above the equator are "in sight" of the uplinks and downlinks on Earth.

Communication with someone you can see has a visceral element that is missing when that person or group of people is not "in sight." Certainly, considerable communication in distance education does not involve face-to-face instruction. The heart of distance education is the concept of separation of teacher and learner. Many say the meeting of students with teachers will soon be a relic of the past, like signal fires. This group touts the convenience of "anytime, anyplace" learning and the power of modern communications technologies to unite learners with instructional events no matter when they are needed and no matter where students may be located.

Others advocate the need for face-to-face instruction. This group stresses the importance of seeing and being seen, and the personal nature of the teaching/learning environment. Some even say that you cannot really learn some topics without being in a specific place with a select group of collaborators.

A third position is advocated by others who say that education should occur using a combination of instructional strategies. Schlosser and Burmeister (1999) wrote about the "best of both worlds," where courses and programs would have varying percentages of face-to-face and distance-delivered learning experiences. Blended or hybrid approaches are probably the most widespread applications of distance education (Daffron & Webster, 2006; Epstein, 2006; Orellana, Hudgins, & Simonson, 2009).

To date, however, no clear and verified process for determining whether face-to-face instruction, distance instruction, or a combination of the two is best. Most instructional designers and instructional technologists know that Richard Clark was correct when he said that media are "mere vehicles," but when courses are designed and instruction delivered, what are the templates, the processes, the approaches to be used to determine whether a module, course, or program should be delivered face to face or online? Or, what percentage of each is "best"? Where is the research? Certainly, decisions about how a course is to be delivered should not be based solely on the "beliefs" of the instructor or the mandates of administrators. Signal fires told of the fall of Troy probably because that was the most appropriate technology available. Today, many technologies are available for instruction of the distant learner. Instructional design processes help the instructor make informed decisions about technology use.

WHY PLAN FOR TEACHING AT A DISTANCE?

Just like other kinds of teaching, teaching at a distance requires planning and organizing. However, teaching at a distance, whether synchronous or asynchronous, requires that greater emphasis be placed on the initial planning phase.

Instructional design should consider all aspects of the instructional environment, following a well-organized procedure that provides guidance to even the novice distance instructor. (See, for example, Figure 5–1.) The instructional environment should be viewed as a system, a relationship among and between all the components of that system—the instructor, the learners, the material, and the technology. Especially when planning for distance education, the instructor must make decisions that will affect all aspects of the system (Moore & Kearsley, 2012).

This chapter presents background information about an organized and systematic way to go about planning instruction. Central to this chapter's organization is the Unit-Module-Topic model for course design (UMT approach). This model is based on best practices in course design and delivery, which will also be presented. This design process allows the instructor to consider elements such as the content, the nature of the learner, the process by which the learning will take place (methodology), and the means for assessing the learning experience. By following through with this process, the instructor will find that teaching at a distance is an exciting and dynamic experience, one that will be welcomed by both the instructor and the learners.

A Look at Best Practice Issues

On October 25 in 1965, downtown St. Louis stopped in its tracks and thousands watched as the last piece of the mammoth Gateway Arch was being put into place. The weight of the two sides required braces to prevent them from falling against each other. Fire hoses poured water down the sides to keep the stainless steel cool, which kept the metal from expanding as the sun rose higher. Some horizontal adjustments were required, but when the last piece was put into place and the braces released, it fit perfectly, according to plan, and no one was surprised (Liggett, 1998). The thousands of onlookers applauded as the sun reflected off the bright span. The architects and engineers who were also watching smiled and went back to their offices.

Just like the Arch, distance education requires a careful process that includes systematic design before implementation. Success is almost guaranteed if all the pieces of the plan receive the same attention as the most obvious. The base sections of the Gateway Arch required more engineering savvy and study than any other component. The last and most visible span that connected the two halves received the most attention from the thousands of onlookers, but success was directly related to how the original supports were positioned.

Design is the fundamental element of effective instruction. Many think that the traditional systematic models of instructional design are not relevant to the online teaching. Some claim that the traditional models of design such as the Dick, Carey, and Carey's model (2011), and its derivative the ADDIE model, cannot be readily applied to instruction that is delivered to distant learners. Some claim that systematic planning is not important or even needed when learner-centered instruction is developed.

In spite of claims, the evidence remains clear that the key to effective instruction is the concept of design, defined by Seels and Richey (1994) as:

> the process of specifying conditions for learning. The purpose of design is to create strategies and production at the macro level, such as programs and curricula, and at the micro level, such as lessons and modules. (p. 30)

At the root of most widely practiced and classic design approaches is the concept of systems. The idea of systems used in instruction is derived from Bertaanffy's General Systems Theory (1968), and Banathy's Instructional Systems (1968, 1991), usually called instructional systems design. This process has served as the intellectual technique of those in the field of instructional technology and distance education for decades.

Instructional designers, the engineers of quality instruction similar to the construction engineers and architects who designed the Gateway Arch, are on the frontlines of distance education implementation. Certainly, modern interpretations of the ADDIE model, such as the Unit-Model-Topic approach have been proposed to clarify and simplify the approaches for the systematic design of distance delivered instruction. However, any approach that makes claims about quality but that does not have the systems approach at its foundation should be considered suspect.

FIGURE 5–1   The instructional systems design model.

Source: Dick et al. (2001). Published by Allyn and Bacon, Boston, MA. © 1996 by Pearson Education. Reprinted by permission of the publisher.

PRINCIPLES OF INSTRUCTIONAL DESIGN SYSTEMS

Systematic Process

The process of systematic planning for instruction is the outcome of many years of research (Dick et al., 2015). An analysis of the application of this process indicates that when instruction is designed within a system, learning occurs. The process of instructional design is a field of study. Instructional design is considered the intellectual technique of the professional who is responsible for appropriate application of technology to the teaching and learning process. In other words, instructional design is to the instructional technologist as the rule of law is to the lawyer, the prescription of medicine is to the medical doctor, and the scientific method is to the chemist—a way of thinking and solving problems (Thompson, Hargrave, & Simonson, 1996).

A critical part of the process is to consider the components of a successful learning system (Dick et al., 2015). These components are the learners, the content, the method and materials, and the environment, including the technology. The interaction of these components creates the type of learning experience necessary for student learning.

The components must interact both efficiently and effectively to produce quality learning experiences. There should be a balance among the components—none can take on a higher position than the others. The attempt to keep the components equally balanced while maintaining their interaction effect is essential to planning quality instruction. Simply stated, a series of activities alone cannot lead to learning; it is only with the careful planning for their balance and interface that learning is the result.

Another critical part of the process is evaluation. For successful learning to take place, it is vital to determine what works and what needs to be improved. Evaluation leads to revision of instruction, and revision of instruction helps secure the outcome of helping students learn (Smaldino, Lowther, Mims, & Russell, 2015). Because of an emphasis on planning and revising, well-designed instruction is repeatable. This means that the instruction can be applied again in another class. For example, instruction designed for a televised, multisite class can be used again with a new group of students at different sites. Because it is "reusable," the considerable initial effort is well worth the time and energy.

Planning for Instruction at a Distance

The process of planning and organizing for a distance education course is multifaceted and must occur well in advance of the scheduled instruction. One "tried and true" approach for planning instruction is to model others. One excellent resource is Pina and Mizell's book *Real-Life Distance Education: Case Studies in Practice* (2014). This book provides research-based case studies about distance education. This book helps to eliminate trial-and-error preparation. Additionally, distance learning faculty should:

▪ Keep in mind that courses previously taught in traditional classrooms may need to be retooled. The focus of the instruction shifts to visual presentations, engaged learners, and careful timing of presentations of information.

▪ In revising traditional classroom materials, consider ways to illustrate key concepts, or topics, using tables, figures, and other visual representations.

▪ Plan activities that encourage interaction.

▪ Plan activities that allow for student group work. This helps construct a supportive social environment. For example, the instructor could present case studies related to theories and concepts covered in the course, and then groups of students could discuss case study questions and reach consensus on a solution to the problem.

▪ Be prepared in the event that technical problems occur. If synchronous equipment fails, it is important for students to have projects and assignments independent of the instructor and alternative means of communication (e.g., fax, phone, e-mail). Discussing with students ahead of time alternative plans in case there is a technological problem will eliminate confusion and loss of productive class time when a problem occurs (Orellana et al., 2009).

In addition to considerations related to planning for instruction, there is also a need to examine issues associated with the separation of instructor and some or all of the students. Time constraints for class delivery, lack of eye contact, visualization of the materials, and planning for interaction require a reconsideration of classroom dynamics. Often instructors use visual cues, such as student facial expressions, within the traditional classroom and conversations with students after class to decide quickly to adjust the instructional approach for a course. These cues give instructors insights that help them personalize the instruction for the students and ensure a quality learning experience for all.

In an online course, it is more difficult to acquire visual clues from and about students. Even when using desktop conferencing technologies, the visual component provides limited information to the instructor. Teaching at a distance eliminates many of these cues. Alternative approaches to ongoing evaluation of instruction must be incorporated. If instructors ignore this area of preparation, planning to teach as they always have, they may feel frustrated. Likewise, students may become alienated and may begin to "tune out" the instructor. The instructional development process must be based on the unique characteristics and needs of students, meshed with the teaching style of the instructor and the course goals and content. Interaction must be maximized, the visual potential of the medium must be explored, and time constraints must be addressed.

ISSUES TO ADDRESS IN THE PLANNING PROCESS

Who Are the Learners?

There are several reasons for bringing students together in a distance learning setting. Students can be pooled into classes of sufficient size to create a critical mass. Students can aggregate for advanced courses in subjects that might not otherwise be available on-site. Distance education can be an important approach to responding to the growing pluralism of learners' backgrounds, characteristics, or unusual learning needs that may require or benefit from specialized instruction. One reason profiles are so important in social media is because people want to know their "friends," or at least know about them. Distance learning students want to "know" their instructor and to be known by their classmates.

Taking the time to learn about the learners in the class yields a more productive learning environment. Knowledge of general learner characteristics can inform the instructor of the nature of the students at local and distance sites. This knowledge can aid the distance education instructor in overcoming the separation of instructor and students.

Along with the general information about the learners, an instructor needs to know the number of students in the class. In video-based distance education classes, knowing how many students are at each site and the number of sites involved in a synchronous distance education class can influence the level of interactivity. For example, in an online class with a large number of participants, it is likely that some students will fail to interact in discussions. Thus, an instructor needs to know his/her students and what technologies are available to them to plan effectively for interactive learning. In addition, it is essential to know the nature of the audience. Are students from urban areas? Rural areas? What is their age range, grade range, and educational background? All this can have a marked impact on the levels of interaction among students. The instructor may have to plan more carefully for the types and levels of interaction to ensure a quality learning experience for all members of the class. The cultural, social, and economic backgrounds of the students also constitute important information for the instructor. In addition, educational expectations of learners can also influence the quality of the learning experience. The attitudes and interests students bring to the class will influence the learning environment. Thus, an instructor who wants to create a quality learning experience for all members of the class, with the ultimate goal of learning as the outcome, will be certain to account for these variables in planning.

Analyze the General Abilities of the Class.   Analysis of the cognitive abilities of the class allows the instructor to observe how students relate to the content of the lesson. Such issues as clearly defining the prerequisite knowledge or skills for the specific learning experience are important to ensure a successful learning experience. The students' prior experience with similar types of cognitive tasks is important.

Further, learning styles have once again become an important area of consideration. With the introduction of Gardner's multiple intelligences has come the resurgence of an examination of learning styles (Gardner, 1993). How students approach learning is as important as how well they can function in the classroom. So knowing more about how students interact with information is important in creating a valuable learning environment.

An instructor can determine students' general knowledge and ability in a number of ways. Pretests and portfolio reviews can provide information about learners' abilities. Because students are coming to the class from a variety of backgrounds and learning experiences, they may be underprepared for the content intended for a particular course, and thus will be frustrated and even unsuccessful in the learning experience. Or, conversely, they may already be familiar with the content and will be bored and uninterested in participating in the class.

By knowing more about students, the instructor can develop supporting materials to individualize instruction. Varying the presentation of materials to match different learning styles (e.g., animation, text, verbal descriptions, and visual messages) can also ensure the greatest potential for reaching all learners.

The instructor can present complex cognitive content in ways that give learners clues, scaffolds, for understanding fundamental concepts, and thereby reach a wider range of individuals. People can remember complex material better if chunks of information are grouped into spatially related locations. Placing similar ideas in a logical sequence can aid retrieval of information at a later date.

Analyze Potential for Learner Interactivity.   Students who are less social may find the distance education environment more comfortable for them. Students may become more expressive because of the perception of privacy and the informative nature of mediated communication. They may perceive the increased and varied interactivity and immediate feedback as a positive input to their interface with the learning experience.

Additionally, students can benefit from a wider range of cognitive, linguistic, cultural, and affective styles they would not encounter in a self-contained classroom. The emphasis should not be on the inherent efficiency of the distance learning, but on the values and services offered to students through their exposure to others (Herring & Smaldino, 1997). Relationships can be fostered, values can be expanded, and shared purposes or goals can be developed. Distance learning experiences can serve as "windows to the world" by providing extended learning experiences.

When special efforts are made, distance education actually can enhance learning experiences, expand horizons, and facilitate group collaboration (Dede, 1990). Students can have more direct experiences with the information (e.g., close-up viewing of an experiment is possible). Time for reflection is possible before responding to the prompts presented, and the ability to work with peers or experts enhances the potential for learning. One of the most effective techniques to promote interaction in distance education is the threaded discussion—instructors post questions related to reading, viewing, and/or listening to assignments, then students post comments in a discussion area. Wade, Bentley, and Waters (2006) have identified 20 guidelines for successful threaded discussions. One critical guideline is the division of large classes into subgroups of 10 to 15 students so that discussions are manageable. A rule of thumb for the instructor's involvement in threaded discussions recommends that early in a course, the instructor should post once for every 4 or 5 student postings, then as students take more responsibility for their own learning later in the course, the instructor might post once for each 10 to 12 student postings—primarily to keep the discussions on track (Simonson, 2007).

Understand Learner Characteristics.   To be effective, it is necessary to understand the learners in the target audience. Willis (1994) suggested that the following questions should be asked prior to development of distance learning environments:

▪ What are students' ages, cultural backgrounds, interests, and educational levels?
▪ What is the level of familiarity of the students with the instructional methods and technological delivery systems under consideration?
▪ How will the students apply the knowledge gained in the course, and how is this course sequenced with other courses?
▪ Can the class be categorized into several broad subgroups, each with different characteristics?

These questions are not easy ones to answer. An instructor should attempt to find the answers prior to the first class meeting. Asking a few well-chosen questions of individual students will help the instructor understand their needs, backgrounds, and expectations. Additionally, students will feel they are important to the instructor. In an online environment, it is often more difficult for the instructor to get information about students; thus it is essential that the instructor plan a way of inviting students to share information about themselves. Be careful to respect their right to privacy, while trying to learn as much as you can about them.

Help Learners Understand the Context of the Learning Experience.   Morrison, Ross, and Kemp (2013) refer to three types of context: orienting context, instructional context, and transfer context. They suggest that the learners need to grasp the intent of the instructor when participating in various types of learning experiences. When the learners have an understanding of the reasons why they are participating in a particular type of instructional activity, they are better able to use that experience to expedite their own learning.

Each of these contexts serves a particular purpose for the learner. The orienting context refers to the students' reasons for being in a course. These reasons vary among the students. For example, a student may be participating in a course for credits toward a pay raise. Or, a student may wish to change positions within a company, which is dependent on completing the particular study area.

Instructional context addresses the learning environment. Scheduling a course to meet at a certain time and location or specifying specific dates for completion of assignments also impact the manner in which the student interacts with the class. Knowing how convenient it is for students to access the resources or to rearrange their own personal and work schedules is important when planning instruction. The third context, transfer context, refers to the way in which the knowledge will be used by students. It is critical when planning that the instructor considers what information is important so the students will apply it to work or school applications. Students will value that information they perceive as useful. Knowing the students and their interests or needs will help the instructor plan useful learning experiences to ensure transfer of learning.

What Is Essential Content?

The content of a course needs to reflect where this content relates to the rest of the curriculum. It is essential to examine the nature of the content, as well as the sequence of information. In any synchronous distance learning environment, one particular issue, that of time constraints, impacts other planning areas. Time constraints refer to the actual online time for delivery, which is often limited and inflexible. The issue of limited time makes it necessary to closely examine the essential elements of the course content. The instructor needs to balance content with the limited time for learning activities and possibly remove extraneous, nonessential information.

Generally speaking, the scope of the content for a course needs to be sufficient to ensure the entire learning experience will lead to the desired outcomes. Concepts, knowledge, and specific skills need to be identified (Dick et al., 2015). Supporting information or knowledge is important to the scope of content analysis. Follow-up and applications of the content should be considered.

The instructor's time is best spent on content analysis if the content is organized within a hierarchy. Starting with the general goals, followed by more specific goals and objectives, the nature of the structure of the content can be made to fall into place. The resulting framework of information about content helps the instructor decide the value and importance of specific information to the total instructional package. It is important to remember that no matter which media formats are used in distance education, the trend is to reduce the "amount" of information delivered and to increase the "interactive value" of the learning experience. Thus, the instructor may need to remove content that had been included in a traditional presentation of a course. Or, the instructor may need to consider delivering information through alternative means, such as additional readings or booklets designed specifically for tasks.

The instructor also needs to examine the sequencing of information. A number of variables—for example, characteristics of the learners, their prior knowledge, content, time, and number of sites involved—are critical when deciding the order of presentation of information. Because the instructor and some or all of the members of the class are separated, the material must be sequenced in a logical fashion for the students.

Goals and Objectives for Instruction.   The challenge of education is to match the content of the subject to the needs of the learners. Broadly stated goals are a helpful starting place for the instructor. The instructor must decide what is appropriate for a group of students and for the individuals within that group. Each instructor constantly must face the challenge of adapting instruction to the student who is expected to learn it. Although content is important, instructors should remember that their focus is on the students. This is critical when establishing goals for any course.

The traditional approach for writing objectives is also effective for distance education courses. Specifically, objectives should state the conditions under which learning should occur, the performance expected of the learner, and the standard to which the performance will be matched. One way to write objectives is as follows:

> Given: *the conditions under which learning occurs,*
> the learner will: *meet some predetermined level of performance*
> according to: *a minimum standard.*

The objectives of a particular lesson may not necessarily change simply because an instructor teaches at a distance. Good instructional goals should form the basis for instruction, regardless of the medium used. Instructional goals and objectives always should be shared with the students, helping both the origination and remote-site students to focus on the parameters of the instruction. This information may be included in course outlines, presentation handouts, or materials presented at the beginning of the course.

What Teaching Strategies and Media Should Be Used?

Students can provide insight into the design of the learning experience. They can give feedback in lesson design and instruction delivery. Using a simple feedback form, students can describe or indicate in some other way their expectations and perceptions of the class structure and the delivery mode. The instructor can examine information students provide to determine if the mode of presentation was effective. Evaluating these responses, the instructor can gain an understanding of how the learners perceived the class experience. An instructor's personal philosophy will influence the approach to teaching at a distance. An individual's philosophical belief will affect selection of goals and curricular emphases, and influence how that individual views himself or herself as a classroom instructor. The instructor who thinks in the philosophical arena of realism, idealism, essentialism, or perennialism will see the instructor as the central figure in the classroom, delivering knowledge and modeling to the student, an instructor-centered approach. On the other hand, the instructor who advocates the philosophies of pragmatism, existentialism, progressivism, constructivism, or social reconstructionism thinks that the student is the central figure in the classroom. The instructor is viewed as the facilitator of learning by guiding, rather than directing the students, thus modeling a student-centered approach.

Although the dynamics of a philosophy will not predict an instructor's success in the distance education classroom, successful teaching at a distance places the recipients' needs before organizational convenience and at the center of planning and decision making. The individual needs of the learners are brought to the forefront in education that uses electronic technology, because separation of learners from the instructor requires students to take more responsibility for learning. Consequently, the learner's opinions and needs play a more important role in decision making than is usual in an instructor-centered environment (Macfarlane & Smaldino, 1997). It is oversimplified to suggest that there is one best way to teach at a distance. In any given content area, there are several potential ways of providing a quality learning experience for the students (Smaldino et al., 2015). However, the one thing that has been repeatedly demonstrated through research is that lecture, or the "talking head" approach, is the least successful strategy to employ in distance education. What is essential in deciding which strategy or strategies to employ is the issue of engaging the learner.

The instructor should to focus on selecting instructional strategies that engage all the learners in active learning. To do this, the instructor may need to de-emphasize the "informative" part of the instruction for more "discovery" of information. The emphasis on keeping the learners engaged in learning ensures that students will be in tune with the class.

Media Selection.   Several models are often used in selecting media (Dick et al., 2015; Holden & Westfall, 2006). The common theme among these models is the learning context, which is the content, the intended outcome, and the nature of the students. Practical considerations such as available resources for creating media and the technologies for delivery of instruction also play a hand in the selection process. Mainly though, the goals and objectives will influence the selection of media. McAlpine and Weston (1994) have come up with a set of criteria for selecting media, whether they are commercial media or media developed specifically for a particular course. The first criterion is to match the medium to the curriculum or content. Other criteria include the accuracy of information, motivational quality, engagement quality, technical quality, and unbiased nature of material. These should be considered in selecting media in order to match student needs to the strategies employed.

Media that are "off the shelf" are often considered sufficient for a quality learning experience in the traditional classroom (Heinich et al., 2004). However, in a distance learning environment, the "ready-made" materials may need to be adapted or modified to accommodate the technologies involved in instructional delivery. Some materials may need to be enlarged or enhanced to be seen by students at a distance. With others, the digital format may need to be changed.

Because of the nature of distance learning and the separation of the instructor from the students, it is essential that the instructor begin to think visually. Too often, instructors do not place enough emphasis on designing and using quality visual materials. Taking the time to develop good visual media will enhance the quality of the learning experience (Heinich et al., 2002).

Visualizing Information.   Visuals provide a concrete reference point for students, especially when they are engaged in an asynchronous learning experience. Even if the visuals are lists of concepts and ideas, they can help students. Visuals also help learners by simplifying information. Diagrams and charts often can make it easier to understand complex ideas. A visual that breaks down a complex idea into its components can show relationships that might be otherwise confusing to students. Also, visuals that serve as mnemonics can assist student understanding. Visuals help students in their study as well. They can use the visuals to prepare for tests and other means of assessing their learning.

When creating visuals, the instructor needs to keep certain things in mind such as legibility. In a televised or computer-based distance learning environment, even with the close-up capabilities of the cameras, the choice of font and size can influence how easily students can read the text. Several "rules of thumb" should be applied:

- Use a large font (e.g., 24 or 36 point).
- Use a sans serif font (e.g., Helvetica).
- Use just a few words per line of text (e.g., six words per line maximum).
- Use only a few lines of text per visual (e.g., six lines per visual).
- Use a combination of both uppercase and lowercase letters; all uppercase is difficult to read.
- Use plenty of "white space" to enhance the readability.

Color can also play an important role in designing visuals. Color can increase the readability of text or graphics. However, the key to good use of color is in the contrast. Use a dark background and light lettering, or vice versa. Make certain to select colors that will not be compromised by the technology used for transmission (e.g., red vibrates in a televised environment). In asynchronous courses where students are learning from media such as videos, graphs, and charts legibility and visibility of content is important.

Two other very important issues should be raised. First is that of copyright. No matter what technologies are incorporated in the distance environment, the instructor needs to respect any copyright restrictions that might apply. For example, in a televised class, the instructor may not be able to use a video without first obtaining permission to display it to the class. In a web-based class, the instructor may need permission to post a journal article. An instructor needs to be responsible in obtaining copyright permissions where appropriate. The second issue is that of access. The instructor cannot assume that all students at a distance have equal access to resources. Students may not have the technologies available. The instructor needs to be certain that all students have similar learning experiences, including access to the materials. For example, if the instructor wishes students to use certain books or journals for outside reading, it is important to check with local libraries to be sure these materials are available.

What Is the Learning Environment?

Educators are familiar with classroom settings. They are comfortable with using the space available to enable learning to take place. It is when the classroom shifts into a distance learning setting that the environment often becomes a challenge to the instructor. Several important elements must be addressed within the distance learning environment.

Technology.   The type of setting, be it place- or time-shifted, will influence planning decisions. Environments that are place-shifted are those that are synchronous but are not in the same location (e.g., a live, video-based distance class). Those that are time-shifted are asynchronous, where students access the class at different times. Assessing the use of technology in a distant setting is essential. In any distance learning environment, the technology becomes an element of concern for the instructor. The instructor must become familiar with the hardware and the nuances of the technology to use them effectively. The instructor needs to balance concern for the operation of the equipment with effective teaching. Once the technology becomes transparent in the educational setting, the instructor can reflect on the lesson quality, the outcomes, and the plans for subsequent lessons.

Several issues are associated with technology when teaching in a distance learning mode. First is the basic operation of the equipment. In a televised distance learning setting, switching between sites is usually a simple procedure, but it does require instructor time to acquire the finesse to operate the switching buttons smoothly—to manipulate cameras, to control sound levels and to change graphic images. Second, using additional cameras in the classroom can create some concern for the instructor. The overhead camera needs to be focused and materials lined up to ensure that learners in all sites can see the material. Third, the instructor should always consider what the student should be viewing during the lesson. Is it better to see the instructor, the visuals, or other students? When an instructor has had experience teaching with the equipment, these decisions become automatic, making learning the foundation for the decisions made (Herring & Smaldino, 1997).

In an online learning environment, the instructor needs to be concerned with the layout of the courseware and the types of resources available to the students learning at a distance. The instructor needs to be certain the material is designed in a way that is intuitive for the various types of learners who may be interacting with it. The instructor also needs to be concerned about student access to the appropriate hardware and software to be successful in connecting to the courseware. Further, the instructor needs to be concerned that the students can complete the tasks expected of them. Finally, the instructor needs to be certain that the students understand the terminology being used. Today at a minimum, the typical distant student needs only a computer with a modern monitor to view course materials

It is essential that the instructor be prepared with alternatives in case of technical problems. What will the students do during a synchronous class being delivered using desk top video such as ZOOM (a proprietary videoconferencing software system) if the technology is not operating properly—or at all? Preplanned contingencies should continue the learning process even though the technology is malfunctioning. Alternative lessons must always be ready, but, it is hoped, never needed. Students need to be prepared to know what to do with those materials. The materials must be designed to be used without instructor intervention. Recording of synchronous sessions is almost always a good idea.

A Look at Best Practice Issues

Assumptions Made by Instructional Designers

An assumption is a position taken until something is proven, or stated another way, assumptions are ideas without evidence—things taken for granted.

Assumptions seem to be the antithesis of the systematic design of instruction— the systems approach generally, and instructional design specifically. The systems approach is based on a premise that aspects of any system should be correctly defined, clearly understood, and well-documented. And, distance education programs are usually planned using the systems approach (Dick, Cary, & Carey, 2015)

Instructional designers do not like to talk about assumptions – about what they "take for granted." However, in the privacy of the design studio, all who plan instruction make assumptions and take things for granted. OK, what are the types of assumptions that form the basis for designing instruction, traditional or online – there are seven:

1. Learners
2. Structure
3. Communication
4. Technology
5. Interaction
6. Literacy—visual and verbal learning

1. Assumptions About Online Learners

Assumptions about learners are what is taken for granted about them. Standards for online instruction often begin with the designers listing of the characteristics of the target audience for the instruction—prerequisite competencies, access to resources, and level of self-motivation, for example.

The massive research data provided by those advocating mastery learning during the 1950s and 1960s provides guidance about learner assumptions (Saettler, 2004). One assumption later supported by research was the idea that any communication between a student and the instructor must be based on what both have in common—language, background, interests, motivation, for example. All models of communication require assumptions about what the sender of a message and the receiver of the message have in common (Simonson, 1984).

2. Assumptions About Online Course Structure

One of the first decisions that online designers must make is time—true individualized instruction holds learning outcomes constant and allows for variations in time (e.g. the student has as much time as they need to meet a course's learning outcomes). Most often however, distance education—teaching and learning at a distance—is time bound (the 15-week semester, or the 8-week term, for example). Once the time issue is resolved, then the structure of the learning experience is decided. At this point the "sticky" decisions about learning theory must be made – behaviorism, constructivist, or combinations of theories. A comprehensive review of online courses and programs shows that behaviorism-based course structures dominate (Simonson, Smaldino &Zvacek, 2015). Courses organized around weeks, or units/modules/topics are most common. Structure decisions are usually decisions without evidence (e.g. assumptions)

3. Assumptions About Communication

Early on, the designer makes decisions about how communication between the instructor, students, and content should occur—and whether this communication be asynchronous or synchronous (Orellana, Hudgins & Simonson (2009). Certainly, there is evidence to help making these decisions, but prescriptive evidence is largely lacking, and the assumptions about communication are often made based on experience or personal preferences. The evidence does support one trend—novice distance educators design their courses with considerable live communication, while more experienced distance educators opt for asynchronous communication (Simonson, Smaldino & Zvacek, 2015).

4. Assumptions About Technology

It is hard to imagine online instruction without instructional technology—so one immediate assumption is that online course design and delivery must be instructional technology-based. The types of communication technology and instructional technology to be used is a critical set of decisions that are made early in the design process.

5. Assumptions About Interaction

The United States Department of Education states that distance education must provide for regular and substantive interaction. Both words—substantive and substantial—are vague and open to interpretation; are assumptions that must be made. Recently, there have been some who have advocated that interaction is not necessary and is an outdated concept—MOOCs supporters, for example (Simonson, 2015). Others, think that the entire distance education experience should begin with the provision for interaction. Certainly, the designer of online instruction must make decisions about interaction, and standards for online education should have clear guidelines about interaction.

6. Assumptions About Literacy—Visual and Verbal

Revisits to Dwyer's (Moore and Dwyer, 1994) relevant-cue research, and Dale's (Dale, 1946) realism theory are critical here. Decisions about text, pictures, motion media, and graphics are critical in any instructional design activity. The individual or team who creates online instruction needs to make many decisions about literacy—how does the medium support the delivery and understanding of content. It is clear that Clark (2012) was correct—media do not directly influence achievement, but it is also a basic assumption that without media it is nearly impossible to communicate at a distance. Assumptions "galore" are made by the designer related to the literacy—visual and verbal—of all involved in distance education.

7. Assumptions About Learning

Actually, this is the most straightforward category of assumptions that are infused in the standards for the design and delivery of online learning. It is clear that 90% of any content area can be successfully learned by 90% of any group of learners, given enough time (Saettler, 2004). However, the six areas of assumptions listed previously directly influence the assumptions about learning—online students will learn assuming that assumptions correct ones.

In summary, an initial design step, and eventually a design standard for online instruction, is for the planner to list the assumptions that are at the foundation of the instructional design plan. Assumptions can be organized into the categories listed here, and should be presented as part of the design plan.

And finally, designers of online instruction can, even must, make assumptions. Scientists interested in distance education should conduct research on assumptions so they become standards—standards are expectations that should, even must, be met—standards without research are still assumptions—ideas without evidence.

Course Management Systems

Course management systems (CMSs) are software systems designed to assist in the management of educational courses for students, especially by helping teachers and learners with course administration. The systems can often track the learners' progress. While usually thought of as primarily tools for distance education, they are also used to support the face-to-face classroom.

A course management system allows teachers to manage their classes, assignments, activities, quizzes and tests, resources, and more in an accessible online environment. Students can log on and work anytime, anywhere. Ullman and Rabinowitz (2004) more succinctly define course management systems as "Internet-based software that manages student enrollment, tracks student performance, and creates and distributes course content."

Proprietary Versus Open Source

In addition to the two ways CMSs are used, there are two categories of CMSs—proprietary and open source. Proprietary, single-vendor systems (such as Blackboard) are software products that are purchased or licensed from one vendor. These systems are installed and used by the school, college, university, or organization. On the other hand, open-source course management systems are free educational software that are maintained by users who implement, even modify, and ultimately support their system to meet local, specific needs. Two major open-source systems are the Sakai Project and Moodle, although there are dozens of open-source CMSs (www.Edupost.ca/pmwiki.php).

The Sakai Project is of particular interest because of its scope and its approach. The project is named after Iron Chef Hiroyuki Sakai, and was started with the purpose of creating an open-source/free course management system that completes and complements proprietary systems.

Five institutions that had created their own CMS met in 2004 and invited other institutions to join in a "Sakai Partners Program." The five institutions—Indiana University, Massachusetts Institute of Technology, Stanford University, the University of Michigan, and UPortal and the Open Knowledge Initiative—were the founders of the Sakai Project. There are now many dozens of educational institutions involved. Members contribute financially and develop programming code for the project and the CMS.

The Sakai CMS has most, if not all, of the features common to course management systems, including course materials distribution, gradebooks, discussion areas, chat rooms, testing, and assignment drop boxes. There are announcement areas, e-mail systems, forums, presentation systems, and a variety of teaching tools such as syllabus posting, content delivery, and editors. The Sakai Project is reported to be growing rapidly as more organizations join. Moodle is another popular open-source system.

First, course management systems are not just for distance education. They are becoming critical components of possible benefit for almost any course. Second, CMSs can be purchased from a single vendor that provides the product and supports its implementation, or CMSs can be obtained free, or at low cost, by adopting one of the many open-source systems that are available. While currently the domain of the CMS is the college or university, it is apparent that the potential of the CMS for K–12 education is real and offers solutions to the many instructional and managerial problems of the school. Finally, the impact of course management systems is yet to be determined. Anecdotal reports indicate there are changes in instructional organization and delivery associated with the use of CMSs. Certainly, a CMS is an essential tool of the distance educator. More generally, the CMS may be one of the most important technological tools now available to education and training.

Resources. The second element to consider in the instructional environment is the resources available to students. What materials will they have at hand? What materials will be available in libraries and laboratories? Will students have access to resources for easy communication with the instructor?

These are the types of concerns that an instructor needs to address when thinking about the learning environment. It is difficult to plan for a particular type of learning activity if the room cannot be adapted or changed in any way. For example, if the instructor plans a group activity in which students will need to communicate to one another, how will this be accomplished?

Planning to Teach at a Distance

Much of what has been suggested in the planning process is not specific to a particular type of distance technology or delivery mode. Rather, the instructional design process is relatively open to any instructional setting. But, when planning to teach on the web, an instructor needs to address some essential considerations. One very important issue is that the instructor is "ready" for the course to begin. It is frustrating for students who begin an online course only to find that all the materials are not prepared or not accessible at the time they need them. It would be an advantage for the instructor planning an online course the first time to consider working 3 to 5 months in advance of the beginning date. This will ensure that the materials will be planned and prepared in a timely fashion. Another important issue when teaching online is that of establishing the communications framework. All too often, instructors of online courses "complain" that students expect them to be available all the time. If you as instructor do not intend to check your course materials daily, indicate that with the initial materials that are distributed. Tell students they can expect a response within a day or that you intend to be online checking the course on specific days of the week. That way both students and faculty will not be frustrated by the interrupted communications process.

Instructors have found that to ensure quality and promptness with online coursework, it is necessary for the students to know exactly when assignments are due. A calendar or timeline is very important. Providing students with rubrics or guides for how to complete assignments well is also very important. The more information students have about completing assignments, the fewer problems the students and instructor will experience during the course.

Finally, when planning to teach online, advise students (and this is a good piece of advice for the instructor as well) to set aside specific periods of time during the week to work on the course. It is so easy to "let it slide" that often the complaint is that there is never enough time to get all the work done. This usually results from someone letting the work pile up before getting to it. With an online course, it is best to plan several shorter periods per week, rather than one longer one. This helps to check things out, do work offline for a period of time, and then to finish up before the time period is up. Part of the initial materials presented to the students should provide guidelines for students to ensure a successful learning experience. When it is noted that a student is falling behind in the work or is not participating at an acceptable level, the instructor should contact that student privately, either by e-mail or by phone, to check to see if there is a reason for nonparticipation. This takes time, but the instructor will find it beneficial for a successful distance learning experience.

How Do You Determine the Quality of the Instruction?

Assessment will be discussed in Chapter 10, and evaluation will be discussed at greater length in Chapter 12. However, there is a need to look at questions an instructor might consider as part of the planning process. These questions revolve around considerations related to the strategies selected, the learners' interaction with the learning experience, and the learning environment.

In the instructional design process, formative evaluation becomes an important aspect. Two questions need to be considered. The first relates to reflection on the action or activity: "Is this approach going to work?" To be an effective educator, it is important to consider what can happen within an instructional event. All experiences, both positive and negative, have some element of surprise. Perhaps expectations were not achieved; perhaps a serendipitous event led to an altogether different, but pleasant, outcome. Whatever the nature of the event, it is essential to reflect upon what has happened.

Reflection may take the form of critical assessment of the events, satisfying curiosity about the nature of those events. Reflection may focus on the success of the learning situation. It helps the instructor understand the learning event. Once the instructor has reflected upon what took place, it is time to move on to the second question of the formative evaluation process.

The second question is, "How can I make this better?" The instructor can examine the instructional event in terms of what worked and what appears to have been a problem. The second phase of the formative evaluation is concerned with helping the instructor ensure a more successful educational experience for students. The instructor needs to consider the learning task, the instructional materials, and the teaching strategies, and also the role that the technology may have played in the instruction.

The instructor needs to consider the elements of technologies and their effect on students. Did the hardware components of the lesson cause the problem? If so, what was the nature of the problem? Can the hardware be improved? Can changes be made in the interactive instructional classroom to aid instruction in the future? If the problem did not relate to equipment, then what was the problem? Perhaps students needed to be better trained about how to use software and equipment. Perhaps the instructor needed to prepare other types of handouts or manipulatives to ensure that the students could accomplish the tasks. Maybe the instructor needed to select an alternative teaching strategy to improve interactivity and student outcomes. Because so many different factors affect the interactive learning environment, reflective teaching practices play a vital role in developing effective teaching practices. The process of determining what has transpired and how to change it creates a dynamic educational experience for both the instructor and the learners. Formative evaluation is essential for successful interactive distance learning experiences.

A Look at Best Practice Issues

What the Accreditation Community Is Saying About Quality in Distance Education

In March of 2006, the U.S. Department of Education's Office of Postsecondary Education released an interesting report titled "Evidence of Quality in Distance Education Programs Drawn From Interviews with the Accreditation Community." What is interesting and important about this document is the approach used to collect information—12 accrediting organizations were asked to identify representatives who had served on evaluation teams for schools offering distance education programs. These representatives were asked to identify "good practices" and "red flags." Their comments make great reading for anyone interested in identifying quality strategies for teaching and learning at a distance.

The report is organized into six sections, each dealing with various indicators of quality: Mission, Curriculum, Faculty, Students, Sustainability, and Evaluation and Assessment. In each category they are dozens of indicators of quality and red flags—danger signs that often indicate a weak or ineffective distance education program.

Some of the most interesting positive indicators are:

- The mission statement contains an explicit statement of the purpose of distance education.
- The regular faculty have oversight of the distance education curriculum.
- The regular faculty are actively involved in course design.
- There is a strong and active faculty development process.
- The university provides instructional design support for distance education.
- There is 24/7 technology support.
- There are academic advisers for distance education students.
- A systematic approach is applied to the growth and management of the distance education program.
- There are clear plans for the future of distance education.
- Evaluation of distance education courses and programs is used for continuous improvement.
- Input from faculty and students is used for program improvement.

Of equal interest and importance are some of the most noteworthy "red flags":

▪ There are two separate approaches, even mission statements, for traditional and distance education.
▪ There are two target populations for traditional and distance education.
▪ There are two course approval processes for traditional and distance education.
▪ Distance education courses are designed using a "cookie-cutter" approach.
▪ Faculty attempt or are encouraged to directly convert traditional courses to distance-delivered courses.
▪ There are two course evaluation systems, one for traditional and one for distance education.
▪ Some student services must be accessed face-to-face by distant students.
▪ Distant students are often confused about contact people at the institution.
▪ The institution has a history of starting and then stopping distance education programs.
▪ Few, other than administrators, know about the institution's distance education program.
▪ There are a large number of distant students who drop out.
▪ There are many complaints from distant students.

OTHER ISSUES TO BE CONSIDERED

As with any planning, some of the aspects of the system that need to be considered are outside of the content, learners, and instructional setting. Three of these issues relate to student handouts, materials distribution, and the site facilitator.

Student Handouts

Even though the topic of student handouts is discussed at greater length in Chapter 8, it is also mentioned here because it is important for the instructor to think about handouts within the context of the planning process. The types of handouts will vary according to the age of the students and the content of the course. But whatever the type, it is important that the instructor realize that in a distance course, handouts are an essential communication link with students. Therefore, during the planning process, the instructor needs to invest time and energy in creating quality handouts for students.

Distribution of Materials

Even within a traditional class, the instructor is concerned with getting materials to the students. Often papers and books are distributed at the beginning of the class period. But when teaching at a distance, this task is rarely an easy one. Often the majority of the class is at a distance, and distribution of materials becomes a logistical nightmare.

An instructor needs to consider the following:

- *Getting the materials to the distant sites on time.* A distribution plan must be established for getting tests and other materials to the remote sites. The technology can be useful in transferring materials.
- *Communicating with the students.* Geographic separation between instructor and students does affect this communication.
- *Dealing with time delays in material transfer.* Students may have to wait a longer time than normally expected to receive assignment feedback. Instructors may elect to use other forms of telecommunications to facilitate this feedback.

MODELS FOR DESIGNING ONLINE COURSES

Traditionally, there are four approaches for the instructional design of courses that are to be delivered asynchronously using the World Wide Web. The four approaches are not entirely new. Two are based directly on the individualized instruction movement of the 1950s and 1960s. The four models are:

1. Linear-designed instruction (Figure 5–2)
2. Branched-designed instruction (Figure 5–3)
3. Hypercontent-designed instruction (Figure 5–4)
4. Learner-directed design (Figure 5–5)

These four designs are depicted graphically. Although they are different in approach and use, they have several similarities. First, instruction is divided into units. Different instructional designers use terms such as *units* or *blocks* instead of *modules,* but all refer to a subdivision of a course's content. Generally, a three-credit college course would have about three units divided into 12 modules, each taking about a week to complete. Designers further divide modules into topics that directly relate to the module. Topics then can be divided into concepts. An example of a unit of instruction—a course—that is divided into units, modules, or topics, would be this book. This book has 12 chapters that identify the major subheadings of content. Each chapter is divided into modules, and modules are supported by major topics.

Linear-designed instruction is based on linear programmed instruction. First, major subdivisions of a course are identified—usually three for a three-credit college course. Next, a content area such as distance education foundations is divided into important ideas. These ideas are called *modules.* Modules of instruction are divided into topics. Each topic has instructional events, or learning experiences, followed by some kind of an assessment. Before students are permitted to continue to the next topic within a module they must successfully complete the assessment. If the assessment is an objective test, they must pass the test. The sequence of topic-related instructional events followed by assessments continues until all topics in a module have been studied. Often, a module-ending assessment must be completed before the student moves to the next module. Similarly, there are often mid-course assessments and end-of-course assessments that require the student to synthesize learning related to many modules. The UMT model is explained in greater detail at the end of this chapter.

Linear-designed instruction is sequential. Students move in the same path through the concepts, topics, and modules, and complete the same assessments and tests.

Branched-designed instruction is similar to linear with two major exceptions. First, assessments are more sophisticated in order to diagnose a student's progress and under-

FIGURE 5–2 Linear design for instruction.

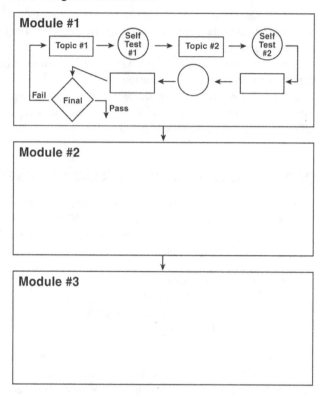

FIGURE 5–3 Branching of design for instruction.

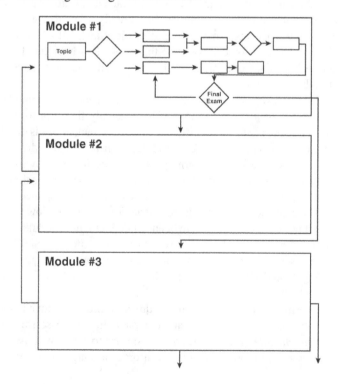

FIGURE 5–4 Hypercontent design for instruction.

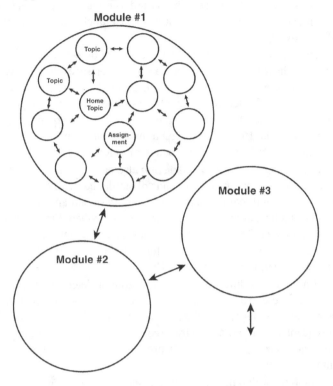

FIGURE 5–5 Learner-directed design for instruction.

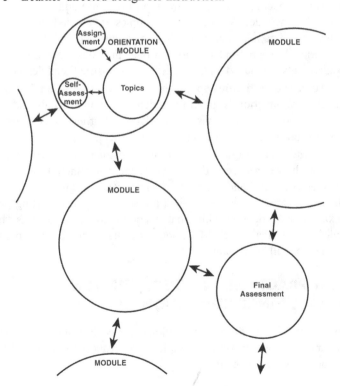

standing of concepts and topics. If a student shows a propensity for topics in a module, it is possible to skip ahead, or branch forward. Similarly, if a student has difficulty, the assessment process will require that the student branch backward, or to remedial instruction, before moving forward in the lesson.

The second distinguishing characteristic of branched-designed instruction is the use of alternative instructional events or learning experiences. In other words, students may interact with different instructional content depending on the results of assessments. Just as a human tutor might decide that an algebra student needs more practice with mathematics, a branched-designed lesson might require a student to complete a drill-and-practice lesson on long division. Branched-designed instruction is difficult and time consuming to effectively produce, and is not often used in distance education.

Hypercontent-designed instruction also has units, modules, and topics. First, modules are identified and organized into units of similar content. Next, topics related to the module are identified and learning experiences are designed and produced. These topics are presented using text, audio, graphics, pictures, and video. Finally, a module assessment activity is developed. This assessment is designed to determine if a student has successfully completed and understands the module satisfactorily. If so, the student moves to the next module in the sequence of modules.

Within the module, there is little instructor-determined sequencing of topics. Rather, the topics and corresponding learning experiences are studied in an order determined by the learner. In other words, the student has control and topics can be studied in a random, nonsequential manner, or in a hypercontent order. Often a course-ending assessment, such as a major paper, presentation, or product, is required. This design approach is the most common model used.

The final design module is the *learner-directed design*. For this approach, the instructional designer identifies units, modules, and topics, including learning experiences, but places no sequence or order on the topics within modules, or among the modules themselves. Learners decide what order of topics are studied, and sometimes even the topics themselves. Learners construct their own instructional strategies and even their own instructional design. Students move through modules in any order they choose. Few, if any, requirements are placed on the student by the instructional designer.

To be successful, this approach requires considerable talent and effort on the part of the learner. Direction is given to students by module goals and by outcome assessment activities. Some constructivists who advocate learner-directed design procedures ask students to construct their own outcome assessments.

Instructional design models for online instruction are evolving. These four approaches draw on the experience and research of the programmed instruction efforts of the past. Some teachers mix and match the four approaches into amalgams of design procedures. The four approaches just described are something of a starting point for course design. Next, literature dealing with what is commonly referred to as "best practices" will be reviewed, and finally the UMT model for course design, a more prescriptive design recommendation, will be explained.

BEST PRACTICES IN COURSE DESIGN FOR DISTANCE EDUCATION

One key to effective distance education is correct instructional design, a systematic process that applies research-based principles to educational practice. If the design is effective, instruction will also be effective.

Distance education has been practiced for more than 150 years, passing through three phases: first, correspondence study, with its use of print-based instructional and communication media; second, the rise of the distance teaching universities and the use of analog mass media; and third, the widespread integration of distance education elements into most forms of education, and characterized by the use of digital instructional and communication technologies. Peters (2002) has suggested that "the swift, unforeseen, unexpected and unbelievable achievements of information and communication technologies" will require "the design of new formats of learning and teaching and [will cause] powerful and far-reaching structural changes of the learning-teaching process" (p. 20). Peters' views are well accepted, but there is also consensus that the most fruitful way of identifying elements of quality instruction may be to re-examine "first principles" of distance education and mediated instruction.

Perhaps the first of the "first principles" is the recognition that distance education is a system, and that the creation of successful courses—and the program of which they are a part—requires a "systems" approach. Hirumi (2005) identified a number of systems approaches but noted a concept common to all: that "a system is a set of interrelated components that work together to achieve a common purpose" (p. 90). He described a system that involved the efforts of faculty, staff, administrators, and students, and consisted of eight key components: curriculum, instruction, management and logistics, academic services, strategic alignment, professional development, research and development, and program evaluation.

Bates (2003, in Foley, 2003) proposed 12 "golden rules" for the use of technology in education. These rules offer guidance in the broader areas of designing and developing distance education:

1. *Good teaching matters.* Quality design of learning activities is important for all delivery methods.
2. *Each medium has its own aesthetic.* Therefore, professional design is important.
3. *Education technologies are flexible.* They have their own unique characteristics but successful teaching can be achieved with any technology.
4. *There is no "super-technology."* Each has its strengths and weaknesses; therefore, they need to be combined (an integrated mix).
5. *Make multiple media available to teachers and learners.* Print, audio, video, and computers should all be available.
6. *Balance variety with economy.* Using many technologies makes design more complex and expensive; therefore, limit the range of technologies in a given circumstance.
7. Interaction is essential.
8. *Student numbers are critical.* The choice of a medium will depend greatly on the number of learners reached over the life of a course.
9. New technologies are not necessarily better than old ones.
10. Teachers need training to use technology effectively.
11. *Teamwork is essential.* No one person has all the skills to develop and deliver a distance learning course; therefore, subject-matter experts, instructional designers, and media specialists are essential on every team.
12. *Technology is not the issue.* How and what we want the learners to learn is the issue and technology is a tool (p. 833).

A number of these guidelines are overlapping. Items 1, 2, and 11 address course and program design. Any examination of "first principles" should first examine instructional design. While it has been noted that instructors, even those new to distance education, can learn to adapt courses and create materials for online delivery (Ko & Rossen, 2010), and the author-editor model has long been an element of correspondence study programs, "what is strikingly missing in these arrangements, usually, is an instructional designer and many good features of the instructional design approach" (Moore & Kearsley, 2012, p. 101). The team-based approach to distance education course development is generally regarded as more likely to result in high-quality materials, experiences, and, hence, more satisfactory teaching and learning experiences (Hirumi, 2005).

Bates's triumvirate of subject-matter expert, instructional designer, and media specialist is the standard core of the course design team, which may be expanded—one source (Hanna, Glowacki-Dudka, & Conceicao-Runlee, 2000) has suggested as many as eight members—based upon the particular needs of the program and the media employed. No one approach to course design is ideal; as Moore and Kearsley (2012) noted, the course team approach results in "materials [that] are usually much more complete and effective. Furthermore, [it] tends to emphasize the use of multiple media in a course" but is "very labor-intensive and therefore expensive, and it involves a lengthy development period" (p. 101-102). Of the two approaches, "the author-editor approach is the only one that makes economic sense if courses have very small enrollments or short lifetimes, while the course team approach is justified for courses with large enrollments and long-term use" (p. 102).

Foley (2003) has noted "there are general principles of good design that can be applied to all distance learning activities" (p. 831), but noted the following influences:

▪ the target audience of the activity
▪ the content of subject matter to be delivered
▪ the outcomes or objectives desired (p. 831).

Other considerations having "profound effects on the design of the learning activities" (p. 831) include:

▪ the cost effectiveness of the system
▪ the opportunity costs of alternative systems and methods
▪ the availability of technology to the provider and to the learners
▪ the geographical location of the learners
▪ the comfort level of the learners with any technology that is used (p. 834).

Foley notes that these factors apply equally well when designing instruction for any given audience, from children to adults. When designing the World Bank's Global Development Learning Network, "results of more than 30 years of research on adult learning were applied to the distance learning programs" (p. 832). The criteria included:

1. They are based on clearly established learning needs and built around succinct statements of outcome.
2. They are based on a variety of teaching and learning strategies and methods that are activity based.
3. Effective distance learning materials are experiential they address the learner's life experience.
4. Quality distance learning programs are participatory in that they emphasize the involvement of the learner in all facets of program development and delivery.

5. Successful distance learning programs are interactive and allow frequent opportunities for participants to engage in a dialogue with subject-matter experts and other learners.
6. Learner support systems are an integral part of any successful distance learning program (p. 832).

The Indiana Partnership for Statewide Education (IPSE, 2000) proposed "Guiding Principles for Faculty in Distance Learning":

▪ Distance learning courses will be carefully planned to meet the needs of students within unique learning contexts and environments.
▪ Distance learning programs are most effective when they include careful planning and consistency among courses.
▪ It is important for faculty who are engaged in the delivery of distance learning courses to take advantage of appropriate professional developmental experiences.
▪ Distance learning courses will be periodically reviewed and evaluated to ensure quality, consistency with the curriculum, currency, and advancement of the student learning outcomes.
▪ Faculty will work to ensure that incentives and rewards for distance learning course development and delivery are clearly defined and understood.
▪ An assessment plan is adapted or developed in order to achieve effectiveness, continuity, and sustainability of the assessment process. Course outcome assessment activities are integrated components of the assessment plan.
▪ Learning activities are organized around demonstrable learning outcomes embedded in course components, including course delivery mode, pedagogy, content, organization, and evaluation.
▪ Content developed for distance learning courses will comply with copyright law.
▪ Faculty members involved in content development will be aware of their institution's policies with regard to content ownership.
▪ The medium/media chosen to deliver courses and/or programs will be pedagogically effectual, accessible to students, receptive to different learning styles, and sensitive to the time and place limitations of the students.
▪ The institution provides appropriate support services to distance students that are equivalent to services provided for its on-campus students.
▪ The institution provides its students at a distance with accessible library and other learning resources appropriate to the courses or programs delivered via technology. It develops systems to support them in accessing and using these library and other learning resources effectively.
▪ It is important to provide the appropriate developmental experiences for faculty who are engaged in the delivery of distance learning experiences.
▪ The institution implements policies and processes by which the instructional effectiveness of each distance learning course is evaluated periodically.
▪ Timely and reliable technical support is vital to the success of any distance learning program.
▪ It is recommended that a system of faculty incentives and rewards be developed cooperatively by the faculty and the administration, which encourages effort and recognizes achievement associated with the development and delivery of distance learning courses.
▪ The institution will communicate copyright and intellectual property policies to all faculty and staff working on distance learning course development and delivery.

▪ The institution complies with state policies and maintains regional accreditation standards in regard to distance learning programs. (www.ihets.org/learntech/principles_guidelines.pdf)

Commonalities between these principles and those suggested by other authors and organizations may be readily perceived. For instance, careful planning and the need for teacher training are cited by Bates (in Foley, 2003), and the emphasis on the unique needs of students in a variety of contexts is mentioned by Foley (2003). The IPSE principles make an important contribution by highlighting the need for consideration of copyright law and policies, intellectual property ownership, faculty incentives, and state policies and accreditation standards.

Because education (including distance education) is a system, each of its elements interacts with other elements, making difficult the isolation of elements. Interaction (its type, quantity, quality, timing, etc.), for instance, cannot be separated from instructional philosophy, choice of media, and other factors.

Whatever media are selected to facilitate instructor–student and student–student interaction, it should be recognized that these forms of mediated discussion should not completely replace the face-to-face element in courses. As Peters (1998) noted, those who think that new, digital media will "supply the interactivity and communication lacking in distance education ??cherish a hope here that will prove to be serious self-delusion" (p. 155). Peters's comments on the topic (in the context of videoconferencing, a relatively rich, "high-bandwidth" form of communication), trenchant and incisive, are worth quoting at length:

> Communication mediated through technical media remains mediated communication and cannot replace an actual discussion, an actual argument, the discourse of a group gathered at a particular location. Mediated communication and actual communication stand in relationship to one another like a penciled sketch and an oil painting of the same subject. What takes place in a discussion between two or more people can only be transmitted in part electronically?. A virtual university that does without face-to-face events by referring to the possibility of videoconferencing can only ever remain a surrogate university?. There is no doubt that to a certain extent [videoconferencing] will improve the structure of communication in distance education—but it cannot ever take the place of personal communication in distance education. (p. 155)

Peters's views on virtual communication have not been significantly modified with time.

> They reduce, surround, parcel out, spoil or destroy experiences gained at school or university. For this reason, it may be concluded, learning in virtual space will never be able to replace completely teaching in real spaces. (p. 104)

The effective use of a variety of media to facilitate communication, combined with critical quantities of well-structured face-to-face instruction and learning, have characterized many distance-delivered programs. They are two key elements of the model of distance education what has been called "the best of both worlds"—a combination of face-to-face and online instruction (Schlosser & Burmeister, 1999).

As important as is the appropriate selection and use of technologies of instruction and communication, technologies are not critical elements in shaping students' satisfaction with their distance courses. Rather, satisfaction is determined by "the attention they receive from the teachers and from the system they work in to meet their needs. Those needs, "what all distant learners want, and deserve" include:

▪ content that they think is relevant to their needs
▪ clear directions for what they should do at every stage of the course
▪ as much control of the pace of learning as possible
▪ a means of drawing attention to individual concerns
▪ a way of testing their progress and getting feedback from their instructors
▪ materials that are useful, active, and interesting

At the same time, it should be noted that frustration with the use of complex, inadequate, or malfunctioning equipment, as well as perceptions of emotional distance engendered by the use of distance education technologies, have negatively affected students' attitudes toward—and, in some cases, achievement in—distance education.

Bates's seventh "golden rule," that "interaction is essential," is well accepted by the field, and is a central element in most definitions of distance education (see, i.e., Keegan, 1996, and Simonson & Schlosser, 2012). Keegan (1996) noted that distance education must offer "the provision of two-way communication so that the student may benefit from or even initiate dialogue" (p. 44). Initial provisions for interaction were primarily for student–instructor interactions, but with the availability of expanded communication technologies in the 1990s came an increasing emphasis on additional forms of interaction. Three forms of interaction are widely recognized by the field: student–content, student–instructor, and student–student. It is this third form of communication, reflecting, in part, andragogical and constructivist perspectives, that has increased dramatically with the rise of online education.

Concurrent with the expansion of online education and the diffusion of new communication technologies, there arose the mistaken belief that if interaction is important, "the more interaction there is in a distance education class, the better" (Simonson, 2000, p. 278). As Simonson (2000) has noted, early research in the field had "demonstrated clearly that the provision for interaction was critical" (p. 278), but later research indicated as clearly that "interaction is not a magic potion that miraculously improves distance learning" (p. 278). Indeed, "the forcing of interaction can be as strong a detriment to effective learning [as is] its absence" (p. 278).

When quantifying and qualifying student–teacher and student–student interaction, perceptions may be less than reliable. In a study comparing distance students' perceptions of interaction (as compared with observations of their interaction), Sorensen and Baylen (2000) noted that in a videoconference class with several sites students accurately noted that across-site interaction was very low, within-site interaction was very high, interaction changes with instructor location, remote site students participate less, and group activities increase interactions. However, students perceived that less interaction occurred over time (when, in fact, interaction increased), and that technology inhibits interaction when, more accurately, it seems to create different patterns of interaction (p. 56).

Although Sorensen and Baylen (2000) examined interaction in the context of an interactive television course, their findings have implications for other distance education modalities. The researchers concluded that a sense of community formed among students at the distant sites, but interaction increased when the instructor was present at a given distant site. Sorensen and Baylen noted that "varying activities and including hands-on exercises and small and large group discussions were instructional methods appreciated by the students" (p. 56). Students in the Sorensen and Baylen study expressed satisfaction with the "distance learning experience," but suggested that the course include "at least one opportunity for students to meet face-to-face" (p. 57).

Distance teaching institutions (and their students) have a wide variety of instructional and communication media from which to choose. These two categories (instructional and communication) may be, to some extent, addressed separately, but they are often one and the same. Bates's fourth "golden rule," that there is no "super-technology," is well accepted and understood by experienced instructional technologists and distance educators, but often less so by those new to the field (and many, many of today's practitioners fall into this latter category). For this reason, it is important to invoke the findings of Clark (1983) explained in an earlier chapter, who noted, decades ago, that "media do not influence learning under any conditions" (p. 446).

If, as Clark (citing hundreds of studies and decades of research) maintains, the application of any particular medium will neither improve student achievement nor increase the speed of learning, what criteria might a distance teaching institution apply in the selection of media for the delivery of instruction and the facilitation of communication? Cost (to both the institution as well as to the student) is an obvious criterion. Less obvious, perhaps, are the culture of the institution and expectations of students (or potential students).

At a very practical level, Ko and Rossen (2017) suggested that, prior to selecting media and instruction for online education, the institution's resources should be assessed and the following questions should be asked:

- What's already in place (what, if any, courses are being offered online; who is teaching them, etc.)?
- What kind of hardware and operating system does your institution support?
- What kind of network has your institution set up?
- What kind of technical support does your institution provide? (p. 19)

As Ko and Rossen noted, "the tools an institution uses and the support it offers very much influence the choices [the instructor will] need to make" (p. 18).

Other guidelines for selection of media for synchronous communication, in the context of one "best practice" in distance education—collaborative, problem-based student work groups—have been offered by Foreman (2003). Foreman noted the usefulness of a wide variety of synchronous technologies: chat, telephone conference, web conferencing and application sharing, voice-over-IP, virtual classrooms, and videoconferencing. Of the technologies at either end of the spectrum—chat and video conferencing—"neither works especially well as a tool for collaborative teamwork" (para. 5) because chat is slow and awkward, and because videoconferencing is expensive, is frequently of low technical quality, and often fails to capture many of the visual cues so helpful for communication. Modern desk-top systems, such as ZOOM, have significantly reduced these problems.

Telephone conferencing, however, "is highly effective for organizing small-team distance learning experiences" (Foreman, 2003, para. 6), as it "provides immediacy, a high rate of information exchange, and complex multiperson interaction facilitated by a familiar audio cueing system." Foreman recognized that telephone conferencing can be expensive, but counters that significant savings may be realized through inexpensive three-way calling options—which, "despite its name, four or more people can use ??at once" (para. 7)—available through most telecom providers and cell phone companies.

In the end, all of the criteria just mentioned are considered and, frequently, a pragmatic approach is adopted. As Bates recommends in his fourth "golden rule," "each [medium] has its strengths and weaknesses, therefore they need to be combined (an integrated mix)" (Foley, 2003, p. 843).

The literature abounds with guidelines for distance education and identified "best practices" of distance education. Sometimes these are based on careful research but are, in the overwhelming majority of cases, the products of practitioners relating practices that have proven successful for that author. Still, some common threads have emerged.

Graham, Cagiltay, Lim, Craner, and Duffy (2001) offered seven lessons for online instruction:

1. Instructors should provide clear guidelines for interaction with students.
2. Well-designed discussion assignments facilitate meaningful cooperation among students.
3. Students should present course projects.
4. Instructors need to provide two types of feedback: information feedback and acknowledgment feedback.
5. Online courses need deadlines.
6. Challenging tasks, sample cases, and praise for quality work communicate high expectations.
7. Allowing students to choose project topics incorporates diverse views into online courses. (http://ts.mivu.org/default.asp?show+article&id=839)

In his eighth "golden rule," Bates notes that "student numbers are critical." While this observation is made in the context of cost and media selection, student numbers are, indeed, critical in at least two other respects: class and working- (or discussion-) group size. Distance education has been embraced, in some quarters, as an opportunity to reduce costs by increasing class sizes. The literature clearly indicates that there are practical limits beyond which the quality of instruction and learning are compromised. As Hanna et al. (2000) noted, "demand for interaction defines the size of face-to-face classrooms and the nature of the interactions within those classrooms; the demand for interaction has a similar effect upon online classrooms" (p. 26). Palloff and Pratt (2003) suggest that experienced online educators can "handle" 20 to 25 students in an online course, while "instructors who are new to the medium, or instructors teaching a course for the first time, should really teach no more than fifteen students" (p. 118). Orellana et al. (2009) have reported that the optimum class size for an online class with one instructor is about 20, if optimum levels of intereaction are desired.

On a larger scale, institutions of higher education should understand that distance education is not the "cash cow" that some have mistakenly suggested. Indeed, the development and support of distance education courses and programs is normally more expensive than similar traditional courses and programs. When exceptions are occasionally noted, it is usually found that a difference in scale could explain the savings, as in the University of California–Davis study that found that preparing and offering a large (430 students) general education course at a distance cost less than the cost of the same course delivered traditionally (Sloan, 2002). A second exception is the instance of the very large distance teaching universities, such as the British Open University, where large enrollments and a long "product cycle" reduce the unit cost per student to about half that common among traditional graduate programs (Moore & Kearsley, 2012).

Care should be taken when schools search the field for suitable models. Schools, then, should clearly identify the type of students they wish to attract, the needs of those students, and the type of university they aspire to be. Distance education is a broad field with a long history. It is important to remember that, the views of some authors notwithstanding, there is no one "right" way to conduct distance education. At the same time, it would be foolish to ignore the insights and recommendations of longtime practitioners of distance education, as well as those whose field is the study of distance education. Distance education has experienced a marked expansion and, to a certain extent, reinvention in the past few years. However, it should be borne in mind that online education is not the sum of distance education, that the field existed long before the web, and that enduring principles of education did not become obsolete with the development of new, electronic technologies.

RECOMMENDATIONS FOR DISTANCE DELIVERED INSTRUCTION—THE UNIT-MODULE-TOPIC MODEL

These recommendations are based on the current literature of the field of distance education (Simonson, 2005b, 2008). These recommended guidelines are intended to provide ways to organize courses and be guiding principles that will make courses with equal numbers of semester credits equivalent in terms of comprehensiveness of content coverage, even if these courses are offered in different programs, cover different topics, and are delivered using different media.

Organizational Guidelines

In the traditional university, the 50-minute class session is the building block for courses. Usually, 15 classes are offered for each semester credit, and a 3-credit college course would have 45 class sessions in a 16-week semester. Distance delivered courses often do not have class sessions. It is proposed that the *topic* be the fundamental building block for instruction. Topics are organized into *modules* that are further organized into *units* that are roughly equivalent to a semester/course credit traditionally offered using 15, 50-minute class sessions (Orellana et al., 2009).

When courses are planned, the designer might want to use the Unit, Module, and Topic approach or model (UMT approach), as explained next.

Unit, Module, Topic Guideline:

▪ Each semester credit = 1 unit
▪ Each unit = 3–5 modules
▪ Each module = 3–5 topics

A typical three-credit course has 3 units, 12 modules, and 48 topics. Working definitions of *unit*, *module*, and *topic* are as follows:

Unit.　A *unit* is a significant body of knowledge that represents a major subdivision of a course's content. Often, one unit of a course would represent 4 or 5 weeks of instruction, and would be equivalent to a semester credit. For example, a unit in an educational statistics course might be Descriptive Statistics.

Module.　A *module* is a major subdivision of a unit. A module is a distinct and discreet component of a unit. Generally, a unit such as Descriptive Statistics might be divided into three to five major components, such as Statistical Assumptions, Measures of Central Tendency, Measures of Variation, and the Normal Curve. Modules generally are the basis for several class sessions and are covered in about a week of instruction and study in a typical 15 week college semester.

Topic.   A *topic* is an important supporting idea that explains, clarifies, or supports a module. A topic would be a lesson or an assignment. Topics in a module on Central Tendency might be Median, Mode, and Mean.

These three terms can be used in a variety of ways. Of importance is the idea that topics form modules, modules form units, and units are the main subdivisions of courses.

Assessment Guidelines

Assessment is defined as the determination and measurement of learning. Ultimately, assessment is used for grading. Assessment is directly related to learning outcomes.

- 1 major assignment per unit
- 1 minor assignment per two to three modules

A typical three-credit course has the following assessment strategy:

- 1 examination
- 1, ten-page paper
- 1 project 3 quizzes
- 3 small assignments (short paper, article review, activity report)
- graded threaded discussions, e-mails, and chats

Learning Outcome.   A *learning outcome* is observable and measurable. Learning outcomes are a consequence of teaching and learning—of instruction and study. Often, learning outcomes are written with three components: conditions under which learning is facilitated (instruction), observable and measurable actions or products, and a minimum standard of expectations. Often, there is one learning outcome for each course topic. For example, a learning outcome for a topic dealing with the median might be:

> After studying the text, pages 51–53, reviewing the PowerPoint with audio presentation on measures of central tendency, and participating in synchronous chats, the Child and Youth Studies student will satisfactorily complete the objective test dealing with measures of central tendency at the 90% level.

Content Guidelines

Traditionally, instructors have offered content by making presentations during face-to-face instruction. Additionally, readings in textbooks and handouts are required of students. Flipped classes, a currently popular approach, expects students to access all course materials, included prerecorded lectures or presentations, as homework. Classes are then devoted to discussions and interactions in the classroom, or during live, synchronous sessions.

In distance teaching situations, readings in texts, handouts, and information placed in the course management system are often used to deliver content. For high-quality courses, there should be an emphasis on the use of various forms of visual media to offer instructional content. Videos, visual presentations with accompanying audio, and other graphical representations of important topics are important to the well-designed course. A variety of

FIGURE 5–6 Online courses should use more media.

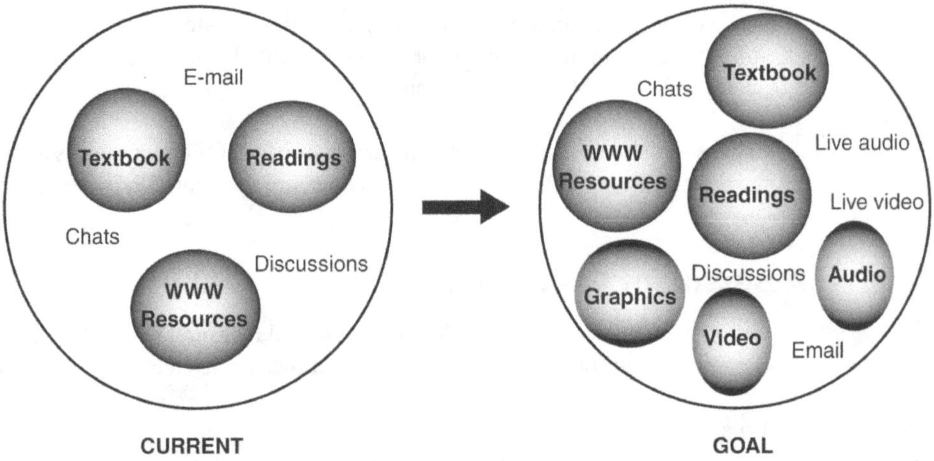

CURRENT → GOAL

delivery systems for content should be considered, including the use of compact discs, electronic files posted to websites, and streaming (Blackinton, 2013). Content is organized for students into *topics*. Topics are combined into *modules* of similar topics, and modules are used to form *units* (Figure 5–6).

Modules might have three to five topics presented in the following ways:

- readings in the text or other written materials
- videos supplied on CD, DVD, or streamed
- audio recordings of speeches or presentations supplied on a CD, as an e-mail attachment, or streamed
- recorded presentations using PowerPoint with prerecorded audio
- synchronous chats with content experts

Instruction/Teaching Guidelines

The pace of instruction for learners is a critical concern to the distance educator. Because many distance education students are employed full-time, it is important to offer instruction in a way that complements their other responsibilities. These guidelines relate to the pace of instruction and the need for continuing interaction between instructors and students in a typical college semester:

- 1 module per week
- Instructor e-mail to students each week
- 1 synchronous chat per week
- 2 to 3 threaded discussion questions per module
- Instructor comments on discussions as part of threaded discussion board
- Progress reports (grades) submitted to students every week or two

These course design guidelines are based on the literature of distance education and are derived from an analysis and review of quality courses delivered at a distance.

The simplicity of the Course Unit (also referred to as the Carnegie Unit) has made it the standard for course design, primarily because it is easy to apply. The Course Unit requires 750 minutes of class time for each semester credit, which translates into 15, 50-minute class sessions. A three-credit college course would meet three times a week for 15 weeks, according to most interpretations of the Course Unit. It is easy to count class sessions in order to determine if a course "measures up." If traditional students are in class for 3 hours per week, they probably spend about 6 hours per week outside of class doing homework, reading, completing assignments, and viewing course materials. Thus, a typical student might be expected to be involved in a typical college three-credit course for somewhere between 100 and 150 hours, or 5 to 10 hours each week in a 15-week semester. This rule of thumb is also explained in Chapter 7. The Unit-Module-Topic approach to course design can be used to meet this "time standard."

COURSE MANAGEMENT SYSTEMS

With the rapid growth of the web in the mid-1990s and keen interest in web technologies on college and university campuses, it was inevitable that products that ultimately would become known as course management systems (CMSs) would appear, and they did. By 1997, web course authoring and management systems in various stages of development included CyberProf, Mallard, and Virtual Classroom Interface (all from the University of Illinois), QuestWriter (Oregon State University), Web Course in a Box (Virginia Commonwealth University), World Wide Web Course Tools (to become WebCT, University of British Columbia), CourseInfo (to become Blackboard, Cornell University), and Canvas (Albright, 1997). At that time, no tested CMS product was available on a nationwide basis, so it was common for universities with programming expertise to develop their own. Numerous others besides those listed here were created. The Wikipedia page on "The history of virtual learning environments" (http://en.wikipedia.org/wiki/History_of_virtual_learning_environments) provides a fascinating history of CMS development and has been offered into evidence to combat Blackboard's claim to a patent on electronic learning technology, which will be discussed near the end of this chapter.

Course management systems, which are known as virtual learning environments in Europe, have now become the de facto standard by which the vast majority of distance education courses are delivered. Course management systems are also commonly used for distributed learning purposes, enabling teachers of conventional face-to-face courses to provide learning resources and conduct course-related activities, such as discussions and testing, outside of normal class time.

More than 40 different products promoted as course management systems were available at the time this chapter was revised for the sixth edition, although some of these focused upon specific tools, such as online discussions or real-time delivery of instruction, rather than providing the full array of CMS tools described in this section. More than half of the course management systems available today are either open source, meaning that adopting organizations can download, install, and modify the software for their own needs without payment of a license fee, or are otherwise free to educational institutions.

Course management systems are often erroneously identified as "learning management systems." Learning management systems (LMSs) are an entirely different genre of product. The primary difference between the two is that the focus of a CMS, as its name implies, *is on the delivery of courses,* while an LMS focuses *upon an individual and tracks the learning needs and outcomes achievement of that person* over periods of time that can be several years in length. Learning management systems first emerged in the corporate and government training sectors as tools that could compare a worker's existing skills with the job skills required for the position, and then guide and/or provide the specific training to enable the employee to become fully qualified. The training itself is often provided via products called learning content management systems (LCMSs), which are the corporate world's equivalent of CMSs.

Learning management systems are also now common at the K–12 level as a means of providing learning experiences and tracking student achievement toward state and federal standards. At the higher education level, LMSs would seem to have excellent potential for tracking student achievement in outcomes-based educational programs, as well as for faculty and staff professional development, but colleges and universities have been slow to adopt these tools. For the purpose of this chapter, know that a CMS is not an LMS, and vice versa.

Components of a Course Management System

The major course management systems all provide essentially the same basic set of components. A CMS typically includes the following tools. The actual pedagogical content for each tool needs to be created and installed by the individual teacher and/or technical support staff, unless it is acquired from a publisher or other third-party vendor.

Course Management.   Course management components may include a syllabus, course calendar, announcements, assignment instructions, learning objectives, a student roster, and a glossary. Some faculty elect not to use the CMS calendar tool and install a detailed calendar that incorporates much more information about course activities, including weekly or daily assignments and due dates for all student work that must be completed online or otherwise submitted. Course management systems also typically provide gradebook tools for faculty to post grades (or for the CMS to automatically post grades in the case of system-scored exams and quizzes) and for students to review their progress. Tools for attendance record keeping are also common and may be linked to the gradebook in the case of courses with face-to-face components.

Readings.   CMSs typically provide a tool for listing required and recommended course readings, with links to those readings that may be found online. These may include links to readings that have been copyright-cleared and reside in library electronic reserve collections or in electronic coursepacks, which will be discussed later in this chapter. References may be listed by topic according to the course schedule.

Content Presentation.   Many faculty maintain archives of presentation notes online for student review. Links to embedded media, such as streamed audio and video, graphics, photographic slides, and PowerPoint presentations, may also be maintained to assist students in their studies outside of the classroom. Course management systems also typically provide pages for annotated links to relevant websites that can be organized by course topic.

Course Communications.   Communication tools normally packaged with CMSs include asynchronous e-mail capabilities at several levels—one-to-one, one-to-several, one-to-all, and within groups. With some CMSs, e-mail is self-contained within the system and is separate from the institution's enterprise-level e-mail system, whereas with others, CMS mail is *only* integrated with the institution's e-mail system and is not self-contained within the course. Most CMS systems also contain chat forums for real-time discussions, typically with white boards and other presentation tools. Some systems now provide instant messaging tools and tools for online journals called weblogs or "blogs." Synchronous videoconferencing software are now commonly included in course management systems, or stand-alone systems such as ZOOM can be used.

Group Project Space.   The need for self-contained work space for groups within the course site has become evident to some CMS vendors. The system allows the instructor to create groups and assign students to groups. Within the group space, the members can chat or exchange e-mail and share documents for group discussion and revision. Some CMS systems even provide tools for groups or individual students to make presentations to the rest of the class in an online environment.

Student Assessment.   Almost all CMSs provide tools for exams and quizzes. Some also enable self-help or practice quizzes that are not part of the grading scheme. Built-in tools allow the instructor to generate questions in a variety of formats (e.g., true-false, multiple choice, multiple answer, matching, short answer, essay), maintain banks of questions, and stipulate that questions be selected randomly from the bank for each student as a means of enhancing security. The instructor can specify windows of time for quizzes to be available to students and set a time limit once a student starts taking the quiz. A very helpful tool packaged with some CMSs is the ability to draw posttest statistical analyses and reports summarizing student performance.

Digital Drop-Box for Assignment Submission.   Many course management systems contain digital drop-boxes for student submission of assignments within the CMS.

Course Evaluation Tools.   Course evaluation tools are relatively uncommon but are included in some CMSs. These tools are specifically for the course itself and not for student assessment. Instructors are able to customize the question sets. The system compiles the evaluations and provides statistical analyses and reports.

Course and System Statistics.   Most systems contain tracking tools that enable the instructor to find out precisely when each student accessed course components (for example content pages), how often, and how much time was spent on task. These tools are extremely helpful to faculty in identifying students who are falling behind in the course. On a broader perspective, some CMSs offer to system administrators detailed information such as total number of courses, instructors, enrolled students, and "hits" on the course server. This information can be compiled for a single day, a month, a year, an academic term, or any other specified date range, and can be tremendously helpful in reporting system use and troubleshooting problems such as server overloads.

Figure 9–2 illustrates an instructor view page in a typical course management system. Note the variety of tools available to the faculty member for customizing the course and obtaining information.

Online Courses Have Three Critical Components
(and Course Management Systems are Not One of Them)

It is happening again. Vendors—and some well-meaning educational administrators—are talking about the power of course/learning management systems and claiming that the technology used to deliver online courses has an impact on student achievement.

How many times have we heard the phrase "put your course in Blackboard, or convert your courses to Canvas," implying that this will make it a better course? The idea seems to be that putting something into an online learning management system makes an online course a good one.

Some may remember the statements of several decades ago about putting a course "on film," "on video," or even "on the computer" to make them relevant or effective or improved. As Clark (1983) so famously noted, "media are mere vehicles that deliver instruction but do not influence student achievement any more than the truck that delivers our groceries causes changes in our nutrition" (p. 446).

Let's be clear. There are really only three critical components of an online course—or any course, for that matter: content, design, and instruction. The learning management system can make an important contribution to course effectiveness, but only to the extent that it appropriately facilitates the "big three" components.

Content, design, and instruction; let's examine each. First, as any publisher will say, content is king. That is why there is education: to provide access to important content and processes.

Next, design—or how the instructor organizes the vast quantity of information that could potentially be presented in a course. While there are many design strategies, those that are based on instructional systems are the most significant and important.

Finally, there is instruction, or what teachers do. This is probably the most important contributor to learning. There are many who argue that teaching is a science, and others who say teaching is an art. Certainly science and art overlap.

There are many issues that need investigation, including:

▪ Are some courses inappropriate for placement in a CMS? If so, how do we decide?
▪ To what degree should courses be redesigned before placement in a CMS?
▪ Does a CMS impose a one-size-fits-all approach that may stifle creativity?
▪ Does the mandated use of a CMS cede academic authority to information technology staff at the expense of the faculty?

One simple measure of what makes a great school lesson, college course, or training session is what is remembered. As for the course management system, unless it impeded learning, no one remembers it.

And finally, as Bill Gates said "technology is just a tool." It is unlikely that putting a course on "this or that course management system" is the path to quality online learning and teaching.

Products for Enhancing Course Management Systems

Instructors are not limited to the tools provided within a CMS, nor must they generate all the content themselves. Products for enhancing course management systems are available from a wide range of vendors.

Course Supplements. Often CMS providers partner with textbook publishers to provide online course materials that supplement the texts and can be integrated into course shells set up on those CMS platforms. These supplements typically contain such features as learning goals and objectives, amplification of the text content to provide learning guidance, updates to the text (which may not contain current information), annotated links to relevant websites, additional course readings, case studies and other types of vignettes for use in class discussions, digitized video and other media, quizzes and tests, discussion questions, and a host of other resources. All components are already copyright-cleared by the publisher for use within the course.

Electronic Coursepacks. Most readers are familiar with the conventional paper coursepack. These are (hopefully) copyright-cleared readings for a course that have been compiled, duplicated, and sold or given to students. Many companies and publishers provide electronic coursepacks to support both distance education and traditional face-to-face courses. Electronic coursepacks can be accessed in digital form through links provided in the course management system or can be sold to students in paper form via partnering area bookstores.

Other Tools Supporting the Management of Online Courses

Other products provided by third-party vendors assist instructors with the management of online courses. They may interoperate with the CMS or be used independently. These occur in many genres. We will discuss the most common here.

Homework Collection and Grading. This product category includes products that enable teachers to collect, grade, and return assignments online.

Electronic Gradebook. The gradebook has also gone online. Gradebooks are built into course management systems such as Blackboard. Now we are seeing standalone gradebook products that interface with administrative student information systems so that students can view their grade reports and transcripts. These systems also have features by which parents of K–12 learners can be sent e-mail messages for reasons such as grade slippages and absences not verified by the parents.

Electronic Testing. Various products outside of CMSs allow instructors to build and store question databases, construct exams, and distribute them to the students; permit students to download and take the exams in a secure environment, then upload them to the teacher; and then score the exams, analyze and report the results, and archive the data. These products are available in a variety of formats and price ranges, and often extend beyond traditional formats for student assessment. Respondus, a new assessment system, was identified previously.

Plagiarism Detection.   Oh my. You think student academic dishonesty was a problem *before* the Internet? The web has provided global access to an unfathomable cornucopia of term papers, essays, and other scholarly works, right there out in the open for purchase or outright theft. The situation is much broader than the acquisition of schoolwork from dubious sources and extends to cheating on virtually every form of student assessment. Studies have repeatedly shown that around three fourths of both high school and college students cheat at least once, and that the majority do so without feelings of guilt or remorse. McCabe (cited in Mengers, 2004) found that the highest cheating rates were among students majoring in business, education, and journalism, three professions in which college graduates should be expected to have high levels of integrity. It is a serious issue, one for which instructors of online courses must maintain a high level of awareness.

Fain and Bates (2003) identified more than 250 "term paper mills" on the Internet, providing various services to students. However, a number of other vendors have seen this situation as an opportunity to market plagiarism detection services, such as Turnitin.com.

In addition to the use of plagiarism detection services, faculty have a number of options at their disposal for combating plagiarism. For example:

▪ Require students to write papers in stages, so that drafts can be reviewed and revisions required along the way.
▪ Require students to submit copies of their references along with the paper.
▪ Require students to write papers in groups, with each contributing sections.
▪ Give students enough advanced warning that they have time to do the research and complete the assignment, which may not deter procrastinators.
▪ Make the guidelines for paper submissions so specific that it is difficult to purchase a paper that meets the requirements.

A Look at Best Practices

Designing an Online Program

Courses are relatively easy to design for online teaching, but for distance education to be successful entire programs need to be designed.

The Perfect Online Course was described by Orellana in 2009. This book of readings clearly presented issues central to course design such as time, organization, production, evaluation, and accreditation. It is an important planning document for the distance educator.

Since then, best practices for course design have become much more widely understood. However, Orellana's book did not explain how to design the "perfect online *program*." Developing an entire program to be offered at a distance is considerably more complex than designing an online course.

Schools, universities, and organizations are moving quickly to offer classes, programs, and training at a distance. Most seem to be gradually making the transition from traditional offerings to distance education by first trying parts of classes, then individual courses, next blended courses, and finally entire distance-delivered programs.

Documenting the process of transitioning from traditional offerings to distance education has not been a priority of those involved in this process. It seems that "trial and error" is the favored approach, rather than a more reasoned process supported by applied research. There are some guides available, if not all in one location. For example, Simonson (2005a) wrote about the eight steps for transforming an organization, with the primary purpose of the transformation being the move to distance delivered offerings. And, in 2012, the development of distance education policy and plans was described. What is missing is a combination of the two approaches—the process of distance education implementation and the artifacts needed to support the move. Certainly, research is needed in this area.

At this point it has become clear that the following two components are needed when an organization plans to infuse distance education as a mission-central approach:

1. First, an academic technology/distance education plan is needed. This plan includes the following components:

▪ A vision statement
▪ A mission statement
▪ Guiding principles
▪ Definitions
▪ Goals
▪ Policy Development Processes
▪ Time Line
▪ Policy Review and Faculty Guidance
▪ References
▪ Resources

2. Next, a process for diffusion and implementation of distance education is needed. This process includes these components:

▪ Development of a sense of urgency by the organization's leaders
▪ Identification and empowerment of a powerful planning group
▪ Identification of a clear, widely understood and agreed on vision
▪ Identification of those willing to act on the vision
▪ Development of plans to guarantee short term successes—successes that are widely publicized
▪ Agreement on the process to combine successes
▪ Development and adoption of successes into models for addition implementation

At the heart of the plan and process is the role of stakeholders, especially teachers, professors and trainers. Certainly, leaders can and must support the transformation process, but those expected to implement changes—the teachers, professors, and trainers—are the groups who will promote or limit success.

The ingredients of a successful, distance delivered academic program include:

▪ A committed and strong organizational leader
▪ An assessment and statement of need

- A technology plan with a detailed program for implementation of distance education
- A steering committee lead by faculty that includes stakeholders such as students, staff, administrators, and alumni
- A detailed timeline
- A formative and summative evaluation plan
- A course design model, such as the Unit-Module-Topic approach
- Full-time faculty to implement the plan
- Instructional designers with media production skills A provision for a help desk for students and faculty
- A distance education policy manual for use by students, faculty, and most important, support staff
- A course management system and media production facilities and equipment Templates for syllabi and course components
- A budget

SUMMARY

It is essential that the instructor take the time to plan and organize the learning experience when engaged in teaching at a distance. The instructional design process provides the framework for planning. Instruction must be at a standard that is acceptable in all venues. The students should be engaged, and the instructor should be satisfied. Planning makes the difference in a successful learning environment.

DISCUSSION QUESTIONS

1. Why is the concept of instructional design so important to the field of distance education?
2. Why is it important to write performance objectives using the three components described in this chapter?
3. Discuss the building blocks for an online course—starting with units, then progressing to modules, and finishing with topics—the U-M-T approach.

REFERENCES

Albright, M. J. (1997). Web course authoring and management systems. *Journal of Academic Media Librarianship*, 5(1), 14–23. Retrieved from http://wings.buffalo.edu/publications/mcjrnl/v5n1/inter.html

Banathy, B. (1991). *Systems design of education*. Englewood Cliffs, NJ: Educational Technology Publications.

Banathy, B. (1968). *Instructional systems*. Belmont, CA: Fearon.

Bertalanffy, L. (1968). *General systems theory*. New York, NY: Braziller.

Blackinton, M. (2013, November). Teaching a "hands-on" profession in an online classroom. *PT in Motion*, 16–23.

Clark, R. (2012). *Learning from media* (2nd ed.). Charlotte, NC: Information Age.

Clark, R. E. (1983). Reconsidering research on learning from media. *Review of Educational Research, 53*(4), 445–459.

Daffron, S., & Webster, E. (2006). Upon reflection: A case study of a simultaneous hybrid classroom. *Distance Learning, 3*(3), 25–34.

Dale, E. (1946). *Audio-visual methods for teaching.* New York: Dryden Press

Dede, C. (1990, Spring). The evolution of distance learning: Technology-mediated interactive learning. *Journal of Research on Computing in Education,* 247–264.

Dick, W., Carey, L., & Carey, J. O. (2015). *The systematic design of instruction* (8th ed.). New York, NY: Longman.

Epstein, P. (2006). Online, campus, or blended learning: What do consumers prefer and why. *Distance Learning, 3*(3), 35–37.

Foley, M. (2003). The Global Development Learning Network: A World Bank initiative in distance learning for development. In M. G. Moore & W. G. Anderson (Eds.), *Handbook of distance education* (pp. 829–843). Mahwah, NJ: Erlbaum.

Foreman, J. (2003, July/August). Distance learning and synchronous interaction. *The Technology Source.* Retrieved from http://ts.mivu.org/default.asp?show+article&id=1042

Gardner, H. (1993). *Multiple intelligences.* New York, NY: Basic Books.

Graham, C., Cagiltay, K., Lim, B-R., Craner, J., & Duffy, T. M. (2001, March/April). Seven principles of effective teaching: A practical lens for evaluating online courses. *The Technology Source.* Retrieved from http://ts.mivu.org/default.asp?show+article&id=839

Hanna, D. E., Glowacki-Dudka, M., & Conceicao-Runlee, S. (2000). *147 practical tips for teaching online groups: Essentials for Web-based education.* Madison, WI: Atwood.

Herring, M., & Smaldino, S. (2001). *Planning for interactive distance education: A handbook* (2nd ed.). Bloomington, IN: AECT Publications.

Hirumi, A. (2005). In search of quality: An analysis of e-learning guidelines and specifications. *The Quarterly Review of Distance Education, 6*(4), 309–329.

Holden, J., & Westfall, P. (2006). Instructional media selection for distance learning: A learning environment approach. *Distance Learning, 3*(2), 1–11.

Indiana Partnership for Statewide Education. (2000). *Guiding principles for faculty in distance learning.* Retrieved from www.ihets.org/learntech/principles_guidelines.pdf

Keegan, D. (1996). *Foundations of distance education* (3rd ed.). London, England: Routledge.

Ko, S., & Rossen, S. (2017). *Teaching online: A practical guide* (4th.). Boston, MA: Houghton Mifflin.

Liggett, R. (1998, October 2). A prescription for telemedicine. *Telemedicine Today,* p. 2. Macfarlane, C., & Smaldino, S. (1997). The electronic classroom at a distance. In R. Rittenhouse & D. Spillrs (Eds.), *Modernizing the curriculum: The electronic classroom.* Springfield, MO: Charles Thomas.

McAlpine, L., & Weston, C. (1994). The attributes of instructional materials. *Performance Improvement Quarterly, 7*(1), 19–30.

McCabe, D. L., & Drinan, P. (1999). Toward a culture of academic integrity. *Chronicle of Higher Education, 46*(8), B7

Mengers, P. (2004, August 9). Keeping it honest as schools battle plagiarism problems. *Delaware County Times.*

Moore, D., & Dwyer, F. (1994) *Visual literacy: A spectrum of visual learning.* Englewood Cliffs, NJ: Educational Technology Publications.

Moore, M., & Kearsley, G. (2012). *Distance education: A systems view* (2nd ed.). Belmont, CA: Wadsworth.

Morrison, G., Ross, S., & Kemp, J. (2013). *Designing effective instruction* (7th ed.). New York, NY: John Wiley and Sons.

Orellana, A., Hudgins, T., & Simonson, M. (2009). *Designing the perfect online course: Best practices for designing and teaching.* Charlotte, NC: Information Age.

Palloff, R. M., & Pratt, K. (2003). *The virtual student: A profile and guide to working with online learners.* San Francisco, CA: Jossey-Bass.

Peters, O. (1998). *Learning and teaching in distance education: Pedagogical analyses and interpretations in an international perspective.* London, England: Kogan Page.

Peters, O. (2002). *Distance education in transition: New trends and challenges.* Bibliotheks- und Informations sytem der Universitat Oldenburg. Carl von Ossietzky University of Oldenburg, Center for Lifelong Leaning.

Pina, A. A., & Mizell, A. P. (2014). *Real-life distance education: Case studies in practice.* Charlotte, NC: Information Age.

Saettler, P. (2004). *The evolution of American educational technology.* Charlotte, NC: Information Age.

Schlosser, C. A., & Burmeister, M. (1999). The best of both worlds. *Tech Trends, 43*(5), 45–48.

Schlosser, L. A., & Simonson, M. (2012). *Distance education: Definition and glossary of terms* (3rd.). Charlotte, NC: Information Age.

Seels, B., & Richey, R. (1994). *Instructional technology: The definition and domains of the field.* Washington, DC: Association for Educational Communications and Technology.

Simonson, M. (1984). *Media planning and production.* Columbus, OH: Merrill.

Simonson, M. (2000). Myths and distance education: What the research says and does not say. *Quarterly Review of Distance Education, 1*(4), 277–279.

Simonson, M. (2005a). Distance education: Eight steps for transforming an organization. *Quarterly Review of Distance Education, 6*(2), vii–viii.

Simonson, M. (2005b). Planning the online course. *Distance Learning, 2*(5), 43–44.

Simonson, M. (2007). Rules of thumb, or DeRoTs. *Distance Learning, 3*(4), 92.

Simonson, M. (2008). And finally … Designing the perfect online course. *Distance Learning, 5*(3), 82–84

Simonson, M. (2015). Regular and substantiate. *Distance Education,* (12(4), 68–67

Simonson, M., & Schlosser, C. (2012). Institutional policy issues. In M. G. Moore (Ed.), *Handbook of distance education* (3rd ed., pp. 437–451). Mahwah, NJ: Erlbaum.

Sloan-C. (2002). *Practice: Comparing the cost-effectiveness of online versus traditional classroom cost per student pass rates.* Retrieved from http://www.aln.org/effective/details5 .asp?CE_ID=21

Smaldino, S. E., Lowther, D. L., Mims, C. & Russell, J. D. (2015). *Instructional technology and media for learning* (11th ed.). Upper Saddle River, NJ: Prentice Hall.

Sorensen, C., & Baylen, D. (2000). Perception versus reality: Views of interaction in distance education. *The Quarterly Review of Distance Education, 1*(1), 45–58.

Thompson, A., Hargrave, C., & Simonson, M. (1996). *Educational technology: Review of the research* (2nd ed.). Washington, DC: Association for Educational Communications and Technology.

Ullman, C., & Rabinowitz, M. (2004). Course management systems and the reinvention of instruction. Retrieved from http://thejournal.com.the/printarticel/?id=17014

U.S. Department of Education. (2006). Evidence of quality in distance education programs drawn from interviews with the accreditation community. Retrieved April 30, 2007, from http://www.itcnetwork.org/Accreditation-EvidenceofQualityinDEPrograms.pdf

Wade, D., Bentley, J., & Waters, S. (2006). Twenty guidelines for successful threaded discussions: A learning environment approach. *Distance Learning, 3*(3), 1–8.

Willis, B. (1994). *Distance education: Strategies and tools.* Englewood Cliffs, NJ: Educational Technology Publications.

Best Practices for Distance Education: Designing the *"Perfect*"* Online Course

Structure (for a 3 semester credit course)

- Instructor time: ~120 hours
- Student time: ~120 hours
- 3 Units, 15 modules,
- 45 Learning Experiences
- Unit = 5 weeks
- Module = 1 week
- Learning Experience = 1 day

Contents (of a 3 semester credit course)

- Syllabus
- Course Management System—WebCT
- Instructor Guidance
  - o Introductory Statement
  - o Monday Morning Memos
  - o E-mails
  - o Telephone Calls
  - o Live Presentations
- Textbooks
- Media
  - o Videos
  - o Audios
  - o Visuals
  - o Animations
- Virtual Materials
  - o Discussions
  - o Chats

Artifacts of Learning

- 3 Major Graded Assignments
  - o Exam
  - o Problem/Scenario/Situation Solution
  - o Research Paper/Portfolio/Blog/Presentation
- 10-15 Minor Graded Activities
  - o Discussion Posting
  - o Chat Participation
  - o E-mails
  - o Wiki Postings
  - o Blog Entries

Unit Contents

- Introduction to Unit
- Readings
- Viewings
- Listenings
- Discussions
- Chat Debate

CHAPTER 6

Teaching and Distance Education

CHAPTER GOAL

The purpose of this chapter is to provide guidance for the instructor when teaching at a distance.

CHAPTER OBJECTIVES

After reading and reviewing this chapter, you should be able to

1. Describe the responsibilities of the instructor in distance education.
2. Explain the importance of creating a learning community.
3. Discuss issues related to course organization.
4. Identify ways to enhance delivery of instruction.
5. Discuss policy issues important to the instructor of distant learners.
6. Estimate the time needed to teach a course delivered at a distance.

QUALITY INSTRUCTION AT A DISTANCE

There has been a dramatic increase in the number of distance education programs throughout the educational enterprise. While previously concentrated at the higher education, post secondary levels, effort has continued in the development of courses and whole programs of study at the middle and high schools levels. More educators are engaging in developing their own versions of distance instruction to meet the learning needs of a highly diverse population.

There has been interest in the design of distance instruction to recognize the value of best practice or instructional integrity. Kidney, Cummings, and Boehm (2007) suggest attributes of quality or elements of best practice in distance education can be characterized within three groups:

- Learners
  - Easy of access and usability
  - Accurate instructions
  - Intuitive navigation and well-integrated tools
- Faculty
  - Ease of instruction and consistent with standards

      ○ Intuitive and customizable course management system
      ○ Ease of preparation and updating
▪ Administration
      ○ Comparable rigor to nondistance classes
      ○ Increased enrollment
      ○ Maintenance of institution's reputation (p. 18).

Well-designed courses draw in the learner, offer engaging activities, and provide opportunities to explore and enhance learning experiences. Quality distance teaching parallels efforts to provide exemplary teaching in any setting. Quality is not a series of checklists or rating scales, but rather the focus on designing effective overall instruction that meet the needs of the learner.

TEACHING THE DISTANT LEARNER

In general, teaching has moved away from traditional approaches in classroom settings. Today, schools, universities, and training organizations are looking for effective learning approaches that focus on students' learning while engaging them in learning content. Well-designed courses provide students with interaction with content using engaging learning experiences.

The shift in location suggests that the participants are not in a single setting, and a shift in time implies that instruction is not "live." But, instruction at a distance can certainly be within a particular location and actually can be in "real-time." These aspects of distance learning present instructional challenges for even the most experienced educators. Distance education is an opportunity to revisit the role of the instructor in the learning environment. Moreland and Saleh (2007) identify faculty concerns related to distance education. They have indicated six from their research:

▪ Concern 1: Faculty size and job security
▪ Concern 2: Quality of distance education
▪ Concern 3: Interactivity in distance education
▪ Concern 4: Plagiarism
▪ Concern 5: Assessment and dishonesty
▪ Concern 6: Credits, clock hours, and student contact requirements

These concerns are not unique to instruction at a distance, but they are often expanded issues within the distance setting. Moreland and Saleh concluded that institutional policies should be in place to relieve the faculty issues and demonstrate support for faculty to ensure their instructional satisfaction and success.

From Teacher-Centered to Student-Centered Learning

Student-centered learning is not a new concept in education. It dates to times when education pioneer John Dewey advocated the personal experience of the learner in the learning process (Conrad & Donaldson, 2012). Further, Dewey supported student collaboration as a way of defining the learning situation. Although Dewey focused on middle-level and high school aged students, Knowles, Holton, and Swanson (2011) expanded Dewey's ideas into ways to approach adults in learning settings. They proposed that adults enter the learning setting as self-directed learners who bring prior knowledge and expect to be engaged in extending their knowledge.

The movement towards distance education has advanced the ideas surrounding active learning for students. When television was the primary vehicle for delivery, it essentially replicated the traditional classroom. And, by its very nature, it allowed for a passive student learning experience, whereby the instructor lectured and the students listened, took notes, and completed tests. This teacher-centered approach continued for many years with the use of video-based technologies. With the shift in technological resources, the instructor's "talking head" began to be eliminated as an instructional strategy in favor of more engaging activities for students.

With the advent of online resources, the student-centered approach to learning fits well into distance education environments. By its very nature, online education demands that students become engaged in the learning process. They cannot sit back and be passive learners; rather they must participate in the learning process. The need to interact with the instructor and other students is important to enhance student learning (Cho & Cho, 2014). Online resources should promote active learning, collaboration, mastery of material, and student control over the learning process. The addition of technology as part of the learning process means that the learner actively communicates within the instructional setting.

Cercone (2008) offered that the design for student-centered instructional practice could be described as shifts in the orientation that focus on instructional considerations. She recommended elements for instruction such as:

- Engaging the learners in active learning experiences
- Scaffold instruction to develop learner self-reliance
- Recognize prior learning experiences
- Facilitate learning as an actively engaged instructor
- Guide learning from prior knowledge to new ideas
- Link learning to application and problem solving
- Provide a collaborative, respectful and informal setting
- Provide self-reflection opportunities throughout the learning experience

The transformation from teacher-centered to student-centered can be seen when the instructor sets aside traditional ideas about teaching and begins to employ creative and innovative strategies. A successful online environment moves away from the teacher to the student as the key to the learning process.

Creating Communities of Learners

Creating a learning community involves both the instructor and the students (Palloff & Pratt, 2007). Everyone must take an active role in the development of a collegial learning situation. Students must understand their role in the progress of the learning experiences (Cranton, 2006; Luppicini, 2007).

Respect for others is an important part of working in groups, especially at a distance (Herring & Smaldino, 2001). Students may need instruction in communication protocols. They may need to be aware of any cultural issues that might be important. In an audio setting, students must be prepared to use microphones or other audio equipment. Further, they need to understand their responsibilities to be courteous and well mannered in their communications with the instructor and their peers. In an online setting, students need to be sensitive to their peers and carefully select appropriate language to express themselves. They should be cautious in the use of humor. Gentle guidance is often all that is necessary to ensure respect for others in the course.

Icebreakers, or sessions in which students get to know each other, serve as a positive experience in developing a community of learners, especially in the distance learning environment. The class is often comprised of a diverse geographic collection of unique individuals. Sometimes an institution can create a cohort of students who study together through the length of their program. The cohort model allows students a greater opportunity to become a community of learners. The single course comprised of a diverse population that may not appear together again brings about a greater challenge in creating the learning community.

Several authors have suggested icebreakers as a means to developing a community among the participants in the class (Conrad & Donaldson, 2012; Herring & Smaldino, 2001). What is fundamental to the concept of an icebreaker is that it serves to humanize the new learning situation. The icebreaker's role is to help build a sense of trust among the members of the group. By gaining knowledge about each member of the class, the opportunities for communications and collaborations are enhanced. An activity as simple as having each student introduce himself or herself and perhaps share favorite books or television programs, personal highlights like honors or awards, or something that the student hopes to accomplish in the future, can be a way to help foster a sense of community among the members of the course. As they move through the course activities, students often build upon that initial information to continue building their community.

Just-in-Time Teaching

Just-in-time learning is a phrase used most often by trainers in private business settings. In the workplace, required skills change frequently. Just-in-time learning most often provides instruction in the form of online modules specific to the topic. Generally, the modules are available at all times and can be easily accessed. This way employees can access the training module they need, when they need it, to learn the new information or skill they require to complete their task. Just-in-time learning makes work-related instruction available for new employees who need to gain a skill or act as a refresher for those who have been working at a task for a period of time. It serves well for those who find themselves with a new and novel situation and need to explore their options for solutions.

Distance Learning Versus Distributed Learning

The concept of distributed learning illustrates how the learner-centered educational model is implemented in today's schools and universities. Sometimes, distributed learning is termed "flipped" because the instruction does not always occur directly in the classroom, but is distributed across learning environments. Not all online learning is necessarily considered to be distance learning. Much of the learning activity involves students and instructors who continue to meet at least part of the instructional time in conventional settings, such as a classroom. Saltzberg and Polyson (1995) offered an early definition:

> Distributed learning is not just a new term to replace the other DL, distance learning. Rather, it comes from the concept of distributed resources. Distributed learning is an instructional model that allows instructor, students, and content to be located in different, noncentralized locations so that instruction and learning occur independent of place and time. The distributed model can be used in combination with traditional classroom-based courses, with traditional distance learning courses, or it can be used to create wholly virtual classrooms. (p.10)

Distributed learning is a broad term that can be, and in fact most often is, associated with face-to-face instruction that incorporates some form of technology-based learning experience, either inside or outside the classroom. In other words, students do not need to be at a distance from their instructor to benefit from distributed learning. Although the primary focus of this book is on distance education, in which students and their instructors are geographically separated, many distributed learning experiences may involve only resources that are at a distance, or that occur at a different time and/or place than the conventional class meeting.

For example, the learning materials can be located on a server anywhere in the world and accessed either by the instructor as part of a class presentation or independently by the students in some interactive setting. Course discussions can take place online and outside the classroom. A class activity can involve tracking a scientific expedition in real time, including interaction with the explorers using live video transmissions. High-speed networks enable sophisticated audio, video, and graphics for real-time learning experiences.

Distributed learning is also represented by what are called blended courses, in which online activities substitute for a portion of the actual "seat time" in a conventional face-to-face course. Blended courses can be employed when the instructor feels that the online activities are more productive learning experiences for students. As the technology resources expand to allow more video and audio capabilities, there is a shift from traditional instructional settings to blended options. And, often the shift involves moving to fully online formats as well.

ASPECTS OF INSTRUCTION

The design of instruction captures those elements that create a learning environment that facilitates student learning. Content is organized and sequenced with an orientation toward prescribed outcomes (Dabbagh & Bannan-Ritland, 2005). Often, decisions related to the content are closely aligned with curriculum or professional standards. Standards alignment is one aspect of the design of instruction.

Another aspect of the design of instruction is the instructor's level of comfort with a variety of methods. Common in higher education is the lecture approach, that serves to provide the same instruction to all participants. In its early years, the lecture approach was common in distance education. The "talking head" is frequently the image that comes to mind when thinking about televised instruction. In online settings, documents have replaced the talking head. With the transition to more student-centered instructional approaches, the lecture is being used less as an instructional strategy and more as a means to convey briefly some information or directions. Instructors need to determine their own comfort levels with the various strategies available.

Structuring Instruction

In any instructional setting, students benefit when they have a clear view of such issues as class organization, expectations, and student responsibilities. The instructor's duty involves organizing the course, including such items as class schedule, grouping for activities, and expectations for interactions and assignments (Vealé, 2009). What is essential is that students understand how the course will function so that they can be better prepared to participate. The more informed the students, the greater the chances for a successful learning experience.

Sorensen and Baylen (2004), and later Cercone (2008), suggested that there a good instructional practice principles that provide a guideline for involving students in quality learning experiences. Their guideline elements include such items as:

- Communication with students
- Collaboration among students
- Active learning experiences
- Prompt feedback
- High expectations
- Respecting diversity

These principles seem logical to most educators, but can become lost in the development of distance learning courses due to the complexities of designing an environment that often involves complex technology. Technologies can often afford the instructor options for engaging learners in unique ways that adhere to these principles, and these strategies may apply in traditional classrooms as well. Blended classes, where the instructor incorporates technology to facilitate communication and interactions among students, permit strategies that enhance learning opportunities for all students.

Organization of Instruction. Issues of format or structure are important to help students quickly and easily become involved in learning rather than trying to puzzle through how the course is delivered (Cercone, 2008; Herring & Smaldino, 2001). The instructor needs to make decisions as to the best way to communicate how the course is organized with the students and the content in mind. When thinking about how to approach learning, does the instructor begin with an activity that requires students to interact with each other? Or, should the instructor begin each class with a brief overview of content? And, at the end of each class or module experience should the instructor consider closing with a summary or questions for the students?

The instructor needs to consider how to begin each session or module. Is a text-based outline or a short video possible for presenting the content or directions? Should the instructor post prompts or questions prior to the actual "beginning" time for discussion so that students can preview them? Or, should students be expected to post questions or prompts prior to the learning experience? The instructor needs to consider how and when to respond to each student's postings. Will the instructor interject comments along the way without specifically responding to all the individual comments? Or, will it be valuable to the discussion to remain quiet, only adding to the discussion when necessary to facilitate the discussion or to bring students back on track?

Students are more comfortable with distance learning when instructors adhere to pre-determined course schedules, making modifications only when necessary (Macfarlane & Smaldino, 1997). If it becomes necessary for the schedule to be adjusted, involving the students in the decisions for the changes is important. For synchronous settings, instructors need to maintain a class schedule that is congruous with the delivery approach. If the class is to meet in a particular classroom periodically, that room will need a prearranged time and the students will know to be in that setting on those dates. For asynchronous distance learning settings, students will need to know when they are expected to post information to the discussions and when assignments are due. The predefined schedule allows students to anticipate due dates and ensures they have ample time to complete the tasks before moving to the next phase of the course. Instructors need to provide time to practice at the beginning to allow students experiences with the technology and how to use their time wisely. For example, to provide experience with communicating with a group and posting to a discussion, an Icebreaker activity can be arranged to give students practice with several critical skills before any actual content discussions or assignments take place. Students need to know where to locate valuable information and materials they will need to access and how to use the resources. A scavenger hunt to find specific items and to respond to specific tasks, including taking a quiz on the location of materials, can help orient students quickly to the course structure.

Students need a clear understanding of their responsibilities within the course. They need to know what is expected of them in terms of their preparation for class and participation in activities. Expecting students to read assignments prior to the learning activity means that the instructor must expand upon the information, not merely repeat it within the experience (Cercone, 2008; Herring & Smaldino, 2001). Thus the types of discussion questions and activities need to extend the students ability to use the information they have read. Students will not read in advance if their learning experiences do not expand their understanding of the content or help them explore additional options. If the instructor has assigned a specific reading selection, then incorporating interactive activities related to that reading assignment reinforces the need to be prepared in advance.

The Syllabus.   The syllabus is the single most important document the instructor can prepare. This is the primary communication tool with students at a distance. An instructor needs to provide enough information within the syllabus that students are able to understand the course structure, expectations, assignments, and the assessment process.

The syllabus helps students understand their role in the distance setting. They need to know what they are to do when having technical or personal difficulties with a course. Students need to assume responsibility for initiating contact with the instructor and need to know the most efficient and alternative ways of doing so. Because of the possibility in a distance setting that the instructor and students may not meet in person, they need to know the best ways to reach the instructor if necessary. When providing students with contact information, be certain to also indicate any restrictions or limitations you might wish to impose, such as, please do not phone after 10 P.M. in the evening or expect a response to e-mail within 24 hours, except on weekends. It is crucial that students have convenient and reliable means of contacting the instructor. An e-mail address or toll-free number are desirable as they do not necessarily impose additional expense to the student.

Additionally, in the syllabus it is important to provide students with the information about resolving technical difficulties. Provide them with the contact information for the organization's technical services department where they can get assistance with hardware or software issues that are confounding their ability to work on the course. Provide students with alternatives for when the technology fails, such as, how to inform the instructor of failed technology or how to time stamp an assignment to ensure it will not be counted late if there are Internet problems for uploading to a course server. Students need to know how to manage the technology and how to address any technical problems that arise. They also need to have a fail-safe or fall-back option if the technology interferes with their ability to connect with the class. When teaching with technology, always anticipate the worst and be pleasantly surprised when everything goes well.

Facilitating Active Learning Practices.   Learners who are engaged in learning are actively participating in their own understanding of the content. The "kiss of death" for any distance course is the lack of student participation. Strategies for active learning range from giving students opportunities to think about a topic and respond to actual hands-on manipulation of learning objects (Sorensen & Baylen, 2004; Tyler 2013). The students who are engaged in learning are reported to remember the content better and for a longer period (Dobbs, Waid, & del Carmen, 2009; Vealé, 2009). In distance learning settings active learning can assume such things as small group discussions, hands-on experiences with available materials, and presentations. Strategies such as case study analysis, structured discussions or debates, or virtual field trips are also options that have been demonstrated to be successful approaches to actively engaging learners. The list of possible strategies for engaging learners in active pursuit of their own knowledge is unlimited. The key to active learning is to keep the learners involved in their own learning, not just staying busy.

Engaged learning involves collaboration among the members of the learning community (Conrad & Donaldson, 2012). Essential to the success of the active learning paradigm are such things as clearly articulated goals, timelines, essential questions, and authentic assessment practices. The instructor needs to work with learners to establish goals for learning, ensuring that the standards or requirements are being met. Further, while it is important to plan in advance of the beginning of any distance learning experience, it may be necessary to negotiate with students the timelines for assignments. Flexibility is critical to successful distance educational experiences, for both the instructor and the learner.

Besides answering student questions and providing authentic learning experiences that lead to products for assessment, learners need to feel comfortable with the expectations (Conrad & Donaldson, 2012). An engaged learning setting assumes that both the instructor and the students are open to adopting strategies that form a dynamic learning community.

Using Instructional Materials.   Instructional materials are an essential element to ensuring quality learning experiences (Herring & Smaldino, 2001; Smaldino, Lowther, Mims, 2019). Media formats for instruction continue to advance with the development of newer technologies. The key to using quality instructional materials is for the appropriate medium to be selected. To select an instructional tool because it is the latest version or the newest idea for instructional materials is not sufficient. Instructional materials need to enhance the learning opportunities for students.

The instructor can design instructional materials to direct students in their exploration of content and to actively engage them in the learning activities. Students learn to rely on these materials as an integral component of their learning process. But not all instructional materials need to be developed by the instructor as new resources. Instructors can rely on existing media to help enhance learning experiences.

Further, instructors can design materials to help students as they participate in the class. While it is often desirable to have all instructional materials prepared at the beginning of a course, it might be wise to consider distributing them over the life of the course. This allows the instructor to make minor changes or adjustments to the directions or resources within the materials to reflect the needs of the students.

It is often better to divide the information into shorter packets than to prepare one long document for students. Some instructors find that giving their students a "condensed" version of their instructional notes or PowerPoint slides facilitates note taking during a video-conference "lecture" session and ensures that students will attend to the content as not all the information is contained in the handouts. Others advocate providing templates and other types of resources for students as they engage in course activities or assignments. By providing students with the outline or learning guides, it is possible to help them understand the expectations for assignments and facilitating the grading process.

Addressing Assessment.   Students need to know how their participation in class discussions is measured. Students who are reluctant to engage in discussion or are unprepared should be ready to accept the consequences of nonparticipation if a portion of the assessment depends on a certain level of participation. Efforts need to be made to provide shy students or students with a non-traditional English language background with nonthreatening means for participating that serve to ease them into feeling confident about their abilities to participate in discussions. Instructors must assume responsibility to meet the needs of students who might be reluctant learners.

Students who are not performing according to the identified standards need to receive private communications from the instructor. Even when students are performing well, it is important for educators to inform students of their successes. Feedback provides students with an understanding for how to continue to improve their performance in a course (Conrad & Donaldson, 2012; Smaldino et al., 2019). Timeliness for feedback is also critical to successful learning experiences (Herring & Smaldino, 2001). Distance cannot be an excuse for failure to communicate with students. Students need to be informed as quickly as possible how well they are doing. Online technologies facilitate this process and might be incorporated into any distant learning course to enhance the communication process with students.

Types of feedback also provide students with the knowledge they need to improve their performance (Conrad & Donaldson, 2012; Herring & Smaldino, 2001). The types of feedback necessary to communicate with students go beyond a simple grade. Feedback should be informative to the student. Feedback provides guidance on what was done well and on areas for improvement adds to the success of the distance learning experience. For example, a short paper that has been reviewed can include comments and edits by the instructor and can help the student understand writing expectations for the next assignment that requires a paper. The earlier the information for improvement of performance is provided, the greater the possibilities students have for success as they move through the course.

Instructional Methods

Teaching methods should be chosen based on the characteristics of the instructor, students, content, and delivery system (Herring & Smaldino, 2001). Because of the increased responsibility for learning placed on the students at a distance, methods that focus on the learners and incorporate interactivity have been shown to be most successful (Miller, 2007; Smaldino et al., 2019). Traditional methods for instruction have a place in distance education. What is of importance when considering instructional choices is that the methods selected for a distance learning setting match the outcomes defined by the objectives and the assessments to be implemented.

Range of Instructional Methods. The instructor needs to determine the appropriate instructional methods to be used in delivering the content. Among the issues to consider is how the choice of a particular method can be used to involve the students in all the instructional settings. There is no ideal way to accomplish this. With some adaptations, the same methods and techniques that are successful in a traditional classroom setting can work well in distance instruction. One key to selection is the way in which the strategy can be used to encourage student interaction.

It has been suggested that if a strategy works in a regular classroom, it probably will work in distance instruction with some adjustment (Herring & Smaldino, 2001). The instructor is responsible for the learning environment created in the instructional setting. Technology used in distance learning should be considered as a tool to deliver the instruction and not as a method. Whatever the choice for creating the learning environment, the instructor should include the fundamental elements of planning, including the effects of the technology in the design. Using distance education technology should not limited the choice of strategies used by instructors, but should open new possibilities for those wishing to enrich their teaching (Smaldino et al., 2019; Westbrook, 2006).

Selecting a variety of techniques is important to creating an interesting instructional environment. An instructor must remember to think of strategies that engage learners in active rather than passive learning experiences (Conrad & Donaldson, 2012; Dabbagh & Bannan-Ritland, 2005; Palloff & Pratt, 2007). Combining techniques is useful, and instructors should not be afraid to experiment, explore, and be creative in their approaches to teaching at a distance. The more actively engaged the students, the more likely learning will occur in the distant setting.

Application of Instructional Methods to Distance Instruction. The type of instructional setting will dictate the appropriate choices for instructional methods. With synchronous (same time) instruction, such as video-conferencing, some approaches are more effective. When teaching online in an asynchronous (different time) format, other approaches facilitate learning. Both environments suggest the need for careful design of instruction (Herring & Smaldino, 2001).

Synchronous Instruction. When teaching in a synchronous environment, many traditional classroom instructional approaches can be incorporated. Lectures, of short duration, are often effective in helping to facilitate the instructional situation. Small and large group activities such as discussions and hands-on activities can fit into the components of the synchronous situation. A key to instruction in a synchronous environment is that the learners can not remain passive for a length of time. Thus, using a variety of teaching strategies seems to work best.

Asynchronous Instruction.   An asynchronous environment requires consideration of the types of instructional strategies that work best to engage the learners over time. Without the convenience of face-to-face instruction, the instructor needs to consider ways of facilitating the learning process and encouraging students to assume responsibility for their learning. The challenge is to select methods of teaching that provide learners with enough interaction to keep them on task while encouraging them to explore their learning experiences. Strategies such as problem solving, collaboration, and student-led discussions work well in asynchronous settings (Smaldino et al., 2019).

Addressing Student Issues

Value of a Schedule.   When designing instruction for a group of students, the instructor needs to consider the members of the class. If working with K–12 students, there are generally things to consider related to their work. Often the courses are divided into segments that reflect the normal grading pattern of the school setting. Thus, when designing a course for a group of students at this level, the assignments and expectations need to be chunked together into a similar pattern. Feedback and grading become an essential expectation for the instructor. Students need to be aware of their level of success, which means the instructor may need to provide shorter assignments and frequent feedback to ensure that the students are successful.

When designing instruction for postsecondary settings, the instructor needs to consider the background and the responsibilities of the students. Often in higher education, students enrolled in online courses are also working adults. For them, the schedule is critical for them to be able to participate. While it may make sense to have a weekly discussion on a topic, it might be wiser to extend the discussion over a 2-week period with periodic additions of issues to be considered in the discussion. And, the due dates for assignments need to reflect the ability of the adults to complete the work and upload it. Many instructors select Thursday nights as the due dates for assignments as that makes it easy for them to grade and provide feedback by the end of the weekend. But, for the working adult in the class, the weekend is often the only available time to complete the coursework. Consider the nature of the students in the class and design a schedule that will make it both efficient and effective for them.

Guide Students at the Beginning.   Even though most students come to distance learning situations with vast experience using technology, it is not safe to assume they can transition directly into a course delivered at a distance. At the beginning of a course it is important to guide students as to expectations for their participation, use of the tools, and location of resources. It helps to provide examples or exercises that model what will be expected in terms of performance. By giving students activities that get them using the resources as part of their introductions or community building activities, they learn to use the tools that will be part of their later learning experiences.

Checking in With Students.   There are times when students may not be participating in a course. It is the responsibility of the instructor to find out what is happening. The instructor generally provides contact information, but the student may not reach out. It then becomes necessary to find ways to contact the student, using e-mail and the phone to find out why that person is not participating. Particularly when working with adults, it is often the case that the individual has had interruptions in his or her life that has made it necessary to set aside the course for a period of time. One way for the instructor to ensure that students' participate is to add a suggested way to manage their time. The course schedule should provide flexibility for minor interruptions in an individual's weekly schedule.

Special Services. There are some times when it is important to know about any special needs of students. Students are not required to provide this information, and in fact there a many stories of successful distance learning experiences where the instructor was unaware of the special needs of a student. But, instructors should provide comfortable ways in which students can identify their special needs. Many institutions offer offices to arrange for considerations once the student has been in contact. The sooner an instructor is aware of these accommodations, the easier it will be to adjust the design of the course. Often the institution offers services to assist the instructor with design recommendations or will help with the actual development of the materials. And, of special note, in all cases of students with special needs, it is imperative that the instructor respects the privacy of the individual. Any accommodations must be handled discretely and with dignity for the student.

TECHNOLOGY CONSIDERATIONS

With any instructional activity heavily invested in technology for the delivery of content, the choice of types of tools is important. There are expanding options available to the instructor. What follows is a brief description of the types of technology tools that can be incorporated into a distance experience.

Course Management Systems

In many formal learning settings, course management systems (CMS) have been available for years. There is a migration away from these more structured online resources to less formal systems but there are aspects of CMSs that make them an easy-to-use and valuable resource for designing instruction.

Most CMS offer components that structure the resources for easy delivery. Built into these systems are such things as a course calendar, announcement area, assignment and discussion areas, student rosters, communications, and grade books. Some faculty elect to not use all the built-in resources, but others have found many of them to be valuable in helping students to be engaged in their learning rather than frustrated in trying to locate and use the system.

For example, to facilitate a dialog, the instructor or student can post a topic and as the members of the class engage in the discussion, it is possible to read postings and respond, review earlier postings, and to facilitate a lively conversation. Testing resources are available as well, with options for multiple choice, true-false, and short essay. Tests can be timed so that they are available at specific times for students, limiting access to them. The results of the tests are automatically placed in the grade book.

The instructor can find it easier to use the assignment tools to upload assignments, grade them, and return them to students with extended feedback. The CMS can connect the grading process to the grade book, which means the instructor spends less time with mechanics and more time with the actual instructional responsibilities.

Another major benefit to using a CMS is that all the material for the course, the syllabus, student assignments, and communications, are managed on a server, which means less chance of loss of the information due to technology issues. Also, because the CMS utilizes a web-based format, the instructor and students can access it from any location where they can connect to the Internet.

MOOCs

A MOOC, massive open online course, offers a broad range of participants an opportunity to participate in an instructional event. The design of the instruction needs to recognize the potential for an unlimited number of participants. It is important to consider the types of interactions, structuring them to ensure that members of groups can collaborate efficiently and effectively. Even a MOOC has specific identified outcomes. The over all instruction encourages discussions and debates on topics or issues within the context of the course content. The instructional materials are often open-source resources that provide opportunities for participants to explore a vast array of ideas. Assessment is a challenging area of instruction within the MOOC, often resorting to objective tests or peer-reviewed comments.

Designing for a MOOC course is very different from designing for a CMS-based course. It is essential that the instructor consider the efficiency of the design to ensure the participants find the learning experience will meet their learning needs. To be effective, the instructor needs to consider how to structure the activities to allow for as much participation as possible while maintaining effectiveness.

Blogs and Wikis

Sometimes when a course management system is not available, the instructor may need to consider other options for designing a distance course. Or, the instructor is considering a blended approach to a course, which opens up other options for the design and student experiences. A blog is often an efficient way to organize discussions online for a group of students. By engaging learners in reading and responding to prompts and discussion, the blog can serve to be an effective means for blending online discussions with traditional classroom work.

A wiki can serve as a means for students to collaborate in their writing. Many times an instructor wishes to have a small group of students work together to prepare a paper or presentation, which they will share with the class. A wiki serves as an easy approach to collaborative writing as all members of the group can have access to the document while it is being prepared. Rather than sharing a document across multiple e-mails, which may "cross paths" in the process, a wiki serves to provide students with a means to access the most current version of the document at all times.

Managing Distance Learning Courses

There are a number of issues related to the design of a distant learning course that will facilitate the management of it during implementation. A well-designed distance education course can be as easy to deliver as a traditional face-to-face course.

Communicate Regularly. Communication is an important component of ensuring successful distance learning experiences. Although you may have provided a schedule of tasks and assignments within the syllabus, regularly remind students of upcoming due dates and activities. By regularly posting announcements of things happening within the next few weeks, even the less organized student will stay on track. One technique demonstrated to be effective especially for asynchronous courses, is the MMM: the Monday Morning Memo (or Saturday Morning Memo). The MMM is a weekly e-mail that summarizes the previous week's class activities and explains in detail what students should be expected to accomplish in the next week. The MMM becomes a guide and progress report that students can count on to direct their learning (Orellana, Hudgins, & Simonson, 2009).

Assignments and Grading.   Because the instructor is often unable to meet with students, it is critical that feedback be an integral component of the grading process. Thus, it might be wise to develop fewer, but more complex, assignments that allow students to demonstrate their knowledge and skills about the topics. Or, tests can be generated and delivered automatically which can save the instructor time.

Rubrics for grading assignments are important to facilitate the communication process and to help outline expectations for assignments. Well-developed rubrics can serve to guide students as they prepare their work and can make grading and feedback easier (Smaldino et al., 2019). The trick is to balance the amount of information within the rubric and keep it reasonably focused on expectations for students to use effectively.

Plagiarism.   The Internet has opened many doors, including ready access to information that is easy to copy into documents. It is not appropriate to think that all students will plagiarize, but it is wise to be prepared to deal with the issue before it happens.

Most schools and universities have policies regarding plagiarism. And, resources are now available to help forestall such practice. Software, such as *Turn-It-In*, allows the student to preview a paper before turning it in to the instructor. The software identifies where a portion of a paper might border on not being a well-prepared paraphrase and more of it a nearly direct quotation. Faculty can also use the software if there is any doubt about the honesty of the student's work.

Faculty have a number of ways to deal with the potential for plagiarism. Among those options are to provide enough time to complete a paper, require students to submit drafts of their papers in stages for review, expect copies of the sources to be made available with the paper, and to make the requirements for the assignment unique to the course such that it would be difficult to purchase a ready-made paper or to copy the work of others.

POLICY ISSUES RELATED TO TEACHING AT DISTANCE

In any academic setting there are issues that need to be addressed related to instruction—issues related to course assignments, faculty teaching loads, expectations, and other institutional matters (Simonson, 2007).

Faculty Issues

Faculty—or labor management—issues can easily be the most difficulty for policy developers, especially if instructors are unionized. Increasingly, existing labor management policies are being used to cover distance education. Clearly faculty need to be recognized for their efforts and expertise in working with distant learners, especially with distance education becoming more mainstream and expected of all instructors. Policies need to be in place that clarify distance teaching responsibilities.

Key issues include class size, compensation, design, and development incentives, recognition of intellectual property of faculty, office hours, staff development for instructors, and other workload issues. Some have recommended that labor management issues be kept flexible since many of these issues are difficult to anticipate. However, faculty issues should be resolved as early as possible to avoid critical problems at a later date. The concept of integrating distance education faculty policy with traditional labor management policy seems to be the best strategy.

Compensation and Support.   A long-term issue has been related to faculty compensation. In many institutions, the expanse of distance education has not been viewed as additional work, but rather something that can easily be assumed within existing responsibilities. Thus, faculty are often not given additional compensation for the workload associated with teaching a course at a distance. Faculty need to negotiate the means for recognition of the additional instructional responsibilities. The compensation can be in the form of additional pay, release from other responsibilities such as committee work, or reduced class sizes (Wolcott & Shattuck, 2007).

Support is an additional issue that needs to be considered. Instructors teaching at a distance not only have to deal with delivery of content, but have to consider the technologies involved in that process. Their experience in the use of the distance technologies may not be sufficient to capitalize on the nuances of the resources. By providing technical support, faculty can focus on instruction and gain necessary skills in using the technologies over time. And, technical support is essential for the distant student as well. Instructors need the assurance that students will have a resource to help them if they encounter technical difficulties in accessing course materials or resources.

Another support issue is access to resources. Faculty need assurance that students will have access to the appropriate resources necessary for their learning. Libraries have been shifting their access portals to provide easy access to the materials necessary for successful study. Most libraries have dedicated staff who serve their distance students exclusively. The instructor needs the assurance that these types of support structures exist within the institution when planning the learning activities within a course.

Qualifications.   The qualifications of a distant instructor are not always articulated. Each institution needs to create guidelines for instructional practice or experience essential for quality teaching at a distance. First-time distance instructors can be highly successful, while others who have taught for many years in traditional classrooms may not be able to adapt to the distance learning environment. Key to quality instruction is an educator who demonstrates flexibility and creativity.

One additional benefit of teaching at a distance is that the instructor often can translate the experience into face-to-face classrooms. The result is a better traditional class experience for the students. Someone who has taught at a distance often understands the needs of students better and is able to bring that appreciation into the classroom setting.

One thing that an institution can do to help faculty to become better distance instructors is to provide them with training in effective instructional practice and the technology resources to be used. Faculty who have taken advantage of professional development opportunities have found their experiences with teaching at a distance to be both positive and successful. One popular theme within the training has been time management; something that is a very important aspect to being a successful distance educator.

Intellectual Freedom and Ownership/Property Rights

In the realm of intellectual freedom, many issues come to bear. Copyright ownership is often in dispute if there is not a clear agreement between the faculty and the institution sponsoring the distance class. Faculty who invest time into the design and development of distance coursework may be compensated for their work by their institution. When this occurs, the perception is that the institution is the owner of materials that are considered "works for hire."

Faculty who are not compensated for their efforts in designing courses may find it appropriate to consider the ownership of the course to be theirs. It is important to clarify the position of the institution regarding ownership of any of the materials designed for the course.

Course Integrity

The quality of any course is contingent on the design and the format for implementation. Faculty who design courses need to have the qualifications in the content area. It helps to have experience with teaching at a distance; however, such experience is not as important as other issues that need to be considered.

Faculty who teach at a distance need to be aware of how a particular course fits into the structure of a program of study. Official courses through an institution should address the standards adopted by the program of study. Students need to know that when taking a course their personal and academic goals will be met.

Curriculum and Standards. One way to ensure quality in coursework is to ensure that the standards or critical criteria are being met (Herring & Smaldino, 2001). Expectations are clarified when the curriculum has included the appropriate content and skill standards. Further, assessments are often easier to design and implement when the curriculum is aligned to standards.

Individual courses can also address standards that might be critical for particular professional or academic areas. Although not necessarily part of a whole program of study, courses aligned with standards often match with whole curricular areas within a field of study.

Course Rigor. An area of concern among institution administrators has been that of the academic rigor or quality. Many administrators have expressed concerns that the courses taught at a distance do not have the same standard of quality associated with the on-campus courses. Wyatt (2005) found that students reported their perception of the quality of online instruction as it related to regular face-to-face instruction to be more academically demanding. Faculty may be over compensating for the issue of assuring the institution of rigor in distance coursework by making the courses more difficult or requiring additional work from students. Wyatt also found that students were very satisfied with their academic experience in an online setting.

Calendar and Schedules. When distance courses are arranged, the issue of scheduling may become a factor. When multiple institutions work collaboratively to offer courses or programs across a distance, they must find ways to compensate for the differences in institutional schedules. For example, a group of schools may cooperate in the delivery of a particular course but may have different spring break schedules. When this happens, the students cannot be penalized for these differences. However, with schedule limitations it may be necessary to consider offering independent study activities or providing online experiences across that take a longer time to complete.

Another issue that can occur with an institution new to distance education deliver is that of ensuring that students meet "in class" for the required number of hours. This concern is often heard with fully online courses. How can the instructor ensure that students have engaged in the course for the required number of hours? Although students will attest to doing more than the usual seat-time in a face-to-face class, the institution may not recognize an asynchronous environment in the same light. Instructors need to consider how they might address this issue.

When conducing an online course, one technical option is "chat," which is a live dialog among the members of the course. With the technology resources available, the discussions can incorporate video or audio conferencing, as well as text-based chats. These types of discussions can be fast paced and seem a bit hectic when there are a significant number of participants, but it is an easy way to bring groups of people together for engaged dialog. One problem with arranging these types of discussions is that the students who enroll in courses may be from a variety of locations, including international settings. Trying to find an acceptable time to meet in an online discussion may prove to be very difficult.

Student Support

Students need to know that they are able to function successfully within a course. They must be able to complete the requirements of the course without undue stress. Considerations such as access to resources and services need to be addressed when designing the course.

When preparing to work with students at a distance, it is necessary to consider the resources available to them. Resources that should be accessed include (also see Chapter 7):

1. Equipment available for student use, such as computers with sufficient memory, scanners, video equipment, et cetera.
2. Available computer software and resource people to assist students at a distance
3. Communication resources students can access, such as e-mail, toll-free phone numbers, fax machines
4. Library and course resources for assignments and out-of-class work
5. Assignment distribution and collection options

This information will provide an instructor with the data necessary for creating opportunities for all students to be successful. It is important for students to feel there is equity among the members of the class regardless of where they are located. This may mean the instructor must create new and different ways of approaching an instructional situation. For example, one instructor liked to begin her traditional classes with a quick quiz designed to measure students' basic knowledge of the content. However, when she converted the class to online, she had to rethink that quick formative assessment process by creating a timed recitation exercise between pairs of students (Macfarlane & Smaldino, 1997). The instructor found this new approach to be a successful means for checking her students that she began incorporating this technique into other courses, even those in traditional settings.

Beyond the mechanics of course options, there are human aspects as well. In a video-based course, the presence of a facilitator in K–12 settings is important in assuring student success (Herring & Smaldino, 2001). The role of the facilitator varies because of location and types of students, but this person can be a valuable asset when working with first-time distant students.

Instructors need to consider ways to communicate with students prior to the beginning of a course. A letter or e-mail to each participant in the class is a way to welcome students and to provide them with initial information about the course structure and schedule. Many successful online instructors have found that a simple letter to students with essential information can alleviate many frustrations on the part of the instructor and the students.

Institutional Aspects

Within the institution there are polices related to issues of delivery for courses and programs of study. The responsibilities for these policies lay principally with several offices within the institution. These policies cover a range of topics, from tuition to types of expenses included in the charges. The central issue behind most fiscal, geographic, and governance policies is one that is institutionally based. The institution has the ultimate responsibility regarding the course or program and is retains the final decision on all matters.

Fiscal and Governance. The key issue in this area deal with tuition rates, special fees, full-time status, state mandated regulations related to funding, service area limitations, out-of-area institutional relationships, consortia agreements, contracts with collaborating organizations, and administration costs.

The institution offering a course or program has considerable expenses associated with offering courses or programs at a distance. Initially, many institutions offered distance courses with additional fees or higher tuition rates to compensate for the additional costs of delivering these courses. The additional revenue went to supporting the additional resources necessary to the quality programming, such as, online library resources, additional technology staff, et cetera. More recently, these costs have been reduced due to the shift in the institutional infrastructure which now supports these additional resources within the traditional institution budgets.

Other issues, such as accepting online courses as part of a full-time student's on campus tuition rate are under consideration at many institutions. Many students find that to maintain a full load of courses, an online option for one course helps them to balance their schedules. In other cases, it is often the only way some classes are now available to students. The institution needs to be sensitive to ensuring that students have the kinds of educational resources that facilitate their successful completion.

Geographic service areas are also difficult to administer. Traditionally, institutions were assigned designated areas to serve. With electronic distribution options, these types of boundaries have become invisible. Regulations that identify geographic limits may need to be clarified or altered when distance education programming is available.

Governance relates closely to geography. The policies related to interinstitutional agreements need to ensure clarification of distance education priorities as well as those considered more traditional in nature.

Legal Issues

Probably the most important legal issue is copyright. Copyright presents a complexity of issues within distance education. It is imperative that the instructor and students understand the copyright laws and the institution's policies. The TEACH Act provides guidelines related to the use of multimedia in courses offered at a distance (Debbagh & Brennan-Ritland, 2005). An institution may have an office that has the responsibility of clearing copy for instructional materials. If there is not a specific office for this purpose, the school's librarian can provide information related to copyright.

Copyright does not restrict students from using materials for their projects. What is important is that they understand the restrictions related to the use of copyrighted materials. Further, they need to provide the appropriate credit in recognition of the authorship of the materials used.

And, finally, plagiarism is an issue that might need to be addressed within the syllabus. Students need to understand the difference between quotations and paraphrases and the appropriate citations regarding the use of information. Most institutions have a policy regarding plagiarism that can easily be applied to the distance setting.

With copyright, "ignorance of the law" is not sufficient. The laws are very specific and there are no excuses regarding infractions. It is best to request permission to use materials rather than to fine oneself in violation of the law.

Technical Policies

Usually an institution owns the distribution network used for distance education or is responsible for its reliability. If a private-sector business is a provider, then clear expectations must be in place, and all members of a consortium should be part of the relationship. If a public agency such as a state department of education or educational organization is the telecommunications service provider, then a very clear chain of command of responsibilities needs to be in place. Often telecommunications policies are not created in the same office as the distance education enterprise, which can generate some issues about services. Policies related to student and faculty needs, such as quality of service, should be established and maintained. Hardware, software, and connectivity minimum requirements should be clearly outlined.

Reliability of Resources. Certainly for those resources provided by the institution, there needs to be access to reliable technology. If necessary, arrangements need to be made in advance to assure that the technology will be appropriate and available within the course timeline.

Students who provide their own technology, such as in an online course, need to understand where the responsibility of the institution lies regarding reliability. It may be that the student may need to acquire additional hardware or software at personal expense in order to maintain quality connectivity. Policies need to be articulated so that all parties are clear about responsibilities.

Technology Requirements. Instructors must be clear about their requirements when delivering distance courses. If they have particular technology needs, they need to identify those requirements prior to the beginning of the course. Also, instructors should be reasonable and specific in their requests. And, just because a certain technology resource is available does not mean that it has to be implemented. Sometimes the use of certain technology resources can inhibit the quality of instruction, so the instructor must make measured choices.

It is when the technology expectations are dependent upon individual resources that complications can arise. Students need to understand the expectations for the types of hardware and software resources they will need to personally supply and those that will be available through the institution. For example, in an online course that uses streaming video, it may be necessary for students to acquire additional memory for their computers in order to view the video successfully. Versions of software can also be important variables that require student access. Communication with students prior to the beginning of the course is a valuable measure to ensure they can prepare their technology for the learning experiences.

TEACHING AND DISTANCE EDUCATION— THE TIME COMMITMENT

Time, specifically the saving of time, may be one of the most significant contributions of distance learning to formal education. College students save time when they do not have to drive to campus, search for a parking spot, and hike across campus to their class setting. High school students save time when they have access to resources in class online and to not have to find their way to the media center. Medical professionals save time when they can consult with specialists about a patient's illness, and professionals save time when they can participate in continuing education or professional development at a convenient location and time rather than traveling long distances.

Most who study distance education issues have documented the potential and real time savings for distant learners. The conventional wisdom is that teaching at a distance takes more time than in traditional settings. Most of the data on teaching time is anecdotal, and is highly individualized. Some instructors spend several hours per day working on their online courses, others may engage in less time.

On average, if an instructor is in a traditional classroom for a 50-minute period, then he or she probably will spend more than an hour in direct instruction. With that, most instructors spend between 2 to 3 hours preparing for that class period. Which means most instructors engage in approximately 4 hours of time for instruction in a course. In a distance course, obviously the instructor is not in the classroom; however, if the course is organized with chats or discussions, it may well be that the instructor is engaged in dialog with students for about an hour. And, participating in asynchronous activities might take another 2 to 3 hours.

Times may vary with the type of course, the extent of the coverage of content, and the expectations for student work. However, the allotment of time can be distributed differently across the time span of the course or training session (Orellana et al., 2009).

SUMMARY

Distance education may be new to both students and the instructor. Preparing students for instruction is important in any teaching mode to maximize learning from class participation. But, it is especially important to prepare students for settings where class participants are separated across distances. Students need to understand their responsibility to ensure a successful learning experience.

Teaching at a distance is a challenge. The instructor needs to be creative and imaginative in the design and structure of the course. One rule of thumb is that successful interactive learning experiences that work in a traditional classroom may be adaptable to the distant learning environment. But, they will require more than just some minor changes to the visuals or the handouts. Those strategies will likely require creative and innovative approaches to engaging learners.

Teaching at a distance can be a pleasurable experience for everyone involved, instructor and student alike. Keeping it interesting and motivating the learners to remain active can make it a valuable learning experience as well as fun.

DISCUSSION QUESTIONS

1. What are some of the institutional factors that an instructor must consider when preparing to teach at a distance?
2. What strategies might be used to facilitate introductions among students?
3. What elements of class structure need to be included when preparing to teach at a distance?
4. Why is it necessary to determine resources available at distant sites when preparing to teach a distance course?
5. How is the instructor's role affected in a distance education environment?

CASE STUDIES

Carol Johnson wishes to begin teaching her high school algebra at a distance. Her students have no experience with taking courses in distance settings. What technology resources should Carol investigate? What are some of the decisions she needs to make when planning to teach her course? What institutional factors does Carol need to consider when preparing to teach this course at a distance?

Tim Wallace will be teaching his philosophy course using the video-conferencing system at the regional community college. His course will involve approximately 20 students located around the county. He has been teaching the same course on campus for several years and wants to ensure his students at the distance will be able to engage in the same types of activities his on campus students have completed. These are predominately discussions and group projects. What can Tim do to facilitate student collaboration? What strategies might he incorporate to help his students work together?

Bill Cunningham has been teaching introduction to Literature and incorporates a very directive style of teaching. After 15 years of teaching face-to-face classes, Bill has been informed is course will be offered online. What does Bill need to consider when moving his course online? How will his teaching style need to be altered to address the online format? What resources does Bill need to identify in advance as he moves his course online?

REFERENCES

Conrad, R., & Donaldson, J. A. (2012) *Continuing to engage the online learner: More activities and resources for creative instruction.* San Francisco, CA: Jossey-Bass.

Dabbagh, N., & Bannan-Ritland, B. (2005). *Online learning: Concepts, strategies, and application.* Columbus, OH: Merrill/Prentice Hall.

Cercone, K. (1008). Characteristics of adult learners with implications for online learning design. *AACE Journal, 16*(2), 137–159.

Cho, M., & Cho, Y. (2014). Instructor scaffolding for interaction and student academic engagement in online learning: Mediating role of perceived class goal structures. *Internet and Higher Education, 21,* 25–30.

Cranton, P. (2006). Fostering authentic relationships in the transformative classroom. *New Directions for Adult and Continuing Education, 109,* 5–13.

Dobbs, R., Waid, C., & del Carmen, A. (2009). Student's perceptions of online courses. The effects of online course experience. *Quarterly Review of Distance Education, 10*(1), 9–26.

Herring, M., & Smaldino, S. (2001). *Planning for interactive distance education: A handbook* (2nd ed.). Bloomington, IN: AECT Publications.

Kidney, G., Cummings, I., & Bohem, A. (2007). Toward a quality assurance approach to e-learning courses. *International Journal on E-Learning, 6,* 17–30.

Knowles, M., Holton, E., & Swanson, R. (2011). *The adult learner: The definitive classic in adult education and human resource development.* Burlington, MA: Elsevier.

Luppicini, R. (2007). *Online learning communities.* Charlotte, NC: Information Age.

Macfarlane, C., & Smaldino, S. (1997). The electronic classroom at a distance. In R. Rittenhouse & D. Spillers (Eds.). *Modernizing the curriculum: The electronic classroom* (pp. 171–195). Springfield, MO: Charles Thomas.

Miller, C. (2007). Enhancing web-based instruction using a person-centered model of instruction. *Quarterly Review of Distance Education, 8,* 25–34.

Moore, M. G. (Ed.). (2007). Handbook of distance education (2nd ed., pp. 391–402). Mahwah, NJ: Erlbaum.

Moreland, P., & Saleh, H. (2007). Distance education: Faculty concerns and sound solutions. *Distance Learning, 4*(1), 53–59.

Orellana, A., Hudgins, T., & Simonson, M. (2009). *The perfect online course: Best practices for designing and teaching.* Charlotte, NC: Information Age.

Palloff, R., & Pratt, K. (2007). *Building learning communities in cyberspace: Effective strategies for the online classroom* (2nd ed.). San Francisco, CA: Jossey-Bass.

Saltzberg, S., & Polyson, S. (1995). Distributed learning on the World Wide Web. *Syllabus, 9*(1), 10–12.

Simonson, M. (2007). Institutional policy issues. In M. G. Moore (Ed.), *Handbook of distance education* (2nd ed., pp. 355–362). Mahwah, NJ: Erlbaum.

Smaldino, S. E., Lowther, D. L., & Mims, C. (2019). *Instructional technology and media for learning* (12th ed.). Columbus, OH: Pearson.

Sorensen, C., & Baylen, D. (2004). Learning online: Adapting the seven principles of good practice to a web-based instructional environment. *Distance Learning, 1*(1), 7–17.

Tyler, R. W. (2013). *Basic principles of curriculum and instruction.* Chicago, IL: University of Chicago press.

Vealé, B. L. (2009). Transactional distance and course structure: A qualitative study. *Open Access Theses and Dissertations from the College of Education and Human Sciences*, 51.

Westbrook, V. (2006). The virtual learning future. *Teaching in Higher Education, 11,* 471–482.

Wolcott, L. L., & Shattuck, K. (2007). Faculty participation: Motivations, incentives, and rewards. In M. G. Moore (Ed.), *Handbook of distance education* (2nd ed., pp. 391–402). Mahwah, NJ: Erlbaum.

Wyatt, G. (2005). Satisfaction, academic rigor, and interaction: Perceptions of online instruction. *Education, 125,* 460–468.

Books, Real and Otherwise

A poem and an essay on the book in distance education

"Crated, carted, cast aside,
printed works have liquefied
in shocking bouts of bookicide.

The printing press is done, perhaps,
and publishers have (boom!) collapsed
to clicky gadgets, gizmos, apps.

Digital books are all the rage,
touchless paper, turnless page.

Stores are only cyber spaces,
cold, electric, faceless places.

Bookshops closed, bookshelves cleared,
paperbacks have disappeared.

The age of print has culminated,
finished, finis, terminated."

—Susan M. Ebbers

Most agree that a book is a series of printed pages, bound together on one side, and with a cover—something real and physical. Almost everyone knows what a book is, and what books are not. But, maybe it isn't that simple. What about virtual books, electronic books, online books? Are they real? Are they books? Or, are they something else—written content? Some textbook publishers would have us think that the electronic book, the virtual book, the online book, are superior to physical books. They are cheaper, more readily accessible, and more modern. But, are they books?

One interesting discussion about books deals with the role the book plays in society. The bestselling book, *The Book Thief*, subtly supports the importance of books. Liesel Meminger is a foster child living in World War II-era Germany. She steals books, including one salvaged from a book burning. Leisel saved and cherished the book. Her book did not burn, and it was a real book.

The reader of *The Book Thief* is left with many conflicting images as the story unfolds, but one stands out; somehow the books that Liesel steals and the books she reads save her and give her life meaning. That may not be the message the Markus Zusak, the author, wants the reader to remember, but books and their impact are certainly central to the story of the book thief. Liesel would just be a lost and lonely girl if she didn't have books.

What about today? All the rage today is the electronic book, one that exists on a server as a recorded file. Electronic books are a great addition to the options available to the reader, but should electronic books replace real ones?

The electronic book file cannot be read without a software package and without a device such as a tablet reader. And, according to some publishers, the electronic book is not owned by you; rather, it belongs to the publisher—who lets you read it for a price.

Why should distance educators be concerned with the status of the book? What difference does it make if we do not have real books, but only have electronic ones? After all, distance educators are in the business of virtual things. Yet, somehow the real book seems important, even critical. Distance learners should read books. Most definitely. But does it matter if the book to be read is only online?

Well, the decision to have real or electronic books is being made for us. One large publisher is no longer offering bound copies (books) of its education titles, only electronic ones stored on a company server that must be accessed using a propriety software reader, and readers only get to rent the electronic book for 6 months (or longer for a bit more money). Is this a good idea?

The role of books in teaching and learning will continue to be an important issue for the distance educator

CHAPTER 7

The Student and Distance Education

CHAPTER GOAL

The purpose of this chapter is to describe the characteristics and responsibilities of the distant learner.

CHAPTER OBJECTIVES

After reading and reviewing this chapter, you should be able to

1. Identify the characteristics of the distant student.
2. Explain the responsibilities of the instructor for ensuring student participation.
3. Discuss the factors that ensure student success.
4. Describe the responsibilities of the student.

AN EMPHASIS ON THE STUDENT

Often in a distance learning situation, much emphasis is placed on the technology. The audience, or the distant learners, are often considered after the planning and organizing of the hardware, the content, and the instructional plan. But it is the learner who is the crucial member of the distance learning system. It is the learner who needs to be considered early in the planning and implementation of a distance learning experience. The more an instructor understands the members of the audience, the better the distance learning experiences will be for all involved (Moore & Kearsley, 2012).

The distance learner can be of any age, have attained any educational level, and have a variety of educational needs. One pervasive characteristic of the distance learner is an increased commitment to learning. For the most part, these learners are self-starters and appear to be highly motivated. Distance learners live in a variety of areas, from rural to metropolitan sites located sufficiently away from where a class is traditionally offered. The students' educational needs are usually specific and may represent low-incidence content areas (e.g., learning a foreign language or technical content knowledge).

One can conclude, after examining the various tools and approaches for distance learning, that there is one primary purpose: to provide a valuable learning experience to students who might not otherwise have access to learning. Dede (1990) suggests that distance education can be useful to the academic institution in a number of ways. One way is to bring together a group of students from various locations to create a class of sufficient size to ensure its economic viability. Offering courses at a distance can also provide a limited resource to students in a low incidence topic of study. Simply stated, there are a number of reasons to bring learners together at a distance. And, because of this idea of bringing together students and resources from an array of different locations to address a common need, it may be necessary to find ways to encourage students to appreciate the value of a distance learning setting. They will need to be motivated to participate and to engage in the types of learning experiences in which they may have little experience.

It is equally important to understand the intent of learners when planning the process for delivery. In any instructional situation, it is important for the instructor to know as much as possible about students in the class. Knowing the students in the class provides the instructor with a better understanding of how to best approach instruction to ensure an optimal learning experience for all. In a distance learning setting, the instructor must learn about students. It can be challenging to get to know the students. Knowledge of the students can assist the distance educator in overcoming the sensation of separation of the instructor and the student and can ensure that the learning experience will be positive for all (Bergmann & Raleigh, 1998; Smaldino, Lowther, Mims, & Russell, 2015).

To begin, the instructor should acquire some basic information about the class as a whole. In a synchronously delivery mode, knowing the number of students and a little about the technologies they are using gives the instructor the "big picture." Equally important is information about the students, such as whether they are located in rural or urban settings. The cultural and social backgrounds of students is also helpful to know. Together, these factors provide the instructor with an overview of the class, which then can lead to learning about individuals in the class. Knowledge of the members of the class is critical to the design and delivery of the course.

Each member of the class is an individual, although each individual may belong to a category of groups, such as, rural or economically challenged. Each individual has a cultural identify, as well as a socioeconomic "standing" in the community. However, each individual is unique and needs to be recognized for those unique characteristics. When the individual is considered, characteristics such as attitude or interest, prior experiences, cognitive abilities, and learning styles will all have an impact. Taking the time to learn about the individual will enhance the learning experience for that individual and for the class as a whole.

TRAITS OF THE DISTANCE LEARNER

Students of all ages are engaging in distance education. As more technology resources are becoming available to educational settings, more students are becoming involved in learning at a distance. There are similarities among the learners, but the differences do exist and those differences need to be addressed when planning instruction.

Adult Learners

Although there are some who would suggest there is little difference among distance learners, adults bring a unique characteristic to a distance learning setting. Theirs is a world of experiences related to learning, life, and their profession. To think that adults bring little to the classroom is to limit the contributions that adult learners can make to any learning situation.

Further, as Benson (2004) would suggest, there are differences among the adult learners in an educational setting. She refers to two categories of what she calls busy adults: "white-collar" and "blue-collar" workers. She further defines the two types of adult learners in terms of their ease of access to distance learning situations. For the white-collar workers, Benson proposes that access is easier and more flexible. For the blue-collar workers, she states that access to distance learning is more complicated, both because of work schedules and limited access to the resources necessary to participate in distance learning. Although this difference is lessening, it is still an essential issue to address. Benson advocates that an instructor needs to be cognizant of these factors when designing distance learning experiences.

Sullivan (2001) further suggests that there is little difference between adult men and women in learning settings. He maintains that both genders identify flexibility, academic achievement, and opportunity for shy students to participate as important reasons for their decisions to enroll in distance education courses and programs. He does note that both genders identify self-discipline and self-pacing as important characteristics, although more women than men suggest these qualities as essential. But, it is in the area of family and children where a significant difference in gender appeared in his study. More women mentioned family as the primary reason for selecting a distance education setting over a face-to-face setting. He suggests that this may imply the woman is a nontraditional student who is often juggling work, school, and family responsibilities. The opportunity to study at a distance makes it possible for members of this group to accomplish their academic goals.

A standard assumption is that adults are more interested in participating in the distance learning situation because of their motivation to apply their learning to their work (Moore & Kearsley, 2012). And, although this is prevalent in most distance learning situations, it is still necessary to consider how to motivate adults to stay active in learning (Conrad & Donaldson, 2012). In addition, most adult learners are "self-starters" and thus require little to get them interested in the course of study, but their focus seems to be on only getting what they need from the learning situation.

K–12 Learners

The younger learners, those in K–12 settings, provide an even more interesting challenge to a distance education instructor. Young people are not necessarily involved in a distant class by choice. They are often seeking a particular course of study, but do not have ready access to a face-to-face class. Thus, they are often put into distance learning situations without consideration of their motivation or self-reliance as a learner.

Further, younger learners bring to the learning setting a wealth of literacy related to "information navigation" described by Brown (2000). Students of all ages now have more in-class experiences with using the Internet for seeking information. They are more facile at moving about in online situations. They are less likely to be patient with instructional settings where they are not motivated or engaged.

It is more likely to find greater diversity among younger learners (Dabbagh & Bannan-Ritland, 2005), and it is probable to find students from a variety of locations participating in an online class. With the advent of the virtual high school, groups of students from around the world can be brought together into one class.

The digital divide identified by Benson (2004) in the adult population has a similar impact on K–12 populations. Access to resources outside a school building may be limited. To require students to participate in an educational experience beyond the normal school day may put undue burden on those students to locate easy access to resources. It is essential that an instructor understand individual access issues within the distance learning group when preparing assignments and out-of-class expectations (Smaldino et al., 2015). It is noteworthy that in one area where the digital divide is significantly level is in the use of mobile technology, especially the digital phone.

FACTORS INFLUENCING LEARNER SUCCESS

A number of factors affect the way in which students approach learning at a distance. Their learning success is dependent on not only understanding those factors but also addressing them as part of instructional planning.

Attitude Factors

Much of what educators know about the classroom applies to a distance learning setting. The student brings to the classroom setting, whether face to face or virtual, a set of characteristics that can influence the success of the instructional plan. Many variables come to play in this situation—factors that can be addressed by the instructor when planning.

Classroom Culture at a Distance. Palloff and Pratt (2007) have devoted much of their research to the study of the development of "learning communities." They advocate that without establishing a community of learners in a distance setting, the potential for instructional success is limited. Palloff and Pratt present a strong argument for taking the time to create a classroom culture that promotes shared learning and teamwork. They suggest that the responsibility for creating this culture in the classroom is the responsibility of all participants, not just the instructor.

Although many distance students are cited as being independent learners, they derive value from collaborative learning experiences (Dabbagh & Bannan-Ritland, 2005). When collaborating, students expand their knowledge, skills, and ability to self-assess their own progress. Working together creates a richer learning experience for the individual participant.

Kanuka, Rourke, and Laflamme (2007) suggest that engaging the learner requires instruction that is well structured, with clear responsibilities for students, and that provokes students to join in deeper levels of discussion. In looking at student interactions in several types of active learning instructional strategies, they found that students who were involved in debates or WebQuests were more likely to be challenged by the learning activity and more likely to show higher levels of collaboration or contributions to discussions. The other instructional strategies they identified—nominal group, invited expert, and reflective deliberation—did not seem to elicit the same levels of engaged involvement as did the debates and Quests.

Etiquette.   More than ever, it is essential that students understand the complexity of the distance education setting in order to be certain to participate in an appropriate manner (Smaldino et al., 2015). With the introduction of a more diverse population, students must become sensitive to all members of the class. It is the responsibility of the instructor to establish the protocols for communications within the course. Students can be held accountable for their actions only if they know what is expected of them. Such things as humor and grammar need to be addressed early in the course. The tone of responses means that it is important for members of the class to refrain from using inappropriate or unacceptable language. There should be courtesy among students. The syllabus can become an important communication vehicle for the instructor in clarifying expectations related to appropriate language in all communications.

Humor is one of those communication aspects that creates the largest challenge. When in a face-to-face setting, humor can often be the "icebreaker" that opens avenues of conversation, but humor frequently "falls flat" in a distant setting (Smaldino et al., 2015). Without all the cues associated with humor—inflection, facial, and bodily gestures—the joke is often "lost." Even using such little devices as the emoticons used in text-based communications—such as ☺ or ☹—humor can go astray. If students wish to use humor, they might begin by stating something to alert others as to their intent, for example, "A NOTE OF HUMOR."

It may become necessary to take a student "aside" and have a private communication related to inappropriate use of language or humor. When working with a variety of students who are enrolled in a distance setting, the instructor needs to be aware of any sensitivities and considerations as early as possible to ensure there is a perception of respect among all participants.

Experience

As has already been mentioned, students today bring an array of experiences to the classroom. Some have prior experience with distance learning; others have had experience with random Internet explorations, and still others may have not had any distance learning experiences at all. Knowing about the backgrounds of students is essential for a successful distance learning situation.

Learning Experiences. All students bring to a class experience with learning. Especially with adults, it is important to consider how these prior experiences will impact the current learning situation. By knowing more about the learners (i.e., their background knowledge, their interests, their goals), it will be possible to design instruction to facilitate successful learning.

Further, if the intent is to facilitate collaborative learning experiences, knowing about prior experience with this type of learning situation is essential. Adult learners who are unfamiliar with the benefit of working with others may not perceive it as a valuable part of their learning. Often, adult learners find working in groups to be unproductive and might express concern that they are expected to work with others who may not be nearby. This attitude can create difficulty for the other learners and the instructor if not clearly articulated at the onset of the course. It might be of benefit to scaffold the collaborative learning experiences for these types of students, starting with less involved collaborative learning experiences before forging into complex group projects (Bergman & Raleigh, 1998). For example, in an online course putting students into a group of collaborative learners to work on an activity that is not academic in nature may help the students build their confidence in the group collaborative experience. In other words, an activity, such as one that asks students to design a new computer input interface (e.g., a better keyboard), will provide them with collaborative experience without having to impinge on each student's personal goal of academic success.

Distance Learning Experiences. An indicator of success in distance education is prior experience (Bozik, 1995; Smith & Dunn, 1991). Students have reported that once they took a distance course, they were willing to enroll in additional classes. Students felt satisfied with the quality of their learning experiences, and the convenience factors reinforced their desire to participate. Students have indicated that they would, if necessary, drive to a centralized campus location to attend classes; however, this was not their preference. An effective instructor who utilizes technological tools in a nonintrusive manner can allay any concerns and encourage students to take advantage of the unique and dynamic learning experiences. But, this does take time and patience on the part of the instructor. It also assumes much in the way of a student's responsibility to grow and adapt personal learning characteristics to a distance learning situation.

Readiness for learning at a distance. Students who are new to distance learning sometimes express concern about their ability to complete the amount of work required to be successful (Dobbs, Waid, & del Carmen, 2009). Students who have not taken a distance learning course, either synchronous or asynchronous, need guidance as to what they are expected to do. It is the responsibility of the instructor, when designing a course, to be certain that there are hints and suggestions, clearly articulated expectations, and information presented in multiple locations for easy access. This helps students by creating redundancy in the presentation of information (e.g., providing the course schedule in the syllabus, displaying an online calendar, and providing weekly reminders of things that will be happening within a 2-week block of time). And, when learners have successful experiences with learning at a distance, they will be more willing to take additional courses. As they become more familiar with the tools and resources, not only will students require less support, but they will also provide help for their classmates.

Elements of Success

To ensure that students at a distance are successful, it is important to consider those elements that can serve as indicators related to achievement.

General Ability.   To be successful it is important that students are in the correct educational setting. There are some students for whom the distance setting is not a viable learning place. Another indicator of success is cognitive abilities (Smith & Dunn, 1991). This is not to suggest that students in distance classes are smarter, but rather that the successful students tend to be capable of initiating their own work and seem to have the desire to complete their study. Students at a distance seem to assume more responsibility for their own learning earlier in the process than do those students who are enrolled in traditional classes. Many authors have indicated the need for the student to assume responsibility for learning (Dabbagh & Bannon-Ritland, 2005; Moore & Kearsley, 2012; Smith & Dunn, 1991; Tuckman & Schouwenburg, 2003; Smaldino et al., 2015). Palloff and Pratt (2007) suggest that the instructor's role is that of facilitator, which implies tat the student must assume responsibility for learning. Since this is not different than what is currently advocated in the traditional educational setting, there is a complexity of responsibility on the part of the instructor to ensure that learners have a clear understanding of expectations and opportunities for participation in a class.

Prior Knowledge.   When an instructor accounts for the background and prior knowledge of students, the learning experience can be more successful. Students of all ages come the educational setting with some knowledge and skills in topics and areas related to the topic of study. It is essential that the instructor have an understanding of what students know and how that relates to the intended instruction.

Often, because of the nature of distance education, students enter into classes with varied learning experiences. It is inappropriate to assume that all students have equal learning backgrounds. A pretest of knowledge or a survey of content covered might be a way of gaining information about what students know to date. Gaining knowledge of students' prior knowledge is a clearly important step in preparing a quality learning experience.

Learning Styles.   Finally, one more indicator of successful learning at a distance is learning styles. For some students, the unique characteristics of distance learning facilitates better learning experiences than in a traditional classroom. For example, in a distance setting the instructor generally places greater emphasis on providing visual cues, whether the technology used is synchronous or asynchronous. When the instructor does provide more visual cues, the visual learner may perform better on tasks. Auditory learners can focus on the instructor's presentation if they can listen to the instructor. Some students are reluctant to participate in class discussions due to language or shyness issues, but find their "niche" in text-based communications such as a discussion board area in the course or through written assignments (Dabbagh & Bannan-Ritland, 2005).

All of this speaks to the need for the instructor to understand the characteristics of the members of the class. The more the instructor knows about the individual student, the more elegant the application of distance tools for the course. The instructor can learn about members of the class in a number of ways. Contacting instructors who have taught the students previously is one way of getting information. This works particularly well if a cohort group is moving through a program of study. As always, caution must be exercised when providing information about previous students in order to not pass on confidential information. Another way of getting information is to simply ask students directly about their own sense of what works for them. Many instructors have added periodic reflection assignments within their courses to gather such information. Students often know what works best for them and will openly express their needs.

A survey or similar type of approach can be distributed to the students prior to the start of the course. This provides the instructor with information that might not be available through institutional records or from other instructors. An additional way to get to know students is to create class-time opportunities for getting to know each other (Conrad & Donaldson, 2012). Not only does this provide additional information to the instructor, but also gives the students a chance to know each other. For example, an instructor could have a first discussion assignment for students to share their favorite books or hobbies, photos, or something of interest about themselves (Macfarlane & Smaldino, 1997). In addition to learning about each other, the students develop a stronger sense of who is part of the class and develop a sense of support among class members. It is wise for the instructor to engage in similar information sharing as that helps to model expectations for the students. Finally, if possible, the instructor can meet with students in person at an optional meeting before the class begins. Private phone conversations and e-mail are alternative ways to spend some private time with each student.

In essence, what is crucial is to become familiar with students in the class and to address their needs as they have identified them. Further, by putting time into this type of discovery of information, the instructor will find that the class will function more as a unit than it otherwise would have. This makes it easier to engage learners in the activities and learning outcomes designed into the class structure.

LEARNER RESPONSIBILITIES

Just as the instructor must take responsibility for learning about students, learners in the distance setting must assume ownership for their learning experiences (Macfarlane & Smaldino, 1997). The type of distance instructional setting will dictate the kinds of responsibilities students need to assume. They will need to know how to respond in a synchronous class or to post responses in a discussion forum, ask questions, or make presentations as the result of assignments; therefore, it is imperative that the students learn to use the tools available in the distance learning setting.

Differences in Settings

With the advent of the advancements in technologies, the resources available for instruction allow for many different types of learning experiences. What is essential is to match the technology to the particular instructional situation.

Online. In an online setting the students need to understand the nuances of the various types of resources available to them. Many students bring a wealth of experience with e-mail and Internet surfing, but may not have the experience with structured instructional tasks such as posting to a discussion board (Bergman & Raleigh, 1998). Also, they may know how to prepare a text document, but not understand how to upload it or save it in a format that is compatible with the course management tools. The instructor's use of Internet tools such as Dropbox, the course management system assignment feature, or an online chat, may cause students frustration or confusion as to how to proceed.

The syllabus can provide students with details on how to operate certain types of tools. It can provide the students with instructions and expectations about uploading files for the course. The instructor may need to be available to handle specific issues related to connectivity and the use of tools. Often a practice exercise, without academic consequence, at the beginning of the course will allow students the opportunity to use the tools without worry of a grade issue. The idea of a scavenger hunt makes this kind of practice fun and gives students a hands-on opportunity to learn to use all aspects of the resources within the course.

Students are responsible for contacting the instructor when there is difficulty with a task or with the technology. The instructor can anticipate many of the probably issues that might arise, but cannot plan for all of them. Even the most carefully planned course will have situations where an individual student will need extra assistance. Thus, the instructor is wise to provide multiple means for seeking assistance when technology problems arise.

Video and Audio.   Video and audio are frequently part of distance classes and have become relatively easy to use. The students may need to learn how to use the tools as they do present unique circumstances in a class. Students will need to learn to use the appropriate tools for responding to the instructor, gaining attention, and how to engage in a private conversation with the instructor or another student during the synchronous class time. Appropriate communication protocols are important when using these types of class interactions. Students will need to learn to keep their comments brief so that others can have a chance to be included in the discussion. Background noises need to be eliminated also.

If video is not available, students may need to identify themselves as others may not recognize their voice when they start to speak, ask a question, or make a comment. Eventually, over time, most participants will learn to recognize individual voices, but initially courtesy is necessary and helps to avoid confusion.

Additional resources and tools that might be available, such as online white boards or video, may require the students to have more sophisticated computer equipment available to them. This would mean that if the instructor intends for students to participate in a class that will use these types of resources, students will need advance notice to be certain they are not disadvantaged when the course begins.

Time for Class

With any course of study, there is a "time" for class to begin. Students need to be aware of their responsibility related to distance class time and how to best balance their personal time. It is appropriate for the instructor to provide students with guidance on how to balance their on-task time for class with their other responsibilities.

Synchronous.   Synchronous class time is similar to the on-campus, traditional arrangement familiar to many students. Students will most likely be at home when participating in a synchronous class. This may mean a need to advise students about optimal locations for them to fully participate in the class. It is wise to suggest a quiet, out-of-the-way location where they will have few distractions from the discussions. A home-classroom is the best solution.

Although synchronous experiences are desirable, they can present some problems when insuring equal access for all members of the class. Time zones differences may pose complications, perhaps causing burden on some to attend a class at a time that might overlap with other responsibilities (e.g. work) or at a time of day that might be extreme (e.g. early hours of the morning). The instructor needs to be aware of these issues when planning the class. It might be helpful to use the first half-hour of the scheduled time as a "hall or office" time, which would allow students who have scheduling or technology issues a chance to get to the class without missing important topics. The "hall time" might be a good time to respond to student questions or to chat informally about recent events.

Asynchronous. In an asynchronous class, meeting times are less of an issue, although there are still some issues that do affect participation. The fact that everyone does not have to be in class at a particular time is one of the advantages of this type of class for very busy people who are unable to rearrange their schedules. It is important that students understand the need to arrange time within their weekly schedule to check into the class and participate in the discussions or group activities. This might be late on a weekend night or early on a weekday morning. The time selected is not important. What is important is that students log into the course regularly and complete the activities within the scheduled time frame (e.g., posting by a particular date in a discussion topic).

There are a number of reasons to ensure that students have a grasp of the schedule for participation. If the instructor has developed a discussion forum which places expectations on all students to have a minimum number of entries, then the student need to know that they are to connect with the class several times over the discussion period. If there are assignments that need to be completed, students must be prepared to upload their materials in a timely fashion. It is imperative that the instructor makes it very clear what students are expected to do to complete a course, but it is the student's responsibility to adjust his or her personal schedule accordingly.

Communication

As with any course, communication between the instructor and the student is important. The instructor has several means to provide information to students such as the syllabus, regular notices or announcements, and feedback on assignments. Students need to be aware of their responsibilities related to communication as well.

Connecting With the Instructor. Distance education means both learning and teaching. The involvement of the instructor in the educational process is critical. It needs to be very clear to the student how to contact the instructor at any point in time through the course of study. The student may need to let the instructor know of a technical or personal issue that delays the submission of an assignment. Perhaps the student will need clarification about an assignment. It is the responsibility of the student to contact the instructor as soon as possible. An instructor can provide information about e-mail and phone contact, with suggestions as to appropriateness of making the contact (e.g., "Please don't call between midnight and 5 A.M."). Another means for students to be able to contact the instructor is through the course management tool such as Blackboard. Here the instructor can provide an Frequently Asked Questions (FAQ) section in the discussion area. Students can post questions and the instructor can respond; however, in this format the questions and answers are available for the whole class to read. Sometimes this is a very efficient means for communicating about questions that may arise during the course.

Whatever the means of communication with the instructor, students need to provide sufficient information to the instructor so that it is clear who is making the contact. "A student in your class" may be insufficient to the instructor, especially when her or she may be teaching multiple courses at a distance. Students need to know that it is their responsibility to make the contact.

Also, the instructor needs to be clear as to the time frame for responses. For example, if you are not going to be available, let the students know. If you do not want to be interrupted during the weekend, let the students know. If you plan to responds quickly, provide a timeline for your response to inquiries (e.g., "I'll reply to your e-mails within 24 hours" or "I'll respond to your e-mails within one working day").

Connecting with other students. Students need to have a sense of community within their classes. Group work is common and an excellent way for students who are working in isolated locations to be connected with others in their class. Once a group is formed and an assignment started, each

student needs to communicate with the other group members. Course management tools provide ways to create group collaboration through the system. Students are given access to several ways to connect with the classmates. As with connecting with the instructor, it is the student's responsibility to initiate the communication.

ENGAGEMENT

Engagement of a learner is defined as emotional and intellectual involvement or commitment—the participation in learning activities via interaction with others in meaningful ways. Engagement theory considers engagement as the process of involving learners in groups or teams working collaboratively on project-based and authentic activities.

Engagement has other meanings, also. For example, an engagement is an agreement to marry. Engagements are hostile encounters between military forces, and engaging is also the act of putting a manual automobile transmission in gear. Engagement is an often-used word important in a variety of contexts.

Okay, what do these definitions have in common? First, they involve more than one person—two people become engaged, armies are of hundreds or thousands, and transmission gears mesh in a predetermined way. Second, they are serious—marriages are to last a very long time, military engagements produce casualties and change people and places, and transmissions are engineering marvels. Finally, engagements are purposeful and result in something of significance or importance—two unite in marriage, armies fight and win battles, and cars with transmissions move more efficiently.

Engagement and engaging are important.

Recently, the idea of engagement has become popular in distance education. When courses are planned, the best instructional designers talk to the subject matter experts—the teachers—about engaging the learner. Designers promote and emphasize instructional strategies that involve team activities, team assignments, and the idea of authenticity of learning events. Student engagement and engaging instruction are important. A purpose of engagement is to expect students to take responsibility for their own learning.

Some techniques that engage learners are:

◼ Group projects—students really do not like group projects, but some team learning in a class can promote engagement.
◼ Peer reviews of assignments—while instructors often say they do not like the use of peer reviews, once again, a modest use of this approach can bring students from isolation to partnerships.
◼ Multiple channels of communication—the use of a number of interaction activities is almost always popular, and promotes engagement.

Specific instructional activities include welcome audios and videos, interviews of classmates by classmates, systematic and regular communication such as the Monday Morning Memo, posting of assignments for class viewing, and group examinations.

One note—the use of social media to promote engagement in an online class may not be the best idea—since social media promote social engagement, using these media for educational engagement may promote a frivolous aspect to the learning process

Class Participation

As in any instructional setting, class attendance is imperative. However, on occasion learners may not be able to attend class because of conflicts, illness, or technical difficulties. The instructor needs to be clear about expectations for participation. It may also be appropriate to provide some guidelines for ways of maintaining participation; for example, the instructor might suggest how many times per week a student should log into the class.

Synchronous. In a synchronous class, a student may be unable to attend. One solution would be to record the class and provide access to it for the learners who missed the class. Although no interaction is possible, at least the student does not lose out on the content of the class. It is wise to inform all the participants of the class that it will be recorded (Macfarlane & Smaldino, 1997).

Class participation, either in a traditional or distance class, always enhances leaning for students (Conrad & Donaldson, 2012). A key to an effective synchronous class is interaction among the members of the class. Some students may not be comfortable participating, either because of their learning styles or because of intimidation by the technology. Instructional strategies that encourage all students to participate are critical for class engagement. Instructors can try several strategies such as pair-share discussions, voting on choices, building consensus through small group discussion, or posing questions.

During discussions, some students may need a brief period to prepare an adequate response to a question or discussion prompt. One solution is to provide the question or prompt prior to class time in order to allow students the opportunity to prepare their responses. Instructors need to engage in strategies that will allow students success and develop comfort levels for participation.

Asynchronous. In an asynchronous class, similar types of considerations are related to the students' responsibilities. Although they are not as specific, the discussions will require some time. It is important that students' responsibilities be made clear for participation in discussions. Online forum discussions are valuable only when all members of the group participate. Logging in to the class the night before the final due date for postings is not contributing to the dialog. Occasionally students encounter problems getting into their online classes, but as a rule, reserving a few hours several times per week is sufficient to be able to actively participate in the class activities. Some instructors suggest that students treat the class as if they are going to campus and to "lock" themselves away in a quiet area of home or office to participate in the class. Too many distractions can contribute to poor participation.

Assignments

It is the responsibility of the student to complete assignments in a timely manner and find an appropriate means to submit them to the instructor. Delay in turning in work can result in delays in grading and receiving feedback. Some instructors use a point penalty approach to discourage delays in submitting materials. It is essential that the student inform the instructor if there is an issue with submitting an assignment on time.

Dealing With the Factors Affecting Completion of Assignments.   An instructor can anticipate some issues related to completion of assignments. These can be identified in the syllabus or in the course overview at the beginning of the class. What is important is that timelines be clearly set and that students understand how to meet them. One suggestion for the instructor is to provide "advance" warning on due dates in calendars or communications with students. Reminding students of an anticipated due date for an assignment might help them with getting the tasks done on time.

Addressing the Grading Issues.   Students like to receive good grades. Often they work hard to deliver what they think is the right response to an assigned task. When they do not meet the expectations of the instructor, there is a need to improve the communication process.

One way of addressing successful completion of the assignment is for the instructor to provide specific instructions on what is expected. Providing rubrics, outlines, and samples often help to eliminate confusion or poorly completed materials.

Further, it is imperative that the instructor considers available resources for students when preparing the assignments. If the assignment requires use of a library, then the instructor needs to be certain that the students have reasonable access to a library or that online versions of the resources are available. This might mean that the due dates need to be adjusted to allow students time to access the resources.

Students need to have a clear understanding of the grading structure and how each assignment fit into that structure. They need to know the balance of expectations so that they can expend the appropriate energies on their tasks. One idea by Herring and Smaldino (2001) is to use a point structure that adds up to 1,000 rather than 100. By "adding a zero" to all assignments within the point structure, students have the perception that there is value to their contributions. In other words, an activity that would have earned 5 points on a 100-point scale now earns 50 points on a 1,000 point scale. It is amazing the differences in students' attitudes toward completing assignments when they have a higher point value. It seems even when they understand how the adjusted point structure works, students still place higher value on each task.

Assuming Responsibility for Own Learning

In any student-centered learning environment, students must assume responsibility for their own learning (Smaldino et al., 2015). It is important that their students know the expectations of the instructor and the requirements to complete the course of study. Further, students need guidance and assurance when they are beginning a course of study at a distance, especially if this is their first time to engage in learning at a distance. They must understand the nuances of the amount of time, the manner of communication, and the means for submitting and retrieving materials. They must focus on their own learning and be able to judge whether they need additional assistance and how to proceed to request it. Generally, students are comfortable with technology for social interactions, but they may not be as comfortable transferring those skills and knowledge to learning settings. It is essential in the design of the course that the information is clear to students. It is often wise to post information in multiple ways to ensure that all students have access to it.

Equipment Requirements and Use

Regardless of the distance instructional setting, it is essential that students know how to use the equipment involved. Students might need to seek assistance from a local vendor or neighbor due to distance issues. The instructor can anticipate some issues and make suggestions as to way to getting help when necessary.

A student who is planning to participate in an online class must be certain that the equipment requirements match what is available. If a student wishes to participate in a class that has very specific technical requirements, then those need to be clearly stated. But it is the student's responsibility to inquire if the requirements have not been identified. Also, it is the student's responsibility to obtain the technology required to be a member of the class.

Technical Know-How. For some online classes, students need to know how to use certain software packages (e.g. Blackboard or SPSS), to use specific types of equipment (e.g., scanners), or to follow technical procedures (e.g. uploading a file to a website). The instructor may assume that students have this type of knowledge. The student may be required to attend special workshops or classes just to prepare for this type of class. It is ultimately the students' responsibility to know how to do these things to ensure full participating in a class.

Technical Difficulties. In any situation where so much technology is involved, problems are bound to occur. When the technology tools do not work, the student has the responsibility to notify the instructor so that adjustments can be made. Sometimes a technician can provide the information necessary to clear up the problem. It is the student's responsibility to let the instructor know about problems. If the student does not assume this responsibility, the instructor may continue under the assumption that the student is not participating because of other reasons. Students should not let a technical problem delay their participation in a course—nor should they let it alter their desire to participate.

GENERATIONS OF LEARNERS

Recently there has been considerable discussion about how there are differences with the current generation of learners. Today's learners have experiences using many social communication tools (Smaldino et al., 2015). They are highly familiar with using mobile technologies and communication tools to exchange information. And more recently, several states have required students to complete an online or blended course prior to high school graduation. These shifts in the background in students may frame a need for an instructor to reframe the strategies necessary to engage students.

At the same time, the instructor may find a class of adults with limited online experience. Thus it is essential to learn as much as possible about the backgrounds of the students who are enrolled in the course before developing the assignments, instructions, expectations, and the resources. With a mix of students representing a variety of backgrounds, the instructor may wish to incorporate a variety of instructional strategies and assignment options. What is important to remember is that all strategies and tasks need to be parallel or equitable.

Social Media and Online Learning—Pros and Cons

Are social media applications empowering or addicting—or both?

Certainly, social media provide a type of interaction and connectivity that was unheard of a few years ago. In the modern distance education era, the quest for interaction and connectivity has been a hallmark of well-designed online learning, and social media applications seem to provide a needed and desirable dimension to online instruction. But it seems that there are pros and cons to the use of social media applications in teaching—empowerments and additions.

Seven positive consequences of social media when used in online instruction come to mind and these seven might be referred to as *the seven empowerments*.

- Social media are *cool*. Sites like Facebook and Twitter give the impression of being modern, so classes that have a social media dimension are perceived as new and generational.
- Social media promote the *ego syndrome* of users. We can access information about our classmates, and they can do the same. Teamwork is promoted.
- Social media promote *self-education*—users can find out what they want quickly and this can expedite the teaching and learning process.
- There is an *instantaneous phenomenon* to social media. When instructors post, students receive, and vice-versa.
- There is a needed match between *instructional design* and social media. If social interaction is a part of a course, a well-planned instructional design strategy is mandatory.
- The *third party* is removed. Social media are if nothing else, personal. We do social media without the need for help, or supervision. The information technology professional's role in social media-based instruction is minimized.
- Social media make instruction seem *friendly*. The whole basis of connecting and interacting is to be social. This works for education also.

Unfortunately, there seems to be a less positive side to the use of social media in online learning. Let's call these seven the seven distractions ("addiction" seems too strong a term). The seven distractions now being referred to in the literature as nomophobias (<u>no</u>-<u>mo</u>bile fears, get it?) are:

1. There is a *greediness* dimension to the use of social media. In other words, users want likes and expect repeated and rapid interaction.
2. *Gluttony* is another of the cons of social media in online learning. There is a need to know everything related to what is being examined and discussed.
3. There is a level of *lustfulness* when social media are used. I want this or that or everything. These three deadly sins—greed, gluttony, and lust—are related and harmful in the extreme.

4. *Pleasure seeking* is a documented consequence of social media use. Learners look for what makes them happy and contented, and this is often not what instructors want. Education must sometimes hurt a little.

5. Some *students are afraid* of social media uses in online instruction. They do not want to interact so often or in the level of detail that others in their class might want. Research shows that if someone is positive in social media, readers perceive this as neutral, and neutral responses are perceived as negative. Truly negative interactions are ego shattering for some.

6. Unfortunately, instructional design, while important and even critical in any online instruction, is often ignored when social media are used. Social media are so easy that *systematic planning is often ignored.*

7. *Feeling left out* happens. If instructors and classmates do not respond in the manner of social media users, some wonder what has happened, or what did I do, or what did I miss.

How do we decide if social media applications have a place in online instruction? The answer is simple; there is no choice, students have already decided. The real key is how distance educators harness the positives and reduce the negatives.

 ## SUMMARY

The students are the core to successful distance learning experiences. Quality learning experiences not only depend on the efforts and preparation of the instructor but they are also largely determined by the efforts and preparation of the distant student. This chapter has identified many of the characteristics, responsibilities, and expectations that students may have when learning at a distance. Also, a learning experience is provided by an instructor and used by a student. Teaching and learning are two sides of the same coin, often referred to as a learning experience. Remember learning experiences for learners should be equivalent, but not necessarily equal.

 ## DISCUSSION QUESTIONS

1. Describe some characteristics of the distant learner. Discuss why these characteristics are important and how they relate to the characteristics of the traditional-setting learner.

2. Why is it important for an instructor to obtain information about distant students?

3. What are some responsibilities of the distant student in a synchronous distance education class? Why are these responsibilities important?

4. What are some responsibilities of the distant student in an asynchronous distance education class? How are these different from those in a synchronous distance class?

 ## CASE STUDIES

1. As Tracy Nelson prepares for her first online course, Introduction to Teaching, she discovers that there are a number of things being expected of her. She notes that are

technical expectations, assignments with specific due dates, and the use of a course management tool she has not used before. What can Tracey doe to make it easier for herself to get started with her studies? What can her instructor do to provide assistance and guidance to help her get started?

2. Ruth Downer and Phyllis Alderman are middle school state history students who have been included in a special invitation-only videoconference class for accelerated students. This is their first time to take this type of class. They are good friends and like to talk with each other, sometimes even in class using text messaging, which does lead them to getting detention What do they need to consider when taking this class related to their studies and their classroom behaviors? What should the instructor consider if their "sharing" becomes an issue?

3. Carl Morris has been enrolled in a program at a nearby university. His program has taken on a blended approach with some courses offered only face to face, although others are totally online. His is aware that because he is a part-time student it will take him longer to complete his program. At this point in his program he is taking a completely online course. What are his responsibilities as a student to be successful? How are his interactions in the online course different than those in the face-to-face classes? What should he expect in this class regarding his performance, that of his classmates, and the instructor's responsibilities?

REFERENCES

Benson, A. D. (2004). Distance education: Reading and willing to serve the underserved? *Quarterly Review of Distance Education, 5*(1), 51–57.

Bergmann, M., & Raleigh, D. (1998). Student orientation in the distance education classroom. *Distance Learning '98: Proceedings of the Annual Conference on Distance Teaching and Learning, 61*–66.

Bozik, M. (1996). Student perceptions of a two-way interactive video class. *T.H.E. Journal, 24*(2), 99–100.

Brown, J. S. (2000). Growing up digital: How the web changes work, education, and the ways people learn. *Change: The Magazine of Higher Learning, 32*(2), 11–20.

Conrad, R., & Donaldson, J. A. (2012). *Continuing to engage the online learner: More activities and resources for creative instruction.* San Francisco, CA: Jossey-Bass.

Dabbagh, N., & Bannan-Ritland, B. (2005). *Online learning: Concepts, strategies, and application.* Columbus, OH: Merrill/Prentice Hall.

Dede, C. (1990). The evolution of distance learning: Technology-mediated interactive learning. *Journal of Research on Computing Education, 22,* 247–264.

Dobbs, R., Waid, C., & del Carmon, A. (2009). Students' perceptions of online courses: The effect of online course experience. *Quarterly Review of Distance Education, 10*(1), 9–26.

Herring, M., & Smaldino, S. (2001). *Planning for interactive distance education: A handbook* (2nd ed.). Bloomington, IN: AECT Publications.

Kanuka, H., Rourke, L., & Laflamme, E. (2007). The influence of instructional methods on the quality of online discussion. *British Journal of Educational Technology, 38,* 260–271.

Macfarlane, C., & Smaldino, S. (1997). The electronic classroom at a distance. In R. Rittenhouse & D. Spillers (Eds.), *Modernizing the curriculum: The electronic classroom* (pp. 171–195). Springfield, MO: Charles Thomas.

Moore, M., & Kearsley, G. (2012). *Distance education: A systems view* (3rd ed.). Boston, MA: Wadsworth.

Palloff, R., & Pratt, K. (2007). *Building learning communities in cyberspace: Effective strategies for the online classroom* (2nd ed.). San Francisco, CA: Jossey-Bass.

Smaldino, S. E., Lowther, D. L., Mims, C., & Russell, J. D. (2015). *Instructional technology and media for learning* (11th ed.). Columbus, OH: Pearson.

Smith, P., & Dunn, S. (1991). Human and quality considerations in high-tech education. *Telecommunications for Learning, 3*, 168–172.

Sullivan, P. (2001). Gender differences and the online classroom: Male and female college students evaluate their experiences. *Community College Journal of Research and Practice, 25*, 805–818.

Tuckman, B., & Schouwenburg, H. (2003). Behavioral interventions for conquering procrastination among university students. In H. Schouwenburg, Lay, C., Pychl, T., & Ferrari, J. (Eds.), *Counseling the procrastinator in academic settings.* Washington, DC: American Psychological Association.

The Home Office

The solitary learner needs a place to learn—a home office (it could also be called a home classroom). The home office is a growth area of the 21st century—more are working from home, and many students are learning from home.

Just what constitutes a home office—is it the couch and 50-inch HDTV? Is it in the garage? Or, can it be my smartphone and the kitchen table. Well, none of these options are going to work, especially when most online courses are designed for the student to spend about 8 hours per week for each course they are taking at a distance. The home office should probably be a dedicated place—a place with "stuff."

Here is a list of what seems to be the consensus of what should be in the home office (stuff)—the Big 20, if you would.

1. A modern computer with monitor
2. Software—MS Office at a minimum
3. A desk
4. A chair
5. Lighting—ceiling and desktop
6. A high speed Internet connection—a cable modem for example
7. A wireless router
8. Telephone with speaker and cordless handset
9. Electrical outlets with surge protectors
10. An all-in-one printer (copier, printer, fax, scanner)
11. Back up drive
12. Uninterruptable power supply
13. File cabinet
14. Storage
15. Firesafe
16. Paper shredder
17. USB webcamera with built-in microphone
18. HDTV connected to cable
19. Supplies
20. Bookshelves

What a list, and oops, we forgot the most important item—a room with doors that can be closed. The distractions in the home are too powerful to be ignored; closed doors keep cats, kids, noise, and the home part of the home office outside.

And finally, as Theodore Roosevelt said "When you play, play hard; when you work, don't play at all." So, when in your home office, don't play at all—or text your friends.

CHAPTER 8

Support Materials and Visualization for Distance Education

CHAPTER GOAL

The purpose of this chapter is to present information about the effective use of support materials in distance education.

CHAPTER OBJECTIVES

After reading and reviewing this chapter, you should be able to

1. Develop a distance education course syllabus.
2. Use interactive study guides.
3. Apply graphic design principles.
4. Develop word pictures.
5. Develop visual mnemonics.

PRINTED MEDIA

What is "trending" in distance education? E-books and e-documents! The printed book has long been a staple of education generally and distance education specifically. The debate over the move to e-books, and electronic course materials at the expense of the printed document is currently a major issue in the field of distance education. Here is a summary of the discussion about e-books

Distance education has its roots in print-based correspondence study. The printed lesson was used to convey content information as well as to assess learning in correspondence study. Today, many people give little credit to the effectiveness of printed materials. Educators sometimes use technological media to replace printed media, even though there is no real need to do so.

Printed materials can enhance teaching, learning, and managing in distance education. In particular, two kinds of instructor-created print media can significantly improve the distance education environment—the course syllabus and the interactive study guide. Additionally, graphic design principles can be applied to develop study guides that use visual mnemonics and word pictures for the visualizations of key instructional ideas.

Best Practices—e-Books

"We will no longer publish printed books in the field of education, we will only publish E-books."
—Statement heard in the executive offices of a large international publisher

"A house without books is like a room without windows."
—Horace Mann

"Many people, myself among them, feel better at the mere sight of a book."
—Jane Smiley

E-books are being proclaimed by some as the next major consequence of the digital revolution. These "futurists" forecast that the printed book and printed materials are destined to go the way of Super-8 film, VHS tape, and 5¼" floppy disk.

E-books, simply defined as electronic versions of printed books, offer the reader many advantages. Certainly, the electronic book, newspaper, journal, class handout, even comic book are here to stay. There are many obviously advantages of electronic publishing. Pastore (2010) listed what are the major advantages of E-books. Some of his more interesting claims are:

▪ E-books promote reading. People are spending more time in front of screens and less time in front of printed books.
▪ E-books are faster and cheaper to produce than paper books, and are often cheaper to buy.
▪ E-books are easily updateable.
▪ E-books are searchable.
▪ E-books are portable. The reader can carry an entire library.
▪ E-books defy time: they can be delivered almost instantly.
▪ E-books can be annotated without harming the original work.
▪ E-books make reading accessible to persons with disabilities. Text can be resized for the visually impaired. Screens can be lit for reading in the dark.
▪ E-books can be hyper-linked, for easier access to additional information.
▪ E-books can read aloud to you.
▪ E-books defeat attempts at censorship.

So, educators generally, and distance educator specifically, are now faced with decisions—the e-book or the printed book? the electronic handout or the printed handout? And, if a favorite text is only available electronically or only in print form, should this influence the adoption decision? Interestingly, some publishers indicate they will make the choice for us –electronic will be the only option.

Is this an important issue? When one thinks about either/or decisions distance educators make, the medium used for the delivery of the printed word does not seem to rise to the level of some other controversial decisions, such choosing between virtual vs. brick and mortar schools, or the issue of open vs. proprietary CMSs.

But, perhaps this apparently simple issue—offering printed materials in ONLY an electronic format, a decision being made by several large publishers—is an issue that may have greater implications than one might expect. Certainly, the advantages of e-books listed by Pastore are important, but why are some left a little cold by the decision by publishers to only publish textbooks in an electronic format? And, if textbooks are all electronic, should there be a move to eliminate all hard copies of materials—to be completely electronic? What is lost compared to what is gained?

Books have always been relatively immune from exclusive ownership. When we buy a book it belongs to us. Public libraries have long offered near universal access, and our ever diligent librarians and media specialists have long guaranteed access.

And, as Thomas Jefferson said, "I cannot live without books."

DISTANCE EDUCATION SYLLABUS

The typical distance education course syllabus is similar to the syllabus used in any other course. The primary difference is in the specificity and completeness of the distance education syllabus as compared with a more traditional one. Normally, the distance education syllabus contains the following:

Course Logistics

- Course title
- Course meeting dates, times, and locations
- Instructor information, including name, office address, telephone number, e-mail address, biographical information, and emergency contact information
- Office hours
- Textbook and course materials

Course Policies

- Attendance policies
- Homework policies
- Participation information

Instructional Activities

- Class schedule with topic
- Topic list and topic organizational concept
- Course goals and objectives
- Reading assignments with links to topics
- Discussion questions for readings (if special discussion sessions are scheduled online, then the timeline for discussing certain topics can be included)
- Assignments
- Test and examination information
- Interactive study guides

Assessment Information

▪ Grading scheme
▪ Project evaluation criteria
▪ Grading contracts, if used
▪ Student precourse assessment
▪ Student postcourse assessment

Additional Information

▪ Student biographical information
▪ Project/assignment examples

The distance education syllabus should be available to students no later than the beginning of the first class, and probably should be distributed much earlier to prospective class members. Often, the syllabus is a recruiting tool for the distance education course. If the syllabus is available online, then the distant learners can access it from wherever they are located. The syllabus is a guide for the student, and can serve as an organizing document for the entire course. Many designers of asynchronous distance education courses use the syllabus to provide the overall structure for the content, delivery, and evaluation of the course.

THE INTERACTIVE STUDY GUIDE

Tom Cyrs and Al Kent are often credited with proposing the interactive study guide (ISG) as an essential tool of the distance educator. Certainly they (especially Tom Cyrs, 1997) are staunch advocates of this technique. Basically, the interactive study guide is a structured note-taking system that leads the learner through a series of concepts, and that requires some active and interactive involvement by the student (Figure 8–1).

There are several reasons why the handout, generally, and the ISG handout, specifically, are important to the distance educator. First, the use of handouts improves student note taking and makes it more efficient. Second, the ISG is a management tool that directs course activities before, during, and after instruction. Finally, the ISG handout can be used in any classroom, including all categories of distance education systems. The ISG is a handout designed to be used by students. It is a highly organized set of student notes, graphics, pictures, graphs, charts, clip art, photographs, geometric shapes, activities, problems, and exercises. It is planned before class or presentation to assist students with note taking and to guide students through a variety of instructional events so they understand the structure of the content of the lesson. ISGs are especially effective when students are viewing prerecorded videos or recorded presentations. Interactive study guides are also meant to show the relationships among ideas and data presented during a class (Cyrs, 1997; Stuart, 2004).

The ISG is different from other handouts because it is more organized and more systematically sequenced than other types. The ISG consists of two parts—the display (with the word picture) and the notes section (Figure 8–2). A series of displays is sequenced (numbered) in the order that each will be discussed or presented. Each display corresponds to one idea or one visual element of the lesson. Sometimes a display is equated to a concept, but most often, displays are less general and more specific than a concept.

FIGURE 8-1   The ISG is a critical tool of the distance educator.

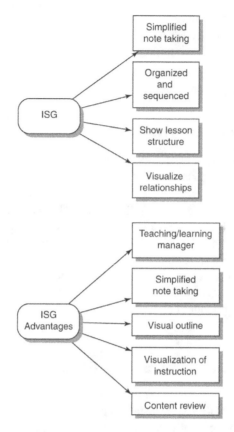

Well-designed displays are made up of word pictures that are graphic representations of concepts, principles, and information derived from various patterns to organize a lesson. The best word pictures are visual mnemonics that relate to the key ideas of the lesson. Mnemonics are ways to remember things, so visual mnemonics are visual ways to remember things.

The ISG is a series of displays presented from the top to the bottom on the left side of the handout page. Normally, three to five displays are presented on each page of the ISG. A display is sometimes referred to as a "chunk" of information that is numbered and then referenced by the student (Cyrs, 1997). A display is similar to a paragraph of information in a written document, but the display attempts to present ideas visually rather than verbally, or at least with a combination of visual elements and words.

Displays can consist of the following:

- Word pictures with fill-ins completed by the student
- Activities or exercises
- A set of directions
- A quote, poem, definition, or other short written item
- Problems—either
- verbal or numerical
- Summaries of data
- Tables or figures

FIGURE 8–2 Interactive study guide components.

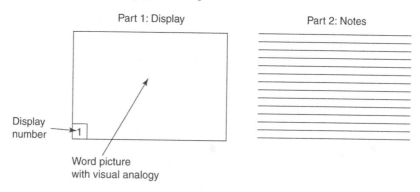

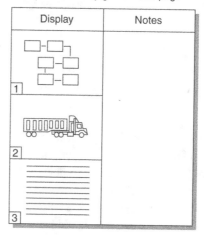

Interactive study guide—one page

- Photographs
- Drawings
- Self-test
- questions
- Lists

An ISG display can contain directions for students to accomplish a task outside of class that is external to the ISG itself. An effective display is clear, easy to understand, and useful to the learner.

Normally, a class session or presentation would require approximately 10-20 displays in an ISG. In other words, displays should be complex enough to require about 3-5 minutes to explain, or conversely, simple enough to cover in 3-5 minutes. This is an estimate. Some displays may take much longer to deal with, and others much less time.

The steps necessary to produce an ISG are as follows:

- Identify the behavioral objectives for the lesson.
- Create a detailed outline of topics that relate to each objective.
- For narrative sections, identify the key words.
- Use geometric shapes to show relationships or visuals to assist the learner in understanding each section.

- Create word pictures for the narrative sections by leaving blanks in the narrative where students will fill in the key words.
- Sequence the displays in the order that they will be presented or that they will be discussed.
- Develop subdisplays for topics that have more than one visual or word picture.
- Produce the ISG using proper graphic design principles.

The production of the ISG requires considerable planning. Once it is developed, the distance education course is considerably easier for the instructor to prepare for and to teach, and is more organized and easier for learners to follow, especially those in distance education courses where live, two-way interactive instruction is not available.

GRAPHIC DESIGN PRINCIPLES

Interactive study guides are often used as the basis for graphics in distance education courses. For this reason it is important to design ISGs to conform to appropriate graphic design principles. The size, font, color and contrast, alignment, and use of uppercase and lowercase in written graphics are critical to successful design (Zelanski & Fisher, 2010).

- *Size.*   Letter size is very closely related to legibility. Large, bold lettering is easier to see and read than is smaller lettering. Certainly lettering should not be smaller than 24 point (1/3 inch), and 32 to 36 point is preferable, especially if computer output is to be displayed on regular television monitors (Figure 8–3). Five words per line and five lines per page are a maximum for an ISG display or a screen of television information.
- *Font.*   Sans serif fonts should be used instead of fonts with serifs, the thin extensions to letters often used in textbooks and printed documents. Serifs often are too fine for display. Bold fonts with thick stems display the best. Also, the same fonts should be used throughout a presentation, and no more than three different fonts should be used for any single display. Two font types work the best, when one is used for one category of information and the second is used for background or secondary information, for example. Fancy typefaces and italics should be avoided unless there is an overriding reason for using them.
- *Color and Contrast.*   Color is often misused online presentations. Colors should be bold and simple and should not be overdone. Some combinations, such as green and red, do not work well together. Avoid saturated colors like red. Use dark letters with a light background, or vice versa. Many instructors like to use bright colors on a black background for displaying computer screens of information. This approach produces very readable displays.
- *Alignment.*   Centering text for video display is not as effective as aligning text to the left. Left-justified text seems to be most legible. (Review the list of single concept videos listed in the Preface to learn more about composing a video/monitor for effective viewing, especially the video dealing with the "rule of thirds.")
- *Capitalization.*   The literature on readability is quite clear that uppercase and lowercase lettering, rather than all uppercase or all lowercase, reads the best.

FIGURE 8–3   The type must be large enough to be easy to read.

	Univers Bold Caps	Univers Bold Caps and Lowercase
9 point	**LEGIBILITY**	**Legibility**
12 point	**LEGIBILITY**	**Legibility**
14 point	**LEGIBILITY**	**Legibility**
18 point	**LEGIBILITY**	**Legibility**
24 point	**LEGIBILITY**	**Legibility**
36 point	**LEGIBILITY**	**Legibility**
48 point	**LEGIBILITY**	**Legibility**
72 point	**LEGIBILITY**	**Legibility**

Elements of Design

Literate, effective visuals for display as part of ISGs or for instructor-led presentations can be developed by applying the elements and principles of design. The elements of design (Figure 8–4) are line, shape, space, texture, value, and color.

▪ *Line* is generally considered to be one-dimensional. Line has length but not width. Line portrays direction, presents objects, and defines the outer shape of something.
▪ *Shape* is used to symbolize objects or to show large or small spaces. Shapes have two dimensions, height and width.
▪ *Space* is either positive or negative. The outline of an object in a visual signifies its positive space. The most common negative shape of something is its background.
▪ *Texture* is the perceived or actual roughness or smoothness of a surface. Texture is used to help define shape or space.

FIGURE 8–4 Elements of design.

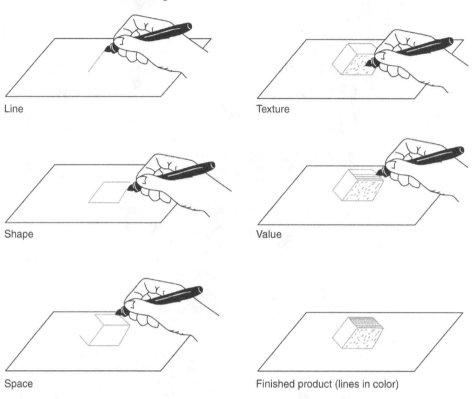

Line

Texture

Shape

Value

Space

Finished product (lines in color)

- *Value* is the degree of lightness or darkness of a surface. Value is accomplished through shading. Value shows changes in space, and is often used to create the illusion of volume or solidity in a graphic object.
- *Color* is related to value and is used to visualize an object realistically or to differentiate an object from another object. Colors have hue, value, and intensity. *Hue* describes a specific color, such as red, green, or blue. Value is the lightness or darkness of a color. Yellow has the highest value. *Intensity* is the strength of a color, such as bright yellow or dull red. Intensity is determined by the purity of a color.

Principles of Design

The elements of design are combined according to the guidelines provided by the principles of design. There are six principles: balance, center of interest, emphasis, unity, contrast, and rhythm (Graer, 2006; Ocepek, 2003, Simonson & Volker, 1984).

- *Balance* is the sense of equilibrium in a visual. The two kinds of balance are formal and informal (Figure 8–5). Generally, a visual should be balanced left to right and top to bottom. Formal balance means that objects of equal size and importance are placed at equivalent distances from the center of the visual (Figure 8–6). Informally balanced visuals are often more interesting to create and to view. Careful planning is important when informally balanced graphics are created. Several small images can be used to bal-

FIGURE 8–5   Formal and informal balance.

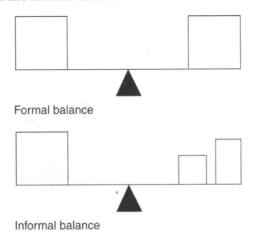

FIGURE 8–6   Formally balanced display.

ance one large object, or words can be used to balance pictures (Figure 8–7). Small, brightly colored objects will balance larger, duller items.

- The *center of interest* is the visual focal point of the graphic and should relate to its purpose. Historically, well-designed visuals did not place the center of interest at the center of the picture. Since most online instruction is viewed on high resolution/high definition monitors it is a good idea to apply the rule of thirds to locate important content—divide the display into thirds horizontally and vertically and place key information along these lines with the intersections of the lines the best places to locate the center of interest. The upper left point of intersection is usually the best place for the center of interest for a graphic involving objects or people.

- *Emphasis* is closely related to the center of interest. The key object should be emphasized so it is apparent to the viewer what is most important (Figure 8–8). There are several ways to emphasize the key element in a graphic, including the following:

FIGURE 8–7   Informally balanced display.

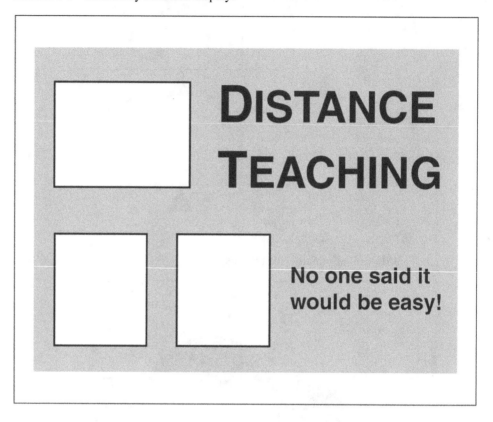

FIGURE 8–8   Rule of thirds, center of interest and how people look at images.

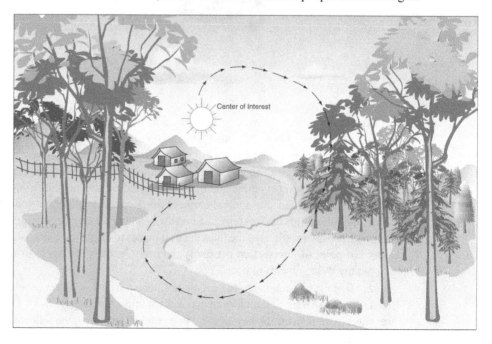

1. Use pointers, such as arrows.
2. Use color to emphasize.
3. Use large objects at the center of interest.
4. Use different shapes for the center of interest.
5. Use more elements of design to create the center of interest for a graphic and fewer for less important elements.

■ *Unity* means that a visual holds together to convey its purpose (Figure 8–9). If several graphics are used as part of a display, they should all convey or pertain to one meaning. Overlapping is a simple technique for promoting unity. Trees overlap buildings and each other. Houses overlap shrubs and people. A single background also promotes a feeling of unity. Another technique to promote the concept of unity is to place an outline or border around the elements of a display. Repetition of shapes, forms, and objects also can promote unity.

■ *Contrast* refers to the characteristics of an object that cause it to stand out (Figure 8–10). Contrast is closely related to emphasis. Most often, contrast is achieved by the use of light- or dark-valued objects. Shapes, forms, and textures can be used to create contrasts and make one object stand out while others seem to recede.

■ *Rhythm* comes from repetition through variety and is used to draw a viewer through the various objects in a visual (Figure 8–11). A row of houses in a display can present a sense of rhythm. The rhythm of a graphic helps tell the story of the picture by leading the viewer's eyes.

An effective graphic should provide visual information related to the topic being learned. The elements of design combined according to the principles of design can assist the distance educator in the development of effective ISGs and handouts that visually explain ideas and that facilitate understanding.

FIGURE 8–9   Emphasis has to do with making the key item stand out.

Arrows or pointers are effective.

A contrasting value can emphasize an area.

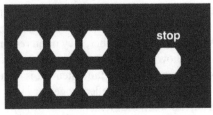

The placement of an item can cause it to be emphasized.

Size can be used.

FIGURE 8–10 Unity involves "oneness" or a tying together of ideas.

A "border" can be used to achieve unity.

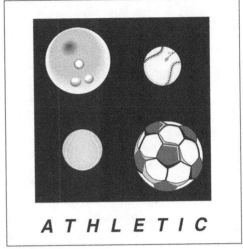

Another technique is to use lines to unify.

Perhaps the most effective method is to overlap a common shape.

FIGURE 8–11 The important part of a display can be made to stand out (contrast) mainly through the use of color, size, value, and shape.

When light and dark values are used, contrast results.

Differences in size can create contrast.

WORD PICTURES

A word picture is a graphic representation of concepts, principles, and information. Each concept, principle, or item of information usually contains key words that can be shown in nodes. A node is a symbol that contains words or stands alone to represent some idea. A node is the central point around which subnodes originate (Cyrs, 1997). The best word picture is a visual mnemonic that helps the learner remember the concept, principle, or item.

Word pictures do not need to be self-explanatory. Rather, they often require additional verbal information. Key words are usually shown in the nodes. Key words are the most significant words in a statement that provide clues to the idea the statement is communicating. Word pictures are graphic organizers that put elements of ideas together in a visual way so the learner can understand the relationship between the elements.

Cyrs does an excellent job of explaining how word pictures differ from other ways of organizing information. Cyrs (1997) says the following about effective word pictures:

1. Emphasis should be placed on the types of symbols used.
2. They should cover chunks of information rather than entire documents.
3. Student attention can be maintained through the use of fill-ins.
4. They emphasize the logical sequence of the class presentation.
5. They provide a complete review of the class content.
6. They can also be used for display by overhead video cameras.
7. They are inexpensive to produce and duplicate.
8. They condense ideas into a few key words.
9. They should be designed to fit the format of television.
10. They apply principles of graphic design.
11. They emphasize communication via the visual sense.
12. They require the instructor to think visually rather than verbally.

Cyrs (1997) discusses various graphic organizers that can be incorporated into word pictures: semantic maps, mind maps, cognitive maps, structured overviews, outlines, patterned note taking, webbing, pyramiding, and information mapping.

- *Semantic maps* are two-dimensional diagrams that use arrangements of nodes and links to communicate ideas and to show the relationships among ideas. Semantic maps use primarily two structures—top down and bottom up (Johnson & Peterson, 1984).
- *Mind maps* use key words or phrases organized in a design that is nonlinear. Mind maps are based on the idea that individuals mentally organize information in a variety of structures, not just top down or bottom up. Rather, mind maps usually start at the center of a page and branch out as individual ideas are presented. Mind maps have the following characteristics (Buzan, 1982):

  1. The main ideas are clearly defined and placed in the center of the graphic.
  2. The relative importance of a subidea is indicated by its proximity to the main idea.
  3. Links between ideas are clearly indicated.
  4. New information is easily added to a mind map because of its nonlinear structure.

- *Cognitive maps* (Diekhoff & Diekhoff, 1982) are organized around the relationship between ideas, and they provide a graphic expression of the structure of a body of knowledge. Many confuse cognitive maps and mind maps. Cognitive maps are more structured and organized than mind maps and are usually developed by the instructor of a class.
- *Structured overviews* use graphics and hierarchical structures showing the relationship of key ideas, concepts, and other information (Figure 8–12). Structured overviews are commonly used for readings or lectures. Austin and Dean-Guilford (1981) define the structured overview as a conceptualized visual-hierarchical type of diagram used to show concept interrelationships within written material.
- *Outlines* are visual displays that are useful in presenting concurrent ideas. Outlines are largely verbal but use visual elements to present clusters of ideas in one display.
- *Patterned note taking* (Norton, 1981) is related to mind mapping. A key word or phrase is placed in the center of a space, and arrows and lines radiate out to subideas. Key words and phrases are used extensively. Lines are used to show relationships.
- *Webbing* is a graphic representation similar to other techniques discussed here. The main idea is at the center, and subordinate ideas radiate out like the spokes of a wheel. Webbing resembles semantic maps.

FIGURE 8–12   Rhythm results when an element is repeated in some systematic manner.

FIGURE 8–13   Word picture: structural overview.

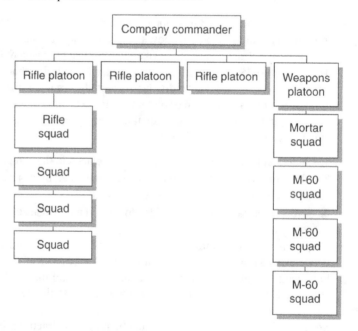

- ▪ *Pyramiding* shows the levels of ideas in a graphic way using a bottom-to-top model (Figure 8–13). Information is grouped according to a hierarchy, such as details at the bottom, concepts in the middle, and principles at the top.
- ▪ *Information mapping* is a method of bringing together current research into a comprehensive materials development and presentation approach. Maps are arranged hierarchically into blocks of information. Each block serves a separate purpose, but all relate to some central theme or idea.

Cyrs (1997) provides an excellent list of organizational patterns for distance education classes. The strategies listed by Cyrs are wonderful starting points for those beginning to develop a personal approach to distance teaching. Several of the most useful approaches are as follows:

1. *Problem Solution.* In this situation, students are presented with a real or contrived problem with elements provided about the situation that caused or have an impact on the problem. Students are then asked, often in online collaborative groups, to make observations about the situation and then propose alternative solutions, including the consequences of each alternative. One effective technique for dramatizing the problem is to use *trigger films/videos,* which are short (2 to 4 minutes) scenarios dealing with the events that produced the problem. Students are then asked to respond to the problem. The film/video "triggers" a response. For example, a trigger film might dramatize a family in financial crisis with a stack of bills that are due at the end of the month. After watching the scenario unfold, financial counseling students would be required to work online in small groups to develop a proposed solution to the situation depicted.

2. *Time Sequence.* This presentation involves organizing information in a list or sequence of events that unfold chronologically. The sequence can be presented by the instructor, or the elements of the sequence can be presented visually and students can be asked to help order the elements and then explain the rationale for their decision. Examples of time sequences include editing video, completing a tax return, building a doghouse, and baking a cake (Hurbais-Cherrier, 2018).

3. *Definitions.* When a presentation is based on definitions, there is usually a statement of the concept to be defined; a listing of its attributes; and examples of how the term, phrase, or item is used. For example, terms in a chemistry laboratory exercise might first be defined by the instructor before students work together to complete the sequence of activities involved in the laboratory experience. Definitions lend themselves particularly well to sequential ISGs. Also review the list of single concept videos (podcasts) listed in the Preface.

4. *Cause and Effect.* In this approach an event and its causes or antecedents are presented (Figure 8–14). For example, the heavy rains in California would be discussed and would be followed by an exploration of why the rains occurred, such as the influence of El Niño water in the central Pacific Ocean. Actual or historic meteorological records could be used, as could weather reports in California newspapers.

VISUAL ANALOGIES

An analogy is a way to describe something that is unfamiliar by comparing it to something familiar. The two things that are being compared seem to be different but have some similarities. Analogies help improve thinking and help learners understand new ideas by giving insights and by allowing new relationships to be explained.

According to Cyrs (1997), analogies have four parts (Figure 8–15): the new subject, the analog, the connector between the analog and the new subject, and the ground.

The *new subject* is the topic that is unfamiliar. The analogy is designed to help provide understanding of the new subject. Subjects normally are described by only a few words. The *analog* is familiar and is something that has been experienced by the learner. It is crucial that the learner knows the analog—the previously understood idea or concept. The *connector* shows the relationship between the two concepts: the new subject and the familiar

FIGURE 8–14   Word picture: Pyramiding—Bloom's taxonomy of the cognitive domain.

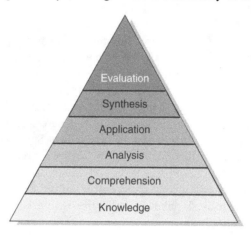

FIGURE 8–15   Word picture: Cause and effect—water cycle.

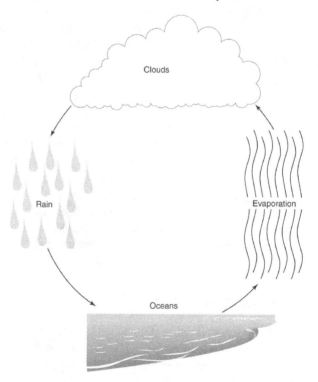

idea, or analog. The connector is the critical element in the analogy and demonstrates the creativity of the author of the analogy. Connectors can be structural or functional.

■ *Structural* relationships show the similarity in appearance and design of the two concepts. Examples of structural relationships include: (a) Sharon is as creative as Leonardo da Vinci; (b) Norman is as soft as a marshmallow; (c) Raindrops looked like balloons.

▪ *Functional* relationships describe what concepts do or how they work. Functional relationships show not only what the subject and the analog have in common but also what they do that is similar.

Connectors that often are used include the following:

tastes like …
resembles …
is comparable to …
feels like …
looks like …
is related to …
is like …

The *ground* relates to the specific set of similarities and differences between the unfamiliar and the familiar. The ground can be verbal or visual, but the more concrete the ground, the more hints it provides and the more likely it will be that the analogy will work. Pictures are often used to help make the analogy realistic (Figure 8–16). Some examples of a ground include these:

▪ Football is like war—it requires strategy, tactics, planning, and trained individuals.
▪ Live, distance teaching is like singing and playing the piano at the same time. It requires simultaneous verbal skills and physical dexterity.
▪ Media are like delivery trucks, since media carry ideas.

When constructing visual analogies one should follow five steps. First, identify clearly what the new subject is, the idea that is not clearly known. Second, identify the appropriate connector, such as "… is like …" or "… is similar to …." Third, identify the known analog—the familiar concept or thing that can be compared to the new idea. Fourth, provide a ground for the comparison of the new and familiar ideas. Describe the similarities and differences between the ideas. Finally, develop a visual way to demonstrate the analogy and provide learners with a visual mnemonic to help them remember the relationship and understand the new subject.

Analogies are difficult to develop. When a good analogy is identified, especially a visual one, it can be the center of an elegant discussion of instructional content. Naturally, the visual analogy should be incorporated as a word picture for an ISG.

FIGURE 8–16 Components of an analogy.

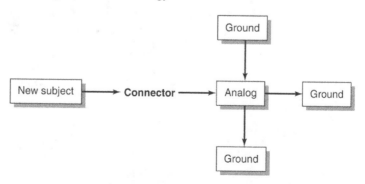

FIGURE 8–17   Example: A visual analogy.

Media are like delivery trucks. They permit the delivery of
ideas to learners.

FIGURE 8–18   Speaking of distance education, this is a graphic display attached to the
Pioneer 10 spacecraft that is hurtling into space. The designers of this display wanted to
convey three ideas to whomever or whatever might find it thousands of years from now:
(1) where the spacecraft came from: the Earth; (2) who inhabited the Earth: men and
women; and (3) that men and women are friendly.

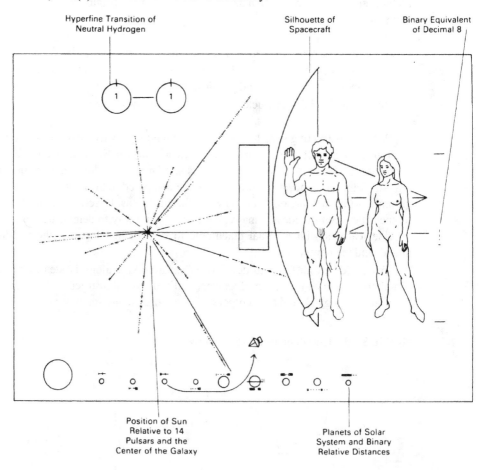

WHAT ABOUT THE FLIPPED CLASSROOM?

Flipping a classroom supposedly refers to recording a class lecture so students watch and listen at home to free up time in the classroom for discussions. What a popular idea (a silly one, too)—teachers have always assigned homework, and then used class time instructor for explanation, review, amplification, and questions.

Of course some instructors still lecture? And, lecturing is okay, probably more so for traditional teachers than for distance educators. Today, it would be unheard of for a distance teacher to have a 50-minute presentation with little or no student interaction, yet flipped classroom advocates seem to promote recording lectures.

The next old idea with a new level of popularity is the single concept lesson—in this case this approach, although classic, is a great one. Single concept teaching is a product of the mastery learning movement of the 1960s and 70s, and is a technique of teaching that uses the single concept as the building block of instruction. Generally a single concept lesson is a relatively short 3–5 minute mediated presentation of an idea with a clear introduction, body, and conclusion.

The epitome of the single concept lesson of the mastery learning generation was the film loop, a 3–4 minute motion picture showing a key idea such as mitosis in biology or the definition of median in statistics. Today, Youtube and Vimeo are loaded with single concept lessons. When single concept lessons are part of a series and can be distributed or pushed to interested viewers as a series they are called podcasts.

One commonality between classroom flipping and single concept teaching is the use of motion media. Film the classic motion medium has inherent disadvantages – cost, training, distribution, duplication, and equipment—all which have become irrelevant in the day of smart phones, free editing software, easy to use storage locations, and digital media.

Thus, it is possible to take the best of these ideas—flipping course content by using short motion media presentations, and organizing the media into a series of related and often sequential single concept lessons. The Unit-Module-Topic approach to course organization provides structure to this approach. The building block of instruction is the single concept—or single topic. Topics/concepts are organized into modules which in turn are collected into course units.

Certainly it is a good idea to use short, "one idea" videos as homework, either created locally or found online. When course content is partially delivered by digital media then regular and substantive interaction can be made available in chats, threaded discussions, and synchronous videoconferences.

Flipping and single concepts— best practices for the distance educator.

And finally, remember back to that great teacher from high school or college—they probably identified key ideas and visualized them in images, even words, organized sequentially. The approaches have not changed as much as the tools.

SUMMARY

Printed handouts and teaching and learning materials are critically important to the effective practice of distance education. First, the course syllabus is the "glue" that holds the course or the learning experience together. Sometimes the syllabus is expanded into the course study guide, which is a document that provides the student with a level of orientation to the distance education experience. Second, the interactive study guide (ISG) is a very important tool that provides the distant learner with a logical sequence for the lesson. The ISG is especially important when the student and instructor communicate asynchronously or when fully interactive two-way instruction is not used.

Interactive study guides are made up of two ingredients—the display and the notes section. The display is made up of a series of word pictures, which are visuals and words that involve student interaction and that attempt to provide the learner with ways to remember the key ideas that are to be learned. In essence, the word pictures are visual mnemonics to help learners remember things. Naturally, for visuals to be meaningful and instructional they need to be designed effectively. The guidelines for effective visual design should be followed.

Finally, printed materials are critical to the practice of distance education (Figure 8–17). Documents provide background information, amplify concepts, and give a sense of direction to instructional events. Printed materials are an important component of the distance education program.

DISCUSSION QUESTIONS

1. Define *visual analogy*. Why are analogies important?
2. Develop a visual mnemonic or word picture for these concepts:
    - Technology as productivity enhancer
    - Pythagorean theorem
    - Definition of distance education
3. Write an analogy for these ideas:
    - Teaching
    - Golf
    - Learning
    - A pet dog
4. Why are interactive study guides are important to the distance educator?

REFERENCES

Austin, R., & Dean-Guilford, M. (1981). *Crashing content reading problems with reading strategies.* Paper presented at the meeting of the Western College Reading Association, Dallas, TX. (ERIC Document Reproduction Service No. ED204703)

Buzan, T. (1982). *Use your head.* London, England: British Broadcasting Corporation.

Cyrs, T. (1997). *Teaching at a distance.* Las Cruces, NM: Center for Educational Development.

Diekhoff, G., & Diekhoff, K. (1982). Cognitive maps as a tool in communicating structural knowledge. *Educational Technology, 22,* 28–30.

Graer, M. (2006). *Inside/outside: From the basics to the practice of design* (2nd ed.). Berkeley, CA: Peachpit Press.

Hurbis-Cherrier, M. (2018). *Voice & vision: A creative approach to narrative filmmaking.* New York, NY: Routledge.

Johnson, D., & Peterson, D. (1984). *Teaching reading vocabulary* (2nd ed.). New York, NY: Holt.

Norton, L. (1981). Patterned note-taking: An evaluation. *Visible Language, 15,* 67–85.

Ocepek, L. (2003). *Graphic design: Vision, process, product.* Upper Saddle River, NJ: Merrill/Prentice Hall.

Pastore, M. (2010). *50 benefits of ebooks.* Ithaca, NY: Zorba Press

Simonson, M., & Volker, R. (1984). *Media planning and production.* Columbus, OH: Merrill Stuart, D. (2004). A picture is worth a thousand megs: Developing music-listening skills by using technology to engage the senses. *Distance Learning, 1*(6), 15–20.

Zelanski, P., & Fisher, M. (2010). *The art of seeing* (8th ed.). Upper Saddle River, NJ: Pearson.

Assessment for Distance Education

INTRODUCTION

If we compressed the instructional design process to a few essential steps, it could be contained within three questions:

1. What will students be able to do as a result of this instruction?
2. How might students demonstrate their progress toward (or mastery of) those goals?
3. What activities could they engage in to advance toward those goals?

The course designer's role, then, is to establish appropriate learning conditions in response to the answers and for this chapter the focus will be on Question 2. Once we have identified what constitutes proficiency (Question 1), we can then consider how to measure student progress toward it, the kind of feedback and guidance we will provide to help them get there, and the evidence of learning that will result from a demonstration of their newly acquired skills. This chapter will address the role of and purposes for assessment, characteristics and types of effective assessments, strategies for creating and implementing assessment activities, deterring cheating and plagiarism, and trends in the assessment arena.

Although the chapter focuses on assessment in distance education, much of the discussion is not exclusive to distance education. Just as exemplary "distance teaching" closely resembles our best models of face-to-face teaching, assessing student achievement has a core of good practice that remains constant across a multitude of teaching-learning configurations. In addition, although many of the examples provided will refer to institutionally based (formal) education, most of the key ideas, strategies, and design consideration could also be applied in a workplace training program, technical certification course, or professional development workshop. Note that although the terms *assessment* and *evaluation* are sometimes used synonymously by other authors, in this text they are treated as activities with distinctly different purposes. This chapter is focused on the assessment of student learning.

PURPOSES FOR ASSESSMENT

In this text, assessment is defined as the process of measuring, documenting, and interpreting behaviors that demonstrate learning. Notice that we have referred to "behaviors" rather than presuming to measure learning directly. The best evidence of learning is found in learner behavior and will likely remain so until cognitive scientists discover a reliable way to determine what knowledge and skills we carry around between our ears just by looking there. So, once we have measured, documented, and interpreted, what can we do with that information? A few of the administrative purposes of assessment results include program evaluation and improvement, justification for funding priorities, identifying and reporting of long-term trends, and providing evidence of productivity and outcomes achievement in academic programs. In a distance education environment, assessment outcomes may sometimes be used to compare the academic performance of remotely-located students with the performance of learners in a more traditional (i.e., face-to-face) classroom. Although not a particularly helpful comparison (we know that even if we could control potentially confounding variables, the results would very likely show "no significant difference" between the groups), it is sometimes necessary to demonstrate the validity of unfamiliar course structures or instructional strategies. Finally, the use of assessment results, together with other educational data sets, to guide decision-making has become somewhat less complicated in recent years and can be especially useful for distance education programs. The use and role of what is now referred to as learning analytics is discussed in greater detail in Chapter 11.

Possibly the most important purpose for assessing learning gains is to provide feedback to learners and instructors. Students gain a sense of control and can take on greater responsibility for their own learning if they know how well they are doing compared with an established set of criteria. Feedback from frequent assessments, informal or otherwise, provides that scale. When students encounter an assessment activity, they not only recall the needed concepts or skills, they also reinforce them through application. This is especially important if course content is highly sequential or hierarchical in nature. Frequent assessments help learners to identify the important points within a course module, while practicing the skills necessary to advance through subsequent material. An instructor, armed with assessment data, can determine if a student needs additional assistance and can provide remediation or coaching. At the same time, this feedback helps the instructor to monitor the effectiveness of the instruction. Many learners struggling with the same concept or skill might signal an instructional design problem. By using assessments carefully, the teacher can identify and address weaknesses or gaps in the instruction.

Assessment activities presented throughout a course or training module can be useful for identifying errors in reasoning and memory that could present obstacles to further progress. Research related to such misconceptions (sometimes referred to as naïve conceptions) suggests that these inaccurate cognitive constructions are frequently stable, persistent, and potentially difficult to dislodge (Hare & Graber, 2007). By incorporating assessments throughout a learning module, especially those that are specifically intended to induce cognitive dissonance in learners holding such misconceptions, errors are more quickly detected and resolved. Waiting until midterm exams to gather feedback about learner understanding, for example, increases the likelihood that misinterpretations of important course content will be solidly embedded and stubbornly resistant to change.

Assessing a learner's readiness to begin an instructional unit can be particularly important in a skills-training environment. Time, effort, and money can be wasted if students do not have important entry-level abilities or if, conversely, they have already mastered many of the desired outcomes. By designing effective entry-level tests (to determine readiness) and pretests (to determine placement), workforce training becomes more efficient and reduces time spent by employees in activities that are either too advanced or an unnecessary review of previously learned material.

Assessments often function as a motivational activity. Most learners want to do well and knowing that they will be held accountable for a body of knowledge or set of skills can be the nudge that keeps them on track. In the distance learning environment an instructor might choose to incorporate frequent discussions, quizzes, or other "small teaching" activities to serve this function. Additionally, in countries such as the United States, where competitive activities (in school and out) constitute a large part of the culture, testing is often seen as an opportunity to pit one's abilities against those of others, while hoping to excel (or at least measure up). Competitive games are a frequently used assessment technique that can motivate, provide opportunities for teamwork, and reinforce important concepts or skills.

For many educators, as well as students, the first purpose for assessment that comes to mind is to enable the instructor to assign grades or sign off on certification/licensure at the end of a course, unit, or lesson. Grades, in and of themselves, provide limited information about learning and although they can be important and may prove helpful in determining how to improve the instruction for future students, there are more direct ways of applying assessment techniques for enhancing teaching and learning before a course or learning module ends.

ASSESSMENT AND INSTRUCTIONAL DESIGN

The role of assessment in the instructional design process is as a corollary to the development of learning objectives, and a precedent to the development and implementation of instructional strategies. In this way, the assessment activities are matched to expectations and instruction is then based on assessment plans. A less formal way of expressing this is: Figure out what learners should get out of the instruction, determine how you will know if they were successful, and then decide what they should do to reach that point. In this manner, "teaching to the test" becomes a desirable basis for instruction because the test (in whatever form it takes) is a measurement of what is considered important.

Unfortunately, this ideal is not always realized and assessments are frequently created after the instruction is planned and often after it has been implemented. This does not preclude the use of objectives as a basis for determining progress, but care must be taken to ensure that the instruction has also been based on the same expectations and has not wandered from the original goals. If students prepare for an examination thinking, "What's going to be on this test?" or face a major project wondering what is expected of them, those questions may indicate that the objectives have been forgotten along the way. Those desired outcomes must act as a continuous thread that binds the instructional process together from beginning to end.

Formative and Summative Assessment

When developing a course, unit, or module, assessment activities can (and should) be incorporated throughout the design. These activities can be categorized as formative or summative and they have different roles in the teaching and learning process. Many instructional designers use a broadly inclusive definition of formative assessment that includes any curricular activity offering the opportunity to practice new skills and get feedback on one's performance. This feedback is a requisite component of formative activities and it allows learners to refine (i.e., "form") their efforts toward accomplishing the goal while, at the same time, teachers can use the results of formative assessments to provide customized assistance when needed. Formative data can also help guide course revisions if, for example, many students misunderstand a task or score badly on one specific concept.

Many instructional activities that fall into the formative assessment realm could also be categorized as *assessment for learning.* Through this lens, such activities resemble what we might think of as teaching strategies or learning experiences and they play that role in the instructional design process. Proponents of the assessment for learning philosophy focus on the active engagement of learners, including the extensive use of self-assessments designed to build a sense of ownership and responsibility within students regarding their learning (Heritage, 2018; Panadero, Brown, & Strijbos, 2016.) This awareness and control of one's own thinking, typically referred to as metacognition, enables students to evolve into autonomous learners and develop skills of self-regulation.

Distance education students who are returning to formal education after a break derive great benefit from the use of ongoing, formative assessment. Ongoing (sometimes called embedded) assessment activities are woven into the fabric of the instructional process so that determining student progress does not necessarily represent to students a threat, a disciplinary function, or a necessary evil, but simply occurs as another thread within the seamless pattern of day-to-day classroom or training events. One advantage of this approach is that any misconceptions held by learners that might interfere with later progress are identified and addressed before they become obstacles to further learning. The American Association for Higher Education encourages this in its classic work, "9 Principles of Good Practice for Assessing Student Learning" (1996), going on to state, "The point is to monitor progress toward intended goals in a spirit of continuous improvement." A natural advantage for the instructor is that the dreaded "crunch" of grading that presents itself when assessments occur in large blocks is avoided; ongoing assessment provides information on student progress in smaller increments over the course of a unit, training module, or academic semester.

Summative assessments are final-outcomes-focused and emphasize the learner's accomplishments or skills at the end of a course or module. Here the emphasis is not on feedback intended to guide progress toward the goal, although student performance data may prove helpful in the long term for self-monitoring and instructional improvement. Standardized, non-course-related exams such as the ACT, GRE, or GMAT fall into this category, as well, because they provide a snapshot of knowledge and skills from which the only feedback is a numeric score and possibly percentile rank. Summative assessments are typically intended for administrative purposes such as assigning grades, reporting the success or failure of specific programs, awarding a certificate or license, or compiling evidence of program quality for accreditation purposes. By definition, summative assessments are almost always comprehensive, measuring the mastery of a specified body of knowledge or completed curricular unit.

Although summative assessments can be beneficial when used appropriately, the misuse of standardized tests (especially in the K–12 arena) has contributed to an overall distrust of how test scores are used, a lack of confidence in their objectivity, and doubt that such exams can actually measure anything of importance. Research suggests that these high-stakes assessments can be demotivating for many learners (Wass, Harland, McLean, Miller, & Nui Sim, 2015), leading to an increasingly large gap between high and low achievers, increased focus on extrinsic versus intrinsic rewards, and decreasing levels of persistence when tasks are perceived as difficult. Obviously, not all summative assessments result in such dire outcomes but the importance of administering and interpreting such tests carefully cannot be overemphasized.

There is a third category—diagnostic assessment—that is sometimes considered its own type of assessment. In this text, however, it has been subsumed into the other two. Diagnostic tests or other tasks may be used in a formative manner to adapt instruction based on learner needs or as a summative measurement to determine readiness for more advanced levels of learning, as in the case of the GRE test, for example. Because diagnostic assessments can be used in both ways, they have not been singled out as a separate category for the purposes of this text.

When designing assessment measures, their usefulness will depend primarily on a clear understanding of whether the resulting information is intended for formative or summative purposes. The assessment techniques used for each type may be quite similar; the distinction lies in how the resulting data are used.

The Affective Domain

Instructional design models are typically focused on the cognitive domain but assessing learner progress also involves an awareness of how our emotional or psychological responses can obscure a student's true abilities. In distance learning programs, where students may be presented with tasks and environments strikingly different from those with which they're familiar, course developers and instructors should recognize how the affective domain can threaten the reliability and validity of assessment results. Two areas in particular—motivation and anxiety—are especially important to understand and recognize.

The role of motivation and its influence on learning cannot be overemphasized and this is especially true for distance education programs that require at least some degree of learner autonomy. For example, when learners lack the confidence that they will be able to master course content, their motivation drops and they are less likely to persist in their efforts to grasp new material. Keller's ARCS-V model (of which "confidence" is the "C") suggests that reinforcing expectations for success, providing opportunities for success, and attributing success to effort and ability will enhance learner motivation (Keller, 2016). Expecting a successful outcome requires that students understand how they will be assessed and what performance criteria will be applied. Opportunities for success might include tasks that are challenging but doable, scheduled early in a course or module, at which learners will succeed if they honestly try. To prevent attribution of their success to luck or instructor bias, feedback offered about individual performance should be specific and clearly tied to the efforts of the learner. Reinforcing student confidence will allow later assessment activities to represent accurately student mastery of course content, by removing obstacles posed by low motivation and anxiety related to fear of failure.

The negative effects of anxiety on student performance have been long recognized, although little research has been done to study its influence on distant students. In early-Internet days, there was concern that the unfamiliarity of the online environment would confound test results, but in an interesting about-face, several studies have shown diminished anxiety for online test-takers over the in-class, pencil-and-paper variety (e.g., Stowell & Bennett, 2010, and Berg & Lu, 2014). Concurrently, there has been an increase in reports of students preferring the use of online exams when given a choice (e.g., Keremedchiev & Peneva, 2017, and Postal, 2015). There are several possible reasons for these results, including the attractiveness of taking an exam in a comfortable setting (e.g., at home) at a time of one's choosing, fewer stress-producing distractions compared to a crowded classroom, or the familiarity of using the computer for course-related activities. As testing applications and learning management systems continue to improve in reliability and interface design these effects are likely to persist if not increase.

Feedback

The overall benefits of feedback to students are well documented and a classic meta-analysis of factors influencing achievement identified feedback as more beneficial to learning than cognitive ability, socioeconomic factors, and class size, for example (Hattie & Timberley, 2007). So, clearly, it's important to provide feedback to learners, yet the nuances of what that feedback should consist of, and when and how it should be delivered are less obvious.

Generally speaking, good feedback is elaborative, balanced, and specific. Elaboration is the degree to which the comments are descriptive and constructive (Van der Kleji et al, 2015). Descriptive feedback goes beyond merely indicating that something is amiss but provides context for why a students' work is inaccurate, unsatisfactory, or simply not quite right. For example, "This timeline doesn't take into account the sub-plots of the novel" or "Although your proposed solution may be workable, it's not supported by the research you've cited." Constructive feedback provides guidance to help students improve their work by recommending helpful resources, referring to the assignment criteria, suggesting alternative perspectives, or posing questions about next steps, for example. Constructive commentary can range from simple hints to fully scaffolded plans for improvement.

Good feedback is also balanced; that is, it addresses strengths as well as weaknesses of the work. While it's easy to focus on areas needing improvement, it's also important to point out the positives and what, specifically, is good about the student's work-in-progress. Do not, however, couch remarks intended to point out errors in vague language ("Well, that's one way to look at it …") hoping to cushion the blow. These cryptic statements are unhelpful and unlikely to result in improved performance.

Feedback needs to be specific and focused on what's most important. General comments at the top of a paper (e.g., "Good job of addressing the issues") are fine but aren't likely to improve the student's next paper. Pointing out the actual instances where the student has "addressed the issues" and how that was done well provides reinforcement and guidance for future work. Specificity, however, is a balancing act between ambiguous commentary and overly controlling input; the first is confusing and the latter demotivating. In addition to being specific, feedback should mainly be given about the key outcomes for the assignment. That is, focus on content, organization, analysis, creativity, or problem-solving rather than spending valuable time pointing out every split infinitive.

Discussions of when feedback should be given often default to, "As soon as possible." However, recent research suggests that although students prefer immediate feedback, in some cases delayed feedback may lead to more learning (Brookhart, 2017; Mullet et al., 2014). Although counterintuitive, this effect appears to be especially important for more complex learning (higher order thinking), while the assessment of factual, declarative knowledge benefits from immediate feedback. Possible explanations for this include that more complex tasks trigger a sense of curiosity that promotes cognitive engagement during the delay and that the delay mimics spaced instruction.

In a distance learning environment, it can be helpful (and efficient) to rely on digital technologies to provide feedback. Text-based assignments can be annotated or commented on directly in the document and in most systems this can be done within the CMS, eliminating the need to download papers, mark them up, and reupload them. Audio comments are also helpful and students find them more satisfying than text-based feedback (Voelkel & Mello, 2014). In earlier versions of MS Word, audio commenting was included with the application, but as of Windows 10 that feature is no longer available. However, third-party apps can be downloaded to utilize this type of feedback for Word and pdf files. Audio or video comments can also be provided with the use of a screen-capture application, such as Screencast-O-Matic (https://screencast-o-matic.com/). In a distance learning environment, it may be useful to reinforce understanding by providing general feedback and review to the entire group in a videoconference setting during which students can ask questions. Individualized feedback can then be provided later.

Finally, although dozens of studies and essays suggest that students pay little attention to feedback (e.g., Crisp, 2007; Gooblar, 2015; Louden, 2017), this effect may be lessened if the feedback is elaborated, balanced, and specific; if the feedback is timed appropriately; or if it is provided in a manner students will attend to. It may also change if students are given the chance to revise and resubmit their work based on that feedback. If comments (even good ones) are provided that *could* lead to a better product, but students don't have an opportunity to apply them, it's no surprise that they go unread.

Assessment and Grading

Once a student assessment is scored or rated, the result may be reported in one of two ways. *Criterion-referenced* grading is used when the learner's performance is compared with that of a predetermined set of standards, drawn from the learning objectives, and is sometimes referred to as outcomes-based scoring. The rater asks, "Did the learner demonstrate mastery of the skills identified in the objectives?" The reported grade reflects the learner's level of expertise by specifying how closely the student's performance matches the ideal. *Norm-referenced* scoring uses the same outcomes but is intended to compare each student with others who have completed the same assessment (and who, theoretically at least, had the same preparation). Keep in mind that the student's raw score (e.g., getting 82 out of 100 questions correct) remains constant; it's the grade or other evaluative mark that differs between criterion- or norm-referenced approaches.

There are appropriate uses for each type of grading. If our goal is to represent how well a student has done relative to the desired outcomes, criterion-referenced grading is the best choice. Norm-referenced scoring, however, is typically used to report long-term trends and to indicate the relative position of a student's performance compared to many others (e.g., students taking the SAT exam), but should never be used to assign grades, award certification or licensure, or determine mastery of content. The term *grading on a curve* reflects this perspective and in this case the rater asks, "How well did this learner perform compared with others?" Grading on a curve tells the teacher and learner how well students did relative to one another but does not offer useful information about whether *any* of them mastered some or all of the content. Unfortunately, this means that a student's grade will depend not on how well they do, but on who else is in the course and those students' performances.

Finally, the topic of grade inflation has captured the attention of the popular media, although the relationship of assessment to grades has largely been ignored. The critical question, then, is, "If grades have gone up over time while actual learning has remained relatively stable, doesn't this indicate that grades, in fact, may not be particularly useful indicators of performance?" Until a reasonable substitute for grades comes along, formal education will continue to expect teachers to distill a complex range of learner abilities, attitudes, and experiences into a single letter. This may suffice for administrative or accountability reasons but offers relatively little useful information to improve teaching and learning over the long term, and for these purposes educators may look to what the assessment of learning gains offers, instead.

CHARACTERISTICS OF USEFUL ASSESSMENTS

As described in the previous section, assessment is one element of the teaching and learning process that evolves from the determination of desired performance outcomes. It follows, therefore, that one of the characteristics of a good assessment tool is that it matches the objectives; learners know what to expect because they have already been made aware of what is important and how they will be expected to demonstrate their mastery of this knowledge or skill. This characteristic is often referred to as *alignment*, indicating an acceptable degree of synchronicity among objectives, instructional activities, and assessment measures. The objectives, ideally, specify what the students will do to demonstrate their mastery of the content, how well they will be expected to perform this task, and under what special circumstances, if any, they should perform it. Objectives should match assessments both conceptually (are you assessing the same content addressed in the objective?) as well as cognitively (are the thinking skills described in the objectives required to complete the assessment successfully?). Occasionally, instructors will find that a test item or exercise they have created does not match the objectives, although they believe it to be an important skill or concept for learners to grasp. In this case, it makes sense to return to the list of objectives and consider the possibility that there are gaps or missing items. This is an excellent reason for creating assessment measures before implementing instruction. This alignment should also extend to matching the cognitive complexity of the assessments to the established outcomes. For example, if one of the outcomes states that students should be able to analyze a research article, that's what at least one of the assessments should require them to do.

An assessment may, on the surface, match the objectives but still not reflect the student's progress. This characteristic, the degree to which an assessment provides an accurate estimate of learning gains, is known as *validity*. If a learner who has mastered the specified body of knowledge does poorly on the test, exercise, or project intended to measure this mastery (or, conversely, if learners who have not mastered the material perform well), that assessment would be said to have low content validity. For example, test items intended to measure analogical reasoning may, instead, reflect the learner's reading ability if vocabulary level is not considered in test design. Or if a project is supposed to demonstrate the learner's ability to design process controls in a laboratory environment, but an unrealistic time limit for completion is imposed, this assessment may indicate that some learners have not mastered the concepts when in fact they simply were not given adequate time to demonstrate their expertise. Criterion-referenced validity, also called predictive validity, has significant implications for workforce training. If an employee successfully completes a series of training units on using a new software package but then cannot apply those skills on the job, the instrument that assessed his or her performance had low predictive validity. This is also important if the content being taught is part of a hierarchically organized series of learning modules in which foundational concepts or basic skills must be mastered before the learner moves on to more advanced tasks.

Reliability refers to the stability of an instrument or activity; this could be thought of as how consistently the assessment measures learning gains. If students perform poorly as a group on one occasion and then do much better later, the predictability of this assessment is called into question. Or if learner mastery is measured by observation and scored by several different raters, the scores must be highly correlated to ensure consistency (also known as interrater reliability). Low reliability signals that the results are not dependable and could vary significantly from day to day, rendering them potentially meaningless.

Assessment measures can be beautifully aligned, valid, reliable, and utterly useless if they are not also practical. Practicality [italicized] requires that we design assessment measures taking into consideration how long it will take students to complete an assignment, the resources available to accomplish it, how long it will take us to score it, and its usefulness as a learning and/or measurement activity. A helpful rule of thumb is that if the instructor can complete an assessment in one hour, plan on two-to-three hours for an average student completion time, although this can vary, of course, on the assignment itself and student readiness. If specialized resources are required, are they sufficient for the number of students and are they readily accessible to more than one student at a time? Countless instructors have bemoaned their short-sightedness after creating assignments only to find that the labor-intensity of reading them and providing meaningful feedback was about to send them to an early grave. A work-around here is to consider the use of peer evaluation and feedback—two techniques backed by years of research supporting their efficacy (see, e.g., Carless et al., 2011; Lu & Law, 2012; Nicol, Thomson, & Bresin, 2014). Finally, it's important to consider whether the information gained from the assessment is worth the time spent creating, completing, and scoring it. Several small, tightly-focused assessment activities may yield useful data more consistently than a cumulative midterm or final examination.

Finally, although there are other criteria for judging the merits of an assessment activity, all are meant to help answer the question, "Does this assessment activity measure learning gains and allow an accurate generalization of results beyond the immediate situation?" In other words, a useful assessment reflects the learner's progress and understanding, as well as the transferability of skills and knowledge. The obvious purpose of an assessment is to document the direct results of instruction, but if a student successfully performs a task in a learning environment but can't replicate it in a real-world setting, what's the point?

ASSESSMENT STRATEGIES

Much of this chapter's content could be applied to any instructional setting, whether online, face to face, or something in between. Likewise, this section will describe several types of assessment activities and their use in distance learning environments, but any of them could be used for face-to-face or hybrid instruction, as well. Only a handful of the many possible types of assessments will be discussed, focusing on those especially well-suited to distance education environments.

Online Quizzes and Tests

Online quizzes, using either a course management system or a dedicated testing application, offer numerous advantages over their pencil-and-paper counterparts. Quizzes can be set up to select questions randomly from a pool, display graphics or video with the question text, provide immediate feedback based on the learner's response, offer spell-checking, allow multiple retakes, and enter the quiz scores directly into an online gradebook, as just a few examples of available features. A variety of question formats are available, including multiple choice, short answer, numeric, and many others. Online quizzes are best used as formative, self-study activities that reinforce important ideas, provide feedback to learners, and motivate them to keep up with course readings. Online quizzes are especially well-suited to reinforce the acquisition of foundational knowledge (i.e., lower order thinking) that supports meaningful, higher-order learning outcomes.

Online testing tools may also be utilized for high-stakes assessments (final exams or licensure tests, for example), but are best administered in a proctored setting. For many distance education programs, hiring test proctors to monitor student exams provides a reasonable element of accountability to offset the unsecure nature of the online environment. Proctored testing centers typically require students to present identification prior to taking an exam and may also elect to install browser lock-down software to prevent printing or copying of the test questions, surfing the web, or interacting with others via e-mail or instant messaging. An additional advantage of integrating proctored assessments into instruction is that student performance levels in a proctored setting that are consistent with scores earned for work completed at a distance will help validate the assessment regimen and enhance credibility.

Asynchronous Communication

One of the most frequently used features in any course management system (CMS) is the asynchronous *discussion forum*. These flexible online utilities can be used for a wide variety of assessment activities. The most obvious approach is to have students respond to questions or discuss course material within the forum environment. Not surprisingly, when learners are given time to think about their responses, the contributions are apt to be more meaningful, on-topic, and well organized than those offered in a traditional classroom environment. Of course, as in all discussions, good questions are more likely to produce good answers. Questions that expect students simply to recall (or look up) the answers won't generate a true conversation and are better saved for quizzes.

One useful strategy is to post a thought-provoking question that encourages higher order thinking; after students respond to the prompt, have them to return to the forum and reply to one or several of their peers' messages. In many cases, students will read all of the messages posted to determine which ones they will respond to, with the ideal result being a discussion in which everyone gets to talk and everyone listens. Additionally, students will often return to the forum yet again to read the comments offered on their initial messages and respond to those posts. Many instructors find it helpful to establish a maximum length on posts (especially at the graduate level) to encourage focused, to-the-point responses and to increase the likelihood of posts being read by peers. Other ways of using the discussion forum include student debates (especially when using groups), student-moderated discussions with questions generated from readings, or using the forum as a repository for student to share their work (in progress or completed) with one another for peer review or support.

Blogs are sometimes used instead of, or in conjunction with, discussion boards in an online class. The advantage of a blog over a discussion is the ability to customize who "owns" the page, who can read it or comment on it, and when. For example, an instructor may choose to establish a blog that a small group can post messages in, but other students are able to read those messages and comment on them if they choose. There is also an affective component to the use of a blog that may provide additional motivation for students to share their ideas. As one instructor explained, "When students use the discussion board they see it as belonging to the entire class, and they're allowed to use it. But a blog seems more like it's *theirs*." This sense of ownership brings with it the responsibility to post meaningful commentary and to engage with other participants who may elect to comment on the blogger's postings.

As an assessment tool, a blog can be used much like a discussion board, with students responding to prompts, posing their own questions, summarizing reading assignments, and so on. Blogs may be part of an integrated course management system or they may be established as free-standing utilities. Although open-access blog tools can be used (i.e., those freely available through providers like Blogger.com), instructors should check with their institution's information security personnel to verify that the application will not compromise student data or pose other unanticipated risks. It's also a good idea to confirm, as well, that there are no institutional policies restricting the use of such third-party applications.

Another asynchronous communication tool especially useful for distant students is a *wiki,* which (like a blog) may be part of a CMS, or function as a stand-alone utility. These online environments allow groups of students to collaborate online, incorporating text, graphics, and other digital materials into a cohesive product. The wiki site (depending upon the software used) can be visible to only a few group members, to anyone in the course, or visible only to members initially, then later made available to others. Permissions for editing and commenting can also be assigned to specific individuals or left open to anyone who's interested. Every version of the site is retained, typically, so if a student inadvertently deletes something important it can be retrieved or if a user determines that an earlier incarnation of the work is preferred, that version can easily be restored.

Using a wiki as an assessment tool has distinct advantages over traditional group work. With the appropriate settings established, the instructor can see which group member made which contributions or edits to the most recent version of the site, thus alleviating one of the major headaches related to student collaboration. Additionally, because all group members can edit the site, students get practice with important teamwork skills like negotiation and consensus-building.

Instructors working with students engaged in field work such as clinicals, student teaching, or internships find *online journals* useful for keeping track of student progress. Journals are usually configured to allow only the teacher or tutor to read the postings and are especially appropriate for assignments or tasks requiring student reflection or activities that occur over an extended period. As with a discussion forum, the instructor will probably need to require students to make regular posts to their journals but it should quickly become a habit. Assigning journal writing provides the distance education teacher an opportunity to model an honest and direct communication style, offer meaningful guidance, and provide sincere and constructive feedback when working with students. Care must be taken, however to ensure that journal topics and assignments are clearly course related and that interactions are never allowed to stray into the realm of confession or counseling.

Synchronous Communication

Communication tools such as desktop videoconferencing, audioconferencing, chat, or instant messaging provide a real-time dynamic for assessment that can offer instructors an immediate sense of how well students grasp the course content. This is especially helpful when specific course objectives require students to apply newly learned skills and content extemporaneously. For example, the ability to speak a foreign language fluently is most appropriately assessed in a real-time, audio- or video-based interaction. Similarly, learners hoping to become successful customer service representatives may be expected to reply immediately (orally or with text-based messaging) to various "unhappy client" scenarios, without the luxury of time to ponder the many possible responses.

Synchronous tools can be used for groups or one-to-one sessions between the instructor and a student, with students calling or logging in individually to a conference site or chat room. Instant messaging also works well for individual interactions and has the added advantage of allowing several simultaneous conversations to occur, each a private exchange between the teacher and one student. Such one-to-one sessions might be used for "oral exam" types of assessments, or to mimic a private office hours appointment. Synchronous communication tools also facilitate the use of student presentations as an assessment option, during which a group of individuals need only log in to view and comment on their peers' speech or other real-time presentation.

One disadvantage to real-time assessments is that only a small group of learners can be actively involved simultaneously. Attempting to conduct synchronous activities with a large group of students (more than a dozen, for example) typically results either in chaos or a substantial percentage of the students lurking passively in the background. One method for avoiding a string of disordered exchanges (or, even worse, none at all) is for the instructor to guide the conversation around a series of discussion questions, with ample opportunity for everyone to respond. Some professors handle this by posing a question in the chat and then "calling on" two or three students to respond. Once these individuals have presented their responses, other students are given the chance to join in and add their ideas or ask follow-up questions, if they choose to. Students have the option to waive a particular question and be called on again, but by keeping track of who has participated throughout, the professor ensures that everyone has a chance to contribute.

Finally, synchronous assessment activities offer two related and especially important capabilities to distance education programs: building a sense of immediacy between students and instructor and facilitating the formation of the learning group. Immediacy refers to the perception of social presence, or that sense of "being with" someone else, and is based on Mehrabian's work (see, e.g., Mehrabian, 1969) on communication and social dynamics. For students working at a distance, possibly in geographic isolation, membership in the learning group offers a sense of belonging and adds relevance to the instructional experience. Synchronous interactions, such as online chats or audioconferences, enhance those perceptions and students often remark that it makes a difference to know that the teacher is "really there, right then" during these sessions. Another possible benefit is that when students feel closer to the instructor or other students, undesirable behaviors, such as responding inappropriately in online discussions or cheating on an assignment, may be less likely to occur.

Portfolios

Portfolios have a long history as summative assessment tools in fields such as graphic design, architecture, and marketing, but are gaining acceptance quickly for their value as formative compilations of work in a much broader range of disciplines. A portfolio might consist of a variety of materials (papers, video clips, photographs, etc.) reflecting generalized learning across disciplines, or it might be a more specific gathering of content-based materials, such as tests, reports, or art projects. One of the key elements of portfolio creation is that the student decides (often with an instructor's guidance) what materials to include in the collection. Self-reflection leading to the development of standards and the determination of criteria to use in selecting these materials are integral components of this process. Identifying what constitutes one's own best work represents a level of self-assessment requiring thoughtful consideration of learning goals and progress toward significant milestones.

For students working at a distance, the development of a portfolio can provide a meaningful connection with the instructor as criteria are established, materials exchanged, and time lines for completion negotiated. Some digital portfolio software packages enable the instructor to integrate rubrics or licensure standards within the site, allowing the student to then link items to each criterion measure to demonstrate mastery. These types of software systems also let portfolio owners to establish permissions for others (potential employers, for example) to view some or all of the portfolio, and to download the materials for storage on a variety of media.

Graphic Organizers

The use of concept maps, infographics, flow charts, and other visual representations to assess student learning is a relatively recent phenomenon. This technique originated in the 1960s (see, e.g., Ausubel, Novak, & Henesian, 1978) but it was not until the diagrams could be created, stored, modified, and shared digitally that their use in education flourished. These models, which may resemble extensive webs, simple line drawings, or content-rich posters, allow learners to organize their thoughts visually and incorporate lines, arrows, drawings, grids, photos, or other visual elements (see Figure 9.1). For many learners, using a visual model to illustrate their understanding will be a freeing experience and lead to more robust and creative thinking; for many topics, creating a graphic image with concepts arranged to denote relationships among the ideas will be the optimal assessment of understanding.

In many cases, students can create visuals individually or collaboratively by using free or inexpensive applications (e.g., Cmap Cloud, Venngage, or Gliffy). This is especially helpful for distance education students because they have an opportunity to collaborate with peers who may live a time zone—or a hemisphere—away. In addition, because students are visually representing their thinking (i.e., how they've organized their new knowledge) the instructor may be able to identify misconceptions or errors quickly that might otherwise be less obvious.

Lab Work

In earlier days of distance education, courses that included lab work were especially challenging to design and manage. Students could be required to participate in these activities at prearranged locations (often with the instructor traveling on evenings or weekends to each of them) or they could be sent equipment and materials (for nondangerous activities) to conduct the work at home. (A classic example is a biology course in which students are sent animals for dissection.) Although many laboratory activities can be safely and effectively accomplished outside of a specialized facility, lab work at a distance remains

FIGURE 9–1 Example graphic organizers.

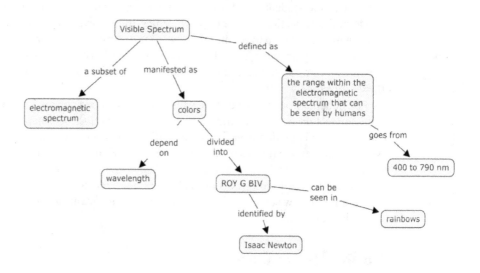

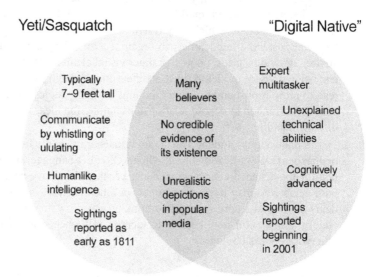

problematic for a significant percentage of courses. Thankfully, advances in computing technology are beginning to address these difficulties.

Increasingly, students are using *remote labs* for courses in science and engineering. Communications technologies enable students to control equipment located a few miles away or around the world through online network applications. Not only do these activities allow students at a distance to engage in laboratory work, they offer many advantages over more traditional, hands-on projects. Students can gain access to equipment that might otherwise be dangerous to work with directly or too expensive for a single institution to purchase, whereas consortium arrangements can facilitate sharing. These remote systems can also alleviate problems with staffing and building access, giving students the opportunity to work when it fits their schedule and from wherever they have Internet access. Additionally, remote experiments can present students with typical "real world" issues such as technical problems or measurement variance, for example. Finally, because the work is done via networking technologies, many of these systems facilitate collaboration even when students are not co-located. Working as part of a team that may be scattered around the globe can prepare students for the professional world they're likely to encounter upon graduation.

Virtual laboratories offer students the opportunity to explore lab work in a low-stakes setting by simulating real events and consequences. As assessment tools, virtual labs make possible a wide range of instructional strategies. For example, a simulated activity can be designed to add complexity as the student becomes more competent, thus reducing cognitive load initially but building in more realistic, potentially distracting, cues over time (deJong, Linn, & Zacharia, 2013). Virtual experiments may also be configured with variables that present a range of scenarios, like flight simulators that can indicate storms, fog, or equipment malfunctions that occur infrequently in real life (fortunately). Continuous, embedded prompts or questions offer multiple opportunities for students to practice and get feedback on nascent skills and as the system gathers data on student progress, instructors can then revise their subsequent teaching to address areas that are especially challenging. Although virtual labs can be time-consuming and expensive to design and develop, once functional the ease and minimal expense of duplication and dissemination can offset upfront costs.

As with remote labs, simulated labs offer significant potential for collaborative work. With lab partners or group members participating at a distance, much as they do in many professional work environments, students must hone their communication skills while they also share the responsibility for completing assigned projects. Virtual labs can include prompts within the activity that encourage (or require) team decision-making, elicit peer feedback, monitor the contributions of each group member, or compare results within and among lab groups, for example. Purposeful development of lab assignments (of any kind) should discourage students from simply "taking turns" or dividing up the tasks then assembling the results like a jigsaw puzzle—true collaboration involves elements of interdependence within the group.

DESIGN CONSIDERATIONS

Designing assessments does not involve only the selection of a strategy, but also characteristics of the activity itself. The following section will describe several decisions to be made as a part of the development process.

Objective and Subjective Measures

Classifying an assessment as either objective or subjective depends not only the activity itself, but more specifically on the nature of the product that results from student performance. Will every successful student end up with the same result? Will the outcomes offer equivalent information regarding student performance but be reflected in individual results? For example, we can assume that if two students complete a multiple-choice test and each scores 100%, their tests (the deliverables) will be virtually identical. However, if those same two students submit term papers, we hope that those products are not identical. Subjective assessments are designed to result in products that are similar from one student to the next, yet demand individual scrutiny to determine the learner's progress and/or score. In contrast, objective measures—that is, the identical-results-type—do not require knowledgeable human intervention to determine whether students achieved mastery. With objective measures, we expect all of the right answers to match.

Objective measures offer significant advantages in ease of implementation. Tests incorporating multiple-choice, true-false, matching, or other types of machine-scorable questions are an efficient way to measure learning, especially if the instructional objectives are written at a low level of cognitive effort, such as remembering or understanding. If the objectives, however, require higher order thinking such as inferring relationships or creating models, multiple-choice test items get more difficult and time-consuming to create. Writing multiple-choice test items that require higher order thinking skills demands creativity and careful attention to the course or unit objectives. For example, a question at the analyzing or evaluating levels might present learners with a written paragraph and then expect them to identify gaps in logical reasoning, recognize data elements relevant to the solution of a problem, or judge which of the statements presented fits a set of given criteria. The students would need to apply their understanding of the course content to demonstrate these skills and would not simply be recalling the correct answer from memory.

Besides the obvious time-savings advantage of machine scoring, objective tests also enable a teacher or trainer to ascertain specifically which concepts within a course, module, or lesson are being mastered and which are not. Item analysis can quickly identify questions missed by many students, for example, and also indicate the likelihood that students simply had not learned the intended concepts, or whether the test items in question appear to be poor discriminators (i.e., items frequently missed by students who know the material and/or items frequently answered correctly by students who do not know the material). Additionally, objective tests created with assessment software (whether specialized or as part of a course management system) can include options such as individualized branching, adapted content presentation, and selective release of test items based on performance. For disciplines requiring meticulous classification of skill attainment and feedback of precise granularity, such customization is highly valued.

Short-answer test items (sometimes called free-response items or supply items) straddle the fence between objective and subjective assessments. These items are written either as direct questions requiring the learner to respond with a word or phrase or as statements in which a space has been left blank for a brief written answer. Because students can fill in any response, care must be taken to create items that are precise and not open to a wide variety of interpretations. This is crucial in many distance education environments; proctors at remote sites cannot be expected to answer questions about test items or what the instructor meant to say. Like multiple-choice tests, short-answer items are easiest to write when students are expected to recall information from memory, rather than analyze complex concepts.

Although objective assessment activities are especially attractive for use in large-enrollment courses, they rarely provide a comprehensive picture of learner progress. Subjective measures (i.e., those requiring human judgment for scoring) include such familiar learning tasks as research papers, essay tests, and projects, as well as more recently introduced strategies such as online discussions, e-portfolios, and graphic organizers (such as concept maps). By providing a mix of assessment types, measurements of student learning are less likely to be confounded by individual learner characteristics or environmental factors that might differentially affect some students.

Subjective assessment methods can work especially well in the distance education environment. For example, although many K–12 school systems have initiated distance education programs, adult learners make up the majority of students involved in distance education overall, whether affiliated with an educational institution, as part of a privately administered training sequence for certification or licensure, or professional development activities offered through their employer's human resources department. These students may have been away from the traditional classroom for several years, and assessment methods typically associated with that environment—pencil-and-paper objective tests, for example—may seem irrelevant or trivial. Many distance education programs (especially those designed for adult learners) have, therefore, adopted a wide array of subjective assessment practices.

The distinction between objective and subjective assessments is useful to the extent that we consider the reason for creating and implementing an assessment activity. Objective assessments are more convenient to administer, easier to score, and frequently are easier to create, as well. They are useful when looking for trends over time (e.g., looking at test scores over a multiyear period) or when making comparisons among disparate groups (freshmen biology students at five different universities). Subjective assessments, on the other hand, are more useful when the transfer of skills to environments outside the classroom is important, or if the process of identifying the correct answer is as important as the answer itself.

Rubrics

One of the major disadvantages of subjective assessment measures is the difficulty of assigning scores or ratings to learner performance. Many instructors use scoring rubrics to facilitate this process and to improve the consistency and fairness of scoring. A rubric is a descriptive framework to guide the evaluation of complex assignments or those requiring individual judgment. Sometimes a rubric consists of a simple list of characteristics or descriptions, aligned with levels of quality, such as *outstanding, good, fair,* and *unacceptable,* or point values given for each level. For example, the criteria for an "outstanding" rating on a set of arithmetic problems could include that the work was submitted on time, completed with at least 90% accuracy, and was written neatly; a rating of "good" might require at least 80% accuracy, submission on time, and written legibly; and so on. Other rubrics may be significantly more comprehensive, developed using a matrix format that includes categories of activities within the task (e.g., vocabulary, organization, etc., for a book report) down one side, and quality levels across the top. The criteria for each mastery level are then included for each cell in the matrix.

Criteria included in a rubric for participating in discussions might refer to elements such as posting messages by the due date or logging in to the chat on time or have a more qualitative emphasis with points given for adhering to the topic at hand, supporting opinions with evidence, or demonstrating a grasp of key concepts. After the rubric is developed, the instructor may wish to provide example answers that demonstrate the various criterion levels and to clarify specifically why points would be deducted from the average or poor responses.

Most course management systems include a rubric tool that enables an instructor or course developer to create a customized scoring matrix that can be attached to a specific assignment or project. These systems allow the instructor to grade the assessment and provide feedback within the rubric that is then transferred to the gradebook for student access. Other options include word processing templates, and repositories of existing rubrics that

FIGURE 9–2 Sample rubric for assessing discussion posts.

	Unacceptable	Getting There...	Good	Outstanding
Clarity	0 points	1 - 2 points	3 points	4 points
	Message is not organized; does not address the original question; includes irrelevant information;	Somewhat organized, but ideas not well connected; may contain irrelevant information; may not have fully answered the question;	Well-organized, with ideas connected; little to no irrelevant information; answers question completely;	Well-organized with ideas clearly connected to one another; no irrelevant information included; question is answered fully and in detail;
Understanding	0 - 1 points	2 - 3 points	4 points	5 points
	Little, if any, understanding demonstrated; does not refer to evidence to support claims;	Limited understanding of important concepts; supporting evidence may be included but is tenuous or unreliable;	Demonstrates solid understanding of key concepts; refers to supporting evidence;	Keen grasp of important concepts bolstered by examples or analogies; supporting evidence is clearly relevant to the argument;
Original Thinking	0 - 1 points	2-3 points	4 points	5 points
	Very little or no original thinking; lacking synthesis or analytical conclusions;	Few original thoughts, mostly reporting of others' ideas; conclusions are not supportable;	Some original thinking demonstrated through interpretation or basis analysis of course content; conclusions may be supportable;	Original thought seen in analysis or synthesis of important concepts; interprets key ideas and draws reasonable, supportable conclusions;
Conversation	0 points	1 point	2 points	3 points
	Does not respond to others' posts or provides only minimal commentary (e.g., "I agree");	Responds to required number of others' posts; provides comments directly related to posts;	Responds to required number of posts or more; comments are constructive and substantial;	Responds to others' posts constructively and substantially; responds to more than minimum required posts;
Style and Mechanics	0 points	1 point	2 points	3 points
	Many errors that make ideas difficult to follow; message and responses may or may not be posted by the deadline;	Several errors in spelling, grammar, etc.; writing is not focused and thoughts appear to ramble; message and responses are posted on or before deadline;	Few errors in spelling, grammar, etc.; writing is focused but may ramble slightly; message and responses are posted on or before deadline;	No errors in spelling, grammar, etc.; writing is focused and concise; message and responses are posted before the deadline;
	< 50%	10 (50%)	15 (75%)	20 points possible

can be customized, such as those collected by the National Institute for Learning Outcomes Assessment (http://www.learningoutcomeassessment.org/Rubrics.htm).

When building a rubric (see Figure 9.2), review the objectives for the task to ensure that scoring is aligned with the stated expectations. This also makes it easy to specify the scoring criteria for the assessment activity, such as "Organization of Ideas" or "Persuasive Elements." Typically, the criteria are listed in the first column of the rubric, along the left side of the matrix. Next, identify how many mastery levels will be included and how these will be identified (e.g., Excellent, Good, Fair, Not Yet). The mastery levels are usually arranged across the top (in the first row), with the highest level to the right. In general, the more complex the assignment, the more levels and greater specificity of criteria are appropriate. This allows for increased granularity when identifying the strengths and weaknesses of student work.

The cells forming intersections between each criterion measure and mastery level can then be filled in with descriptions explaining each level of quality. That is, describing what "Excellent" looks like for "Organization of Ideas" so that it's distinct from the "Good" category. Once the descriptions are filled in, determine how many points will be possible for each criterion measure, keeping in mind that these should be weighted based on their relative importance. For example, a research paper rubric might include criteria for the thesis statement, appropriateness of cited research, analysis of readings, and organization, in addition to mechanics such as grammar and spelling. Most instructors would agree that these criteria are not equally important, so the point values should reflect this. For major assignments with high point values, consider assigning a point range for each mastery level to enable greater flexibility and granularity in scoring.

A frequent error when creating simple rubrics can result in student work being "under-rated." If there are three mastery levels, it may seem obvious to assign 1, 2, and 3 points (or an equivalent) to each. However, a student receiving a middle rating of 2 on each criterion would end up with a score of 66% which is a failing grade in many programs. When creating any rubric, be sure to verify that the point values are aligned with the established grading scheme.

Rubrics should always be shared with students before they engage in the assessment activity and this can be done in many ways. One clever professor distributed the rubric that would be used for students' research papers along with some sample papers, and the students worked in pairs to grade one of the papers using the rubric. This helped students understand how their papers would be assessed and gave them practice applying evaluative criteria, as well as providing the instructor with feedback about the clarity and usability of the rubric. Another instructor enlisted the students' help in creating a rubric to score discussion postings, leading to greater buy-in and increased participation.

Authenticity

Authentic assessment refers to tasks that reflect genuine problems or challenges within a discipline. Mueller, on his *Authentic Assessment Toolbox* website (http://jfmueller.faculty.noctrl.edu/toolbox/), describes an effective authentic activity as one in which students "perform real-world tasks that demonstrate meaningful application of essential knowledge and skills." These assessments emphasize the transfer of skills to unfamiliar situations beyond the classroom and are often embedded in problem- or case-based instructional modules.

Assessments that are authentic can provide robust evidence of learning and heighten a sense of relevance for students—an important factor supporting intrinsic motivation. Wiggins (2014) pointed out that authentic assessments, "Are enabling, pointing the student toward more sophisticated and important uses of skills and knowledge." This type of higher order task relies on foundational knowledge but applies those concepts to activities that are meaningful beyond the scope of an individual course or academic program.

Structuring Assessments

An important consideration when designing assessments is ensuring clarity of expectations. For example, are the instructions clearly explained, has information about scoring

FIGURE 9–3   Transparent Assignment Template (Winkelmes, 2013). Used with permission.

Transparent Assignment Template·

© 2013 Mary-Ann Winkelmes

This template can be used as a guide for developing, explaining, and discussing class activities and out-of-class assignments. Making these aspects of each course activity or assignment explicitly clear to students has demonstrably enhanced students' learning in a national study.[1]

Assignment Name
Due date:

Purpose: *Define the learning objectives, in language and terms that help students recognize how this assignment will benefit their learning. Ideally, indicate how these are connected with institutional learning outcomes, and how the specific knowledge and skills involved in this assignment will be important in students' lives beyond the contexts of this assignment, this course, and this college.*

Skills: The purpose of this assignment is to help you practice the following skills that are essential to your success in this course / in school / in this field / in professional life beyond school:

> *Terms from Bloom's Taxonomy of Educational Objectives may help you explain these skills in language students will understand. Listed from cognitively simple to most complex, these skills are:*
> o   *understanding basic disciplinary knowledge and methods/tools*
> o   *applying basic disciplinary knowledge/tools to problem-solving in a similar but unfamiliar context*
> o   *analyzing*
> o   *synthesizing*
> o   *judging/evaluating and selecting best solutions*
> o   *creating/inventing a new interpretation, product, theory*

Knowledge: This assignment will also help you to become familiar with the following important content knowledge in this discipline:

> 1.
> 2.

Task: *Define what activities the student should do/perform. "Question cues" from this chart might be helpful: http://www.asainstitute.org/conference2013/handouts/20-Bloom-Question-Cues-Chart.pdf. List any steps or guidelines, or a recommended sequence for the students' efforts. Specify any extraneous mistakes to be avoided.*

Criteria for Success:

Define the characteristics of the finished product. Provide multiple, annotated examples of what these characteristics look like in practice, to encourage students' creativity and reduce their incentive to copy any one example too closely. With students, collaboratively analyze examples of work before the students begin working. Explain how excellent work differs from adequate work. It is often useful to provide or compile with students a checklist of characteristics of successful work. This enables students to evaluate the effectiveness of their own efforts while they are working, and to judge the quality of their completed work. Students can also use the checklist to provide feedback on peers' coursework. Indicate whether this task/product will be graded and/or how it factors into the student's overall grade for the course. Later, asking students to reflect and comment on their completed, graded work allows them to focus on changes to their learning strategies that might improve their future work.

criteria been included, or mention of specific resources that should be consulted. The *Transparent Assignment Template* (Winkelmes, 2013) is a guide to the development of assessment activities that help students understand why they're engaging in the activity (purpose), what they're expected to do (task), and how their performance will be measured (criteria). (See Figure 9.3.) Purpose has two subsections for information about the skills and knowledge students will be acquiring. Although an instructor or course designer can use the template as is and fill in the sections as appropriate, the format is less important than ensuring that the three types of information (purpose, task, and criteria) are communicated.

Students working at a distance may be at a disadvantage (compared to face-to-face students) when faced with assignments because it can be more difficult or take longer to get clarification about requirements. Making expectations and intentions clear (i.e., "transparent") can reduce anxiety (Zeidner, 2014) and has been shown to enhance college student success, especially among first-generation, low income, and underrepresented students (Winkelmes, et al., 2016). In addition, clearly-articulated assessments improve the validity of the exercise by ensuring that students are actually demonstrating what the instructor had intended.

Facilitating Student Collaboration

Collaborative work is the norm in many professions, and it is the rare individual who works entirely alone without relying on others for input or assistance. Unfortunately, many students are more familiar with schools in which competitive models of education reign and collaborative learning looks to them like a risky venture. The ideal collaborative project requires interdependent work by students, during which reciprocal, social interactions result in positive outcomes for the entire group. Projects that are not easily broken into discrete tasks work well, to prevent students from simply completing each portion individually and assembling the pieces like a jigsaw puzzle. Although a significant body of research supports the use of collaborative learning and its benefits, many instructors and an even greater number of students prefer not to engage in such activities. Two reasons typically emerge when one asks students why they avoid collaborative group work: logistical difficulties and—as one student rather bluntly exclaimed, "Slackers!" Logistical issues are significantly alleviated with the use of online tools such as wikis and discussion boards, but teachers share their students' concerns about scoring, and worry that they'll never be able to assign grades fairly when an individual student's efforts may be masked by the good, or not-so-good, work of his or her teammates.

Strategies to mitigate concerns about scoring group work include defining the grading criteria at the outset, monitoring the group's progress throughout the process, and not relying on collaborative work for the majority of a course or unit grade. Defining the criteria will reinforce exactly what the expectations are and how performance will be rated. Monitoring student progress by using a CMS provides instructors with the opportunity to see at a glance who's contributing to wikis or discussions, who's asking important questions, or who's producing work to be shared among the group for feedback.

Some instructors also invite students to assess the contributions of their teammates, by assigning percentages or point values to each group member. Another method is to ask students, midway through the project, to report on how well their group is working, in terms of task sharing, negotiating consensus, communication, and related criteria. Although the initial resistance to collaboration may prove daunting, ultimately these valuable work skills will be a practical addition to any student's abilities.

ACADEMIC MISCONDUCT

In any discussion about assessing learner progress it is inevitable that the conversation will turn to the many ways that students can (and will) undermine our efforts by cheating, plagiarizing, or otherwise breaking our teacherly hearts. While there appears to be no single, agreed-upon definition of academic misconduct, it may be that, like art, "you know it when you see it." Most institutions have policies stating what, for their students, constitutes academic misconduct—misrepresentation, plagiarism, disruption of classes, et cetera—and how infractions will be handled. Unfortunately, such policies seem to have little effect as deterrents to unethical behavior. Speculation about why students cheat typically includes such reasons as "pressure to succeed" (and its twin, "fear of failure") and the sense that everyone is doing it coupled with the perception that if other students are cheating, those who do not will be at a competitive disadvantage.

Although cheating and plagiarism are not problems exclusive to the distance education domain, the use of advanced communications technologies, coupled with the perceived absence (at least geographically) of an authority figure, has led to what many teachers and trainers consider a growing problem on campus and off. As public awareness of academic misconduct has grown, arguments are inconclusive concerning whether the number of occurrences has actually increased, or if an increase in reported occurrences is responsible for the perception of rampant dishonesty. Refreshingly, several studies suggest that students in online classes cheat less (Peled, Eshet, Barczyk, & Grinautski, 2017) or no more than (Beck, 2014) their face-to-face counterparts. What everyone can agree on is that cheating and plagiarism are serious problems and that they have never been easier to commit, thanks to the increased technological literacy of our students and the wide availability of online services facilitating questionable behavior.

Plagiarism

Clarifying precisely what constitutes plagiarism and having clear policies for dealing with it are two strategies suggested by the Council of Writing Program Administrators for alleviating this problem (2010). Instructors should also attempt to distinguish between plagiarism (i.e., the intent to claim as one's own someone else's words or ideas) and the simple misuse of sources resulting from ignorance or carelessness. Unfortunately, many students do not understand when or how to cite sources appropriately and few instructors are willing to take time away from course content to teach them. The good news is that there are several excellent online tutorials such as Indiana University's Plagiarism Tutorials and Tests site (https://www.indiana.edu/~academy/firstPrinciples/index.html).

It is important to know your institution's policies on dealing with suspected plagiarism and share this information with students. Some instructors are uncomfortable confronting students if there's a suspicion of wrong-doing, but it's important to address the problem and to alert the proper administrators of the issue when appropriate. Too many students leave a trail of infractions throughout their academic program, never facing the consequences for their actions because instructor after instructor chose to not report them.

The ease of relying on the work of others has fueled interest in plagiarism detection services, whether integrated with a CMS or stand-alone. These tools compare papers turned in by students (at one's institution or worldwide) to those already included in databases of previously submitted papers, as well as thousands found publicly online or in digital library collections. While there is no denying that this helps to detect plagiarism, such methods may pit students and teachers against one another in adversarial roles—not the ideal learning relationship. Additionally, because such services often retain student papers to add to their databases (with which to compare papers submitted in the future), many educators have concerns about the intellectual property rights of students and some have denounced the use of these tools, suggesting that better writing instruction and assignments will do more to combat misconduct than simply catching and punishing students who plagiarize. For example, many instructors deal with these concerns by requiring students to submit rough drafts to the plagiarism detection system, thereby alerting students to potential problems with citations or direct quotes. At a minimum, if instructors anticipate using a plagiarism detection system, they should notify students of this in writing, explaining why the software is used, how their work and private information is protected, and whether they are allowed to opt out of the process.

Of the technologies that have influenced cheating and plagiarism, the most frequently cited as troublesome are the online sites where (allegedly) literate entrepreneurs sell papers for students to claim as their own work. Although purchasing prewritten essays or term papers is hardly a recent phenomenon, the relative anonymity of the online marketplace has contributed to the boom of companies offering these products. In the past, the danger of being caught buying a term paper might deter the faint of heart, but now a credit card and an e-mail address will connect a potential buyer with an eager seller. In addition, yesteryear's purchased paper often had to be completely retyped in order to present an original-looking copy to the instructor. Now that few instructors accept hard-copy papers even this minor inconvenience has vanished.

Term paper mills, those online businesses that will, for a fee, provide the customer with a (supposedly) custom-written paper have found a lucrative niche in cyberspace. A quick Google search turns up hundreds of sites dedicated to relieving students of the tiresome burden of writing their own papers. Each company hastens to reassure potential customers that the papers they buy will be completely plagiarism-free. Of course, this completely ignores the fact that as soon as students (the customers) claim the papers as their own work they've committed academic fraud. Many paper mill services rationalize this by claiming that they are only providing sample papers for students to use as models when writing their own original papers and others go so far as to warn of the dire consequences of hiring the services of other "fraudulent" paper-writing companies. Of course, students just might get exactly the grade they deserve if they purchase a paper from a site that claims, "We make non-plagiarized cheap essays for sale" that are "written papers of the top notch quality" (SmartWritingService, 2018).

Cheating

To a great extent, teachers assume that students are honest individuals. For example, few instructors in a face-to-face classroom environment would consider checking identification to verify that each person sitting in that room is, in fact, who they claim to be. So it is with distance education programs, that when students submit assignments, participate in discussions, or request instructor assistance they are rarely questioned as to their identity. However, as discussed earlier, proctored exams provide a checkpoint to balance the perceived anonymity of learning at a distance, ensuring that the student upon whose transcript the course credit and grade will appear, or whose license validates their abilities, is actually the student doing the work and demonstrating their mastery of the objectives.

Technological options to combat cheating on tests include randomizing the order of test items, randomly selecting a percentage of items from a test pool, utilizing browser lock-down software, and implementing a monitoring program using the computer's built-in video camera to record learners taking tests, although many instructors find this last method objectionable and many consider it intrusive. These measures can all be defeated, of course, when students are taking tests in an unproctored setting, but their use sends a reminder that cheating is unacceptable. Instructional or logistical means to alleviate these problems might involve requiring students to take exams in a proctored setting, expecting or allowing students to work collaboratively on a test (thereby turning a problem into a learning strategy), imposing time limits for test taking, or simply abandoning the use of objective tests for other assessment methods. Heightened awareness of unethical behavior may be a signal for course designers and instructors to rethink what types of tests (if any) are most useful and how tests might be deployed most appropriately.

Finally, it is helpful (albeit depressing) to learn about the many options students have available if they decide to cheat or plagiarize. A rudimentary online search will reveal services ranging from selling papers (from short essays to entire dissertations), providing test banks (individual course tests up through professional licensure exams), and offering to take tests and/or entire online courses for a fee. Awareness of these questionable sources of assistance can help instructors think carefully about their assessment practices and how they might design assessments that discourage students from such temptations.

Deterring Academic Misconduct

Distance education programs walk a fine line between creating a climate of suspicion and mistrust, and condoning a completely laissez-faire attitude toward serious transgressions, particularly when students feel removed both geographically and psychologically from the educational process. Notwithstanding the popular media attention given to academic misconduct (see, e.g., Lodhia, 2018), evidence remains questionable as to whether instances of cheating, plagiarism and other forms of dishonesty among students are skyrocketing. As media reports of unethical behavior in politics, business, journalism, and other professions escalate, the perception that "it's no big deal" may, in fact, lead to greater honesty in self-reported academic misconduct, and may also unwittingly encourage such activities.

An analogy of how instructional design might deter academic dishonesty is that of the person who decides to learn a foreign language before moving to another country. Would that student cheat on assignments, avoid studying, or duck out of tutoring sessions? Not likely! When the assessment activity is relevant to a student's need (practice with new vocabulary) and the end result is tied directly to a desirable outcome (speaking in the new language) cheating is, at best, a self-defeating activity. Or, maybe your neighbor decide to build a deck on her house. Would she have someone else attend the workshop to learn how to do it? Would she avoid opportunities to practice using the appropriate tools and get helpful advice? Here again, the example may sound ridiculous, but the need to design relevant assessment activities that result in meaningful outcomes is not exaggerated.

Another instructional strategy that may circumvent dishonesty is to incorporate many small assessments throughout the unit, course, or module. These ongoing activities can reduce student anxiety and alleviate the one-chance-to-prove-myself pressure that may nudge students over a line they should not cross. These might include short exercises over course readings, requiring students to participate in a weekly poll about topics relevant to the course content, or a version of the "1-minute paper," during which students write a summary of what they considered the most important concepts of that unit (Angelo & Cross, 1993). These motivational activities also encourage students to keep up with their work and they provide valuable feedback with minimal effort for teachers or students.

Many schools have adopted honor codes as one way to reinforce the concepts of academic integrity. These codes typically require students to sign a pledge (once or each time they submit a major assignment or test) and involve a peer judiciary to deal with infractions. Research conducted under the auspices of the Center for Academic Integrity at Duke University suggests that these codes can deter academic misconduct, although their influence appears to have lessened over time (McCabe, Butterfield, & Treviño, 2012). At a time when society seems to present dishonesty as the norm, an honor code may, at the very least, reinforce the notion that cheating is considered aberrant behavior and will not be tolerated.

A straightforward approach, coupled with understanding, may prove beneficial, as well. Some instructors directly address the topics of cheating and plagiarism at the start of the term to make it clear that they are fully aware of the many questionable options available and that infractions will be taken seriously. At the same time, however, many of these tough-love practitioners suggest to students that if they find themselves on the verge of a decision they might later regret, they can call the instructor to talk about it. As one faculty member put it, "You will probably get caught, if not now then later, and no grade is worth the damage you'll do to your academic standing—and to your self-image—if you decide to cheat." Utilizing tools such as browser lock-downs during online tests or secure logins can help, but the real issues related to cheating and plagiarism may be cultural. Many teachers are now questioning the increased emphasis on cheating because of the us-versus-them atmosphere it can generate and are advocating a more moderate approach that promotes trust and balances the seriousness of the offense with only as much attention as it deserves. Spending large quantities of valuable time chasing after a small number of cheaters can quickly lead to diminishing returns. In the end, as ingenuous as it may seem, it really is the student who loses out by avoiding opportunities for scholarly growth.

TRENDS IN ASSESSMENT

A promising array of technological, pedagogical, and theoretical advances forecast enhanced flexibility for assessing learning and greater credibility for assessment results, whether at a distance or in traditional environments. The following trends are those currently getting a lot of attention and generating insightful discussions about how our design and use of assessments may change and how they may change our institutions, as well as our ideas about teaching and learning.

Automated Feedback and Scoring

The often-controversial use of automated essay scoring was discussed in an earlier edition of this textbook (Simonson, Smaldino, Albright, & Zvacek, 2012). Technological advances and the increased use of these systems for other types of student work merit a brief update.

Automated feedback and/or scoring, at its core, is the comparison of student work with an established standard, typically through the use of software applications. While objective assessments have been scored this way for decades, the use of automation for subjective measures that rely on artificial intelligence and natural language processing technology is still not widely accepted, at least for anything beyond an initial review of surface features. In a review of research about automated feedback generators, Keuning, Jeuring, and Heeren (2016) found that the majority of these systems provided little beyond the identification of mistakes, although newer tools may incorporate guidance and suggested resources for improvement (see, e.g., Burstein, Klebanov, Elliot, & Molloy, 2016).

Research in this area has broadened and now includes, for example, studies related to the combined use of instructor with machine-generated feedback and student acceptance of the systems. Some promising results include the finding that a combination of automated and instructor-provided feedback resulted in higher-level instructor comments. By relying on the software to identify low-level errors the instructors could use their limited time to offer more meaningful input to students (Wilson & Czik, 2016). Peterson (2017) found that students not only responded positively to automated feedback, but were more likely to use the feedback to revise their work, possibly due to the perceived impartiality of the system.

Unlike traditional coursework, most online programs establish timelines for the prompt return of student work and the adoption of an automated system may ease the labor-intensity of feedback for writing-intensive courses. Continued improvements to these systems and dissemination of positive research outcomes may also result in a greater acceptance of technology-mediated instruction, overall.

Adaptive Assessment

Adaptive assessment is not actually a new technology; its roots were firmly established in the mid-1900s, but its use in formal education programs is much more recent. These assessments rely on data generated during online tests and use this information to determine which questions each test-taker will get and how many. In its simplest form, the system presents questions of varying difficulty, based on the test-taker's previous responses. When questions are answered correctly, the following questions will be more challenging; if answered incorrectly, the difficulty level drops. (In practice, the algorithms are much more sophisticated than this.) These types of tests are often built in to adaptive learning platforms that use response results to tailor the presentation of instructional materials and activities.

Adaptive testing system developers focus on two decision points: (a) next item (branching based on the test-taker's response, and (b) termination (how many questions are required to determine the test-taker's ability accurately). Although adaptive testing has not yet been widely adopted, it forms the backbone of many tutoring platforms such as ALEKS, YiXue, and Smart Sparrow, is used in the GRE and GMAT exams, and is in development for the ACT and SAT tests.

The three main advantages of adaptive testing are efficiency, accuracy, and test security. There is some research support for the claim that fewer test items are needed (efficiency) to obtain a clear picture of student knowledge or abilities and that test results are more granular and thus more accurate (e.g., Martin & Lazendic, 2018). Test security is heightened as a result of the non-linear and customized presentation of test items to each student, although an entire pool of items could still be at risk from hackers. Research results on student attitudes have been mixed. Some test takers have reported feeling discouraged because there aren't enough questions that they can answer easily, i.e., there may be too many challenging items (Kimura, 2017). Test-takers might also be frustrated because the design of the exam typically prohibits changing their answers to earlier questions.

Adaptive assessment shows great promise, particularly in the ability to customize test items to the individual, whether high-performers who would otherwise "max out" on an exam, or struggling students who could end up completely discouraged. It's only a matter of time before the major CMS platforms accommodate (or build in) adaptive testing, as well as full-blown adaptive learning applications.

Games for Assessment

Game-based, and its cousin gamified, teaching can be valid instructional strategies that facilitate learning while enhancing motivation and time-on-task learning. There is now a growing body of research focused on the use of digital/online games for assessment. When playing a game, mastery of increasingly difficult tasks is tied directly to success, as in any kind of mastery learning program. Games typically include formative assessments designed as small challenges that provide immediate feedback and an opportunity for players to reflect on their decisions. These challenges may include extraneous clues or distractions, requiring the player to define a problem and distinguish between useful and irrelevant information. A summative assessment could be the major hurdle that determines whether a player moves to a higher level, for example (Lookadoo et al., 2017).

Game designers will find it helpful to work collaboratively with a subject matter expert and an instructional design to clarify the desired learning outcomes. The designer can then explore ways in which players will, within the game context, demonstrate mastery of those objectives. This is supported by research by Lee et al. (2013) who found that games with built-in formative assessment resulted in greater success (students reached higher levels) and faster play than games without. This type of designed-in approach is often referred to as *stealth assessment* and defined as "assessments that are woven directly and invisibly into the fabric of the gaming environment" (Shute & Ventura, 2013, p. 31). It is also important that the tasks within the game are moderately challenging; too easy or too difficult and players quickly lose interest and are less motivated to continue.

Games may be especially useful in a distance education course for several reasons. First, they are accessible at the learner's convenience and offer flexible pacing to accommodate busy schedules. Second, student progress through the game can be recorded down to each mouse-click, offering the instructor valuable insight about where students are struggling, which may be harder to determine without the opportunity to observe learner activity directly. Finally, games are designed specifically to engage the player and encourage persistence. Students who feel somewhat disconnected in an online course (a factor highly correlated to dropping out) may benefit from these motivational elements.

SUMMARY

Assessment is the means of measuring learning gains and can be used to improve the teaching-learning process in distance education settings, as well as traditional environments. Determining content mastery and transferability of skills helps teachers and students identify gaps in learning; it gives feedback to the teacher about the instruction and feedback to the student on their strengths and weaknesses relative to the desired outcomes. It also can reinforce content and identify misconceptions, and act as a motivating force that prods learners toward content mastery. In times when political pressures call for greater institutional accountability, assessment can produce evidence of student learning to justify state or federal funding, as well.

Some final conclusions and recommendations remain. First, assessment must be an integrated and transparent component of the instructional process. Aligning the desired learner outcomes, instructional activities, and assessment tools provides clear expectations and a sense of relevance for student participation. In any instructional environment, assessments should reinforce course content, provide opportunities to practice newly acquired skills, result in meaningful feedback, and motivate learners to succeed. Second, instructional designers, teachers, and program planners need to pay attention when news reports suggest that academic misconduct, in the form of cheating and plagiarism, is being reported at record levels. Students are more likely to cheat when assessment activities are considered irrelevant, trivial, or unfair, and although a few individuals will behave unethically in any circumstance, there is reason to think that the majority of such behavior can be deterred with a combination of approaches. Finally, good quality assessment practices require attention to possible confounding effects of the learning environment, mediating technologies, and instructional strategies, as well as interactions among these factors and student characteristics. Designing with an awareness of the constraints and opportunities faced by learners at a distance ensures that each student's progress will be recorded accurately and fulfill the purposes of diagnosis, reinforcement of concepts, feedback, and motivation.

Distance education can serve as a catalyst for change and growth in the education arena. By rethinking our ideas about what a classroom is, what teaching and learning are, where learning can occur, and how to measure it most effectively, we can use the best of what we know that works and discover new ways to facilitate this change. Distance education can be more than doing the same old things in many places instead of just one, and we need not feel bound to emulate worn-out models. Assessment, as a component of the instructional design process, can explore new ideas and refine the old as we reflect on our best practices for teaching and learning in whatever environmental configurations may confront us in the future.

DISCUSSION QUESTIONS

1. Although instructional design models prescribe the development of assessment instruments or activities prior to instruction, many (if not most) teachers wait until after instruction to do this. What are some reasons this occurs, and how might it affect the assessment results?
2. An assignment that incorporates peer feedback can be an excellent instructional strategy when used appropriately. How would you structure such an activity to ensure that it's a learning experience for both the giver and receiver of the feedback?
3. Although scoring rubrics are generally considered useful for grading subjective assessments, they are not used as frequently as they might be because of the difficult of creating instruments that are reliable and fair. Why is this so difficult and are there ways that the process could be streamlined?
4. Academic misconduct is considered a critical problem in education today. What measures might you undertake to deter cheating, plagiarism, or other unethical practices?

REFERENCES

American Association for Higher Education. (1996). *9 Principles of good practice for assessing student learning.* Retrieved from http://www.learningoutcomesassessment.org/PrinciplesofAssessment.html

Angelo, T. A., & Cross, K. P. (1993). *Classroom assessment techniques: A handbook for college teachers* (2nd ed.). San Francisco, CA: Jossey-Bass.

Ausubel, D., Novak, J., & Hanesian, H. (1978). *Educational psychology: A cognitive view* (2nd ed.). New York, NY: Holt, Rinehart and Winston.

Beck, V. (2014). Testing a model to predict online cheating: Much ado about nothing. *Active Learning in Higher Education, 15*(1), 65–75.

Brookhart, S. (2017). *How to give effective feedback to your students* (2nd ed.). Alexandria, VA: ASCD.

Burstein, J., Klebanov, B., Elliot, N., Molloy, H. (2016, July). *A left turn: Automated feedback & activity generation for student writers.* Proceedings of Language Teaching, Learning and Technology Workshop, San Francisco, CA.

Carless, D., Salter, D., Yang, M., & Lam, J. (2011) Developing sustainable feedback practices. *Studies in Higher Education, 36*(4), 395–407. doi:10.1080/03075071003642449

Council of Writing Program Administrators. (2010). Defining and avoiding plagiarism: The WPA statement on best practices. Retrieved from http://wpacouncil.org/positions/WPAplagiarism.pdf

Crisp, B. (2007). Is it worth the effort? How feedback influences students' subsequent submission of assessable work. *Assessment & Evaluation in Higher Education, 32*(5), 571–581.

deJong, T., Linn, M., & Zacharia, A. (2013). Physical and virtual laboratories in science and engineering education. *Science, 340*(6130), 305–308.

Engel, P. (2013, June 24). Organized 'crime rings' have stolen billions of dollars from federal student aid programs. *Business Insider.* Retrieved from http://www.businessinsider.com/organized-crime-rings-have-stolen-billions-of-dollars-from-federal-student-aid-programs-2013-6

Gooblar, D. (2015). Getting them to read our comments. Pedagogy Unbound. *Chronicle of Higher Education.* Retrieved from https://chroniclevitae.com/news/1129-getting-them-to-read-our-comments

Hare, M., & Graber, K. (2007). Investigating knowledge acquisition and developing misconceptions of high school students enrolled in an invasion games unit. *The High School Journal, 90*(4), 1–14.

Hattie, J., & Timperley, H. (2007). The power of feedback. *Review of Educational Research, 77*(1), 81–112.

Heritage, M. (2018). Assessment for learning as support for student self-regulation. *The Australian Educational Research, 45*(1), 51–63.

Keller, J. (2016). Motivation, learning, and technology: Applying the ARCS-V Motivation model. *Participatory Educational Research, 3*(1), 1–13. Retrieved from http://www.perjournal.com/archieve/issue_3_2/1-per_16-06_volume_3_issue_2_page_1_15.pdf

Keremedchiev, D., & Peneva, J. (2017). *Comparison of online and traditional in class exams in computer science courses.* Proceedings of the National Conference on Education and Research in the Information Society. Retrieved from http://eprints.nbu.bg/3516/1/ERIS2017-book-p07.pdf

Keuning, H., Jeuring, J., Heeren, B. (2016). Towards a systematic review of automated feedback generation for programming exercises. Retrieved from https://www.researchgate.net/publication/305081685_Towards_a_Systematic_Review_of_Automated_Feedback_Generation_for_Programming_Exercises

Kimura, T. (2017). The impacts of computer adaptive testing from a variety of perspectives. *Journal of Educational Evaluation for the Health Professions, 14*(12). doi.org/10.3352/jeehp.2017.14.12

Lodhia, D. (2018, May 1). More university students are cheating—But it's not because they're lazy. *The Guardian, US Edition.* Retrieved from https://www.theguardian.com/education/2018/may/01/university-students-cheating-tuition-fees-jobs-exams

Lookadoo, K., Bostwick, E., Ralston, R., Elizondo, F., Wilson, S., Shaw, T., & Jensen, M. (2017). "I forgot I wasn't saving the world": The use of formative and summative assessment in instructional video games for undergraduate biology. *Journal of Science Education and Technology, 26,* 597–612.

Louden, K. (2017). Delaying the grade: How to get students to read feedback. *Cult of Pedagogy.* Retrieved from https://www.cultofpedagogy.com/delayed-grade/

Lu, J., & Law, N. (2012). Online peer assessment: Effects of cognitive and affective feedback. *Instructional Science, 40*(2), 257–275. Retrieved from https://doi.org/10.1007/s11251-011-9177-2

Martin, A. J., & Lazendic, G. (2018). Computer-adaptive testing: Implications for students' achievement, motivation, engagement, and subjective test experience. *Journal of Educational Psychology, 110*(1), 27–45.

McCabe, D., Butterfield, D., & Treviño, L. (2012). & Butterfield, D. (1999). *Cheating in college: Why students do it and what educators can do about it.* Baltimore, MD: The Johns Hopkins University Press.

Mehrabian, A. (1969). Some referents and measures of nonverbal behavior. *Behavior Research Methods and Instrumentation, 1*(6), 205–207.

Mueller, J. (2016). *Authentic assessment toolbox.* Retrieved from http://jfmueller.faculty.noctrl.edu/toolbox/whatisit.htm

Mullet, H., Butler, A., Verdin, B., Borries, R., & Marsh, E. (2014). Delaying feedback promotes transfer of knowledge despite student preferences to receive feedback immediately. *Journal of Applied Research in Memory and Cognition, 3*(3), 222–229.

Nicol, D., Thomson, A., Breslin, C. (2014). Rethinking feedback practices in higher education: A peer review perspective. *Assessment & Evaluation in Higher Education, 39*(1), 102–122. doi:10.1080/02602938.2013.795518

Panadero, E., Brown, G., & Strijbos, J. (2016). The future of student self-assessment: A review of known unknowns and potential directions. *Educational Psychology Review, 28*(4), 803–830.

Peled, Y., Eshet, Y., Barczyk, C., & Grinautski, K. (2019). Predictors of academic dishonesty among undergraduate students in online and face-to-face courses. *Computers & Education, 131,* 49–59.

Peterson, E. (2017). *The impact of computer-generated feedback on student perceptions of revision process.* Masters of Arts in Education Action Research Papers, 247, St. Catherine University. Retrieved from https://sophia.stkate.edu/maed/247/

Postal, L. (2015, March 30). Majority of Florida students prefer computer tests over paper ones, survey shows. *Orlando Sentinel.* Retrieved from http://www.orlandosentinel.com/features/education/school-zone/os-florida-students-computer-tests-versus-paper-post.html

Shute, V., & Ventura, M. (2013). *Stealth assessment: Measuring and supporting learning in video games.* Cambridge, MA. MIT Press.

Shute, V., Leighton, J., Lang, E., & Chu, M. (2016). Advances in the science of assessment. *Educational Assessment, 21*(1), 34–59.

SmartWritingService. (2013). Retrieved from https://smartwritingservice.com/

U.S. Department of Education. (2008). *Higher Education Opportunity Act–2008.* Retrieved from https://www.gpo.gov/fdsys/pkg/PLAW-110publ315/pdf/PLAW-110publ315.pdf

Van der Kleji, F., Feskens, R., & Eggen, T. (2015). Effects of feedback in a computer-based learning environment on students' learning outcomes. *Review of Educational Research, 85*(4), 475–511.

Voelkel, S. & Mello, L. (2014). Audio feedback—Better feedback? *Journal of Bioscience Education, 22*(1), 16–30.

Wass, R., Harland, T., McLean, A., Miller, E., & Nui Sim, K. (2015). 'Will press lever for food': Behavioural conditioning of students through frequent high-stakes assessment. *Higher Education Research & Development, 34*(6), 1324–1326.

Wiggins, G. (2014). Authenticity in assessment, (re-)defined and explained. *Granted, and ... thoughts on education by Grant Wiggins.* Retrieved from https://grantwiggins.wordpress.com/2014/01/26/authenticity-in-assessment-re-defined-and-explained

Wilson, J., & Czik, A. (2016). Automated essay evaluation software in English language arts classrooms: Effects on teacher feedback, student motivation, and writing quality. *Computers & Education, 100,* 94–109.

Winkelmes, M. (2013). Transparent assignment template. Retrieved from https://www.unlv.edu/sites/default/files/page_files/27/Provost-Faculty-TransparentAssgntTemplate-2016.pdf

Winkelmes, M., Bernacki, M., Butler, J., Zochowski, M., Golanics, J., & and Harriss Weavil, K. (2016). A teaching intervention that increases underserved college students' success. *Peer Review, 18*(1/2). Retrieved from https://www.aacu.org/peerreview/2016/winter-spring/Winkelmes

Zeidner, M. (2014). Anxiety in education. In R. Pekrun & L. Linnenbrink-Garcia (Eds.), *Educational psychology handbook series. International handbook of emotions in education* (pp. 265–288). New York, NY: Routledge/Taylor & Francis Group.

PART 3

Managing and Evaluating Distance Education

CHAPTER 10

Intellectual Property: Ownership, Distribution, and Use

CHAPTER GOAL

The purpose of this chapter is to discuss the implications of laws relevant to the creation, use, and protection of intellectual property for teaching in distance education environments.

CHAPTER OBJECTIVES

After reading and reviewing this chapter, you should be able to

1. Describe what is meant by "intellectual property" and explain why laws are necessary to protect it and how those laws evolved.
2. Explain the basic tenets of copyright law, including the rights granted to copyright holders in the United States, the four criteria for determining fair use, when and how a work might enter the public domain, and guidelines for use of others' work in a distance education environment.
3. Request permission from a copyright holder to use his/her work for a distance education course. and
4. Describe the licensing options available via Creative Commons and how to identify open educational resources available for use in a distance education course.

INTRODUCTION

Educators routinely create instructional materials in a variety of formats as a part of their jobs, although they may not fully understand the laws and legal guidelines pertaining to that intellectual property. This chapter will address the ownership and legal protections afforded those creative products, as well as how the legally protected works of others may be used for educational purposes. For those who want to encourage others to use their original work, information is provided on how to waive specific rights to those materials and how to identify works that are openly available for use. Please note: the authors of this book are not attorneys and this information should not be considered legal advice.

INTELLECTUAL PROPERTY

Intellectual property (IP) is a blanket term for "creations of the mind," such as literature, inventions, designs, brand names, and product logos, for example (World Intellectual Property Organization, n.d.). These works are protected by a system of laws for copyrights, patents, trade secrets, and trademarks. In the business world, these creations are considered valuable assets and are rigorously protected from unlawful appropriation and use, but the education environment has traditionally been more focused on the "intellectual" part of IP than the "property" part. This, in addition to the complex legalities inherent in the system, results in many educators having only a vague understanding of their own IP rights or the rights of others.

Conflicts over IP rights have become increasingly common with institutions asserting ownership claims on patented inventions, research data, and online courses, so it benefits faculty and course developers to understand the policies and practices at their own institutions. Having a clearly stated policy delineating the rights of all parties can alleviate such conflicts, although there will always be gray areas requiring case-by-case resolution. Since at least the mid-20th century, however, there has been nearly unanimous agreement that rights to instructional materials used in traditional, face-to-face environments belong to the teachers that create those works, even if developing those materials is considered part of the teacher's job. In fact, Ahmadi (2017) suggested that some institutions may have adopted policies favoring faculty ownership as a way to attract and retain top scholars in their fields. Although the "teacher's exception" granting IP rights to instructors has been recognized as a matter of tradition and supported by case law, there is, in fact, no provision within copyright statutes granting teachers these rights. This is rarely a problem when traditional courses rely heavily on an individual instructor's planning, classroom presence, delivery of content, and/or interactions with students.

With the growth of online distance education programs and the ease with which schools can reuse and repurpose courses this issue has garnered substantial attention. Fully developed online courses that can be taught multiple times by multiple low-paid adjunct instructors have significant market value beyond that of their face-to-face counterparts. This only works, however, if the institution owns the IP rights to the course, including the right to reproduce, distribute, modify, and license it (i.e., provide access for a fee, such as tuition). Although these rights might be shared, most institutions prefer to safeguard their investment in course development by preventing faculty members from packing up "their" online course to offer it elsewhere.

A popular method of clarifying online course ownership is to pay the individual faculty course developer under a separate "work for hire" contract that specifies the rights and responsibilities of all involved. This can reduce ambiguity, such as that related to scope of employment (is course development considered just another part of the faculty member's job?) or the degree to which use of institutional resources (network access, computer, office, etc.) influences determinations of ownership. Unfortunately, there may be additional complicating factors, such as when courses are developed by a team of subject matter experts, instructional designers, and multimedia developers or when a faculty member repurposes instructional materials created for a face-to-face class to use in an online course. Many distance education programs rely on agreements, rather than official contracts, but any such document should include, at a minimum, the items found in Figure 10-1.

Just as difficult is determining how one might use the intellectual property of others— books, articles, test banks, or videos—for instructional purposes. Copyright law can seem to be little more than a series of statutes that boil down to, "*Don't do this!*" and it is not surprising that many educators throw their hands up in frustration and simply hope they are not infringing on someone's rights or, if they are, to not get caught. The following sections will explain what copyright is and how it affects the design of distance education coursework. Note that the following information deals almost exclusively with U.S. copyright law; similar statutes exist in nearly all countries, worldwide. International treaties, most

FIGURE 10–1   Course development agreement information.

Category	Example Information
Course Description	Course Title and Number Credit Hours
Development Timeline	Begin/End Dates Milestones and Intermediate Deadlines
Payment Details	Total Payment Amount Payment Schedule Penalty for Late Delivery
Deliverable(s)	Full Course or Individual Components/Modules Original Content or Use of Pre-existing Materials
Quality Control Procedures	Design Guidelines Reference to Criteria for Approval (typically within a separate evaluation rubric) Evaluating Team
Institutional Services Provided	Instructional Design Assistance Multimedia Development Copyright Clearances
Rights of All Parties	Institutional and Individual Claims Permission to Duplicate, Distribute, Modify, Reuse, or License
Right of First Refusal	Teaching Course Revisions

notably the Berne Convention for the Protection of Literary and Artistic Works, protect works beyond their borders of origin.

COPYRIGHT ESSENTIALS

Most educational content resources (books, videos, test banks, etc.) are protected by copyright, a collection of statutes guaranteeing the creators of the resources exclusive rights to reproduce, sell, distribute, modify, use, and/or perform those works. Copyright holders may, however, voluntarily relinquish one or more of those rights in order to facilitate the reuse of their IP by others (to be discussed later in the chapter). Understanding what copyright is and does can help course developers avoid misconceptions that could limit their instructional creativity or lead them into dangerous legal territory.

Misconceptions About Copyright

Myth 1. *I can use materials without permission if they aren't registered with the U.S. Copyright Office.* Any work meeting the criteria specified in the copyright law receives protection as soon as it is fixed in a tangible medium of expression. For example, an original manuscript is protected as soon as it is written by hand or when the digital file is saved or printed. Inclusion of a copyright notice or the copyright symbol © is not required. Registration with the Copyright Office is optional although a work must be registered before a plaintiff can collect statutory damages in the event of an infringement.

Myth 2. *Materials that I find online are in the public domain, so I can use them as I wish.* Nothing could be further from the truth. Original works of authorship placed on the Internet are protected by copyright just like any other works meeting the law's criteria. A useful analogy is that books in a public library are freely available for use but are also entitled to protection under copyright law.

Myth 3. *As long as I'm not making any money from it, I can use copyrighted materials without obtaining permission.* Copyright infringement can be claimed whether there was financial gain involved or not. In addition, a civil judgment in the case of copyright violation may consider the actual or potential damage to the market for the original work when determining penalties for infringement.

Myth 4. *I can use copyrighted materials for educational purposes without having to obtain permission because this is covered under "fair use."* As a blanket statement, this is perhaps the biggest myth of all. Education is one of the purposes for which fair use may apply, but fair use can be determined only after careful consideration of four significant criteria. Many educational applications are completely beyond fair use and require permission from the copyright holder—for example, the development of most course-packs of readings, whether hardcopy or electronic.

Myth 5. *I can digitize copyrighted materials and place them on a course website without permission, as long as the site is password protected.* Recent legislation has expanded the scope of materials that may be digitized and placed on a password-protected course website, but fair use criteria still apply. For example, although a fair use case may be made for scanning a limited number of images from a text to incorporate into course website, it is easy to stray well beyond fair use without realizing it.

Myth 6. *If I make a few changes to a copyrighted work I can claim it as my own and use it without obtaining permission.* The act of taking someone else's work and modifying it is considered creating a "derivative work" according to copyright law. The right to create derivative works belongs to the copyright holder unless specific permission has been granted for this.

Myth 7. *I won't get caught.* Yes, it is possible to step on someone's rights and never get caught doing it, although it has become increasingly likely that you will, especially with the advent of web-crawlers used to search out infringements. However, it may also be useful to consider whether the benefit is worth the risk and if ignoring the law and behaving unethically sets an appropriate example. (Good luck explaining to students why they should not cheat on exams.)

History of Copyright

The first U.S. copyright legislation, adopted in 1790, was modeled after a similar statute enacted by British Parliament in 1714. The law, Title 17 of the U.S. Code, has undergone several major revisions, the latest in 1976 as Public Law 94-553. Section 102 specifies that copyright protection subsists in original works of authorship fixed in a tangible medium of expression, now known or later developed, from which they can be perceived, reproduced, or otherwise communicated, either directly or with the aid of a machine or device.

Thus, two critical conditions must be met before a work is eligible for copyright protection. First, copyright applies to works of authorship representing the tangible expression of ideas, requiring originality and some degree of creativity. Copyrighted works of authorship in a distance education course—by instructors or students—may include notes, e-mail messages, comments made in online discussions and chats, images, digital audio and video files, animations, presentation graphics such as PowerPoint files, and/or printed materials reproduced for student study. Copyright protection similarly extends to original content and comments posted on blogs, the content of wikis, podcast files, video files posted on YouTube, tweets, and any other original content posted on the web by anyone, as long as it meets the fundamental criteria for copyright protection. Copyright protection does not extend to facts, titles, names, familiar symbols, standard forms, procedures, and works consisting of common property, although some items in these categories may be eligible for patent or trademark protection.

Second, the work must be fixed in a tangible medium of expression. The previous examples are self-evident because they can be perceived, reproduced, or otherwise communicated (the actual terminology used in the law). Copyright would not apply to comments made in a live, face-to-face classroom discussion unless the interaction were recorded or otherwise transcribed. However, the situation is different in an online course, because online discussions are typically fixed in digital form. Even synchronous communications using audio- or videoconferencing systems are fixed in a tangible medium of expression if they are recorded and archived for on-demand access at a later time, and therefore fall under copyright protection. As with other works, courses themselves are eligible for copyright protection if they are fixed in a tangible medium (such as residing on a server) and include original content.

Exclusive Rights of Copyright Holders

The law grants copyright owners the exclusive rights to do, or to authorize others to do, any of the following:

- Reproduce the copyrighted work
- Prepare derivative works based on the copyrighted original
- Distribute copies of the copyrighted work
- Perform the copyrighted work
- Display the copyrighted work publicly

Fortunately, Congress recognized that the use of protected materials without permission from the copyright holder should be acceptable within certain circumstances. In fact, limitations on exclusive rights consume the majority of Chapter 1 of Title 17. Two sections are of particular importance to distance educators: Section 107, which provides the criteria for fair use and Section 110, which addresses public performance and display.

Fair Use.   According to Section 107, "the fair use of a copyrighted work ... for purposes such as criticism, comment, news reporting, teaching (including multiple copies for classroom use), scholarship, or research, is not an infringement" (Copyright Act of 1976). In other words, you can use copyrighted materials for these purposes without asking for permission. *However,* House Report No. 94-1476 issued that same year noted that no adequate definition of the concept of fair use had emerged, and that no generally applicable definition was possible. Rather, the doctrine should be viewed as "an equitable rule of reason," with each case to be decided on its own merits against the criteria provided in the law. This has not changed in the intervening years.

The phrasing here is critically important. Section 107 does not grant educators wholesale permission to use copyrighted materials simply because they work in nonprofit educational organizations. Rather, fair use can be determined only after four essential criteria have been considered. These considerations are:

- ▪ **"The purpose and character of the use, including whether such use is of a commercial nature or is for nonprofit educational purposes...."**   Uses in a nonprofit, educational setting are more likely to be fair use than those in a corporate training or proprietary/for-profit school setting, as are those considered transformative. Reproduction for purposes of criticism or commentary may be considered more favorably, also, even if for commercial purposes.
- ▪ **"The nature of the copyrighted work...."**   Nonfiction works are more likely to be considered fair use than fictional or artistic works containing a higher degree of creative expression. Published works are generally favored by courts more than unpublished materials, and printed works more than audiovisual materials. Publications designed to be consumable, such as workbook pages or standardized test forms, should never be reproduced without permission.
- ▪ **"The amount and substantiality of the portion used in relation to the copyrighted work as a whole...."**   The law itself does not provide specific limits or percentages, although criteria have been set in negotiated guidelines that will be discussed later in this chapter. The case for fair use can be enhanced if no more of the published original is taken than is deemed necessary to meet the user's needs. This criterion also has a qualitative component in that reproduction of even a small proportion of a work may exceed fair use if that portion contains the heart or essence of the original.
- ▪ **"The effect of the use upon the potential market for or value of the copyrighted work...."**   In infringement suits, the courts consider whether and to what extent the use might harm the existing and future market for the original work.

Congress deliberately wrote these criteria in broad, general terms to provide a flexible structure that could be applied across a multitude of potential scenarios without the need for constant revisions to the law. No single criterion of the four is enough to deny fair use. Even if one criterion weighs against, the use may still be considered fair if the other three weigh in favor. As mentioned earlier, countries outside the U.S. have their own copyright statutes and this holds true for fair use exceptions, as well (e.g., the "Fair Dealing" provisions enjoyed by British Commonwealth nations).

Public Performance and Display.   Section 110 of the copyright law permits the performance or display of a work during the face-to-face teaching activities of a nonprofit educational institution, in a classroom or similar place devoted to instruction, with a lawfully made or acquired copy (if applicable). This has become known as the "face-to-face teaching exemption." Section 110 covers activities such as the reading aloud of literature, performance of dramatic works by class members (but not by actors from outside the class), performance of compositions in music classes, and display of video recordings and other audiovisual materials that takes place in the face-to-face classroom.

House of Representatives Report 94-1476 noted specifically that the face-to-face teaching exemption did not extend to the transmission of audiovisual materials into the classroom from a location outside the building. For many years, this restriction was quite problematic for libraries and media centers that transmitted videotapes from centralized collections into classrooms via school networks, if transmission and reception occurred in separate buildings. The distribution of materials in this manner required specific licensing agreements with the rights holders.

Of greater concern for distance educators for a quarter century after the 1976 revision was the problem of incorporating video recordings and other audiovisual media (defined in the law as works that consist of a series of related images which are intrinsically intended to be shown by the use of machines or devices such as projectors, viewers, or electronic equipment) into courses transmitted to remote sites via distance education delivery systems, including both video- and Internet-based distribution. Such use clearly was outside the limits specified in Section 110. Passage of the Technology, Education, and Copyright Harmonization (TEACH) Act by Congress in 2002, which will be discussed in detail later in this chapter, alleviated this situation.

Section 110 cannot be applied to training events that take place in for-profit settings, for example, in proprietary institutions and private-sector industry. Classroom display of materials such as video recordings in these for-profit locations should be covered by licensing agreements when the materials are purchased.

Duration of Copyright

Several formulas have been devised to help determine when copyright protection expires on specific works and they move into the public domain. Terms of protection vary according to the date of creation, whether the work was published, whether ownership resides with an individual or an employer or other legal entity, and whether the original copyright on an older work was renewed. Generally speaking, however, works created before 1923 are definitely in the public domain, works published between 1923 and 1977 may be protected up to 95 years from the date of publication, and works from 1978 or after are protected for the life of the creator plus 70 years. Everything that was published in 1923 will be in the public domain as of January 1, 2019. (For more detailed information on copyright duration, see Lolly Gasaway's website at https://www.unc.edu/~unclng/public-d.htm)

The task of determining the actual term of copyright is compounded by the layers of protection that may exist for a given work. For example, Mozart's symphonies have long been in the public domain, but a 1998 recording of his Symphony No. 41 is likely to be protected for longer than the owner of the recording can find equipment on which to play it back. A textbook photo of an artwork may be copyrighted at several levels: by the publisher, the photographer, and the owner of the original work, for example.

Public Domain

Any work in the public domain may be used freely in a distance education course. Works may enter the public domain several ways, most often simply through expiration of copyright protection. Most materials published by the U.S. federal government are specifically excluded from copyright protection by Section 105 and are in the public domain from the date of creation. However, works developed by or for state agencies, including video recordings and other audiovisual materials, may be declared public domain according to the state's policies but are more likely to be copyrighted.

Another means by which works enter the public domain is for owners to abandon their copyrights. For example, as Myth 2 previously illustrated, a popular and widespread misconception holds that materials posted to the Internet become public domain because the Internet is such a public and uncontrolled medium. Abandonment of copyright actually requires an explicit and overt statement from the copyright holder—and rarely occurs. More information about public domain can be found in the section on releasing rights.

GUIDELINES

As the 1909 copyright law was undergoing revision in the mid-1970s, Congress recognized that the nonprofit educational community could benefit from guidelines to help define acceptable practices under fair use. The House report contained guidelines for classroom copying and educational uses of music that had been negotiated by educator and publisher groups. A third set of guidelines was approved in 1979 to cover off-air recording of broadcast programming for educational purposes.

Although the authors of the law tried to accommodate future technological developments with vague terminology such as "fixed in a tangible medium of expression, now known or later developed" and "with the aid of a machine or device," they had no way of anticipating the phenomenal growth of digital media authoring, storage, and distribution systems, or the incredible range of technology now easily available to both educators and consumers. As a result, application of a 1976 statute in the 21st century is often the source of considerable frustration and confusion.

In September 1994, the U.S. Department of Commerce convened the Conference on Fair Use (CONFU), bringing together information proprietors and user groups in an attempt to develop fair use guidelines addressing new technologies (Lehman, 1998). Over a two-and-a-half-year period, representatives of more than 100 organizations met as a whole and in smaller work groups to draft guidelines for distance learning, image collections, multimedia, electronic reserves, and interlibrary loan. By May 1997, only the first three work groups had developed formal proposals, and none of the three garnered widespread support in the education community. Ultimately, CONFU elected neither to endorse nor to reject any of the proposals but to continue the negotiation processes. Even though the CONFU drafts were never operationalized, they are useful because they may represent the limits to which the rights-holder community considers fair use. On the other hand, education and library organizations are quick to point out that the limits of fair use may in fact extend beyond the guide-lines and can only be determined by the courts.

COPYRIGHT-RELATED LEGISLATION

The copyright law itself is a document in a perpetual state of change and has been amended many dozens of times since the Copyright Act of 1976. Typically, more than 20 acts are introduced in each 2-year congressional session. Most of these never become law, and of those that have survived the process and been enacted, few have been significant for the education community. Two that have, however, are the Digital Millennium Copyright Act (DMCA) and the subsequent legislation it spawned, the TEACH Act.

Digital Millennium Copyright Act

The DMCA, 59 pages long in its PDF version, has been the most comprehensive revision of the 1976 copyright law of interest to educators to date, with significant implications for distance education. The act was intended to bring the United States into compliance with two treaties agreed on by the World Intellectual Property Organization in 1996. Three components of the DMCA are particularly relevant to this chapter.

Infringement Liability Protections. The DMCA specifies that if a copyright infringement is discovered on a website maintained by an Internet service provider (ISP), the rights holder may request that the ISP block access to or take down the infringing material. The DMCA offers to these service providers what is known as "safe harbor" protection, releasing the ISP from liability for such infringements. Many school districts and most higher education campuses provide Internet access for their faculty, staff, and students, and thus fall into the category of "service provider." (For the remainder of this section, service provider will refer to the school, district, or higher education institution providing Internet services for its internal constituencies. This responsibility is normally placed within an instructional or information technology department.)

If, for example, a faculty member has placed copyrighted material on a course website without the appropriate clearance or legitimate fair use claim, the copyright owner can request that the service provider remove it, or at least block access to it. These "takedowns requests" typically result in immediate action (blocking or removal), because if the service provider does not, it may be liable for the infringement along with the teacher. The ISP must also give notification of the takedown to the person who placed the infringing material on the website. To be eligible for liability protection, the service provider must have been previously unaware of the infringing activity and cannot receive any financial gain from the infringement.

The DMCA lists several protective measures that schools and colleges must take to limit their liability as service providers:

▪ A designated agent must be registered with the Copyright Office to receive copyright infringement complaints and respond appropriately. Instructions for registration of an agent and a list of agents may be found at the Copyright Office website. Procedures for contacting the agent must also be posted on the service provider's website.

▪ A current copyright policy for the ISP's Internet users must be in place and posted on the organizational website. The policy must contain provisions stating that access privileges will be terminated for repeat offenders.

▪ The ISP must maintain an ongoing program for educating its Internet users about copyright and requirements for obtaining appropriate permissions before placing protected material on institutional web pages, including course websites.

Education and library groups have pointed out that taking down course materials that are the target of infringement complaints may have serious implications for fair use and academic freedom, not to mention a potentially deleterious impact on student learning. The DMCA permits the faculty member to serve a counternotification that she or he believes the initial complaint was filed erroneously, for example, in a claim of fair use. Unless the copyright owner takes legal action as the result of the counternotification, the service provider must restore access to the materials in question within 10 to 14 working days, or essentially within 2 to 3 weeks. However, filing the counternotification could place the faculty member at risk of litigation, and the period of time during which the materials are offline may jeopardize the lesson plan.

Unfortunately, the creators of the DMCA severely underestimated the potential for abuses of this system. False takedown requests reportedly number in the tens of millions each year (Binder, 2018), many due to the copyright owner's lack of understanding regarding fair use provisions, but the majority of this rapidly-increasing number is generated en masse by bots. In addition, a small (but not insignificant) number of these are malicious claims in which the copyright owner files the notice to block legitimate critique of their work, for example, or simply as a hostile act against the alleged infringer (Antkers & Miller, 2018). Although penalties awarded for misrepresentation have been rare, the courts have, in an increasing number of cases, ruled in favor of the accused.

Circumvention of Technological Protection Measures. The DMCA addresses measures taken by copyright owners to control both access to and reproduction of their protected materials. Related to websites, the DMCA not only prohibits the sale and use of devices that circumvent access restriction methods such as password protection, but it also makes illegal the act of informing others how to circumvent these measures and linking to sites that provide this information.

However, as with the infringement liability issues described above, the education and library communities have protested the circumvention limitations of the DMCA as threats to fair use and academic freedom. Specifically, these organizations hoped for broader access to such materials as literary works and video materials that exist online but require fee payment before access is granted. The Electronic Frontier Foundation put it bluntly in their whitepaper, *Unintended Consequences: 16 Years Under the DMCA* (Electronic Frontier Foundation, 2014) when it stated, "In practice, the anticircumvention provisions have been used to stifle a wide array of legitimate activities."

Distance Education Study. Section 403 of the DMCA required the Copyright Office to collect information from all stakeholders and make recommendations to Congress on how to promote the use of digital technologies in distance education. The Office's Report on Digital Distance Education was released in May 1999 (U.S. Copyright Office, 1999). Most of its recommendations focused on amending Section 110 of the copyright law to extend the exemptions granted in face-to-face instructional situations to distance learning environments.

The Report on Digital Distance Education led to the introduction of several related acts in both the House and Senate. Another major impetus leading to this legislation was the highly acclaimed report of the Web-Based Education Commission compiled for the president and Congress, entitled *The Power of the Internet for Learning: Moving From Promise to Practice* (Web-Based Education Commission, 2000), which considered the challenge of providing 21st century distance education with obsolete copyright laws as analogous to trying "to manage the interstate highway system with the rules of the horse and buggy era" (p. 97).

Technology, Education, and Copyright Harmonization (TEACH) Act

This is the legislation in response to the DMCA that ultimately emerged to address distance learning issues. The TEACH Act was enacted by Congress and signed into law by President George W. Bush in November 2002. The Act was a long-anticipated blessing for distance educators because it amended Section 110 and loosened restrictions. However, strings were attached. The changes provided by the TEACH Act do not apply unless two critical institutional requirements are met. First, the provisions only apply to accredited nonprofit educational institutions, at both the K–12 and higher education levels. Accreditation is an important qualification. Second, the educational organization must have a published policy regarding teacher use of copyrighted materials and an ongoing copyright training program in place for faculty, staff, and students. In other words, the organization must comply with the DMCA.

Other requirements of the act relate to teacher use of the materials and the materials themselves.

- Access to the digitized materials must be restricted to students enrolled in the course.
- Digitized materials must be used in the same manner in an online course as they would be in a face-to-face (f2f) course. For example, if a video segment would have been displayed by the teacher in the face-to-face setting, it may be digitized for the online course. If students would have viewed the video independently in a learning resources center instead of the f2f classroom, the TEACH Act would not apply. Moreover, the digital materials must only be available to the students during approximately the same time period in which they would be available to an f2f class, a particularly troublesome requirement for an asynchronous course.
- In the case of a video recording, only the essential portions that the teacher would display in the f2f classroom may be incorporated into the online course. In many cases, that would not be the entire production.
- Materials must have been lawfully acquired.
- Students must be notified of the relevant copyright information for the materials and that the materials are protected by copyright law.
- Materials may be digitized for online use only if digital versions are not already available.

If these provisions are met, the TEACH Act may open the door to a wider range of instructional technologies for distance education than were permitted by the old Section 110 by allowing performances of nondramatic literary and musical works and "reasonable and limited portions" of dramatic and audiovisual works for online classes. The Act also eliminated the requirement that students receiving the instruction be located in a classroom or other site devoted to instruction. Unfortunately, although the intent was to increase the options for use of copyrighted materials and clarify existing guidelines, teachers, librarians, and course developers at many institutions maintain that the legislation is inflexible and has not been as beneficial as was originally hoped (Fruin, 2012).

User Training

The Digital Millennium Copyright Act requires educational institutions to engage in an ongoing program to educate its Internet users about copyright issues. How should that training be conducted? Is it enough to post the copyright policy on the organization's website? That alone is required by the DMCA, but more should be done. Optional workshops about copyright are likely to set new institutional records for nonattendance, but these topics could also be addressed in faculty meetings or in a campus newsletter. Discussing copyright matters within the context of other institutional issues may encourage faculty attention, as well. Frequently asked questions web pages (FAQs), even if they are asked only by the author of the FAQ column, can be helpful if applied to practical situations, but they should be located and maintained within websites visited by faculty on a regular basis.

Providing copyright training to students may be an even greater challenge. Students do not attend workshops on this topic and are unlikely to read and respect printed guides to "safe copyright." In addition, the proliferation of sites that will buy course materials from students (e.g., study guides, test questions, or PowerPoint handouts) has increased the chances that a student might run afoul of copyright law. Increasingly, universities are adopting policies that also make such distribution (for financial gain or not) a violation of academic integrity codes. An example syllabus statement might read:

The materials you are provided in this course are copyrighted and the intellectual property of [instructor] and/or third parties. This may include, for example, the syllabus, study guides, handouts, and tests. Please respect [instructor's] rights and do not distribute (for free or for pay) any course materials. Likewise, your coursework belongs to you; neither your instructor nor [institution] will reproduce or distribute your work without written permission. Violations (on either side) may be punishable under the [institution] Academic Integrity Code.

COPYRIGHT APPLICATIONS IN DISTANCE EDUCATION

What are the major implications of U.S. copyright law for distance education? This section will address, in broad terms, how copyright law applies to different types of instructional materials and their use in distance education programs. Although detailed information concerning how much of any particular work is allowable is beyond the scope of this chapter, guidelines can be found in Circular 21 of the U.S. Copyright Office, *Reproduction of Copyrighted Works by Educators and Librarians* (https://www.copyright.gov/circs/circ21.pdf). As a reminder, the authors of this book are not attorneys and this chapter does not constitute legal advice.

Printed Materials

Regardless of the delivery vehicle, teachers of distance education courses may want their students to have copyrighted articles and other printed materials in hand for study purposes. In most cases, these materials would be digitized and posted on the course website or incorporated into digital coursepacks. The guidelines mentioned above permit limited reproduction and distribution of copyrighted materials (no more than one copy per student in the course) as long as the tests of brevity, spontaneity, and cumulative effects are met. Brevity refers to the suggested limitations for amount to be used and the test of spontaneity requires that the inspiration to use the work and the moment in time of actual use in the course do not allow for a reasonable attempt to obtain permission. The latter effectively prohibits use of the same materials in subsequent academic terms without the copyright holder's approval. The cumulative effects test caps the number of items copied for a single course at nine per academic term.

The criteria specified in the guidelines help determine what can be reproduced without the need to seek permission. The development of coursepacks, particularly those including the same materials term after term, normally requires licensing and payment of fees. The licensing of printed materials is not an overwhelming task. The Copyright Clearance Center (see URL at the end of this chapter) has been established as the reproduction rights organization (RRO) for the United States and serves this clearinghouse function. Since its founding in 1978 to provide book and periodical clearance services in response to the then newly revised copyright act, the Copyright Clearance Center has evolved into a comprehensive organization that has managed millions of clearances in more than 180 countries and distributed royalties in excess of one billion dollars.

The concept of the electronic coursepack is not exclusive to the Copyright Clearance Center. For-profit companies such as XanEdu and University Readers also have emerged to help distance educators incorporate electronic works into their courses. With services such as XanEdu, for example, faculty create accounts and identify the publications they wish to include. The service provider then obtains the appropriate permissions, compiles the coursepacks, sets prices, and sends access information to the faculty member, who forwards it to the students. Students set up their own accounts with the service provider, pay the fee, normally by credit card, and receive immediate online access to the coursepack materials.

Electronic coursepacks purchased by students should be used only when the same content is not available for free (whether through an online source or through a subscription service provided by the institution's library, for example). A wide variety of reports and other documents published by government and nonprofit agencies, as well as by many commercial organizations, are also freely available online, as are many conference papers posted by their authors or the conference organizers.

Video

Many faculty use video resources in their conventional, face-to-face classes and want to use the same resources in their courses delivered at a distance. The TEACH Act sets specific guidelines for the use of video in a distance education environment, but the requirement that the materials must be "lawfully acquired" is not as straightforward as it appears. The most obvious response is that the original recording has been purchased or rented by the educational organization for the specific purpose of supporting instruction. Distributors of these products, however, typically do not include online use in their license agreements without a separate, specific permission. Many (if not most) educational videos are now offered via streaming services on a subscription basis, however, and institutions are streaming videos via course management systems to ensure that only students who are enrolled in the course will have access. Even with these access constraints, it is not yet clear if this can be considered "fair use." The most recent ruling on this practice (in November, 2012) dismissed charges of copyright infringement against the University of California, Los Angeles brought by the Association for Information Media and Equipment (*AIME v. Regents of the University of California*, 2012), but Judge Consuelo Marshall reminded the involved parties, "Notably, no court has considered whether streaming videos only to students enrolled in a class constitutes fair use, which reinforces the ambiguity of the law in this area" (p. 11). To be sure, the final chapter of this saga has not yet been written. Ultimately, it will be the courts that define what is fair use, what is not, and under what conditions.

Photographs and Digital Images

The reproduction of photographs, illustrations, graphic designs, and other still images for use in a distance education course presents a perplexing copyright dilemma because IP may be involved at several levels. For example, a teacher may wish to digitize a textbook photograph. The book and the photograph may be copyrighted separately, and depending on the subject matter, the original object may also be protected. Moreover, the chain from the original to the photo in the book may involve intermediate steps, each entitled to copyright protection. Even if the original object is in the public domain, the photograph and book may not be.

Section 110 of U.S. Copyright Law permits the classroom display of photographic material that has been lawfully acquired, such as digital image sets purchased for educational use from a distributor authorized by the rights holders. The "lawfully acquired" condition may also apply to images that have been scanned locally from books and magazines. Circular 21 indicates that one picture per book or periodical issue is permissible. Guidelines for the educational use of digital images were drafted by one of the CONFU working groups but were quite restrictive and failed to garner much support in the educational community. The draft does provide some insight into the limits to which some copyright holders perceive fair use. The guidelines include the following selected provisions:

- Only lawfully acquired analog images may be digitized.
- Educational institutions may not digitize images that are already available in usable digital form for purchase or license at a fair price.
- Educational institutions may display and provide access through a secure electronic network to images digitized under these guidelines, provided that access is controlled via a password or PIN and restricted to students enrolled in the course.
- Use of images digitized from a known source may be used only for one academic term; subsequent use requires permission. If permission is not received, subsequent use is subject to the four-factor fair use analysis.
- If the rights holder is unknown, the image may be used for 3 years from first use, provided that the institution conducts a reasonable effort to identify the rights holder and seek permission.
- Images digitized under these guidelines may be used in face-to-face teaching, independent study by students, and research and scholarly activities at the institution.
- The images may not be used in publications without permission.

E-Mail, Websites, and Other Internet Resources

Materials placed on the Internet, whether e-mail messages, postings to subscription mailing lists, websites, blogs, wikis, podcasts, and other digital resources, represent IP fixed in a tangible medium of expression and are entitled to copyright protection like any other work of authorship. From a legal perspective, placement of the material on the Internet is no different from any other form of distribution, except that access and the potential for abuse are both greatly expanded. Posting documents or other materials online does not imply an abandonment of copyright. Materials with expanded usage rights via Creative Commons licensing will be identified as such.

Is it necessary to obtain permission before linking to someone else's website? Although some purists insist that the answer is yes, most authorities feel that freely linking to the websites of others not only is legal but is encouraged, and that those who object to setting up hyperlinks are essentially missing the point of the web. Generally speaking, it is not necessary to obtain permission prior to installing links to external resources within a course website. Indeed, faculty who fail to do so may be missing some excellent opportunities to expand student access to valuable online resources and promote learning in the course content areas. From a strictly logistical perspective, linking to an online article, image, video, or other item is typically preferable to uploading them into a course management system where storage capacities may be limited or performance compromised by large files. If a website specifically states that linking to it requires permission, it is considered courteous to request permission but it is not legally required.

OBTAINING PERMISSION

If guidelines are not applicable, fair use cannot be determined, and the TEACH Act does not apply, distance educators should obtain permission from rights holders before using copyrighted materials in their courses. Although this may seem daunting, it is not difficult although it may be time-consuming. The three steps for getting permission are described below (Digital Media Law Project, 2014).

1. Begin by identifying who holds the copyright for the work. In most cases this is not difficult, but it's important to keep in mind that the original creator of the work might not be the copyright owner. It may be necessary to search online for information, contact a copyright collective (e.g., Copyright Clearance Center), or request help from a reference librarian.

2. Contact the copyright owner by e-mail or telephone and describe the circumstances of your request. You should provide your name and contact information, identifying details of the work in question (title, URL, author, etc.), the reason for your request (e.g., for instructional purposes, the name of the course, etc.), and how you intend to use the work (posting in a password-protected CMS, for example).

3. Get the permission in writing. The copyright holder may give an informal okay, but it is important to have an official record of your communications, the date permission was granted, and any conditions.

Obtaining permission is not complicated but it may take time to identify the copyright owner and/or to hear back from them. It's a good idea to plan ahead and start the process as early as possible.

Copyrighted Materials and Course Management Systems

As discussed throughout this book, many (if not most) distance education courses and programs, particularly in higher education and corporate training settings, are now offered using a course management system such as Canvas, Blackboard, or Moodle. The copyright implications described are equally applicable in these settings, even though most of the systems require passwords that restrict access to the enrolled participants. Placing full text of copyrighted documents, such as journal articles, behind password protection strengthens the case for fair use, but until the courts rule otherwise, this practice is risky without the proper permissions or licensing. Publishers and copyright management organizations are acutely aware of the potential for copyright infringement within course management systems, and some provide copyright guidance for faculty teaching within that context (e.g., Copyright Clearance Center, 2011).

Content resources (for example, supplementary readings) that are publisher-provided and integrated into the CMS within a proprietary cartridge typically require the adoption of an accompanying textbook for access. These resources do not require permission because copyright clearances are included and the materials might even be automatically disabled or deleted at semester's end to prevent accidental infringement. Materials that an institution licenses on a subscription basis, such as e-journals or commercially produced videos for streaming, may be accessed by linking to them from within the CMS. Finally, course content for which an instructor holds copyright, resources that are in the public domain, or works that grant usage permission through Creative Commons may be placed within the CMS for direct student access.

In many cases it's helpful to have a quick reference resource for instructors who have basic copyright and fair use questions. Figure 10-2 provides a sample portion of such a resource.

FIGURE 10–2   Portion of a quick reference guide for faculty.

Do This	Not That
Use the [CMS] system to organize your course materials and make them available to students. This relieves you of the responsibility of ensuring that appropriate security and authentication measures are in place.	Do not post copyrighted materials on a website outside of the [CMS] system. Even if the site is password-protected, you may be at risk of a copyright violation.
You may provide access to copyrighted materials only to students registered for the course and other instructional staff (teaching assistants or guest lecturers, for example). Students may have access to these materials throughout the academic term.	Do not allow students not enrolled in the course to have access to copyrighted materials. Instructional staff (e.g., teaching assistants) should have a direct affiliation with the course. Do not extend student access beyond the end of the academic term.
Fair Use guidelines stipulate that copyrighted works may be used "in support of curriculum-based instructional activity." Include such resources within course modules that integrate associated readings, discussion questions, and assignments.	Do not provide access to copyrighted materials if they aren't justifiably in support of clearly-articulated learning outcomes.
Provide attribution for both the original creator and the copyright holder (these may be different entities) when using the work of others.	Do not assume that if materials lack a copyright notice © that they needn't be cited or are in the public domain. (They do and they probably are not.)
Whenever possible, link to materials that already reside online.	Do not link to works that appear to have been posted online illegally by someone else.

RELEASING RIGHTS TO CREATIVE WORKS

Copyright is not the only form of intellectual property protection. For those who would like to release some rights but not all, the two most popular options are Creative Commons or Copyleft, although the latter is used almost exclusively for software programming. Creative Commons (CC) is a nonprofit organization created to facilitate sharing of intellectual property by providing free legal tools and advocacy for educational, scientific, and cultural projects supporting open access to knowledge and creative works. Creative Commons was founded in 2001 and released their initial series of licenses late in 2002. By 2003, more than 1 million items had CC licenses and that number climbed to more than 1.4 billion works worldwide by the end of 2017 (Merkley, 2018). CC offers a variety of licensing options that extend beyond the standard "all rights reserved" nature of copyright while also avoiding the "no rights reserved" result of public domain works. All CC licenses require attribution (i.e., credit where credit is due), and copyright holders can also allow the creation of derivative works based on the original, require derivatives to be publicly shared, permit commercial use of the work, or any combination (or none) of these options.

A CC license does not negate the legal protections of copyright but is, instead, a way for individuals to relinquish some of their rights to enable others to use, modify, and/or distribute the item in question without obtaining permission from the copyright holder. Creative Commons licenses are only applicable to works already protected by copyright and

FIGURE 10–3 Creative Commons licenses.

Attribution
CC BY

All CC licenses require that others who use your work in any way must give you credit the way you request, but not in a way that suggests you endorse them or their use. If they want to use your work without giving you credit or for endorsement purposes, they must get your permission first.

ShareAlike
CC BY-SA

Attribution + You let others copy, distribute, display, perform, and modify your work, as long as they distribute any modified work on the same terms. If they want to distribute modified works under other terms, they must get your permission first.

Attribution-
NonCommercial
CC BY-NC

Attribution + You let others copy, distribute, display, perform, and (unless you have chosen NoDerivatives) modify and use your work for any purpose other than commercially unless they get your permission first.

Attribution-
NoDerivs
CC BY-ND

Attribution + You let others copy, distribute, display and perform only original copies of your work. If they want to modify your work, they must get your permission first.

"The Licenses," Creative Commons, Attribution 4.0 International license.

are intended primarily for use with material that is available online, to facilitate easy sharing. The types of licenses and their associated permissions are described in Figure 10-3. Note that these license types can be combined (e.g, CC BY-SA-NC-ND), depending on what you will allow others to do with your work.

Licensing a work through Creative Commons is relatively easy and simply requires selecting the ways others can use the item in question and marking the work with the appropriate CC icon(s). Optional information can be appended to add machine-readable metadata that will help others attribute the work to you. A series of questions helps the owner/creator to identify which licensing option is the best fit and the appropriate html is automatically generated to attach to the work, alerting others of how they might use it.

In some situations, content creators may want to relinquish *all* of their IP rights, including attribution, by marking their works with the CC0 (CC-zero) icon, thus entering the work into the public domain. This option can be thought of as a "no rights reserved" alternative to copyright or CC licensing. Although it is also possible to relinquish all rights to a work by applying a public domain mark (PDM) to it, the CC0 license may be a better option for several reasons, including the inconsistency of how public domain is defined internationally. It's important to note that releasing all rights includes the possibility that the work will be claimed by others specifically for financial gain through sales or licensing.

Additional information about licensing, CC0, and the public domain can be found at the Creative Commons website (creativecommons.org), including human readable (i.e., understandable by nonlawyers) descriptions of the licenses in addition to their official, legal code versions. For those who wish to use CC licensed works created by others, the website also provides examples of how to cite these resources as well as information on how to mark adaptations of an original.

THE OPEN EDUCATION MOVEMENT

The open education movement grew out of a broad combination of philosophies that had earlier laid the groundwork for open source software, open data, and open design standards, for example. This culture of sharing and collaboration, intended to reduce duplication of effort and improve outcomes, has been widely adopted throughout the education community, although logistical and philosophical concerns have been acknowledged. Early initiatives include the establishment of the MERLOT learning object repository in the late 1990s and MIT's Open CourseWare project in 2002, in which online materials and learning activities from 50 courses were made freely available. Within the education environment, labeling a work as "open" typically implies no cost (or low cost) access to the material as well as fewer restrictions on use, adaptation, and sharing than copyright allows and it is typical for these works to be labeled with Creative Commons licenses.

Materials created or repurposed for public sharing are known as Open Educational Resources (OER). Examples of OER include: full courses, course modules, syllabi, lectures, homework assignments, quizzes, lab and classroom activities, pedagogical materials, games, simulations, and many more resources contained in digital media collections from around the world. (Institute for the Study of Knowledge Management in Education, 2018). Some examples of these repositories include OER Commons (www.oercommons.org), The Internet Archive (archive.org), and OpenStax CNX (cnx.org), where content resources are organized by topic and grade level, and typically are searchable on a range of more specific criteria. In addition, some of these collections allow users to evaluate materials and provide feedback about their usability and validity.

Adopting, adapting, or creating open resources has many advantages over traditional textbook-based resources, with cost savings to students the most obvious benefit. OER can also shorten the time between the creation and distribution of resources by eliminating many of the delays inherent in traditional publishing, and enable experts in specialized fields to contribute resources that might have too small an audience to be attractive to publishers. Finally, the open education movement relies on an informal ideology of collaboration that can result in improved materials as they're shared and improved upon. These positive outcomes would be difficult (if not impossible) to attain under the constraints of copyright.

LOOKING FORWARD

Many homes, workplaces, and schools today are equipped with advanced telecommunications systems integrating telephone services, Internet access, and television programming, and other features not yet realized or imagined are on their way. Distance education will play a central role in that future, as technology-delivered curricula are increasingly available on a global basis to anyone, anywhere, at any time. For those instructional initiatives, current IP policies and copyright laws will likely prove insufficient for dealing with the enormous complexity of protecting ownership rights of individuals while at the same time providing access to the creative works needed to provide high-quality learning experiences.

Any collection of laws as complex as those related to IP will take time to create and enact, so it is not surprising that these statutes lag behind technological, societal, and cultural advances. In fact, at the completion of the last major copyright overhaul in 1976, the head of the U.S. Copyright Office, Barbara Ringer, candidly described it as "a good 1950 copyright law" (cited in Pallante, 2013). In March, 2013, Maria Pallante, then register of copyrights, addressed the Congressional Subcommittee on Courts, Intellectual Property, and the Internet and called for a major rethinking of IP laws.

> I think it is time for Congress to think about the next great copyright act, which will need to be more forward thinking and flexible than before. Because the dissemination of content is so pervasive to life in the 21st century, the law also should be less technical and more helpful to those who need to navigate it. Certainly some guidance could be given

through regulations and education. But my point is, if one needs an army of lawyers to understand the basic precepts of the law, then it is time for a new law. (Pallante, 2013)

Certainly, the basic concepts of copyright and fair use need to be reconsidered, but a more probable intermediate solution for distance education providers will likely include a combination of enhanced subscription services to extensive databases of content, an increase in the use of Creative Commons licensing and open repositories, and improved technologies to prevent or deter unauthorized reproduction and distribution of copyrighted materials.

Meanwhile, although the present law may be inadequate, educators must abide by its provisions or face the consequences. The penalties from civil litigation can be substantial (e.g., statutory damages of up to $150,000 per instance), but the more relevant deterrent to violating another's IP rights should be based on the ethical variables inherent in such situations. Appropriating the property of someone else—even for a noble cause—is wrong. If, as educators, we hope to model the behaviors we would like to see in our students, respecting the value of others' work is an excellent place to begin.

DISCUSSION QUESTIONS

1. What did you read in this chapter that alerted you to copyright infringements you have witnessed, either in the workplace or at your own educational setting? What was the most blatant copyright violation you've ever seen, and what was done about it?

2. What did you read in this chapter that will change the way in which you use the IP of others?

3. You have been appointed chair of a committee to develop a copyright policy for your organization. This policy will cover employee and student use of IP for which ownership rests outside the organization (i.e., your organization does not own the copyright). What would you argue are the most important points to make in the policy?

4. In order to comply with the requirements of the Digital Millennium Copyright Act, an educational organization must provide copyright training to its membership on a regular basis. What do you think would be the most effective means of providing that training, so that the participants "get it" and follow the organization's copyright policy?

5. What are the potential advantages and disadvantages of promoting the use of open educational resources? Might some content creators feel that this devalues the work put into developing instructional materials?

REFERENCES

Ahmadi, S. (2017). Faculty rights to courses and digital courseware. *New Directions for Higher Education, 177*, 25–37.

AIME v. The Regents of the University of California. Case No. 2:10-cv-09378-CBM (U.S. District Court, Central District of California. Nov. 20, 2012). Retrieved from https://cases.justia.com/federal/district-courts/california/cacdce/2:2010cv09378/489296/16/0.pdf?ts=1376973726

Antkers, A., & Miller, S. (2018j, March 2). Fair use and the Digital Millennium Copyright Act. [Blog post]. Retrieved from https://www.authorsalliance.org/2018/03/02/fair-use-and-the-digital-millennium-copyright-act/

Binder, M. (2018, August 6). *Fraudsters are abusing Google with fake copyright complaints and it's getting worse.* Retrieved from https://mashable.com/article/google-fake-dmca-takedown-requests/#KmyNGO1FXaqN

Copyright Clearance Center. (2011). *Using course management systems: Guidelines and best practices for copyright compliance.* Retrieved from http://www.copyright.com/wp-content/uploads/2015/04/Using-Course-Management-Systems.pdf

Digital Media Law Project. (2014). *Getting permission to use the work of others.* Retrieved from http://www.dmlp.org/legal-guide/getting-permission-use-work-others

Electronic Frontier Foundation. (2014). *Unintended consequences: 16 years under the DMCA.* Retrieved from https://www.eff.org/files/2014/09/16/unintendedconsequences2014.pdf

Fruin, C. (2012). Struggles and solutions for streaming video in the online classroom. *The American Journal of Distance Education, 26*(4), 249–259.

Institute for the Study of Knowledge Management in Education. (2018). *OER Commons.* Retrieved from https://www.oercommons.org/

Lehman, B. (1998). *The conference on fair use: Final report to the commissioner on the conclusion of the conference on fair use.* U.S. Patent and Trademark Office. Retrieved from https://www.uspto.gov/sites/default/files/documents/confurep_0.pdf

Merkley, R. (2018). State of the commons. Retrieved from https://stateof.creativecommons.org/

Pallante, M. (2013). The register's call for updates to U.S. copyright law. Statement of Maria A. Pallante, Register of Copyrights, United States Copyright Office before the Subcommittee on Courts, Intellectual Property, and the Internet. Retrieved from https://www.copyright.gov/regstat/2013/regstat03202013.html

Roper, J. L. (2017). *A heuristic approach to creating technological fair use guidelines in higher education* (Doctoral dissertation). Retrieved from NSUWorks, College of Engineering and Computing. (1016) http://nsuworks.nova.edu/gscis_etd/1016.

Stim, R. (2004). *Getting permission: How to license & clear copyrighted materials online & off.* Berkeley, CA: Nolo.

U.S. Copyright Office. (1999). Report on copyright and digital distance education. Washington, DC: Author. Retrieved from www.copyright.gov/reports/de_rprt.pdf

U.S. House of Representatives. (1976). Copyright Law Revision Report 94-1476. Washington, DC: Author.

Web-Based Education Commission. (2000). *The power of the Internet for learning: Moving from promise to practice.* Washington, DC: Author. Retrieved from www.ed.gov/offices/AC/WBEC/FinalReport/WBECReport.pdf

World Intellectual Property Organization. (n.d.). *What is intellectual property?* Retrieved from http://www.wipo.int/about-ip/en/

HELPFUL WEBSITES ON COPYRIGHT AND INTELLECTUAL PROPERTY ISSUES

Copyright Law

U.S. Copyright Office: Online source of Copyright Office publications, forms, and other information, including status of pending copyright legislation and full text of the copyright law. (http://www.copyright.gov/)

UT System Crash Course on Copyright: Georgia Harper's widely acclaimed guide to copyright, including applications in distance learning, maintained by the University of Texas System Office of General Counsel. Libraries. (http://guides.lib.utexas.edu/copyright)

Fair Use

Stanford University Libraries: Extensive online listing of copyright resources created by Rich Stim, with a special emphasis on fair use. (https://fairuse.stanford.edu/overview/fair-use/)

EDUCAUSE: An extensive collection of resources about fair use and related topics. (https://library.educause.edu/topics/policy-and-law/fair-use)

Intellectual Property

Kathy Schrock: A robust collection of links to resources about intellectual property in education, including sites related to students. (http://www.schrockguide.net/intellectual-property.html)

American Association of University Professors (AAUP): Information about copyright, distance education, and intellectual property. Includes helpful sample forms, templates, and examples of policy language. (https://www.aaup.org/issues/intellectual-property/resources-copyright-distance-education-and-intellectual-property)

Copyright Clearances

Copyright Clearance Center (CCC): Website for the reproduction rights organization serving the United States. (http://www.copyright.com)

RightsDirect: The international subsidiary of CCC, established to facilitate copyright compliance throughout beyond the United States. (https://www.rightsdirect.com/)

Open Educational Resources

Creative Commons: Nonprofit organization providing a variety of licensing options to allow creators of intellectual property to share their works with others. (http://creativecommons.org)

OER Commons: A content hub with links to resources available for use, re-use, adaptation, and distribution. (http://www.oercommons.org)

CHAPTER 11

Managing and Leading a Distance Education Organization

CHAPTER GOAL

The purpose of this chapter is to describe the functions and professional concerns of an administrator of distance education programs.

CHAPTER OBJECTIVES

After reading and reviewing this chapter, you should be able to

1. Describe the typical job functions of a distance education administrator.
2. Discuss the major areas of interest during the planning stage for distance education programs.
3. Identify the major distance education readiness issues related to the educational organization, faculty training, technology infrastructure, and policy development.
4. Discuss the procedures that can help ensure quality control of a distance education program.
5. Identify and discuss the regulatory issues that can affect a distance education program.
6. Describe the most critical issues related to the support of students enrolled in a distance education program.

THE DISTANCE LEARNING LEADER

It is one thing to participate in distance education as a student or teacher and quite another to manage and provide leadership for a distance education program. As more institutions have established such programs, or expanded the ones they already had, they've also recognized the need for centralized leadership and management. Fredericksen (2017) found that the majority of these administrative positions in higher education settings have been created in the years since 2011. This chapter will describe the functions of a distance education manager/administrator and explore the current issues that an administrator will need to address and will be useful to those starting (or considering) such a career.

While the concept of leading a distance education organization is implied in the role of administrator or manager, there is a growing body of literature that differentiates the leader from the manager. This chapter will focus on managing, but the role of leader should not be ignored. Figure 11–1 shows the pyramid of competencies needed by the distance learning leader. The pyramid has the broad base of knowledge about distance education at the bottom and is topped by

FIGURE 11–1 The distance learning leader pyramid of competencies.

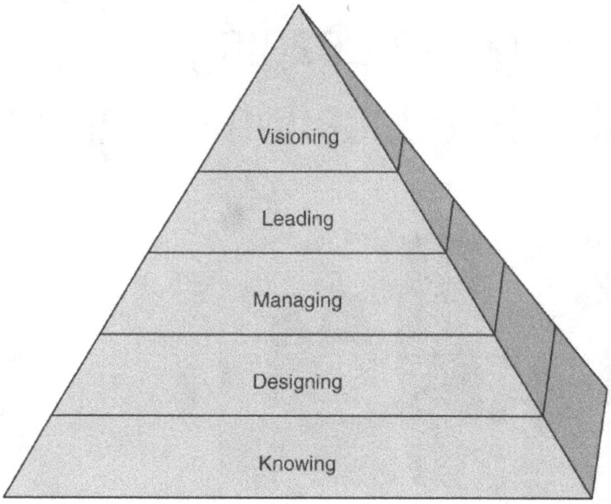

a clear vision for distance education within the organization. Simonson (2004) defined the distance learning leader as:

> A distance learning leader is a visionary capable of action who guides an organization's future, its vision, mission, goals, and objectives. The leader guides the organization and its people who have faith in the leader and have a clear understanding and acceptance of the organization's worthwhile and shared vision and goals. A distance learning leader has competence in knowing, designing, managing, leading, and visioning distance education. (p. 48)

MANAGEMENT WITHIN THE CONTEXT OF READINESS

At the very heart of the distance education administrator's responsibility is the matter of readiness—institutional readiness, faculty readiness, and student readiness. Abedor and Sachs (1978) felt that organizational development activities, that address institutional readiness issues, and faculty development activities, that address faculty readiness concerns, should precede instructional development, in this case the development and delivery of courses and programs at a distance, to help maximize the chances for an instructional innovation to be successful. While distance education is hardly an innovation this far into the 21st century, it remains an alternative to conventional classroom instruction and still has many skeptics among mainstream faculty and academic administrators. Therefore, it is imperative that distance education activities take place in an environment most conducive to achieving success. Leading the initiatives to attain organizational and individual faculty readiness should be central to a distance education administrator's duties.

ORGANIZATIONAL READINESS

Abedor and Sachs (1978) identified organizational structure, a receptive reward system for faculty, the availability of resources, and institutional policies that encourage instructional innovation among the most potent factors in achieving organizational readiness. You will see these themes recurring throughout this chapter. We will also discuss other readiness issues directly applicable to distance education, such as planning, quality control, accessibility, regulatory concerns, and costing.

Leadership and Direction for the Distance Education Program

If an educational organization plans to engage in distance education activities, a qualified individual at an appropriate administrative echelon should be designated with responsibility for providing leadership, direction, oversight, quality control, and accountability for those courses and programs. Figure 11–2 lists common functions of a distance education administrator and illustrates the scope of tasks that may come with the position. Achieving success with distance learning initiatives will be difficult unless one individual is tasked with overall accountability to see that these functions are accomplished and is given the authority to ensure quality outcomes.

Planning for Distance Education

No organization should enter the distance education marketplace without a clearly thought-out plan that has gained the consensus approval of all key players. In addition to the general plan, each individual academic program to be delivered at a distance should have a realistic business plan that justifies the existence of the program, clearly identifies the intended student population and describes how it will be recruited, describes the means of course delivery, and projects the anticipated cash flow at a level acceptable to the organization. The absence of a realistic business model is the main reason for the failure of many online learning ventures and several prominent universities in the United States have strolled right into this tar pit.

Analysis of Potential Markets.   Distance education has rapidly turned into a saturated marketplace. At a time that higher education enrollments overall in the US continue to drop, the number of students taking at least one online class grew by more than 5% (estimated conservatively) between 2015 and 2016 (Seaman, Allen, & Seaman, 2018). Add to this the estimated 2.7 million K–12 students that were enrolled in online courses during the 2014–15 academic year (Herold, 2017), and it is obvious that distance education represents a serious market. As impressive as these statistics are, however, supply ultimately could overwhelm demand, reinforcing the value of needs assessments to determine what market niches may remain underserved and what students in those niches need and expect. It is far better to spend $100,000 on a market analysis to learn that a market is not there than to assume it is, discover the hard way that it is not, and make a high-dollar mistake (not to mention the negative publicity that such a failed investment would generate). It's also important to determine whether the potential market exists in an academic content area consistent with the core mission and values of the host organization. Online programs developed simply to jump onto the online learning bandwagon or to make a few dollars can be a red flag to accreditation agencies.

Other Planning Concerns.   Once the presence of an appropriate, receptive market has been confirmed, planning should then turn to institutional and faculty readiness issues. Is the organization collectively ready to offer and support distance education programs?

FIGURE 11–2   Typical functions of a distance education administrator.

Administrative Functions:

- Provides strategic leadership and direction for distance education programs.
- Participates in organizational planning to ensure that policy development is congruent with the needs and priorities of distance education programs and initiatives.
- Helps academic units develop business plans based on market analyses and other relevant data to ensure the viability of proposed distance learning programs.
- Promotes distance education programs to intended student populations.
- Ensures that information about distance education programs is readily available and up-to -date.
- Provides information and program referrals to prospective students interested in the organization's distance education programs.
- Ensures that students enrolled in the organization's distance education programs are provided with support and guidance to facilitate their academic success, including navigating administrative procedures, using course delivery technologies, and accessing learning resources, for example.
- Develops and manages budgets to support distance education initiatives and programs.
- Seeks out and applies for external funding to support the organization's distance education initiatives, as appropriate.
- Recruits, hires, and leads distance education support staff, ensuring efficient and effective utilization of human resources.

Academic Functions:

- Coordinates development of programs and individual courses for delivery via distance education.
- Hires, or consults with academic units in the employment of, instructors for distance education courses.
- Ensures that all distance education course content, tools, and support services meet appropriate accessibility standards.
- Provides appropriate training/professional development activities for distance education faculty and affirms instructor readiness.
- Ensures that distance education faculty have continuing access to responsive technological and pedagogical support.
- Oversees quality control of distance education courses and programs and conducts appropriate activities to assess course/program effectiveness and facilitate necessary improvements; facilitates a comprehensive evaluation of every distance education program on a periodic basis.
- Ensures organizational compliance with appropriate standards, guidelines, and regulations, including those required by the institution's accreditation agencies.

Specifically, is the technology infrastructure sufficiently robust to support distance education at the desired level? Is the organization ready to support faculty who will be teaching in the program and the off-campus students who enroll? Will institutional policies accommodate distance education courses and programs?

Procedural questions must also be addressed. How will quality be assured? What procedures will be implemented to make sure the courses are well designed, taught effectively, and updated as needed to ensure academic rigor? How will tuition and fees, if applicable, be determined? A thorough analysis of the up-front and ongoing costs of the program, strategies for recovering those costs, and generation of additional revenue (if that is a goal of the program), is imperative as part of the planning process.

SCOPE OF TASK IN DEVELOPING DISTANCE COURSES AND PROGRAMS

Another important readiness issue that must be addressed in the planning stage is whether the organization has the resources, or can obtain the resources, to accommodate the scope of the task in developing and supporting courses and programs to be delivered at a distance. If the scope is relatively small, for example just a few courses, a careful assessment can determine whether course development and ongoing support can be accomplished with existing resources. However, the development of a large-scale program will likely require additional resources and these funding needs will have a significant effect on the cost analysis.

For example, a common scenario is to put an associate's degree fully online at a community college, or a 2-year degree completion program at a baccalaureate institution targeted toward students who have associates degrees. Two-year online degree programs typically require roughly 60 semester hours' worth of courses. That is the equivalent of 20 three-credit-hour courses that must be developed and supported, not counting optional elective courses across the variety of academic departments that service the major. The actual hours and resources required to develop each course could vary significantly depending on the amount of research time involved, how much development of learning activities and content objects will be needed, the involvement of instructional development staff in addition to the instructor's own time, whether licensing of learning materials or additional technology is necessary, how much instructor training, if any, is required, and so forth.

Suffice to say that the development of a single course can be an extraordinarily time-consuming venture. Then multiply that by the number of courses required to deliver the program and provide ongoing support to the instructor and students. Then double that total if the institution wishes to mount a 4-year online program. Without the necessary assets readily available to bring off such an effort, or the willingness to dedicate additional resources to achieve this goal, an organization has no business even considering offering online programs. Organizational readiness, in such a case, has not been established.

Student Support

The quality of student support services available and easily accessible to a distant learner will play a major role in determining whether that student learns about the program, enrolls, and persists through to completion. This is an essential organizational readiness concern. Students enrolled in online courses and programs should be able to expect that:

▪ They will receive the same access to support services, delivered by the same administrative units, as on-campus students.

■ As much information as possible will be provided online.

■ Contact information related to student services will be easily accessible, as well as the contact people themselves.

■ Services and support will be self-service to the greatest degree possible, with transactions conducted online.

■ Services and support will be personalized, rather than generic (e.g., replies from a real person rather than computer-generated responses or form letters).

■ Requests for information or assistance will be addressed accurately and promptly.

A project developed by the Western Cooperative for Educational Telecommunications (WCET), Guidelines for Creating Student Services Online, provides excellent guidance for identifying service areas and facilitating student support in an online environment. Although this project (originally funded by a FIPSE grant) was done in 2002, the ideas remain relevant to today's institutions and to student needs. The essential model is depicted in the form of a "Web of Student Services for Online Learners" included in the project report (WCET, 2002). See Figure 11–3. This model organizes student services into five general areas—Administrative Core, Academic Services, Communications, Personal Services, and Student Communities—and identifies examples of student support that should be provided under each.

Student training and ongoing guidance is another critical student support issue that could fall under "technical support" in the WCET model but merits special attention here. Students need clear instructions regarding all technologies they will use while enrolled in

FIGURE 11-3 WCET's "Web of Student Services for Online Learners." Reprinted with permission.

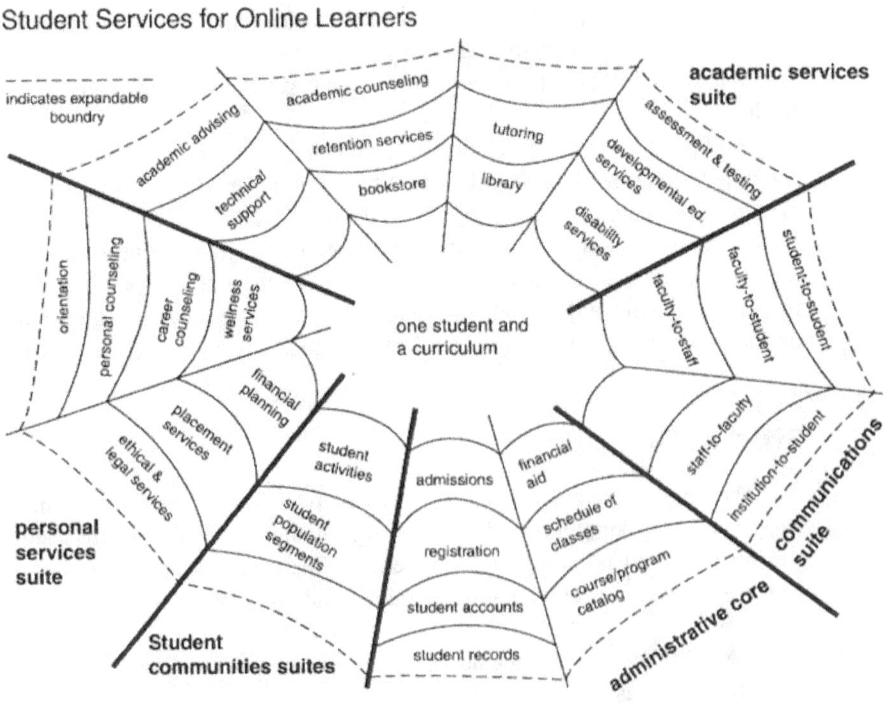

Student Services for Online Learners

the program, from the course management system to online library services to all web and other software applications that faculty might employ, such as a blogging site or plagiarism detection service. Even though today's students are often assumed to be extraordinarily tech-savvy, research suggests that the majority exhibit beginner-level technology skills, even when working with basic productivity tools (see, e.g., Judd, 2018).

Therefore, it cannot be assumed that they will be able to use these applications without at least some guidance. Moreover, students also need to have clear instructions for institutional procedures, such as admissions, advising and course registration, paying their bills, and obtaining transcripts. Collaborating with the central offices that coordinate these systems can clarify the game plan for students and ensure that these tasks can be accomplished without undue hardship, such as requiring an in-person visit.

Readiness of the Technology Infrastructure

The institution's technology infrastructure must be sufficiently robust, reliable, and well supported to accommodate the increased demands from a new or expanding distance learning program. If this is not the case, there must be a firm commitment, backed up with the necessary funding, to bring campus technology to this level or higher. Inadequate and/or unreliable technology is one of the quickest ways to kill a distance education program, so it is critical that candid discussions with IT personnel occur early in the planning process to determine if systems need to be improved or expanded. Factors to be assessed include:

Capacity and Quality of Network Infrastructure. In planning for a web-based distance education program, including those delivered synchronously via videoconferencing systems, the entire network infrastructure should be reviewed. Although many institutions now rely on managed hosting or cloud-based arrangements in which their course management system and its associated databases are maintained elsewhere, bandwidth to and from these systems must be considered. Whether on-campus or off, does the network have sufficient bandwidth to accommodate local users effectively, as well as to allow off-campus students to connect without service slowdowns? This is a particularly important concern if courses utilize streaming audio or video or other bandwidth-intensive learning objects or applications. Does the organization (or its contracted host) have reliable Internet access of its own, sufficient server capacity, adequate routers, servers for redundancy in the case of server failure, emergency generators during power failure, and a file backup system with off-site storage? The same network security issues that apply in intra-organizational computing also are applicable to distance education programs. Off-campus students have an even greater need than residential students, for example, to be able to conduct campus business transactions over a secure network.

Quality of the Administrative Computing System. As we noted above, remote-site students enrolled in distance education programs need to conduct as much institutional business as possible online. This begins with the admission and financial aid application procedures and continues through advising, course registration, access to student records, and business office services. These systems must be user-friendly, secure, and rigorously maintained. An educational organization that fails to provide these core administrative services effectively and expeditiously to its distant students sends them a distinctly negative message.

Availability and Quality of Academic Technologies.   Most educational institutions now use course management systems (CMSs) to deliver their online courses and to supplement and support blended/hybrid and face-to-face courses. Course management systems themselves have been discussed at length elsewhere in this book and will not be explored in detail here. Suffice to say that the robustness and reliability of the CMS is an essential organizational readiness concern, as is, of course, the skills with which course instructors utilize the CMS tools to promote student learning. In addition, the organization may provide or license other technology applications, such as those used for audio and/or video streaming; recording, editing, and storing audio and video files, electronic course-packs, plagiarism detection services, or electronic portfolios, for example. This collection of systems and applications, as well as their integration within the overall institutional technology infrastructure, should be central to the technology readiness assessment for distance education.

Overall Staffing Support.   Does the organization maintain the technology staffing level that will be required to support the distance education program at an effective level? If not, what additional staffing will be needed, and how will it be funded? A vitally important consideration is help desk support. The availability of timely technical assistance for distant learners is another hot button for accreditors. Students frequently need assistance with matters beyond interrupted access and forgotten passwords. Many requests for help will involve some aspect of the course management system or other relevant delivery system (for example, videoconferencing tools for synchronous communication). For this reason, help desk staff should be well versed in navigating and troubleshooting technology applications supported by the institution for instructional purposes. Detailed user guides for all campus technologies used by students should be posted on relevant websites and also made available to the help desk staff for convenient reference. These guides and searchable online databases (typically referred to as knowledge bases) can also be extremely helpful to students and faculty, especially when the help desk is closed.

Working Relationship Between Distance Education and Information Technology.   In many cases, information technology support for distance education programs will be provided by a department administratively independent of the office managing distance education programs. Does an effective working relationship exist between the administrative office for distance education and the IT unit? Students who cannot connect because of server or network failure are likely to contact the instructor first, who then would contact the distance education office for resolution of a problem that may fall under the responsibility of the IT office. Not only must communication channels be wide open, but monitoring and problem resolution systems must be in place to address issues as soon as they occur and to minimize down time. The lack thereof is another serious red flag for accreditors.

Repair and Replacement Funding.   An organization that does not annually budget for repair and replacement of hardware, or for upgrading software, will have serious difficulties sustaining a successful distance education program. This is another important readiness issue. At some institutions, these replacements and upgrades are funded with fiscal year-end "budget dust," hardly a reliable approach. Much information technology equipment, such as servers and routers, should be replaced every 4 to 5 years at a maximum and software upgrades need to follow industry standards for reliability and security. The organization's technology plan should include schedules for replacements and upgrades, so that the "refresh" is systematic and institutionalized, and funding needs can be anticipated in the planning process for upcoming budget cycles.

Institutional Policies

A review of existing institutional policies that have implications for distance education is imperative when assessing an organization's readiness and some current policies may require revision. Policies that could affect a distance education program, its faculty, or students may be related to intellectual property rights, student fees, on-campus office hours, or access to network resources, to name a few. The review may also act as a catalyst for the development of new institutional policies in areas such as accessibility of digital materials or use of student data, for example.

Distance Education Policy

Policy development and implementation, as well as revision of existing institutional policies when appropriate, is an important topic to be addressed when an organization considers offering distance courses and programs. Gellman-Danley and Fetzner (1998) identified seven critical areas of policy development for distance education: academic, fiscal, geographic, governance, labor-management, legal, and student support services. Figure 11-2 presents a modified version of this original list to include categories and issues related to current priorities and technological advances. Keep in mind that these are internal policies within the organization.

It may be most appropriate for the organization to develop an omnibus distance education or online learning policy, if one does not already exist. This document can include links to relevant sections of other existing institutional policies and incorporate new policy areas as appropriate. Such a policy should be drafted by those administering the distance education program, in collaboration with appropriate administrative offices, governance bodies, and faculty representatives, and be vetted and approved through the organization's

FIGURE 11–4 Policy development areas for distance education.

Policy Area	Key Issues
Academic/Curricular	Quality assurance, academic calendar, student academic misconduct, program/course approval, student grades; library resources and access, course development and modification, enrollment caps
Administrative	Admissions criteria, budgetary priorities, service areas, tuition and fees, software licensing/procurement
Faculty Concerns	Training/certification; teacher evaluation; faculty hiring, oversight, and compensation; workload; promotion and tenure
Student Support	Advising, technical support, financial aid, transfer credit,
Legal	Data security, intellectual property rights, liability, accessibility
Technology Use and Management	CMS access and management, 3rd-party software, acceptable use of technology resources, accounts and passwords

normal policy development procedures. The following sections briefly discuss these policy areas as identified above.

Academic Policies.   The distance education/online learning policy will likely refer to existing institutional academic policies but may emphasize how some are specifically applied in distance/online course situations. For example, the policy might:

▪ Require that the academic rigor of all courses delivered by distance education must be maintained at least at the level expected for traditional classroom-based courses.

▪ Specify that distance education courses are expected to conform to the same academic calendar as traditional classroom courses and follow the institution's standard schedule for drops, adds, last day for credit/no credit grading, course withdrawals, and resolution of Incomplete grades; state that flexible course scheduling is possible and encouraged when justified.

▪ Specify the use of on-campus or institutionally monitored systems (within a CMS or elsewhere) for recording grades or conducting other activities involving student data, to avoid compromising student privacy.

▪ Indicate how remote-site students gain access to library resources, including hard-copy materials, and how reference services will be provided. Policies should also address the appropriate use of multimedia resources (e.g., videos) within online courses.

▪ Establish enrollment caps for distance education courses, ideally 20–25 per section.

This section of the policy should also specify the requirements and timeline for preapproval of distance education courses and programs. The timeline for course approval is very important. Courses to be offered at a distance must be included in the official course schedule, which is compiled and made available well before the registration period for that academic term. Distance education marketing staff need early identification of courses so they can be promoted effectively to the intended student populations. Identification in the course schedule also benefits residential students who may wish to take online courses because of scheduling conflicts or for other reasons such as instructor preference.

Administrative Issues.   A critical part of the administrative policy section will specify how the organization approaches the matter of tuition and fees paid by students at a distance, if applicable. For example, should students enrolled in distance education programs pay the same tuition and fees as residential students? Should they pay a surcharge to help cover the cost of the delivery technologies, or should they pay less, because remote-site students are unlikely to use as many of the on-campus services as face-to-face students? The policy should refer to the appropriate web page where current tuition rates and fee schedules are maintained. Procedures should be identified for canceling courses that do not meet minimum enrollments or for merging sections if two or more are offered.

Other administrative policy statements might refer to the organizational structure of the distance learning management unit, issues related to student admission into online programs, and service area designations, if applicable. These policies may also address issues of fiscal responsibility for software licensing, obtaining competitive bids for procurement of services and products, and budgetary prioritization, for example.

Faculty-Related Issues.   A variety of faculty-related issues may be addressed in a distance education/online learning policy. Referrals to other official institutional policies (such as those related to faculty contracts, faculty evaluation, promotion and tenure, ranks and titles, and workload) will be common in this section, but matters such as the following may receive special attention in this policy. These are examples only and will not reflect the official position of every institution.

▪ It is the organization's first priority to assign core (i.e., full-time, tenure-track) faculty to teach distance education courses; if core faculty are unable or unwilling to teach these courses, the teaching assignments will be given to adjunct faculty.

▪ The development and utilization of distance education courses shall never be used to reduce or eliminate core faculty positions.

▪ The teaching of distance education courses will be considered part of an instructor's normal workload and will not merit additional compensation unless assigned as an overload.

▪ Instructors will not be approved to teach online courses until after successfully completing the required orientation and training program.

▪ The teaching of distance education courses shall be considered during the promotion and tenure approval process according to the same standards as for conventional classroom teaching. No faculty member shall ever be penalized during the promotion and tenure process for teaching distance education courses.

▪ Instructors teaching distance education courses shall maintain "virtual" office hours for students completing these courses at a distance. This includes physical office hours for student phone calls, as well as timely response to electronic mail messages. The use of other electronic communication tools, such as texting or videoconferencing to interact with students is strongly encouraged.

▪ Instructors teaching distance education courses will be evaluated by students at least once per term and should expect that their teaching strategies and student interactions will be reviewed at some point during the term, with advance notice provided.

Student-Related Policies. This section of the distance education/online learning policy should refer to policies relevant to all students (on-campus and at a distance), but may also do the following:

▪ Require that accounts and passwords for electronic mail, course management system, administrative databases for student use, and any other technologies utilized by students at a distance be established as soon as new students are admitted into these programs, or when new nonmatriculated students are enrolled in individual courses, as appropriate. The policy may also specify the procedure for new students to be informed of their account access and given guidance for using these systems.

▪ Specify the information to be collected from a new student at the time of application or registration as a nonmatriculated student, such as complete name, primary contact e-mail address, complete home address, and home and/or cellular phone numbers, and designate responsibility for collecting this information. This is particularly important for making initial contact with these students and providing essential information for course access, well before courses begin, such as via welcome letters.

▪ Limit the number of distance education courses that may be taken simultaneously during a single academic term.

▪ Establish procedures for submission of student concerns or complaints regarding distance education courses and programs.

Legal Issues. Legal issues are commonly addressed in other organizational policies that apply to all programs and courses, faculty and students, not just to those at a distance. However, those policies themselves should be identified and referenced in the distance education/online learning policy. For example:

▪ As described in the previous chapter, "ownership" matters related to distance education courses and course materials should be addressed in the institution's intellectual property (IP) policy.

▪ The intellectual property policy should also address ownership and rights related to works created by students for a course, such as assignments. This includes all student comments made in an online discussion forum.

▪ The use of materials copyrighted by others in distance education courses should be addressed in the organization's copyright policy. Copyright is discussed at length in Chapter 11 of this book. It is particularly important that the copyright policy establishes institutional requirements regarding compliance with the Digital Millennium Copyright Act (DMCA) and the TEACH Act.

▪ The distance education/online learning policy should also require that all distance education courses offered by the organization follow the accessibility standards specified by the Americans with Disabilities Act and the Rehabilitation Act. This legislation will be discussed more extensively later in this chapter.

Technology Use and Management. Virtually every educational organization maintains policies governing who can use institutional technologies, how they can be used, and the rights and responsibilities that accompany this access. For example, typically there are prohibitions on the use of such resources for commercial and illegal purposes, restrictions about software installation, and rules forbidding e-mail that is harassing or discriminatory. Of paramount importance to online students are the policies related to account security and the need to keep passwords safe. All students need to be made aware of these policies and the consequences for violating them.

In addition to the organizationwide policies for technology use, guidelines should be established to clarify how the course management system will be administered. Many of these statements might rely on already-existing organizational policy (e.g., those related to intellectual property rights), but would be interpreted to apply to the CMS. These guidelines may include information about:

▪ How soon students will have access to an online course prior to the beginning of the term and how long they'll have access after the end of the term;

▪ When, if ever, a student not enrolled in a course may be added to the course roster;

▪ File size limitations for uploaded course materials;

▪ Whether the CMS may be used for noninstructional purposes, such as managing faculty senate business;

▪ Who has the right to "observe" an online course by examining the content materials, instructional activities, and/or interactions between and among the instructor and students; or

▪ Who can authorize third-party software integrations, version upgrades, or license revisions.

Accessibility

According to the National Center for Educational Statistics (2017), more than 11% of all undergraduate students have some type of disability requiring support services and/or accommodation. These include learning disabilities; mobility, hearing, and vision impairments; and other types of disabilities or limitations. With more than five million undergraduates enrolled in distance education classes during the fall 2016 term, this translates to more than one-half million students who've reported a disability and does not include the many who choose not to disclose that information.

The Americans with Disabilities Act (ADA), passed in 1990, and Section 504 of the Rehabilitation Act, enacted in 1973, require that "standard assistive technologies" be made available to persons with disabilities. Congress expanded the Rehabilitation Act in 1998 to add Section 508, requiring that all federal government websites be fully accessible by June 21, 2001. Section 508 also applies to educational organizations that receive federal funding, including most school districts as well as private and public colleges and universities. If the moral/ethical arguments for addressing accessibility issues don't sway some institutional administrators, the recent increase in complaints—up 10% between 2016 and 2017—filed with the Department of Education's Office of Civil Rights may get their attention (Diament, 2018).

Course management system vendors claim that their products are compliant with Section 508. However, organizations that provide distance education courses must be aware of possible limitations of CMS products as well as of other technologies that may be deployed. Updates to Section 508 (adopted in 2018) that are relevant to online learning include language specifying that software support documentation be accessible and readily available, that software must interoperate with assistive devices, and that tools and resources must be aligned with WCAG 2.0 standards. Distance education administrators should review all of their technology applications and be ready to provide accommodations to students, as necessary.

The web can be an important tool for disabled students. Students at a distance, however, can be at a greater disadvantage if they are without easy access to campus-based disability resources and advocacy for web-ready resources. Beyond the accessibility of these resources and availability of consultation, however, distance education providers have limited obligations regarding a disabled student's home or off-campus workplace situations. If the program requires that all students are responsible for equipment or software that enables them to participate in the course, the institution is not required to provide assistive equipment. This is based on a popularly-accepted interpretation of ADA, however, and there has not been a court case testing that assumption as of 2018.

For an overview of accessibility considerations, EDUCAUSE has compiled a list of 19 "risk statements," indicating areas of concern for many institutions, each accompanied by documentation related to relevant court cases or settlements. These statements include risks that are especially meaningful for online programs, such as references to video captioning, faculty awareness of accessibility resources, and accessible instructional materials (EDUCAUSE, 2015).

Quality Control

Quality control of distance education programs is an area of specific interest for accreditation agencies. In March 2006, the Office of Postsecondary Education (OPE) of the U.S. Department of Education released a report entitled Evidence of Quality in

FIGURE 11–5   Interregional guidelines for the evaluation of distance education (online learning) (C-RAC, 2011).

Interregional Guidelines for the Evaluation of Distance Education
(Online Learning)

1. Online learning is appropriate to the institution's mission and purpose.

2. The institution's plans for developing, sustaining, and if appropriate, expanding online learning offering are integrated into its regular planning and evaluation process.

3. Online learning is incorporated into the institution's systems of governances and academic oversight.

4. Curricula for the institution's online learning offerings are coherent, cohesive, and comparable in academic rigor to programs offered in traditional instructional formats.

5. The institution evaluates the effectiveness of its online learning offerings, including the extent to which the online learning goals are achieved, and uses the results of its evaluations to enhance the attainment of the goals.

6. Faculty responsible for delivering the online learning curricula and evaluating the students' success in achieving the online learning goals are appropriately qualified and effectively supported.

7. The institution provides effective student and academic services to support students enrolled in online learning offerings.

8. The institution provides sufficient resources to support and, if appropriate, expand its online learning offerings.

9. The institution assures the integrity of its online learning offerings.

Distance Education Programs Drawn From Interviews With the Accreditation Community (OPE, 2006). The report was derived from a series of meetings with eight regional and five national accrediting associations and described what these agencies considered "best practices" related to distance education. Using this document as a starting point, as well as Best Practice Strategies to Promote Academic Integrity in Online Education (2009), the Council of Regional Accrediting Commissions (C-RAC) released their Interregional Guidelines for the Evaluation of Distance Education (Online Learning) in 2011 (Figure 11.5). Although more than 10 years have passed since the discussions that led to development of the guidelines, they are still used to evaluate quality in online course and program offerings and have been endorsed by all six regional accrediting agencies' assessment frameworks. *(A fuller discussion on accreditation can be found later in this chapter.)*

Minimum Course Expectations.   While respecting academic freedom, an institution may set minimum expectations for courses offered a distance, such as requiring course learning outcomes that emphasize higher cognitive levels and application of course content to real world needs, problems and issues; use of a course's discussion forums and other online resources to facilitate critical thinking and student engagement in the learning process; standards for course organization and structure; standards for student assessment; and a requirement for instructor commitment to monitor student participation and follow up with students who do not participate on a regular basis. These may be published in the distance education/online learning policy.

Instructor Training and Certification Requirement.   Another widely implemented quality control measure is a requirement for all instructors of distance education courses to receive appropriate training and be "certified" before being allowed to teach these courses. Appropriate faculty training is an absolutely imperative readiness concern. The distance education/online learning policy will likely vest in the distance education program administrator the authority to determine what this training will include and the procedure for instructors to be certified. We will discuss faculty training more extensively later in the chapter.

Mandatory Course Evaluations.   Every course offered at a distance should be evaluated by students at or near the end of every term using a well-designed and validated survey instrument. Many institutions are now recommending mid-term evaluations, as well, to address concerns while the course is in progress, rather than waiting until it's too late to make changes. Program administrators should use student responses to provide constructive feedback to the instructors and set goals for course and/or teaching performance improvement. Faculty with consistently poor evaluations should not be permitted to teach subsequent courses at a distance, keeping in mind that student evaluations with low response rates may skew results unfairly.

Periodic Program Evaluations.   Although program evaluation is discussed in detail in Chapter 12, it is important to mention it here as a component of readiness. The distance education administrator should work with departmental academic administrators to evaluate the programs on a periodic basis. The distance education/online learning policy should specify the frequency for these reviews, typically every 5 to 7 years, although the policy may require new programs to be evaluated more frequently, perhaps every 3 years. Such reviews might fall under the purview of the institution's program assessment office, in which case the distance education administer should work closely with these staff members to ensure results that are useful and comprehensive. A small selection of possible review questions is provided below as examples; many more would be used to guide an actual program evaluation.

Institutional Context/Overall Effectiveness

▪ Is the program in alignment with the institution's mission and strategic objectives?
▪ Is the intended student population responding with applications and enrollments?
▪ How do the program costs compare with program revenues?
▪ What are the measurable results of the program thus far?
▪ Is the academic "home" department satisfied with the students and their achievement?

Overall Program Quality

▪ Are students satisfied with the quality of instruction they're receiving?
▪ Are employers of the program's graduates satisfied with the quality of their preparation?
▪ What percentage of students continues in the program through to graduation (if applicable)?
▪ Does the academic department or distance education administrative unit request feedback from students who leave the program? If so, has that feedback been used to identify areas for improvement and remediation?

Student Support

▪ Are students satisfied with support services (e.g., library, help desk, etc.)? What services, if any, are missing?
▪ Are students able to use course technologies effectively? If not, are resources available to assist them?
▪ Are students satisfied with processes for admission, advising, registration, and other administrative procedures?
▪ Do students feel that they are part of the institutional community?

Regulatory Issues

Regulatory matters may affect an organization's readiness for distance education in any number of ways. We have already addressed policy at the local level. Policy in a much broader perspective is also determined by those who regulate distance education. Regulation occurs at several levels—by the federal government, state governments, and by regional and professional accreditation agencies.

Federal Government. The U.S. Constitution delegates the primary responsibility for public education to the individual states. However, the federal government has considerable influence on distance education policy and practice. Here are a few examples.

Student Financial Aid. Historically, it has been difficult for students enrolled in distance education programs at the postsecondary level to obtain federal financial aid, a situation dating from abuses in the correspondence course era that continued into the age of instructional television in the 1960s and 1970s. Enactment of amendments to the Higher Education Act in 1996 began to ease the restrictions, and most remaining rules were eliminated by congressional action in 2006, largely as a result of intense lobbying by for-profit and predominantly online educational institutions. The easing of these restrictions also greatly assisted conventional nonprofit colleges and universities with large online programs by enabling a much greater number of students to enroll.

Unfortunately, the downside of these changes has meant big-dollar consequences for higher education. Many online programs have attracted the attention of thieves (often referred to as "Pell runners") who pose as students (or as several different students), enroll in online programs, and collect financial aid monies, only to disappear with the funds that remain after paying tuition. A sample of government actions taken (i.e., convictions and sentencing) against perpetrators of such fraud between October 2017 and March 2018 represented losses of $3,973,900 (U.S. Department of Education, 2018).

Schools with low tuition rates are especially attractive to these scammers because the balance of the remaining funds may be greater after paying for tuition. Such instances of fraud can create serious financial problems at the targeted institutions if they are required to pay back the monies if students drop out of school (as they inevitably do). Student aid professionals across the United States have been struggling with similar crimes for decades, but the frequency and sophistication of the latest wave has grown rapidly with the increase in online programs where it is easier to assume multiple identities, for example.

Not surprisingly, measures to confirm student identity and the means to authenticate students when logging in to course management systems are of increasing importance to federal and state government, as well as accrediting bodies. The Higher Education Opportunity Act requires,

> An institution that offers distance education to have processes through which the institution establishes that the student who registers ... is the same student who participates in and completes the program and receives the academic credit. (2008, Sec. 495)

Sophisticated programs for student authentication are gaining acceptance in educational settings as pressure to validate student identity increases. Some of the more advanced systems utilize biometric authentication measures that rely on artificial intelligence to prevent a proxy student from logging in to take an online test, for example. These software utilities also employ rigorous data analytics to spot suspicious behaviors, such as multiple students logging in from the same IP address. Other systems mine databases of publicly available information to create customized identity check questions, such as, "Which of these addresses have you never lived at?" For an institution that has been targeted by Pell runners, these systems can be invaluable in identifying and heading off potential problems, while also improving the odds that the person taking a test or submitting an assignment is actually the student who is enrolled in the course.

Copyright. Many face-to-face courses are enriched by the display or performance of copyrighted materials in the classroom through the application of Fair Use guidelines. Unfortunately, these allowances do not apply to the delivery of content at a distance. Although the TEACH Act expanded the rights of teachers and course developers to share such works with students at a distance, there are still significant restrictions in place, especially for audiovisual content. More detail regarding copyright and the TEACH ACT can be found in Chapter 10 of this text.

School and Public Access. The federal government has significantly increased access to Internet-based instruction, including distance education opportunities, at the K–12 level through enactment of the Telecommunications Act of 1996 and its resulting Universal Service Fund, distributed through the E-Rate. Created by the Telecommunications Act of 1996, the Universal Service Fund has provided more than $48 billion dollars to schools and libraries for improvements in their telecommunications infrastructure, with a differentially positive effect for low-income areas that have fewer resources, otherwise. Changes to the program in 2014 included a simplified application procedure and an emphasis on advanced technologies, leading to optimistic projections for the adoption of bandwidth-intensive applications. The E-Rate has enabled almost every school and library in the United States to receive high-speed Internet service, greatly increasing student access to online distance learning opportunities. This fund is supported by the charges for "universal service" on consumer telephone bills.

Data-Gathering.   The federal government maintains a massive data collection capability. For example, the National Center for Educational Statistics tracks trends in distance education in postsecondary institutions and the Department of Education's Office of Inspector General compiles information on state and accreditation agency controls over distance education programs. These are just two of many examples, although concerns over the potential for invasion of privacy may bring even educational data collection under increased scrutiny.

State Governments.   Individual states maintain the right to establish their own rules regarding education, and this extends to the delivery of distance education programs into those states by educational organizations based in other states. Historically, states have used the yardstick of "physical presence" to determine whether education programs offered by out-of-state entities come under their jurisdiction. These situations were obvious when colleges and universities established physical locations for such purposes as instruction, laboratory activities, student assessment, tutoring, recruiting, and admissions. The ubiquitous directional signs to University of Phoenix facilities in most U.S. states serve as an example. Phoenix is licensed in those states.

How, though, do physical presence standards apply in the cases of distance education programs that cross state lines? This question has been an issue since the early 1960s, when educational programming was distributed to multiple states via broadcast television, and it became even muddier during the 1970s and 80s, when courses delivered by communications satellites could be viewed virtually everywhere in the country, including Alaska and Hawaii. The web extended the marketplace to worldwide proportions and brought the cost of delivering distance learning programs down to affordable levels for almost any educational entrepreneur with a server. In 2011, the Department of Education issued a requirement that institutions gain program authorization for every state in which they had one or more enrolled students. This requirement applied whether an institution had a physical presence in the state or not and allowed the institutions less than a year to comply. Eventually, in July of 2012, the Department of Education eliminated the deadline for obtaining authorizations, but did not remove the requirement, itself.

In an attempt to streamline the existing labyrinthine processes for state-by-state approvals, a commission was established in 2012 with the development of a state reciprocity plan as its first major task. This system was designed to be "based on the voluntary participation of states and institutions to govern the regulation of distance education programs" (Commission on the Regulation of Postsecondary Distance Education, 2013, p. 3). The resulting program—informally referred to as SARA (State Authorization Reciprocity Agreement)—established procedures for state-level reciprocity and is administered by four (pre-existing) regional compacts: WICHE, MHEC, NEBHC, and SREB. These procedures provide consistent definitions and standards for authorizations among the states that choose to participate and have eliminated the need for state-by-state approvals. Another bonus is that states agree to not levy additional fees on other SARA-participating institutions, thus producing savings that can be passed along to students. For more information about SARA, visit the website of the National Council for State Authorization Reciprocity Agreements at www.nc-sara.org.

Prior to (and since) SARA's establishment there has been discussion at the federal level regarding state authorization of postsecondary programs, including those offered at a distance. After several years of committee work, negotiation, and clarification, federal regulations for State Authorization of Postsecondary Distance Education were to be put into effect on July 1, 2018. On July 3, 2018, the Department of Education announced a delay until July 1, 2020 (Program Integrity and Improvement, 2018). There is concern that these additional regulations will restrict financial aid options for many students and impose burdensome requirements on institutions. It remains to be seen (at least until 2020) whether they will go into effect at some point.

Accreditation Agencies. The United States has six regional accreditation agencies (e.g., the North Central Association of Colleges and Schools), two of which have separate agencies for K–12 and higher education, for an actual total of eight. In addition, the Council for Higher Education Accreditation (2018) identifies 54 national accreditation organizations, divided into the categories of faith-related, career-related, and programmatic (or discipline-specific).

Depending upon their respective missions, these commissions accredit entire institutions and schools, and/or individual degree and diploma programs. Their primary emphasis is on program quality and improvement through self-regulation, with reviews conducted primarily by peers. In particular, the regional accreditation agencies are increasingly included among distance education administrators' best friends in promoting distance education and upholding quality standards. All are making every attempt to understand distance education and put themselves in a position to evaluate it effectively. As described earlier, these groups have a shared set of guidelines for distance education programs (Inter-regional Guidelines for the Evaluation of Distance Education [Online Learning]) that are used in conjunction with their existing evaluation standards.

It is important to note that, as this text goes to press, the Higher Education Act (HEA) is scheduled for reauthorization. (The HEA, among other things, requires that institutions hoping to participate in federal financial aid programs be accredited.) Although it is too early to know exactly how the updated act will affect distance education programs, at least one version of the proposed bill removes stipulations that require distance education programs to be accredited as separate entities. They would, instead, be evaluated with their more traditional counterparts. Some are interpreting this as a sign that distance education has gained acceptance as a sound model for postsecondary education, although there are concerns that decreased scrutiny could open the door to low-quality programs, resulting in less public trust than ever before.

Individual degree programs in postsecondary education are typically accredited by professional associations (included in the 60 national organizations identified by the Council for Higher Education Accreditation). These organizations can be more conservative and protective of the status quo and are more likely to offer resistance to distance education programs. Those associations that have reservations about distance education have at their disposal an extremely effective tool for controlling academic programs: the power to deny accreditation, although in reality this rarely happens on the basis of distance education programs alone.

Cost Issues

The costs of delivering distance education and ensuring return on investment are foremost concerns of many distance education administrators. Few organizations can afford to "hemorrhage" large amounts of money supporting programs that aren't successful, and skeptics of distance education are quick to point out the failures in recent years of distance education ventures by high-profile universities and consortia. As the price for nearly all types of postsecondary education has risen to record levels compared to inflation and to family income, increased government scrutiny is likely to increase, as well. The savvy distance education administrator will keep a sharp eye on budgets during these times.

Distance education is expensive but has long been considered a low-cost delivery option and a way for colleges and universities to make money. In fact, at a national meeting of 150 state legislators, *not even one* thought distance education courses cost more to design, develop, offer, and support than face-to-face courses, and a large majority of those lawmakers thought it costs less (Poulin & Straut, 2018). For a more realistic perspective, look back several pages to the resources necessary to plan, deliver, and evaluate distance education programs. The costs range from basic operation of the administrative office for distance education to faculty salaries to instructional design and technical support personnel to student support personnel to the delivery technology infrastructure, and to course and program promotion, including advertising. Although it might seem that instructional technologies drive up expenses, personnel costs typically represent the bulk of the total budgets for distance education programs. Even if these costs are prorated portions of the overall organizational budget, they can be extraordinary, depending upon the size of the program. The distance education business plan must account for all these expenses, and then balance them against revenues and other benefits of the program.

A detailed discussion of costing distance education is far too broad a topic for this chapter. As a cautionary note, however, any cost analysis method must recognize the risks of estimating expense and income that depends on data from other, potentially dissimilar, organizational structures or institutions. Without a broadly-accepted lexicon defining variables related to delivery systems, faculty compensation, or course development (as just a few examples), relying too heavily on the outcomes of other programs for make-or-break decisions may prove disastrous. Take into consideration the financial practices of other programs, but use these models primarily as clues – or warnings – and establish estimates based on local circumstances.

FACULTY READINESS

Depending upon the scope of the distance education programs offered by an organization, the administrator may be in a position to hire instructors, or at the very least should work with academic program directors to select faculty who will teach courses at a distance. It is important that the instructors hired or designated to teach these courses exhibit characteristics that facilitate effective teaching at a distance. In a classic article, Savery (2005) described the characteristics of successful distance education faculty members using the acronym VOCAL. That is, they are:

- Visible: They create a sense of "presence" through a variety of communication channels;
- Organized: They provide detailed instructions, clearly sequenced course content, and specific expectations for assignments and other learning activities;
- Compassionate: They build a sense of trust among the learning group to overcome the potential isolation of learning at a distance;
- Analytical: They design multiple types of assessments that are aligned with specified outcomes; and they
- Lead by example: They provide constructive feedback, model desirable learning strategies, and follow through on promised timelines or activities.

This is not to suggest that instructors who do not exhibit these attributes cannot be successful in teaching courses at a distance, only that they are likely to find the endeavor more challenging. If the selected faculty are making the transition from conventional classroom teaching for the first time, they will need to understand that the distance education environment is different in some ways from the one with which they are familiar. For example, the demands on their workload will likely increase, probably significantly. A distance education course, particularly an online course, will need much more organization, structure, and detail than typical classroom courses. Students, especially those new to distance education often need precise, detailed instructions to guide their activities throughout the course and keep them on task, and this structure and detail must be in place from the first day of the class.

Faculty Support

Faculty support in a distance education environment is of particular interest to accreditors. The readiness of the institution regarding the impact of online courses and programs on faculty workload, compensation, and the institutional reward system must be addressed. Other faculty issues such as training, course development support, and technology support must be evaluated and addressed.

Training.   Considering that few postsecondary instructors have any formal teacher training (i.e., to teach in any environment) before their faculty appointment, it's not surprising that in a survey of college and university distance education administrators, the most frequently cited challenge was, "Faculty development and training" (Fredericksen, 2017). Unfortunately, faculty training programs for distance education often begin and end with workshops on using the delivery technologies, such as the course management system, but many instructors need additional assistance in implementing instructional strategies that are specifically effective in the distance education environment. In addition to hands-on training with the CMS, the training curriculum should include the following topics, at a minimum:

- the unique attributes and needs of distance learners;
- pedagogies that promote higher order thinking;
- online discussion facilitation, management, and assessment;
- effective use of embedded technologies such as videoconferencing, plagiarism detection, or assignment mark-up tools;
- assessing learner progress at a distance;
- course evaluation resources and requirements;
- administrative factors such as office hours, copyright compliance, and student support concerns and resources; and
- instructional design for online courses (depending on the institution).

These offerings may be provided via intense workshops that often are online themselves, putting the instructors in the role of online learners while the workshop leader models effective online teaching methods and course structure. Or, they might consist of a series of in-person activities, supplemented with online resources and hands-on practice with the CMS. Another option that many instructors find useful is to pursue certification "externally" from distance education organizations (e.g., Learning Resources Network, Quality Matters, or Online Learning Consortium) or from institutions that provide online training as part of their continuing education or extension programs (e.g., Michigan State University, University of Colorado-Denver, or Texas Southern University). Adjunct instructors might find these especially valuable for two reasons: a) participating in training at the institution where they're teaching may be difficult, especially if courses are assigned shortly before the term begins; and b) an "official" certificate course is often considered more credible than an in-house program and can be an asset when applying for jobs.

Assistance With Course Development and Delivery. Effective training can equip instructors with the essential skills for course development, delivery, and assessment, but many can also benefit from working with a professional instructional developer. Course development specialists may be tasked with guiding instructors who are creating courses, creating some of the course components (such as multimedia content objects), or developing an entire course on their own to be taught by the instructor of record. In these ready-made-course situations, some or all of the instructional modules and materials may be locked down, to prevent revisions that could change course outcomes or create inconsistencies among multiple sections.

Technology Support. As discussed earlier, a competent, well-informed, dedicated help desk staff can provide essential technical support to both faculty and students. Some institutions have separate units to handle faculty/staff and student concerns, although there may be cost efficiencies to consider if choosing that model. For distance education students, who may be engaged with coursework late at night or in the very-early morning, having access to technical help 24/7 can be a grade-saver, although this may be an expensive proposition for schools with a small IT staff. Another attractive option is to contract with the CMS vendor to provide technical help on an ongoing basis, especially since most of the problems are likely to be related to that system in some way.

Workload, Compensation, and Reward Systems. Teaching at a distance also presents sensitive questions related to faculty workload, compensation, and, especially in postsecondary education, promotion and tenure. Faculty are (understandably) very concerned about the amount of time required to develop an online course, as well as the additional time required to teach it.

Compensation can be a challenging issue. Because of the extra workload, many faculty members feel that developing and teaching distance education courses should rate additional compensation. Or, as an alternative, they may seek release time that they can dedicate to course development and delivery. Release time essentially means that a percentage of the faculty member's time is "bought out" for this purpose, such as a one-course reduction in the professor's teaching load. This results in a financial strain for someone in the budget chain, because another faculty member must be assigned to teach that class on an overload basis, or an adjunct instructor must be hired to teach the course. Many online programs, including those that duplicate an on-campus version of the program, rely heavily (or even entirely) on adjunct faculty, rather than assigning full-time, ranked faculty members to those classes. Unfortunately, the talent pool for these contingent instructors is large enough that institutions don't have to pay well. It's not uncommon (in 2018) to be paid between $2,500 and $5,000 for teaching a three-credit online course per semester, without benefits such as health insurance. Assuredly, in disciplines that are typically higher paying, such as medicine, business, or law, that per-course amount can be much higher.

The institution's reward system is another important faculty concern. Colleges and universities, as well as school districts, have policies related to retention, tenure, and promotion, most of which were written long before distance education became a gleam in the dean's eye. For the most part, these policies do not accommodate instructional innovation in general, and do not forgive faculty for spending a disproportionate amount of their time teaching online. Many pretenure instructors are actively discouraged from teaching online due to the time demands—time that, in most faculty reward systems—would be better dedicated to writing, research, or grant-seeking. Distance education managers must work with faculty unions, academic senates, and administrators to revise their respective reward systems to provide incentives for teaching in a distance education environment.

STUDENT READINESS

According to a 2018 survey by the Pew Research Center (Anderson & Jiang, 2018), 95% of teens have a smartphone or access to one, although ownership of or access to a computer is somewhat lower at 88%. Of the 743 teens interviewed, 45% "say they are online on a near-constant basis," up (way up) from 24% in 2014. A 2017 survey of more than 43,000 college and university students from 124 higher education institutions conducted by the EDUCAUSE Center for Applied Research (Brooks & Pomerantz, 2017) found that 95% brought a laptop to campus, 97% owned a smartphone, and 30% owned a laptop, smartphone, and tablet. Unfortunately, the ownership and use of such devices does not imbue these alleged "digital natives" with the skills needed for success in online courses, or few other courses, for that matter.

Assessing Readiness

The distance learning administrator should help ensure, either through self-assessment tools or personal interviews, that incoming students have the appropriate level of readiness, including commitment, self-discipline, and time management skills to be successful in an online environment. Many providers of online courses and programs provide "readiness checks" on their web sites, intended to assist potential students in deciding whether online learning is right for them. One popular instrument is the SmarterMeasure Learning Readiness Indicator (www.SmarterMeasure.com). This survey is intended to measure individual attributes, as well as technical competencies, typing speed and accuracy, and reading abilities. A wide variety of other models, many developed "in house" for specific programs or institutions, rely on similar factors, as well as self-efficacy, technology access, attitudes, and communication skills, for example (Doe, Castillo, & Musyoka, 2017).

Surveys like these can be useful, but it's important to understand the possible problems inherent in their design and interpretation. First, most (if not all) of the instruments rely on self-report and the debatable assumption that responders can or will be completely objective and honest about their strengths, behaviors, or beliefs. Second, although these surveys aren't valid predictors of student success, it's difficult to ignore the connotation implied by "unreadiness." Wladis and Samuels, studying survey results from more than 24,000 undergraduates who had expressed interest in online coursework, found that students with low readiness scores were less likely to enroll, even though the variables in question were not correlated with academic achievement or persistence (2016). Finally, few of the surveys accurately differentiate between readiness for online learning and readiness for postsecondary coursework of any kind, but are labeled and promoted as if they do. What is needed are instruments that can identify students who are at increased risk specifically within the distance education environment. The judicious use of a readiness survey, taken in consultation with a program advisor, can inform and become part of a broader conversation about student goals, expectations, study habits, and learning opportunities to boost those skills needing improvement.

Student Orientation to the Distance Education Program

As we have stressed, it is also imperative that students be supported throughout their time in the program with guidance in navigating administrative systems and course design that leads to academic success, for example. Many distance education programs also provide orientation systems or short courses and may require new-to-online-learning students to complete or successfully test out of these activities. McGowan (2018) examined online learning orientations offered at 65 institutions across the U.S. and categorized the topics that were included in each into six categories. Each category has several subareas, samples of which are provided in the list below.

- *Getting Started:*   Welcome, user account instructions, introduction to and overall navigation of the LMS
- *Technical Requirements:*   Hardware and software (e.g., browser) requirements, managing access across firewalls
- *Success Strategies:*   Time management, communication tips, advising resources, academic support (e.g., writing center)
- *Help Resources:*   Technical support, disability services, textbook purchasing/access
- *Institutional Information:* Distance education-specific fees, proctoring requirements, contact information for the distance education support office
- *Orientation Support:*   Tutorials, knowledge base, guides, orientation quiz

With the abundance of distance education programs available, student support can be a significant differentiator for those choosing an academic program. These services may mean the difference between a sustainable program and one that faces financial uncertainty, so it is critical to provide and maintain systems, led by qualified professionals, to assist and encourage students in their academic endeavors.

LOOKING FORWARD

The role of a distance education manager requires dedicated attention to trends and hot topics in the field. Two areas gaining traction within education in general that have even greater relevance for online learning programs are *microcredentials* and *learning analytics*.

Microcredentials

Whether they're referred to as badges, stackable credentials, or nanodegrees, the idea of recognition for highly focused learning and competencies holds great appeal for many potential online students. These types of microcredentials are filling a gap between informal or one-off learning experiences (e.g., conference workshops) and a full academic degree program. The key difference between the old-school paper certificate presented at the completion of an educational or professional development experience and its digital counterpart is the metadata embedded in the badge awarded, articulating the specific competencies or achievements that it represents. This background information enables the learner to compile a portfolio of credentials that have meaning beyond a course title or workshop description and present a coherent array of competencies. In their earliest incarnations, many badges were awarded for trivial or meaningless "accomplishments" (e.g., attending a conference but demonstrating no engagement or actual learning), leading to speculation that they may have a demotivating effect on learning, as with other extrinsic reward systems (West & Randall, 2016). Efforts are underway, however, to increase collaboration among badge providers to develop an agreed-upon framework for microcredentials that would build consistency, enhance transferability, and bolster credibility.

What does this have to do with distance education? Consider that many of the people who are interested in obtaining industry-specific certifications or licenses are already working full-time and may have competing priorities, such as families or social obligations. Add to this the mobility of modern-day professionals who may not be able to attend face-to-face courses at one institution long enough to complete a degree, and microcredentials look more and more attractive. Online courses can be a perfect fit for these individuals and open up new markets for non-degree-based offerings. In addition, many such credentials are intended to be hierarchical and lead to a higher certificate, license, or degree (Wilson, 2016). Any distance education program offering high quality courses (or other instructional experiences) that result in microcredentials is likely to have an automatic advantage over other programs. Finally, it's important that distance education managers become acquainted with this trend in light of the opportunities for increased student enrollments in degree completion programs.

Learning Analytics

The other area of interest is learning analytics. The most-commonly cited definition of learning analytics describes it as "the measurement, collection, analysis and reporting of data about the progress of learners and the contexts in which learning takes place" (Siemens et al., 2011). With online learning, in particular, the mouse clicks, assignment submissions, discussion board postings, and other quantifiable data points can identify trends or patterns to aid in decision-making. Many institutions are now using software applications intended to identify at-risk students by continually analyzing factors such as frequency of logins and time spent in the CMS or whether content resources have been opened, for example. Many also rely on predictive modeling that incorporates additional factors (e.g., demographic data) held in institutional repositories. These indicators do not necessarily mean that a student is, in fact, at risk of failing the course but the instructor can be alerted to determine if a personal check-in with the student would be prudent.

While the convenience and information-crunching power of these systems can be attractive, it makes sense to explore first whether the CMS itself archives useful data that can be exported for analysis with less expensive statistical software. Some of the analyses that may prove useful for decision-making or research might include, for example, whether specific content objects are linked to higher (or lower) scores on related assessments, if increased participation in online discussions correlates with success in group-based projects, or whether female students are more likely to ask female instructors for assistance than male instructors. Although it's usually preferable to define the questions to be answered prior to compiling data, the distance education manager may also choose to explore a variety of data pools that could suggest relationships among factors that might otherwise go undetected.

As with any technological innovation, there should be a review of existing (or needed) policy regarding the use of learning analytics and the data generated. Determining who will have access to these reports, how they may be used, and how student privacy will be ensured *must be decided before proceeding*. Finally, even though it may be helpful to track the progress and behaviors of individual students, it's important to recognize that the true long-term value of learning analytics will be from analysis of accumulated group data as the outliers and other quirks are smoothed out in the aggregated set, all while keeping in mind that the analyses can only suggest possible relationships among factors and should be viewed accordingly.

The Future of Distance Learning Administration?

This chapter dealt with responsibilities and job functions of a distance education administrator who is employed by the institution offering online (or other distance-delivered programs), but there is another model that is garnering interest in postsecondary education. This is the use of a for-profit entity to help develop and administer online degree programs, typically at the master's level and primarily in high-demand disciplines. These online program management companies (OPMs) take care of marketing, student enrollment, curriculum development, course design and development, delivery system technologies, faculty training, and technical support for new or re-envisioned online degree programs. The two most common business models for these companies are: (a) revenue-sharing, in which the company assumes the up-front costs of marketing, program development, and faculty development for a sizable cut of the tuition and fees generated over an extended period, often as high as 60% for 10 years based on guaranteed (sometimes startlingly high) enrollments; and (b) fee-for-service, an unbundled model in which the institution contracts with an online program management company for one or more services at market rates.

Three of the largest OPMs that work on a revenue-sharing basis are Pearson Online Learning Services, 2U, and Wiley Education Services (Hill, 2018), although many smaller groups have entered the market. It's likely, however, that the field will see several mergers/partnerships and that some of the smaller players will close up shop before the dust settles. Although there can be advantages to working with an OPM, questions about the academic bona fides of these businesses and the perception that they operate on a scale-before-quality platform have many educators concerned (Riter, 2017). The next 5 to 10 years may see a tipping point, forward or back, for these models.

The Road Ahead

In a 2017 survey of 295 online program administrators and 1,500 students, several trends emerged that may signal changes in the upcoming distance education landscape (BestColleges, 2018). The first of these is that online learners, as a group, are continuing to get younger. One interpretation of this is that distance education is increasingly seen as a flexible, high-quality option for students who, in the past, might have chosen a more traditional environment right out of high school. In terms of delivery systems, 2017 saw a noticeable increase in students reporting the use of synchronous communications technologies in their courses, possibly due to advances in videoconferencing that make it an easy-to-use, inexpensive option for real-time teaching, a trend that is likely to continue. Finally, 76% of the program administrators reported an increase in demand for online courses at their institutions. It is clear that, even with overall postsecondary enrollments stagnating, distance education continues its upswing in the higher education sector.

Technologies for delivering coursework, facilitating communication, assessing learner progress, and managing the varied components of online instruction will continue to evolve and present opportunities to stretch our thinking about what constitutes teaching and learning in a digital age. The challenges and rewards for distance education administrators make this an exciting career track at all levels and in many environments.

DISCUSSION QUESTIONS

The following six questions all are based upon the same scenario. Assume that the administration/management of your organization has made a commitment to a major new distance education program, and you have been appointed its director. (For the purpose of these questions, you select the specific program and target student population.)

1. What would be your highest priorities in getting the program off the ground, and where would you start? Why are these the highest priority for you?
2. Specifically, how would you approach the planning issues related to faculty? Assume that instructors for the program would be drawn from existing faculty in the organization. What issues do you need to address, and how would you address them?
3. Assume that you would be the person responsible for selecting and training the program's faculty. What specific characteristics would you look for in these individuals, and why?
4. What procedures will you follow to effectively train the program faculty? What topics would you include and how would you structure the training, and why would you do it this way?
5. How would you approach the planning issues related to student support services for the new program? In other words, how would you determine if the existing student support infrastructure is sufficient for the program? If it isn't, what would you do? Assume that the organization has funding limits.
6. What steps would you take to ensure quality control of the new program?

REFERENCES

Abedor, A. J., & Sachs, S. G. (1978). The relationship between faculty development (FD), organizational development (OD), and instructional development (ID): Readiness for instructional innovation in higher education. In R. K. Bass & D. B. Lumsden (Eds.), *Instructional development: The state of the art* (pp. 2–19). Columbus, OH: Collegiate.

Allen, I. E., & Seaman, J. (2013). *Changing course: Ten years of tracking online education in the United States.* Wellesley, MA: Babson College. Retrieved from http://sloanconsortium.org/publications/survey/changing_course_2012

Anderson, M., & Jiang, J. (2018). Teens, social media, & technology 2018. Retrieved from http://www.pewinternet.org/2018/05/31/teens-social-media-technology-2018/

BestColleges. (2018). Online education trends report. Retrieved from https://www.bestcolleges.com/perspectives/annual-trends-in-online-education/

Brooks, D. & Pomerantz, J. (2017). ECAR study of undergraduate students and information technology, 2017. Research report. Louisville, CO: ECAR. Retrieved from https://library.educause.edu/~/media/files/library/2017/10/studentitstudy2017.pdf

Commission on the Regulation of Postsecondary Distance Education. (2013). Advancing access through regulatory reform. Retrieved from http://www.nc-sara.org/files/docs/Commission-on-Regulation-of-Postsecondary-Distance-Education-Draft-Recommendations.pdf

Council for Higher Education Accreditation. (2018). 2018-2019 Directory of CHEA recognized organizations. Retrieved from https://www.chea.org/2018-2019-directory-chea-recognized-organizations-pdf

Council of Regional Accrediting Commissions. (2011). Interregional guidelines for the evaluation of distance education (on-line learning). Retrieved from http://www.msche.org/publications/Guidelines-for-the-Evaluation-of-Distance-Education-Programs.pdf

Diament, M. (2018, February 23). Ed department logs sharp rise in disability complaints. Retrieved from https://www.disabilityscoop.com/2018/02/23/ed-department-rise-disability/24761/

Doe, R., Castillo, M. & Musyoka, M. (2017). Assessing online readiness of students. *Online Journal of Distance Learning Administration, 20*(1). Retrieved from https://www.westga.edu/~distance/ojdla/spring201/doe_castillo_musyoka201.html

EDUCAUSE. (2015). IT accessibility risk statements and evidence. Retrieved from https://library.educause.edu/~/media/files/library/2015/7/accessrisk15-pdf.pdf

Fredericksen, E. (2017). A national study of online learning leaders in US higher education. *Online Learning, 21*(2). Retrieved from https://files.eric.ed.gov/fulltext/EJ1149347.pdf

Gellman-Danley, B., & Fetzner, M. J. (1998). Asking the really tough questions: Policy issues for distance learning. *Online Journal of Distance Learning Administration, 1*(1). Retrieved from http://www.westga.edu/~distance/danley11.html

Herold, B. (2017, June 12). Online classes for K–12 schools: What you need to know. *Education Week.* Retrieved from https://www.edweek.org/ew/articles/2017/06/14/online-classes-for-k-12-schools-what-you.html?intc=EW-TC17-TOC

Higher Education Opportunity Act, Pub. L. No. 110-315, 122 Stat. 3080, (2008), U.S.C. §495. Retrieved from https://www.gpo.gov/fdsys/pkg/PLAW-110publ315/pdf/PLAW-110publ315.pdf

Hill, P. (2018). Online program management: Spring 2018 view of the market landscape. e-Literate. Retrieved from https://mfeldstein.com/online-program-management-market-landscape-s2018/

Judd, T. (2018). The rise and fall (?) of the digital natives. *Australasian Journal of Educational Technology, 34*(5), 99–119.

McGowan, V. (2018). An investigation into web-based presentations of institutional online learning orientations. *Journal of Educators Online, 15*(2). Retrieved from https://www.thejeo.com/archive/2018_15_2/mcgowan

National Center for Educational Statistics. (2017). Characteristics and outcomes of undergraduates with disabilities. Retrieved from https://nces.ed.gov/pubsearch/pubsinfo.asp?pubid=2018432

Office of Postsecondary Education, U.S. Department of Education. (2006). Evidence of quality in distance education programs drawn from interviews with the accreditation community. Retrieved from http://www.ysu.edu/accreditation/Resources/Accreditation-Evidence-of-Quality-in-DE-Programs.pdf

Parry, M. (2010, January 17). Online scheme triggers new fears about distance education fraud. *Chronicle of Higher Education.* Retrieved from http://chronicle.com/article/Online-Scheme-Triggers-New/63532/

Poulin, R., & Taylor Straut, T. (2018). The economics of distance education: Boxing match or productive dialogue? *Change: The Magazine of Higher Learning, 50*(1), 14–23. doi:10.1080/00091383.2018.1413900

Program Integrity and Improvement, 83 Fed. Reg. 128 (July 3, 2018). Retrieved from https://www.federalregister.gov/documents/2018/07/03/2018-14373/program-integrity-and-improvement

Riter, P. (2017). Five myths about online program management. *EDUCAUSE Review.* Retrieved from https://er.educause.edu/articles/2017/3/five-myths-about-online-program-management

Savery, J. (2005). Be VOCAL: Characteristics of successful online instructors. *Journal of Interactive Online Learning, 4*(2), 141–152.

Seaman, J., Allen, I., & Seaman, J. (2018). Grade increase: Tracking distance education in the United States. Babson Survey Research Group. Retrieved from https://www.onlinelearningsurvey.com/highered.html

Siemens, G., Gasevic, D., Haythornthwaite, C., Dawson, S., Shum, S., Ferguson, R., … Baker, R. (2011). Open learning analytics: An integrated & modularized platform. Society for Learning Analytics Research. Retrieved from http://www.elearnspace.org/blog/wp-content/uploads/2016/02/ProposalLearningAnalyticsModel_SoLAR.pdf

Simonson, M. (2004). Distance learning leaders—Who are they? *Distance Learning, 1*(3), 48.

U.S. Department of Education, Office of Inspector General. (2018). Semiannual Report to Congress, No.76: October 1, 2017 – March 31, 2018. Retrieved from https://www2.ed.gov/about/offices/list/oig/semiann/sar76.pdf

West, R. & Randall, D. (2016). The case for rigor in open badges. In L. Muilenburg & Z. Berge (Eds.), *Digital badges in education: Trends, issues, and cases* (pp. 21–29). New York, NY: Routledge.

Western Cooperative for Educational Technologies. (2002). Guidelines for creating student services online. Boulder, CO: Author. Retrieved from http://wcet.wiche.edu/wcet/docs/beyond/overview.pdf

Western Cooperative for Educational Technologies, UT Telecampus, & Instructional Technology Council. (2006). Best practices to promote academic integrity in online education. Retrieved from http://wcet.wiche.edu/wcet/docs/cigs/studentauthentication/BestPractices.pdf

Wilson, B. (2016). *Stackable credential policy toolkit.* National Skills Coalition. Retrieved from https://www.nationalskillscoalition.org/resources/publications/file/Stackable-Credential-Policy-Toolkit-1.pdf

Wladis, C., & Samuels, J. (2016). Do online readiness surveys do what they claim? Validity, reliability, and subsequent enrollment decisions. *Computers & Education, 98,* 39–56.

CHAPTER 12

Evaluating Teaching and Learning at a Distance

CHAPTER GOAL

The purpose of this chapter is to present approaches for evaluation of distance education courses, programs and systems.

CHAPTER OBJECTIVES

After reading and reviewing this chapter, you should be able to

1. Differentiate between research and evaluation.
2. Define *evaluation.*
3. Explain the six categories of evaluation information: in measures of activity, efficiency, outcomes, program aims, policy, and organizations.
4. Describe the AEIOU approach to evaluation and its five levels—accountability, effectiveness, impact, organizational context, and unanticipated consequences.

RESEARCH AND EVALUATION

> The best way to find things out is not to ask questions at all. If you fire off a question, it is like firing off a gun—bang it goes, and everything takes flight and runs for shelter. But if you sit quite still and pretend not to be looking, all the little facts will come and peck around your feet, situations will venture forth from thickets, and intentions will creep out and sun themselves on a stone; and if you are very patient, you will see and understand a great deal more than a person with a gun does. (Huxley, 1982, p. 20)

This marvelous quote from Huxley's *The Flame Trees of Thika* illustrates a metaphorical rationale for a major refocusing of procedures for evaluation of distance education systems. Traditional evaluation models have concentrated on the empirical and quantitative procedures that have been practiced for decades (Fitzpatrick, Sanders, & Worthen, 2004; Stufflebeam & Shinkfield, 2007). More recently, evaluators of distance education programs have begun to propose more qualitative models that include the collection of many non-numerical types of information (Rovai, 2003; Sherry, 2003).

Because it is easy to think of them as being the same thing, it is important to differentiate between theory-based research and evaluation. Simonson, Schlosser, and Orellana (2011) provided a review of distance education literature including research on and about distance education. This review summarized distance education research as follows:

■ Distance education is just as effective as traditional education in regard to learner outcomes.

■ Distance education learners generally have more favorable attitudes toward distance education than traditional learners, and distance learners feel they learn as well as non-distant students.

■ The research clearly shows that distance education is an effective method for teaching and learning.

Evaluation, as contrasted to research, is the systematic investigation of the worth or merit of an object. Program evaluation is the systematic investigation of the worth of an ongoing or continuing distance education activity (Yarbrough, Shulha, Hopson, & Caruthers, 2011). Martinez, Liu, Watson, and Bichelmeyer (2006) discuss the importance of evaluating distance education programs. Evaluation of programs is used to identify strengths and weaknesses as well as the benefits and drawbacks of teaching and learning online. They asked students, administrators, and instructors to evaluate course management categories, such as registration, support services, advising, and sense of community. One important finding of this study was the equivalence of the distance education program to the traditional program (Martinez et al., 2006).

This chapter focuses on approaches to evaluation for the purpose of improving distance education and determining the worth of distance education activities. Rose (2000) identified a number of databases related to evaluation of distance education courses that are available on the World Wide Web. These online databases provide a repository of up-to-date information about online courses. Additional information related to evaluation and distance education is available in Ruhe and Zumbo (2009) Clark and Barbour (2015), Thompson and Irele (2007), Cyrs and Smith (1990), Fitz-Gibbon and Morris (1987), Fitz-patrick et al. (2004), and Rossi, Lipsey, and Freeman (2003).

EVALUATION AND DISTANCE EDUCATION—FIVE STEPS

Evaluation procedures are becoming of critical interest to trainers and teachers who are adopting distance education (Peak & Berge, 2006). As new distance education systems are being planned and implemented there is considerable concern that the time and effort required to move to distance delivery of instruction produced a valuable educational experience, thus, evaluation is regularly a part of plans to move from traditional face-to-face instruction to distance education. Kirkpatrick and Kirkpatrick's (2006) evaluation approach with its four levels of evaluation, supplemented by Phillips (2003); the fifth evaluation level—return on investment—seems to be the preferred approach of many trainers, and some educators.

Kirkpatrick and Kirkpatrick's evaluation approach has been traditionally used to evaluate classroom training and teaching, especially in the private, government and military sectors. It is a straightforward approach that produces usable information for the trainer. The four levels of the approach are designed to obtain answers to commonly asked questions about training—Did they like it? Did they learn it? Will they use it? Will it matter? (Simonson, 2007).

Level 1—Reactions (Did They Like It)

As the word reactions implies, evaluation at this level measures how participants in the training program feel about the educational activity. Students are asked what they liked and did not like about training, sometimes several times during a course or program. Students are required to use checklists, Likert responses to statements, and open ended comments, all to determine if the training was perceived positively by participants.

Level 2—Learning

At this level, evaluation strategies attempt to determine more than learner satisfaction. Rather, evaluators assess the extent to which learners have advanced in skills, knowledge, or attitude. What and how much did participants learn? What new skills do they possess? And, what new and appropriate attitudinal positions have been produced.

Methods include objective testing, team assessment, and self-assessment. Often pretest, posttest change is used as a measure at Level 2.

Level 3—Transfer

At this level, evaluators attempt to determine if the skills, knowledge and attitudes learned as a result of training are being transferred to the work place or to actual learner activities. Evaluation questions deal with the use of new skills, or the application of new knowledge to events. Timing of the evaluation at this level is critical, and problematic, since it is difficult to know when transfer actually occurs.

Level 4—Results

Evaluation activities at this level attempt to measure the success of the training or teaching program in terms of increased productivity, improved quality, lower costs, and for businesses, even higher profits. Trainers are increasingly being ask to demonstrate the direct and indirect impact of training on the success of the organization and to relate training to mission accomplishment. In schools, Level 4 evaluations often look at enrollments in additional courses, learning motivation, and educational achievement.

Level 5—Return on Investment

Increasingly, many training and educational organizations that are adopting distance education are interested in the concept of return on investment—converting training results from eLearning activities into monetary values and comparing these costs to the cost of the training program to determine a return on investment. Phillips (2003) describes a five step process to determine return on investment.

1. First, it is necessary to collect Level 4 data to determine if there is a change in job or educational performance that is positive and also measurable? This assumes that there were evaluation data collected concerning the first four levels of the Kirkpatricks' model.

2. Second, evaluators need to identify the training that contributed to the change in performance. Testing can be used, as can control groups that receive different training, or no training at all.

3. Third, it is necessary to convert the results of training or education into monetary values. This often means a relatively subjective process must be undertaken to quantify outcomes related to the training.

4. Next, the evaluation process requires the determination of the total cost of training. This includes trainer costs, facilities expenses, materials purchased and other expenses.

5. Fifth, return on investment, or ROI, is determined by comparing the monetary benefits to the costs. In this manner, it is possible to quantify the impact of training, the effectiveness of education and the value of the instruction.

The ROI process is time consuming, requires a skilled evaluation team, and is sometimes criticized because it produces evaluation results that look at what has happened, rather than what will happen. Peak and Berge (2006) also recommend that not everything needs to be measured. Rather, leaders should determine what they think is important and then trainers evaluate those areas.

While evaluation has always been somewhat important in corporate and military training and of interest to a lesser extent in education, the recent phenomenal growth of distance education has made many leaders want to know what the implications are of moving to training and teaching that is not face-to-face. Thus, Kirkpatricks' and Phillips' evaluation approaches have received increased attention, especially since most evidence clearly demonstrates distance education works academically to produce required achievement gains. The evidence is clear that students learn just as effectively when they are taught at a distance as compared to when they learn in a traditional classroom (Simonson, 2007). Thus, it can be generalized that traditional training and eLearning work equally well. The question for evaluators then becomes the determination of the advantages, if any, of moving to an eLearning environment? Evaluators are looking at cost savings, time savings, increased motivation and satisfaction, economies of scale, and other nonachievement outcome metrics. Evaluation of eLearning should provide leaders evidence they need to support or to refute training decisions.

EVALUATION AND THE OPEN UNIVERSITY

Program evaluation at the Open University of Great Britain is the systematic investigation of the merit of a particular distance education program, curriculum, or teaching method, and how it might be improved compared with alternatives. As part of evaluation procedures for distance education by the Open University (Woodley & Kirkwood, 1986, 2005), two alternative strategies have been merged. The first is the traditional, positivist-empiricist approach to evaluation. This represents an attempt to apply the rules and procedures of the physical sciences to evaluation. The second is a more eclectic view of evaluation that incorporates qualitative and naturalistic techniques for the evaluation of distance education.

The traditional strategy normally includes an experiment that determines the effectiveness of a distance education strategy. The distance education project is structured from its beginning with the requirements of the evaluator in mind. Carefully matched samples are picked, controls are established, and variables are selected for which comparison data will be collected. Next, objective tests of variables are selected or constructed. Data are collected before, during, and always after the instructional event or procedures. Then the evaluator takes the data and prepares the evaluation report, which is submitted weeks or months later.

The primary outcome of this type of evaluation is the comparison of the data collected from the two or more categories of learners. For example, the distant learners are compared with those taught locally, and conclusions about the effectiveness of the distance education activity are made.

This approach represents the traditional process for the evaluation of distance education. Recently at the Open University and elsewhere, a countermovement has emerged (House, 2010). Advocates of this counterapproach are united in one primary way: They are opposed to the traditional, quantitative procedures for evaluation. Increasingly, evaluation activities are incorporating more naturalistic methodologies with holistic perspectives. This second perspective for evaluation uses focus groups, interviews, observations, and journals to collect evaluation information in order to obtain a rich and colorful understanding of events related to the distance education activity.

From a practical standpoint, most evaluators now use a combination of quantitative and qualitative measures. Certainly, there is a need to quantify and count. Just as certainly, there is a need to understand opinions and hear perspectives.

According to Woodley and Kirkwood (1986, 2005), six categories of evaluation information can be collected about distance education activities:

1. **Measures of Activity.** These measures are counts of the numbers of events, people, and objects. Administrative records often provide data for activity questions. Activity questions are ones such as:

   - How many courses were produced?
   - How many students were served?
   - How many potential students were turned away?

2. **Measures of Efficiency.** Measures of efficiency are closely related to measures of activity, and often administrative records can be the source of efficiency information. Efficiency questions often asked are ones such as:

   - How many students successfully completed the course?
   - What was the average student's workload?
   - How many students enrolled in additional courses?
   - How much did the course cost?
   - How much tuition was generated?

3. **Measures of Outcomes.** Measures of adequate learning are usually considered the most important measures of outcomes of distance education activities. Often, interviews with learners are used to supplement course grades in order to find students' perceptions about a distance education activity. Mail surveys are also efficient ways to collect outcome information from distant learners. Other outcome measures include documenting the borrowing and use of courses and course materials by other institutions as an indicator of effectiveness, and the enrollment by students in additional, similar courses as indicators of a preliminary course's success.

4. **Measures of Program Aims.** Some distance teaching programs specify their aims in terms of what and whom they intend to teach, and evaluation information is collected to establish the extent to which these aims were met. One common aim of dis-

tance education programs is to reach learners who otherwise would not be students. Surveys of learners can be used to collect this type of information.

5. **Measures of Policy.** Evaluation in the policy area often takes the form of market research. Surveys of prospective students and employers can be used to determine the demand for distance education activities.

   Policy evaluation can also include monitoring. Students can be surveyed to determine if tuition is too high, if appropriate courses are being offered, and if there are impediments to course success, such as the lack of access to computers or the library. Sometimes policy evaluation can be used to determine the success of experimental programs, such as those for low achievers or for students who normally are not qualified for a program. The purpose of policy evaluation is to identify procedures that are needed or that need to be changed, and to develop new policies.

6. **Measures of Organizations.** Sometimes it is important to evaluate a distance education institution in terms of its internal organization and procedures. Evaluators sometimes are asked to monitor the process of course development or program delivery to help an organization be more efficient. This category of evaluation requires on-site visits, interviews, and sometimes the use of journals by key organization leaders.

These six categories of evaluation are not used for every distance education activity. Certainly, some modest evaluation activity is almost always necessary. It is important that the activities of evaluators be matched to programmatic needs. Woodley and Kirkwood (1986, 2005) have summarized evaluation in distance education as being a fairly eclectic process that utilizes procedures that should match program needs to evaluation activities.

QUALITY SCORECARD AND QUALITY MATTERS

Evaluating Programs and Courses

Two widely used and standardized evaluation instruments are the Sloan Consortium's Quality Scorecard for the Administration of Online Education Programs, and the Quality Matters Rubric Standards. These two instruments can be used to evaluate online programs and courses and are also effective for use when courses are designed—as models for effective programs and courses (Quality Matters, 2013; Sloan-C, 2013)

The Scorecard deals with issues such as institutional support, technology support, course development and instructional design, course structure, teaching and learning, social and student engagement, faculty support, student support and evaluation and assessment. Quality Matters provides a rubric for courses, including the course overview, learning objectives, assessment and measurement, instructional materials, learning interaction and engagement, technology, learner support and accessibility. Both tools are excellent.

Often, local institutions will prepare their own evaluation systems that are based on guidelines and approaches they expect all online courses in include. Generally, these kinds of course evaluations are divided into four sections:

1. Course Introduction
2. Course Organization and Accessibility
3. Learning Activities and Interaction
4. Assessment

Multiple subsections are usually included in each section. One example are guidelines developed by a task force at Nova Southeastern University (Orellana, 2018)

THE AEIOU APPROACH

Fortune and Keith (1992) proposed the AEIOU approach for program evaluation, especially the evaluation of distance education projects. The effectiveness of this approach has been demonstrated through evaluating the activities of the Iowa Distance Education Alliance Star Schools Project (Simonson & Schlosser, 1995a; Sorensen, 1996, Sorensen & Sweeney, 1995, 1996, 1997; Sweeney, 1995), a multiyear, statewide distance education activity. Additionally, the model has been used to evaluate a number of other innovative projects, such as the Iowa Chemistry Education Alliance in 1995, the Iowa General Chemistry Network in 1994, and the DaVinci Project: Interactive Multimedia for Art and Chemistry (Simonson & Schlosser, 1995b). More recently, a major distance education initiative in South Dakota used a modified version of the AEIOU approach (Simonson, 2005).

The AEIOU approach is similar to Woodley and Kirkwoods' in that it is an eclectic one that uses quantitative and qualitative methodologies. It has two primary purposes as an evaluation strategy. First, the model provides formative information to the staff about the implementation of their project. Second, it provides summative information about the value of the project and its activities. The AEIOU evaluation process provides a framework for identifying key questions necessary for effective evaluation. Some evaluation plans use only parts of the framework, whereas other, more comprehensive plans use all components. Some examples of evaluation questions asked in comprehensive distance education projects are presented next.

Component 1—*Accountability*

Did the Planners Do What They Said They Were Going to Do? This is the first step in determining the effectiveness of the program, project or course and is targeted at determining if the project's objectives and activities were completed. Evaluation questions typically center on the completion of a specific activity and often are answered "yes" or "no." Additionally, counts of numbers of people, things, and activities are often collected.

Questions such as the following are often asked to determine project accountability:

- Were the appropriate number of class sessions held?
- How many students were enrolled?
- How many copies of program materials were produced, and how many were distributed?

Methods Used: Accountability information is often collected from project administrative records. Project leaders are often asked to provide documentation of the level of completion of each of the project's goals, objectives, and activities. Sometimes evaluators interview project staff to collect accountability data.

Component 2—*Effectiveness*

How Well Done Was the Program, Project, or Course? This component of the evaluation process attempts to place some value on the program, course or project's activities.

Effectiveness questions often focus on participant attitudes and knowledge. Obviously, grades, achievement tests, and attitude inventories are measures of effectiveness. Less obvious are other ways to determine quality. Often, raters are asked to review course materials and course presentations to determine their effectiveness, and student course evaluations can be used to collect reactions from distance education participants.

Examples of questions to determine effectiveness include:

▪ Were the in-service participants satisfied with their distance education instruction?
▪ Did the students learn what they were supposed to learn?
▪ Did the teachers feel adequately prepared to teach distant learners?

Methods Used: Standardized measures of achievement and attitude are traditionally used to determine program effectiveness. Surveys of students and faculty can be used to ask questions related to perceptions about the appropriateness of a project or program. Focus groups (Morgan, 1996) also provide valuable information. Participants are systematically asked to respond to questions about the program. Finally, journals are sometimes kept by project participants and then analyzed to determine the day-to-day effectiveness of an ongoing program.

Component 3—*Impact*

Did the Program, Course, or Project Make a Difference?   During this phase of the evaluation, questions focus on identifying the changes that resulted from the program's activities, and are tied to the stated outcomes of the project or course. In other words, if the project had not happened, what of importance would not have occurred? A key element of measurement of impact is the collection of longitudinal data. The impact of distance education courses is often determined by following learners' progress in subsequent courses or in the workplace to determine if what was learned in the distance education course was useful.

Determinants of impact are difficult to identify. Often, evaluators use follow-up studies to determine the impressions made on project participants; and sometimes in distance education programs, learners are followed and questioned by evaluators in subsequent courses and activities.

Questions might include:

▪ Did students register for additional distance education courses?
▪ Has the use of the distance education system increased?
▪ Have policies and procedures related to the use of the distance education system been developed or changed?

Methods Used: Qualitative measures provide the most information to the evaluator interested in program impact. Standardized tests, record data, and surveys are sometimes used. Also, interviews, focus groups, and direct observations are used to identify a program's impact.

Component 4—*Organizational Context*

What Structures, Policies, or Events in the Organization or Environment Helped or Hindered the Project in Accomplishing its Goals?   This component of evaluation has traditionally not been important even though evaluators have often hinted in their reports about organizational policies that either hindered or helped a program. Recently, however, distance educators have become very interested in organizational policy analysis in order to determine barriers to the successful implementation of distance education systems, especially when those systems are new activities of traditional educational organizations, such as large public universities.

The focus of this component of the evaluation is on identifying those contextual or environmental factors that contributed to, or detracted from, the project or course's ability to conduct activities. Usually these factors are beyond the control of the project's participants. Effective evaluation of organizational context requires the evaluator to be intimately involved with the project or course in order to have a good understanding of the environment in which the project or course operates.

Questions typically addressed in evaluating organizational context include:

▪ What factors made it difficult to implement the project or to successfully complete the course?
▪ What contributed most to the success or failure of the program, course, project, or the students in the course?
▪ What should be done differently to improve things and make the course more effective?

Methods Used: Organizational context evaluation uses interviews of key personnel such as faculty or students, focus groups made up of those impacted by a program, and document analysis that identifies policies and procedures that influence a program or course. Direct participation in program activities by the evaluator is also important. Sometimes evaluators enroll in distance education courses. More often, a student is asked to complete a journal while enrolled in a course. By participating, the evaluator is confronted directly with the organizational context in which a program exists, and can comment on this context firsthand.

Component 5—*Unanticipated Consequences*

What Changes or Consequences of Importance Happened as a Result of the Program, Course, or Project That Were Not Expected? This component of the AEIOU approach is to identify unexpected changes of either a positive or negative nature that occurred as a direct or indirect result of the program, course, or project. Effective evaluators have long been interested in reporting anecdotal information about the project or program that they were evaluating. It is only recently that this category of information has become recognized as important, largely because of the positive influence on evaluation of qualitative procedures. Often, evaluators, especially internal evaluators who are actively involved in the project or course's implementation, have many opportunities to observe successes and failures during the trial-and-error process of beginning a new program. Unanticipated consequences of developing new or modified programs, especially in the dynamic field of distance education, are a rich source of information about why some projects are successful and others are not. Central to the measurement of unanticipated outcomes is the collection of ex post facto data.

Examples of questions asked include:

▪ Have relationships between collaborators or students changed in ways not expected?
▪ Have related, complementary projects been developed?
▪ Were unexpected linkages developed between groups or participants?

▪ Was the distance education system used in unanticipated ways?

▪ Did the distance education system have an impact on student learning other than that expected?

Methods Used: Interviews, focus groups, journals, and surveys that ask for narrative information can be used to identify interesting and potentially important consequences of implementing a new program. Often, evaluators must interact with project participants or course students on a regular basis to learn about the little successes and failures that less sensitive procedures overlook. Active and continuous involvement by evaluators permits them to learn about the project as it occurs.

Sweeney (1995) advocates an eclectic approach to evaluation, an approach also supported by Fitzpatrick et al. (2004). The AEIOU model is a dynamic one that permits the evaluator to tailor the process of program evaluation to the specific situation being studied.

PROGRAM EVALUATION: EXAMPLES

South Dakota

South Dakota has a network for distance education that connects every school in the state. Currently, hundreds of classrooms are connected to the Digital Dakota Network (DDN). The DDN was funded using state monies and grants from telecommunications providers, such as QWEST Communications.

Implementation of the DDN was called the Connecting the Schools project. As the network came online and began to be used, it was decided that a comprehensive evaluation effort was needed. Evaluators used the AEIOU approach and collected both quantitative and qualitative information (Simonson, 2005; Simonson & Bauck, 2001).

Quantitative information was collected using a locally developed survey called the Connecting the Schools Questionnaire (CSQ). The CSQ asked respondents to provide four categories of information: demographics, information about personal innovativeness, questions about organizational innovativeness, and questions about distance education.

Demographic information was collected in order to obtain a profile of the teachers in the state, and included questions about age, years of experience, gender, academic background, and professional involvement. The second part of the CSQ was a modified version of Hurt, Joseph, and Cook's (1977) innovativeness scale (Simonson, 2000). The innovativeness scale is a standardized measure of how innovative a person thinks he or she is. Part three of the CSQ was a modified version of Hurt and Tiegen's (1977) Perceived Organizational Innovativeness scale. The scale is a standardized measure of a person's perception of his or her employer's organizational innovativeness. The final section of the CSQ asked questions about distance education. These questions were to find out how much South Dakota teachers knew about distance education and to determine their general feelings about the impact of distance education on teaching and learning.

The qualitative portion of the CSQ evaluation in South Dakota used focus groups, participant observations, interviews, and site visits. Three questions were at the heart of the quantitative evaluation. First, evaluators tried to determine what educators thought would be the greatest benefits provided by implementing distance education. Second, attempts were made to determine what was preventing individuals from becoming involved in distance education. Next, school superintendents were selected randomly and interviewed to determine their perceptions of the impact of distance education and the Digital Dakota

Network on education in their school districts (Calderone, 2003). Finally, questions were asked about the impediments to distance education.

When quantitative data were combined with qualitative information, a rich understanding was provided to education leaders about South Dakota's ability to adopt distance education (Learning at a Distance: South Dakota, www.tresystems.com/projects/). Complete results of the evaluation were reported in Simonson (2005). In general, the evaluation of the South Dakota project verified that Rogers's (2003) theory concerning the diffusion of innovations was directly applicable to distance education efforts in South Dakota and that this theory could effectively serve as a model for promoting the adoption of innovations, such as the DDN specifically, and distance education in public schools, more generally.

Iowa

Several years ago, it was decided that a three-phase plan should be implemented to establish distance education classrooms throughout the state of Iowa. Recently, hundreds of sites were connected to this distance education infrastructure, which was named the Iowa Communications Network (ICN).

As part of the implementation plan for the ICN, a comprehensive evaluation program was put into action. This program utilized the AEIOU approach and collected data from thousands of sources and individuals. The evaluation approach went through several stages during the 5 years it was used. First, evaluators concentrated on evaluating the construction, connection, and implementation of the ICN's physical infrastructure. Records related to classroom design, construction schedules, and dollars spent were collected and reviewed, and summary results were reported. This related to the accountability component of the AEIOU approach.

Next, those involved in the decision-making process for establishing the network were interviewed and completed surveys. Evaluators used the results to develop reports on the effectiveness of the processes used to construct the ICN. To determine impact, evaluators conducted follow-up investigations of classroom utilization and examined records of how the system was used.

The program evaluators examined many interesting organizational issues, such as who made decisions about where classrooms were located, how funds were obtained and spent, and who controlled access to the system. One interesting outcome was related to the use of the distance education classroom, which were typically locked. Utilization of this classroom was related to who had the room key, with the second highest usage for locked room when the school library media specialist had the key. If the principal had the key, usage was relatively low. Highest usage occurred when the room was *not* locked during regular school hours.

Finally, program evaluators identified unanticipated outcomes. One of the most significant was the infusion of several millions of dollars from federal, state, and local sources to support the development of the network. How these funds were obtained and used added to the importance of the evaluation report.

Once the network was built and a plan for its continued growth was put into place, evaluators shifted their primary focus to the human side of the growth of distance education in the state. Staff development, technical training, curriculum revisions, and school restructuring became the focus of network planners and funding agencies, so program evaluators used the AEIOU model to obtain information about these activities. The approach was used to provide formative information about the development of programs and their impact on teachers and learners, and also to provide information on outcomes, or summative information, to document the successes and failures of various program activities.

A true understanding of activities of evaluators of this statewide, multiyear project can only be gained by reviewing the yearly reports they submitted. However, it is important to note that the evaluation plan provided the following information:

Accountability.   Evaluators checked records, interviewed staff, and visited classrooms to determine the status of the development of the ICN, both as a physical system and as a tool used by teachers to deliver courses to distant learners. The accountability focus shifted during the project as its activities shifted from construction to implementation and finally to maintenance.

Effectiveness.   Evaluators conducted interviews and focus groups to determine what impact the availability of the ICN had on classroom education. Surveys were sent and reports were generated that helped education leaders to better understand what role distance education was playing.

Impact.   As the network became widely available and the number of courses and activities increased, it became possible to determine the impact of the ICN and distance education events on education in the state. Students were tested and grades reported. Most of the achievement data showed that learning occurred and good grades were obtained. More important, the availability of new learning experiences grew considerably.

Organizational Context.   From the beginning of the ICN project, the role of the state as compared with local educational organizations was a focus of evaluation activities. One outcome was to identify where cooperation between agencies was necessary, such as in scheduling, and where local control, such as in course selection, should be maintained. Project evaluators identified and reported on what the data seemed to indicate were the barriers and the contributors to the effective growth and utilization of the ICN.

Unanticipated Outcomes.   During the project, scores of unanticipated outcomes were identified and reported. Among the most interesting were:

- The movement of the ICN into the role of Internet service provider
- The role of the ICN in attracting external grants
- The role of distance education and the ICN in the movement to restructure schools
- The impact of the ICN on positive attitudes toward technology in education
- The emerging role of the public television station in Iowa education

There were also many other unanticipated outcomes. The AEIOU approach was useful in helping the state's educators in evaluating the role of distance education as an approach and the ICN as an infrastructure. Evaluation played a significant part in the positive implementation and use of this new technology in the state of Iowa.

STUDENT EVALUATION OF DISTANCE EDUCATION COURSES

The purpose of a course evaluation is to fulfill accreditation requirements and to provide a means for reporting course and instructor effectiveness. Standardized course evaluation forms are available that have already been developed and have gone through rigorous psychometric analyses. The literature suggests course and instructor evaluation models that focus on six constructs:

- Teaching and learning
- Developing a community of learners
- The instructor
- The student
- Implementation of the course
- Technology use

Evaluation instruments should possess the psychometric characteristics of standardized measures, meaning they should be valid, reliable, administered in a consistent manner, and have normative tables so scores can be compared.

Valid instruments measure what they are supposed to measure, in this case the effectiveness of online courses and online teaching. Reliable measures are consistent. In other words, if the measure was administered a second time the scores should be very similar. Consistent administration of course evaluations ensures that more or less favorable conditions of testing do not influence the results. Finally, scores for any course evaluation are difficult to decipher if there is no comparison data. Often, scores from evaluations for many courses are collected so that the scores for any individual course and instructor can be compared with others. Usually, any identifiers for comparison courses are removed. It is important to remember that course and instructor evaluations are to be used for continuous improvement, and to provide input for course revisions.

A sample evaluation instrument to collect students' perceptions about the six constructs, the Online Course Evaluation Instrument (OCEI, pronounced ooh-see), is shown in Figure 12–1.

SUMMARY

As distance education in the United States increases in importance, evaluation will continue to be a critical component of the process of improvement. Certainly, the literature is clear. Eclectic models of evaluation such as the ones advocated by Woodley and Kirkwood (1986) and Sweeney (1995) are most applicable to distance education program evaluation. Evaluators should use quantitative and qualitative procedures. Distance education programs and even single courses should be accountable to their goals, should be at least as effective as alternative approaches, and should have a positive impact. Evaluators should attempt when possible to identify what organizational contexts support effective distance education systems, and unanticipated events both should be shared with interested readers and should be used to improve courses.

If you are very patient, you will see and understand. (Huxley, 1982, p. 20)

REFERENCES

Calderone, T. (2003). *Superintendents' perceptions of their role in the diffusion of distance education* (Unpublished doctoral dissertation). Nova Southeastern University, Fort Lauderdale, FL.

Clark, T., & Barbour M. (2015). *Online, blended and distance education in schools: Building successful programs.* Sterling, VA: Stylus.

Cyrs, T., & Smith, F. (1990). *Teleclass teaching: A resource guide* (2nd ed.). Las Cruces, NM: Center for Educational Development.

FIGURE 12–1   An evaluation instrument.

ONLINE COURSE EVALUATION INSTRUMENT (OCIE)

Course Name:

Gender: ____ Male	**Class Size:** ____ Class size 1 to 10
____ Female	____ Class size 11 to 20
	____ Class size 21 to 30
Age: ____ Years	____ Class size 31 to 40
	____ Class size 41 and above
Class Level: ____ Undergraduate	
____ Master	**First Experience in an Online Course** ____ Yes ____ No
____ Doctorate	

Class Term: ____ Summer
____ Fall
____ Winter

Please rate each item using the following scale:

5 – Strongly agree
4 – Agree
3 – Neither agree nor disagree
2 – Disagree
1 – Strongly disagree

Teaching and Learning

1. The course has clearly stated objectives _____
2. The course activities are consistent with course objectives _____
3. The course syllabus is an accurate guide to course requirements _____
4. The course materials are a helpful guide to key concepts covered in the class _____
5. The course projects and assignments build understanding of concepts and principles _____
6. The course presents appropriate skills and techniques _____
7. The course is current with developments in the field _____

Developing a Community of Learners

1. Collaborative work is a valuable part of this course _____
2. There is opportunity to learn from other students _____
3. Differing viewpoints and discussions are encouraged in this class _____
4. Mutual respect is a concept practiced in this course _____
5. Each student has an opportunity to contribute to class learning _____

The Instructor

1. The instructor clearly states the methods of evaluation that will be used to assess student work _____
2. The instructor uses a variety of methods to evaluate _____
3. The instructor shows respect for the various points of view represented in this class _____
4. The instructor makes learning interesting and motivates students to learn _____
5. The instructor uses technology in ways that help learning of concepts _____
6. The instructor responds to questions with consideration _____
7. The instructor displays a clear understanding of course topics _____

Fitz-Gibbon, C., & Morris, L. (1987). *How to design a program evaluation.* Newbury Park, CA: SAGE.

Fitzpatrick, J., Sanders, J., & Worthen, B. (2004). *Program evaluation: Alternative approaches and practical guidelines* (3rd ed.). Upper Saddle River, NJ: Pearson/Allyn & Bacon.

Fortune, J., & Keith, P. (1992). *Program evaluation for Buchanan County Even Start.* Blacksburg, VA: College of Education, Virginia Polytechnic Institute and State University.

House, E. (Ed.). (2010). *New directions in educational evaluation.* Lewes, England: Falmer Press.

Hurt, H., Joseph, K., & Cook, C. (1977). Scales for the measurement of innovativeness. *Human Communications Research, 4*(1), 58–65.

Hurt, H., & Teigen, C. (1977). The development of a measure of perceived organizational innovativeness. *Communication Yearbook I* (pp. 377–385). New Brunswick, NJ: International Communications Association.

Huxley, E. (1982). *The flame trees of Thika: Memories of an African childhood.* London, England: Chatto and Windus.

Kirkpatrick, D. (1994). *Evaluating training programs: The four levels.* San Francisco, CA: Berrett-Koehler.

Kirkpatrick, D., & Kirkpatrick, J. (2006). *Evaluating training programs: The four levels* (3rd ed). San Francisco, CA: Berrett-Koehler

Martinez, R., Liu, S., Watson, W., & Bichelmeyer, B. (2006). Evaluation of a web-based master's degree program: Lessons learned from an online instructional design and technology program. *Quarterly Review of Distance Education, 7*(3), 267–283.

Morgan, D. (1996). *Focus groups as qualitative research.* Newbury Park, CA: SAGE.

Orellana, A. (2018*). FCE online course design guidelines.* Davie, FL: Fischler College of Education.

Peak, D., & Berge, Z. (2006). Evaluation and eLearning. *Turkish Online Journal of Distance Education, 7*(1), Article 11.

Phillips, J. (2003). *Return on investment* (2nd ed.). Burlington, MA: Butterworth-Heinmann.

Quality Matters. (2013). Quality matters rubric standards 2011-2013 edition. Retrieved from https://qualitymatteres.org

Rogers, E. M. (2003). *Diffusion of innovations* (5th ed.). New York, NY: Free Press.

Rose, E. (2000). An evaluation of online distance education course databases. *DEOSNEWS, 10*(11), 1–6. Retrieved from http://www.ed.psu.edu/acsde/deos/deosnews.deosarchives.asp

Rossi, P., Lipsey, M., & Freeman, H. (2003). *Evaluation: A systematic approach* (7th ed.). Newbury Park, CA: SAGE.

Rovai, A. P. (2003). A practical framework for evaluating online distance education programs. *Internet and Higher Education, 6*(2), 109–124.

Ruhe, V., & Zumbo, B. (2009) *Evaluation in distance education and e-learning.* New York, NY: Guilford.

Sherry, A. (2003). Quality and its measurement in distance education. In M. Moore & W. Anderson (Eds.), *Handbook of distance education* (pp. 435–459). Mahwah, NJ: Erlbaum.

Simonson, M. (2000). Personal innovativeness, perceived organizational innovativeness, and computer anxiety: Updated scales. *Quarterly Review of Distance Education, 1*(1), 69–76.

Simonson, M. (2005). South Dakota's statewide distance education project. In Z. L. Berge & T. Clark (Eds.), *Virtual schools: Planning for success* (pp. 183–197). New York, NY: Teachers College Press.

Simonson, M. (2007). Evaluation and distance education. *Quarterly Review of Distance Education, 8*(3), vii–ix.

Simonson, M., & Bauck, T. (2001). *Learning at a distance in South Dakota: Description and evaluation of the diffusion of an innovation.* Proceedings of Research and Development Papers presented at the Annual Convention of the Association for Educational Communications and Technology, Atlanta, GA. (ERIC Document Reproduction Service No. ED47103)

Simonson, M., & Schlosser, C. (1995a). More than fiber: Distance education in Iowa. *Tech Trends, 40*(3), 13–15.

Simonson, M., & Schlosser, C. (1995b). *The DaVinci project.* Paper presented at the Iowa Computer-Using Educators Conference, Des Moines.

Simonson, M., Schlosser, C., & Orellana, A. (2011). Distance education research: A review of the literature. *Journal of Computing in Higher Education, 23*(2), 124–142

Sloan-C. (2013). Quality scorecard for the administration of online programs: A handbook. Retrieved from http://sloanconsortium.org/quality_scorecard_online_program

Sorensen, C. (1996). *Final evaluation report: Iowa distance education alliance.* Ames, IA: Research Institute for Studies in Education.

Sorensen, C., & Sweeney, J. (1995). ICN Technology Demonstration Evaluation. *USDLA Education at a Distance, 9*(5), 11, 21.

Sorensen, C., & Sweeney, J. (1996, November). *AEIOU: An approach to evaluating the statewide integration of distance education.* Paper presented at the annual meeting of the American Evaluation Association, Atlanta, GA.

Sorensen, C., & Sweeney, J. (1997, November). *A-E-I-O-U: An inclusive framework for evaluation.* Paper presented at the annual meeting of the American Evaluation Association, San Diego, CA.

Stufflebeam, D., & Shinkfield, A. (2007). *Evaluation theory, models, and applications.* Hoboken, NJ: Jossey-Bass

Sweeney, J. (1995). *Vision 2020: Evaluation report.* Ames, IA: Research Institute for Studies in Education.

Thompson, M., & Irele, M. (2007). Evaluating distance education programs. In M. G. Moore (Ed.), *Handbook of distance education* (2nd ed.). Mahwah, NJ: Erlbaum.

Woodley, A., & Kirkwood, A. (1986). *Evaluation in distance learning.* Paper 10. Resources in Education. (ERIC Document Reproduction Service No. ED304122)

Woodley, A., & Kirkwood, A. (2005). *Evaluation in distance learning: Course evaluation.* Retrieved October 14, 2013, from http://www1.worldbank.org/disted/Management/Benefits/cou-02.html

Yarbrough, D. B., Shulha, L. M., Hopson, R. K., & Caruthers, F. A. (2011). *The program evaluation standards: A guide for evaluators and evaluation users* (3rd ed.). Thousand Oaks, CA: SAGE

SUGGESTED READING

Cronbach, L. (1982). *Designing evaluations of educational and social programs.* San Francisco, CA: Jossey-Bass.

Index